A TEXT-BOOK

OF

MATERIA MEDICA

AND

THERAPEUTICS.

CHARACTERISTIC, ANALYTICAL, AND COMPARATIVE.

BY

A. C. COWPERTHWAITE, M.D., Ph.D., LL.D.,

PROFESSOR OF MATERIA MEDICA AND THERAPEUTICS IN THE STATE UNIVERSITY OF IOWA;
AUTHOR OF "A TEXT-BOOK OF GYNECOLOGY," "INSANITY IN ITS
MEDICO-LEGAL RELATIONS," ETC., ETC.

SIXTH EDITION. ENTIRELY REWRITTEN AND REVISED.
WITH CLINICAL INDEX.

CHICAGO:
GROSS & DELBRIDGE.
1892.

COPYRIGHT, 1891,
BY GROSS & DELBRIDGE.

ELECTROTYPED BY THE WERNER PTG. & LITHO. CO., CHICAGO, ILL.–AKRON, O.

Volume 2

Publishing Statement:

This important reprint was made from an old and scarce book.

Therefore, it may have defects such as missing pages, erroneous pagination, blurred pages, missing text, poor pictures, markings, marginalia and other issues beyond our control.

Because this is such an important and rare work, we believe it is best to reproduce this book regardless of its original condition.

Thank you for your understanding and enjoy this unique book!

KALI NITRICUM. 431

GENERAL ANALYSIS.

Kali Nitricum acts directly upon the spinal system, paralyzing the spinal cord and the heart, arresting the action of the latter in its diastole. It also produces an antiplastic and spoliative effect upon the blood. It acts upon the kidneys, and upon the respiratory and alimentary mucous tracts as a decided irritant, in the former producing excessive action, diuresis, the solid constituents being also increased, and in the latter irritation, leading to congestion and inflammation.

CHARACTERISTIC SYMPTOMS.

Mind.—Difficult thinking in the morning. Anxiety; ennui, melancholia, weeping mood (Natr. mur., Nux m., *Ign., Puls.*)

Head.—Confusion of the head; vertigo. Dullness, stupefaction and heaviness of the head. Violent pressive headache, especially in forehead. Constrictive pain in back of head; parts feel as if stiff; forcing to bend head backward; better after tying up the hair. Hot spots on the head. Headache on vertex, like pulling of the hairs. Sensitiveness of the scalp to touch (Carb. v., Cinch., Merc., Natr. mur., Nitr. ac.). Small, scurfy spots on head; itching.

Eyes.—Transient blindness. Rings of varigated colors before the eyes. Burning in eyes, lachrymation, and aversion to light, especially in morning; after washing in cold water.

Ears.—Deafness; rushing, ringing and roaring in the ears (Cinch., Merc., Sil., Sulph.). Stitches in ear worse at night, and when lying on the affected side. Tensive pain behind the ear.

Nose.—Loss of smell, with coryza; sneezing; mucus passes through posterior nares into fauces. Sore pain in upper part of right nostril. Nosebleed; dryness and stoppage of nose. Nostril swollen and painful to pressure. Bones of nose sore to touch. Swollen feeling in right nostril.

Face.—Pale, sickly expression; sunken; nose cold (Ars., Camph., Verat. alb.). Acute tearing pains in cheeks (*Cinch., Chin. s., Spig.*).

Mouth.—Gums red, swollen; bleed easily (Merc., Nitr. ac.). Throbbing, tearing toothache; worse from cold things

(Ant. crud., Calc. c., Staph.). Disagreeable, disgusting taste. Sour taste in throat, in morning, on rising. Dryness of mouth and tongue (*Ars., Bry., Nux m.*). Tongue burns at tip, as if cut; burning pimples. Tongue coated with white mucus. Offensive odor from the mouth (*Ars.,* Hep. s., Merc., Iodi., *Nitr. ac.*).

Throat.—Burning in throat; cutting pains, with impeded deglutition. Hawking of sweetish, tough mucus from throat. Rawness and scraping in throat (Amm. carb., Caust.). Sore throat; uvula and tonsils red (Bell.).

Stomach.—Violent hunger, or loss of appetite. Violent thirst °Cannot drink for want of breath, drinks in sips. Nausea; qualmishness; violent vomiting of mucus, with blood. *Faint-like weakness at pit of stomach* (*Cimic., Ign., Petrol., Puls.*). Cold feeling or burning in stomach; inflammation. Sharp, sticking pains; hinder breathing. Pressure and gnawing in pit of stomach.

Abdomen.—Violent colic, worse on right side; griping and cutting about the umbilicus (*Coloc.*). Abdomen distended with much rumbling (*Carb. v., Cinch., Lyc., Sulph.*); emission of offensive flatus.

Stool.—Watery, thin, fæcal; soft with colic. Bloody; with tenesmus. Stool containing membranous portions of intestines mixed with blood. With great pressure. °Diarrhœa from eating veal. Constipation.

Urinary Organs.—Frequent urination, and discharge of much pale urine, with reddish clouds. Mucous sediment, salts increased; sp. gr. 1030–1040. Dysuria; frequent desire, with burning, only a few drops at first; °after irritating medicines; °gonorrhœal extensions.

Male Organs.—Violent erections, with increased desire.

Female Organs.—Menses suppressed; too early and profuse. Menstrual blood black as ink (*Croc., Cycl., Sabin.*); pains in abdomen, small of back and thighs (*Cimic., Puls.*).

Respiratory Organs.—Aphonia; roughness and scraping in larynx with hoarseness. °*Cannot drink for want of breath; has to take drink in little sips;* little children take hold of the cup with both hands, and take greedily one sip after another. Constriction of lungs in morning in bed. Burning in forepart of chest. Burning in morning extending into throat, expectoration is loosened. °Paroxysms of difficult and rapid breathing, evening and night; less in morning; oppressed breathing on ascending stairs (*Ars., Ascl., Calc. c., Merc.*). °Asthma; cannot lie in horizontal position; violent gasping and suffocation (*Ars., Ipec., Samb.*). Cough; awakens at 3 A.M. with violent, stupefying headache; in open air; worse ascending, or when holding breath; with cutting and stitches in chest; expectoration of coagulated blood; after hawking mucus. Dull tightness and constriction of chest, as if lung were constricted from back. Stitches on drawing long breath, or coughing (*Bry.*). Congestion to chest. Heaviness and tightness of chest, like a great load, pressing thorax together; dyspnœa to suffocation; the latter out of proportion to the slight congestion or hepatization. °Suppuration of lungs, with profuse (colliquative) sweat (*Hep. s., Phos.*).

Heart and Pulse.—Palpitation on rising or moving about quickly, with heat of face and oppression of chest. Violent audible palpitation (*Spig.*), with dyspnœa and great anxiety; has to sit up in bed (*Acon.*). Pulse usually full, hard, accelerated; slow, mornings, weak and thready.

Neck and Back.—Stiffness and paralyzed feeling in neck and back. Small of back feels bruised. Pressure and burning in back, relieved by motion. Drawing pain in region of kidneys.

Limbs.—Trembling, lameness and paralytic feelings in limbs. Rheumatic pains; stitching pains at night. Parts feel as if made of wood. Paralysis of limbs; debility of limbs.

Generalities.—Twitching and trembling of muscles over whole body. Great exhaustion and debility; tremulous weakness. Sensation as if parts, or whole of body were of wood. Formication; constrictive feeling in many parts. Hæmorrhages of bright-red blood (*Acon., Erig., Ham., Ipec., Sec.*). Sudden swelling of body, neck, thighs.

Skin.—Itching pimples; small pustules. Pricking like needles, then burning. Burning vesicles filled with yellow serum; on scratching they burst.

Sleep.—Yawning and drowsiness. Restless sleep at night; sleepless after midnight; nightmare.

Fever.—Chill and coldness in afternoon and evening; increased from motion; passing off when lying. Chill, with subsequent sweat; no intervening heat. Coldness and shivering, with thirst. Heat at night, without thirst, and without subsequent sweat. Debilitating sweat from least exertion (Calc. c., Chin. sulph., Hep. s., *Merc., Phos.,* Sulph.). Profuse, cold, clammy night sweats (*Ars., Phos., Merc.*).
Compare.—Acon., Ars., Canth., Tereb.
Antidotes.—Nitr. sp. d. Camph. increases the pains. Nitr. relieves strangury after abuse of Canth., turpentine and the abuse of condiments.

THERAPEUTICS.

Has not been so extensively used as other Potash salts. Has cured mucous polypus of right nostril. Diarrhœa after eating veal. Dysentery after Acon. when that remedy fails to relieve the cutting pain, great thirst and cold hands and feet. Peritonitis. Dysuria. Enuresis. Diabetes insipidus. Pneumonia, with excessive heat and thirst. Asthma with great dyspnœa, stitching pains, rather free expectoration. Useful in all stages of phthisis, but particularly for acute exacerbations, with much cough, pain and dyspnœa. Acute rheumatism with endocarditis. Other cardiac diseases with symptoms mentioned.

KALMIA.

Synonym.—Kalmia Latifolia. *Natural order.*—Ericaceæ. *Common name.*—Mountain Laurel. *Habitat.*—An evergreen shrub growing on rocky hills and damp soil from Maine to Ohio and Kentucky. *Preparation.*—Tincture from the fresh leaves.

GENERAL ANALYSIS.

Acts prominently upon the heart, diminishing the force and frequency of its action and causing a slow, weak pulse. It also acts upon the nervous and upon the muscular system; producing neuralgic and rheumatic pains, tingling, numbness and restlessness.

KALMIA.

CHARACTERISTIC SYMPTOMS.

Head.—Vertigo, with pains in the limbs. Tearing pains in head and neck (Cimic.), neuralgic pains extending from forehead into roots of right upper molars or into eye teeth or down the neck.

Eyes.—Glimmering before the eyes. Vision imperfect. Pain in eyes, worse on turning them (Bry.). *Sensation of stiffness around the eyes, and in the eyelids* (Rhus tox.).

Face.—Neuralgia of the face, mostly on the right side; rending, agonizing pains. °Anxious expression of countenance in rheumatism of heart.

Stomach.—Nausea; everything becomes black before the eyes, with pressure in the throat; incarcerated flatulence; oppression in breathing, and rheumatic pains in the limbs. Pressure in pit of stomach; worse when sitting bent over; better when sitting erect, with the sensation as if something would be pressed off below the pit of stomach. °Crampy pain, with eructation of wind, palpitation, gastralgia, angina pectoris.

Urinary Organs.—Albuminuria; also with pains in lower limbs. Frequent micturition of small quantities of urine which feels hot.

Respiratory Organs.—Tickling in the trachea. Difficult and oppressed breathing. Stitches in the lower part of the chest. Shooting through chest above the heart into the shoulder blades (Kali carb.), with pain in the left arm (Acon., Rhus tox.). Dyspnœa and pain; °angina pectoris.

Heart and Pulse.—*Palpitation of the heart,* with anxiety and oppressed breathing (Acon., Ars.); with faint feeling. Fluttering of the heart; on slowly ascending stairs. Rheumatic pains in region of heart (Rhus tox., Spig.). Pulse slow and feeble; irregular; quick but weak.

°Hypertrophy and valvular insufficiency, or thickening after rheumatism. °Shooting, stabbing pain from heart through to left scapula, causing violent beating of the heart; rheumatism of the heart.

Back.—Pain in back at night in bed. Constant pain in spine, sometimes worse in lumbar region, with great heat and burning. Sharp or drawing pain in loins; worse from motion; worse evenings. Paralytic pain and lameness in loins in evening in bed.

Limbs.—Pain in left arm (Acon., Rhus tox.). *Pressure in left arm.* Joints hot, red, and swollen. Rheumatic pains in the limbs; from hip to feet. Neuralgic pain from neck down right arm to little or fourth finger.

Generalities.—Bruised feeling all over the body. Restlessness and frequent turning. Rheumatic pains all over the body; often changing their position. Pains worse from sitting bent, yet a feeling that he must do so; relieved by sitting or standing upright. Weakness the only general symptom, with neuralgia. Pains worse during early part of night; or soon after going to bed. Pain occurring at regular times, continuing for no definite period, coming suddenly or gradually, and leaving as uncertainly. Neuralgic pains, sometimes attended with numbness, or rather succeeded by numbness, of the parts affected.

Fever.—Rapid alterations of chill and heat. Shivering, with or without coldness.

Compare.—Acon., Bell., Cimic., Digit., Hep. s., Kalies, Spig., Rhus tox. Kalmia follows Spigelia well in heart disease.—*Hering.*

Antidotes.—Acon., Bell.

THERAPEUTICS.

Kalmia has been found most useful in rheumatism and in organic diseases of the heart. Chronic, subacute articular rheumatism, pains shifting from one joint to another. Acute inflammatory rheumatism, shifting pains and numbness. Rheumatic endocarditis. Hypertrophy and valvular insufficiency, or thickening, after rheumatism. Always in cardiac disease violent shooting, stabbing pains, great dyspnœa and slow, weak pulse. Angina pectoris. Neuralgic pains, accompanied by great weakness, and attended with or succeeded by a sort of paralytic numbness of the parts affected (Aconite). Facial neuralgia following herpes zoster (Mezer.). Gastralgia in sudden paroxysms. Retinitis. Albuminuric, during pregnancy. Sclerotitis, especially in rheumatic subjects. Sclero-choroiditis, especially anterior. Muscular asthenopia. Bright's disease, with heart symptoms. Albuminuria during pregnancy.

KREOSOTUM.

Synonym.—Creosotum. *Common names.*—Creasote. Kreosote. Wood Tar. *Preparation.*—One part of Kreosote made from beech-wood tar is dissolved in ninety-nine parts of Alcohol to make the 2x dilution.

GENERAL ANALYSIS.

Kreosote acts upon the lymphatic system, and especially upon the mucous membranes of the digestive and female generative organs and upon the skin, producing catarrhal conditions, with tendency to disorganization, ulceration, and destruction of the parts involved. The chief characteristic of Kreosote is the corrosive, acrid character of its secretions.

CHARACTERISTIC SYMPTOMS.

Mind.—Weakness of memory (*Agar., Ambr., Anac.,* Led., *Merc., Nux m.,* Natr. miur., Phos. ac.).

Head.—Vertigo. Painfulness in the head, as after a carouse (*Nux v.*). Throbbing pains, especially in the forehead.

Eyes.—Sight confused, as when looking through a veil (Caust., Croc., Hyos., Petrol., Phos., *Puls.,* Rhus tox.). Heat and burning in the eyes, and lachrymation (Acon., Ars., Merc. cor.). The tears are acrid like salt water. Swelling of the eyelids and their margins (*Puls.,* Staph.).

Ears.—Roaring in the head; also humming and difficulty of hearing before and during menses.

Nose.—Offensive smell before the nose (Calc. c.). Frequent sneezing, especially in morning. Catarrh, fluent or dry, with much sneezing. °Chronic catarrh with old people.

Face.—Pale face; bluish tinge; bloated. Upper lip feels sore and is cracked. Flushes of heat, with circumscribed redness of the cheeks (Sang., Sulph.). °Burning pains; worse talking or exertion; better lying on unaffected side; nervous, excitable.

Mouth.—Tongue coated white (*Ant. crud., Bry., Nux v., Puls., Sulph.*). Drawing pains in the teeth (*Merc.*). °Gums bleed readily; scorbutic, spongy, and ulcerated (*Merc.,*

Nitr. ac., Phos.). °Putrid odor from the mouth (Arn., Iodi., *Nitr. ac.*, Nux v.).

Stomach.—Bitter taste, especially in the throat. °Water after it is swallowed tastes bitter. Nausea; like that of pregnancy (Nux m., Kali c., Puls.); with burning in mouth; with spitting of saliva and general chill, without heat or thirst. Urging to vomit, nothing but saliva results. Retching; morning when fasting. Vomiting; of sweetish water, in morning, fasting; of food. Painful, hard spot at or to the left of the stomach.

Abdomen.—Feeling of fullness, as after having eaten too much (*Lyc.*). Pain like electric shocks from abdomen to vagina. Constriction of hypochondria (Acon.). Cannot tolerate tight clothing (Calc. c., Carb. v., Graph.). Distension of the abdomen (Ant. crud., Bry., Caps.). Colic, resembling the pains of labor.

Stool.—Constipation; stool hard, and expelled only after much pressing (*Bry., Nux v., Sulph.*).

Urinary Organs.—Frequent urging to urinate (Acon., Apis, Canth.); *always with great haste and passing a great deal* (Merc.). Urine offensive (Benz. ac., Calc. c., Sulph. ac., Nitr. ac.) colorless (Ign., Phos. ac.); reddish sediment (Bell., Lyc., Carb. v., Sep., Graph.).

Female Organs.—Menses too early, too profuse and too protracted (Calc. c.). *Leucorrhœa of a yellow color, staining linen yellow, with great weakness* (Carb. an.), *in legs;* acrid, causing itching and biting on external genitals. White leucorrhœa, *having the odor of green corn. Burning between the pudenda on urinating. Soreness between the pudenda; also between the thighs and pudenda, with burning, biting pains. Violent itching of the labia; also of the vagina* (Canth., Coni.); *obliged to rub the parts; external genitals swollen; hot, hard and sore. Soreness and smarting between the labia and vulva* (Sep.). °Nausea during pregnancy; ptyalism; very offensive excoriating lochia. °Dwindling away of the mammæ (Iod., Kali iod.), with small, hard, painful lumps in them.

Respiratory Organs.—Scraping and roughness of the throat, with hoarseness (Mez., Nux v.). Shortness of breath (Acon., Ars., Phos.). °Convulsive cough, with inclination to vomit

KREOSOTUM. 439

(Ant. tart.). °Paroxysmal, moist cough, caused by a crawling behind the sternum. *Burning in the chest* (Ars., Nux v.). Stitches in the chest, just over the heart (Lil. tig., Kali c.). Frequent blood spitting; severe pains in chest; afternoon fever and morning sweat.

Neck and Back.—Glands of neck swollen (*Bar.*, Calc. c., Merc., Hep. s., Iod.). Pains in small of back, like labor-pains (Cimic., *Puls.*).

Limbs.—Bruised pain in the limbs (Arn.). *Pain in the left thumb, as if sprained and stiff.*

Generalities.—General weakness and prostration. Faintness in morning, when rising earlier than usual. °Hæmorrhages; small wounds bleed much (Phos.). Numbness; loss of sensation. Rapid emaciation. Excoriation of mucous surface (*Hydras.*). Most symptoms better in the open air.

Skin.—Itching; becomes exceedingly violent toward evening. Pustular eruptions over the whole body (Crot. tig., Iris).

Sleep.—Great desire to sleep, with frequent yawning. Sleeplessness; tosses about without any apparent cause.

Conditions.—Suitable for old women. For tall, lean persons.

Compare.—Ant. tart., Ars., Carb. ac., Carb. v., Calc. c., Graph., Hep. s., Ipec., Iod., Merc., Nitr. ac., Petrol., Phos., Sec. c., Sulph. (followed well by Sulph., also Ars. in cancer). After Carb. v. it disagrees.

Antidotes—Acon., Ars., Cinch., Ipec., Nux v.

THERAPEUTICS.

In Kreosote the acrid and fœtid (from decomposition) character of the secretions, especially from mucous surfaces, and the extreme burning pains are very characteristic and of great clinical importance. So also is the general tendency to hæmorrhage and destruction of tissue. The drug is especially useful in scrofulous affections, putrid ulcers, gangrene and gangrenous tendencies of ulcers in general, with horrible odor, burning pain, etc. Senile gangrene. Cancer, with very offensive discharges, burning pain, etc. Carbuncles. Catarrhal conditions with acrid, very irritating and offensive secretions. Blepharitis with moderately profuse discharge and much smarting in eyes. Acute aggravation of chronic Keratitis, hot, smarting lachrymation. Chronic inflammation and swelling of lids and margins, with agglutination. Humid eruption about the ear, with swelling of cervical glands. Epithelioma and lupus of nose, lips and face, with burning pain. Scorbutis; gums spongy and bleeding; rapid decay of the teeth. Children's teeth begin to decay as soon as they appear. Persistent vomiting in infants; in dyspepsia, food is not retained. Sympathetic vomiting, as of phthisis, cancer of liver or uterus; pregnancy, chronic kidney disease, etc. Seasickness. Diarrhœa, offensive, acrid stools, nausea and vomiting. Thin, fœtid, bloody, sometimes dark and clotted stools during typhoid fever, with great prostration. Cholera infantum. Chronic enuresis. Diabetes. A valuable remedy in inflammation, erosions and ulcerations of the uterus, cervix and vagina, characterized by offensive, excoriating discharges. One of the most valuable remedies for an acrid offensive leucorrhœa. Cancer of uterus or soft parts, with characteristic discharges and violent burning pains. Putrid state of the uterus after parturition; offensive lochia. Apthous or inflammatory state of external parts, symptomatic of ovarian or uterine disease. Malignant induration and ulceration of stomach. Hæmatemesis. Gastro malacia. Hæmorrhages from the uterus change to ichorous leucorrhœa, and then back again to blood and so on. Menorrhagia. Metrorrhagia. Pruritus from acrid leucorrhœa. Sterility caused by acrid leucorrhœa. Dwindling of the mammæ, with small, hard, painful lumps in them. Chronic laryngeal and bronchial catarrh, with symptoms already given. Whooping cough. Winter cough of old people, spasmodic at night. Chronic pneumonia or phthisis with violent burning pains in chest, spasmodic cough, etc. Gangrene of the lungs. Urticaria, extremely violent itching towards evening; after menstruation.

LACHESIS.

Synonym.—Trigonocephalus Lachesis. *Natural order.*—Ophidia. *Common name.*—Lance-headed Viper of Brazil. *Preparation.*—Triturations of the venom.

GENERAL ANALYSIS.

Acts upon the cerebro-spinal system, and more especially upon the pneumogastric. The nerve centres are poisoned, and as a result, prostration, convulsions and unconsciousness ensue, while from the influence of the pneumo-gastric we obtain irritable conditions of the throat, larynx, bronchi and heart, yet not passing into distinct inflammation. As a further result of the poison, the blood becomes inoculated, decomposition sets in, the fibrin of the blood is destroyed, and we have, resulting ecchymoses, hæmorrhages, asthenic inflammations, abscesses, malignant inflammations, gangrene, pyæmia; and with all, and as a result of all, a general typhoid condition. The chief characteristic of Lachesis is the aggravation of all its symptoms after sleep.

CHARACTERISTIC SYMPTOMS.

Mind.—Memory weak (Agar., Ambr., *Anac.*, Kreos., *Merc.*, Natr. mur., *Nu.v m.*, Phos. ac.); makes mistakes in orthography (Lyc.). Confusion as to time. Great mental activity, ideas crowd rapidly (*Coff. c., Cinch.*). *Loquacious;* in the evening. Constantly changing from one subject to another (Cimic.), with mocking jealousy, satire, ridiculous ideas, frightful images (Hyos.). Indifference. Great sadness and anxiety on awaking in the morning (Natr. mur.). °Proud (*Plat., Stram.*); *jealous* (Apis, Hyos.); suspicious. °Thinks herself under superhuman control.

Head.—*Vertigo in the morning on waking* (Alum., Phos., Nitr. ac.); *momentary, on closing the eyes* (Thuja). *Headache, extending into the root of the nose* (Merc. iod.). Headache with flickering before the eyes. Rush of blood to head. Heat in head. Pressive headache, with nausea. Headache in left frontal eminence; deep internal. Headache over the eyes and in the occiput, every morning on rising. Throbbing headache over right eye. One-sided headache; pains intense, extend to neck and shoulders, with tension in muscles. Neck stiff (*Rhus tox.*); tongue paralytic. Pressing, bursting pains in the temples; better when lying down. Sticking and boring in vertex. Heaviness, like lead, in the occiput (Carb v., Chel.); can scarcely raise head from pillow, with vertigo. Sensitiveness of scalp in left temple from vertex down, and left side of face on touch or moving muscles, a sensation as if sunburnt. Numbness and crawling on left side of head, when touched or on moving the muscles in the evening and morning with crawling. °Hair falls off (*Graph., Merc., Nitr. ac.*, Phos., *Sep., Sulph.*); worse during pregnancy; aversion to sun's rays (Bell., Glon., Natr. carb.).

Eyes.—*Dimness of vision; black flickering before the eyes;* often makes reading difficult. Fog before the eyes (Kali iod., Merc., Puls., Sulph.); bright blue rings, filled with fiery rays, about the light; zigzag figures. Sensitive to light. Lachrymation. Sticking, drawing pains in and above the eyes.

Ears.—*Pain in ears, with sore throat. Tearing, extending from the zygoma into the ear.* Whizzing, as from insects in the ear. Hearing diminished.

Nose.—Coryza, preceded by headache (Hydras.); and stiffness of nape; discharge watery, with red, sore nostrils; scabs in the nose (Merc.). Nosebleed; blood thick and dark. °Nosebleed in amenorrhœa, typhus, etc. °Paroxysms of sneezing in hay asthma. Many symptoms end with catarrh.

Face.—Pale, earthy, gray color of face (Ars.). Erysipelatous inflammation of the face (Bell., Graph., Hep. s., *Rhus tox.*). Heat and redness of the otherwise pale face. *Tearing in zygoma, extending into the ear. Left side of face and lower jaw swollen and sensitive to touch.* Trifacial neuralgia, left side, orbital; heat running up into the head. Feeling of stiffness of the malar bone, coming from the cervical glands. Itching of the face.

Mouth.—Toothache, tearing, jerking, sticking (Puls.); *often extending through jaw to ear; periodic; after waking; after eating* (Ant. crud., Nux v., Staph.); *from warm and cold drinks.* Feeling as if the teeth were too long when biting them together. Gums bleeding; swollen; spongy. °Tongue dry, red, black, stiff, cracked (Bapt., Bell., Naja, *Rhus tox.*); swollen and covered with blisters. °Difficult speech; tongue heavy (Mur. ac.); cannot open mouth. °Tongue trembles when protruded, or catches behind the teeth. Burning pain and rawness in mouth, then apthous and denuded spots. Mouth sore, parched, dry, apthous (*Borax*, Hydras., *Merc.*, Iodi.).

Throat.—*Hawking of mucus, with rawness in the throat. Dryness in throat at night on waking, without thirst.*

(Apis, Nux m., Puls.). *Throat seems swollen, as if two large lumps came together, on empty swallowing; better from swallowing food. Feeling of a crumb of bread left sticking in the throat,* obliging her to constantly swallow. *Tonsilitis; worst on left side; choking when swallowing; or when swallowing, pains from throat to ear* (Ambr., Bell., Kali bi., Hep. s.); *neck sensitive to touch* (Apis). Pain and soreness begin left side of throat. *Liquids cause more difficulty in swallowing than solids* (Bell.). *External throat very sensitive to touch* (not painful, but an uneasy sensation); *in evening on lying down, with suffocative sensation; even to touch of linen.*

Stomach.—Appetite variable; at times good, at others no appetite at all. Thirst, with dry tongue and skin. Desire for oysters. Eructations, which relieve; amounting to vomiting. Dyspepsia; worse after eating (*Cinch., Nux v., Puls.*). Stitches extending into the chest. Gnawing in stomach; relieved after eating, but returns when stomach gets empty. Painless gnawing. Pressure in stomach; after eating; with weakness in knees. Great discomfort of having clothes tight around the waist (Bry., *Calc. c.*, Crot.).

Abdomen.—Tearing and cutting pains in right side of abdomen. Abdomen distended and hard; hot; sensitive; painful (*Acon., Bell.*). Sensation as if ligaments from stomach were stretched, *so that she must wear clothes very loose.* Drawing from anus to umbilicus. Feeling of emptiness in the abdomen. Ulcerative pain about liver; inflammation and abscess. °Swelling in cæcal region; must lie on back, with limbs drawn up; typhlitis. °Abdomen hot, sensitive; painfully stiff from loins down thighs; peritonitis; pus formed.

Stool and Anus.—Burning in anus during and after stools (*Ars., Canth.*, Merc., Natr. mur., Sulph.). Constriction of rectum; of anus. Protrusion after stool. *Beating in the anus, as with little hammers.* Stool lies close to anus without passing and without urging. Spasmodic pain in anus before and after stool. Closed feeling in anus. °Tormenting, constant urging in the rectum, not for stool Stools watery offensive, dark (Ars.); watery, frequent, sudden, about midnight, offensive, ammoniacal; soft, bright yellow; pasty putrid. Obstinate constipation (*Alum., Nux v., Op., Plumb.*). Hæmorrhoidal tumors, protruding (Aloe, Calc. c., Mur. ac., *Puls.*), °with stitches at each cough or sneeze.

Urinary Organs.—Urine frequent, °foaming, black. Pressure in bladder, with frequent urging. Sticking, cutting pains, or soreness in fore part of urethra. Inefficient urging to urinate.

Female Organs.—°Menses scanty, feeble, but irregular; blood black. Labor-like pain during menses (*Caul., Cimic., Puls.*). °Uterine and ovarian pains; relieved by a flow of blood. °Pains, like a knife thrust into abdomen. Uterus will not bear contact even of bed clothes; they cause uneasiness. °Hot flashes; metrorrhagia and other troubles *during climacteric period* (Sang.).

Respiratory Organs.—Hoarseness; rawness, scraping and dryness in larynx (Acon., Caust., Cham., *Phos.*); *sensitive to touch* (Acon., Spong.); necessity to swallow; constant necessity to hawk. Voice will not come because something in larynx prevents, which cannot be hawked loose, though mucus is brought up. °Suddenly something runs from neck to larynx, and interrupts breathing; awakens him at night; spasm of glottis. *Larynx and throat painful on bending head backward.* Pain in sternum at night, with burning in chest; under left heart. Larynx sensitive; cannot bear anything about the throat (Apis); causes suffocation. *Cough worse after sleep; caused by pressure on larynx; dry and hacking; caused by touching the throat;* from tickling the throat; from crawling in ulcers in throat; from contact with open air, from smoking (Ign.); in evening on lying down. *Constantly obliged to take a deep breath* (Ign.); worse when sitting. After a long wheezing cough, suddenly spits up profuse, frothy, tenacious mucus. Shortness of breath; attacks of suffocation (Acon., Ars., Apis, Ipec., Phos.). Oppression of the chest; in sleep. Spitting large quantities of ropy mucus.

Heart.—Constriction about the heart (*Cact.*). *Cramp-like pain in the præcordial region, causing palpitation, with anxiety.* Feels beating of the heart, with great weakness. Irregularity of beats in the heart (Cact., Laur.). °Restless,

LACHESIS. 445

trembling anxiety about the heart; suffocation on lying down; weight on chest; heart feels constricted; rheumatism of heart. °Fainting, with pain in heart; nausea; pale face; vertigo.

Neck and Back.—Stiffness of the nape of the neck (Kali c., Ign., Phos., Rhus tox.); sensitive to external pressure. Pain in small of back, as if lame and weak (Rhus tox.). Drawing pains in small of back; extending into hips and legs.

Limbs.—Great weakness in both arms and legs. Aching pains in shin bones. Weakness in knees after eating. Ulcers on lower extremities (Ars., Lyc.). Perspiration on feet. Red, bluish, painful swellings of legs and feet.

Generalities.—*Weakness of whole body in morning on rising.* Emaciation with suffering and weakness. Trembling as from anxiety, without anxiety. Sudden jerking of whole body when sitting. Starting from below. Necessity to do everything rapidly. *Great physical and mental exhaustion,* in mornings. Fainting, with pain in heart; nausea; pale face; vertigo. Pricking, pulsating, tearing pains (Puls.). °Convulsions; epilepsy (*Bell.,* Calc. c., Cupr.). Affected parts look bluish. °Restless tossing about, with moaning in children with sore throat. Restlessness and longing to get into the open air. Great inclination to lie down, especially after eating. Rheumatic pains, first in the left side, then in the right. Feels bruised in the morning after waking. Slight touch intolerable. °Complaints mostly on left side of body. *Obliged to wear clothes loose; cannot bear the contact.*

Skin.—*Sore spots become fungoid, dark-red, brownish,* with whitish spots, burning on wiping. Superficial ulcers, foul at the bottom (Merc., Nitr. ac.); black-bluish appearance. Miliary eruption; rash appears slowly, or turns black or bluish. Erysipelatous eruptions. Carbuncles, with purple surroundings. Old scars break open and bleed; the open spots dark-red, looking like a flat sponge. Itching over the whole body.

Sleep.—Sleepiness, without being able to sleep (Bell., Cham., Op.). Tossing and moving during sleep. *Lively and wide awake* in the evening. Restless sleep, with many dreams and frequent waking. *Waking in fright at a trifle.* Amorous dreams. Dreams with meditation.

Fever.—*Chilliness in back* (Abies can.); *commence in small of back* (Caps., Eupat. perf.). Coldness in evening, with chattering of teeth. Shivering during the heat. Chill runs up the back: on alternate days. Icy coldness of the feet; with oppression of chest. Heat as from orgasm of blood; mostly at night (Calc. c.). Heat particularly in hands and feet, evenings; burning in palms and soles (*Sulph.*). Perspiration at night (Calc. c., *Cinch., Phos.,* Phos. ac., Sil., *Sulph.*). °Intermittents, recurring every spring, or after suppression in the previous fall, by quinine.

Aggravation.—*After sleep;* in morning; in evening; after eating; from acids or alcoholic drinks; from sun's rays; from extremes of temperature.

Amelioration.—*From loosening the clothes;* from eructations.

Conditions.—*Often useful in women during climacteric period.* In persons of a phlegmatic constitution, with disposition to melancholia and indolence. Persons with dark eyes and dark complexions.

Compare.—*Apis, Ars.,* Bell., Caust., Cinch., Hep. s., Lactic ac.. Lyc., Merc., Naja, Nitr. ac., *Phos., Puls.,* Rhus tox., Sulph., Tarent.

Antidotes.—Ars., *Bell., Merc.,* Nux v., Phos. ac.; Heat, Alcohol, Salt. Acids disturb the curative action.

THERAPEUTICS.

A knowledge of the general clinical range of Lachesis is very readily inferred from the preceding general analysis and pathogenesis. It is especially useful in diseases characterized by blood decomposition and tissue degeneration on the one hand, and the peculiar nervous phenomena upon the other, while the two combined present a perfect picture of the general action of the drug, only applicable, however, in the individual case when the symptoms of the latter correspond with those of the drug. It is a valuable remedy in all adynamic and typhoid types of disease, where the symptoms correspond, whether the case be a true typhus or typhoid fever, or the condition accompanying asthenic inflammations, ulcers, suppurating wounds, abscesses, malignant diseases, eruptive or otherwise, gangrene,

LACHESIS. 447

pyæmia, etc. The discharges, whether from the bowels or from ulcers, etc., are always offensive, and in case of local inflammations of whatever nature the affected parts present a bluish or dark purplish appearance. Tendency to ecchymosis and bed sores. In typhoid fever hæmorrhages of decomposed blood. Purpura hæmorrhagica. Indolent ulcers. Varicose ulcers. Carbuncles. Erysipelas. Pustular and other eruptions, which turn black or bluish. Fungus hæmatodes. Yellow fever, with characteristic hæmorrhages, etc. Scarlatina of a malignant type, dark eruptions, or none at all, virulent throat symptoms, advanced stages, signs of blood poisoning, great prostration. Lachesis is valuable in a great variety of nervous troubles. Convulsions epileptic and hysterical. Chorea. Tetanus. Paralysis; left-sided; after apoplexy, or cerebral exhaustion. Progressive locomotor ataxia. Neuralgia of the spine. Coccyodynia; myelitis; neuritis; sciatica. Mania. Dementia. Melancholia. Delirium tremens. Mania after over-study. The characteristic delirium is of a low, muttering type. In mania loquacity predominates. Neuralgic headaches. Meningitis. Threatening apoplexy, especially in drunkards. Retinitis apoplectica, whether idiopathic or secondary; absorbs the hæmorrhage. Hæmorrhages into optic nerve, also in eye chambers. In these and other similar eye affections dimness of vision is the most prominent symptom. Defective sight after diphtheria, a paralysis of accommodation, requiring far-sighted glasses (Gels.). Keratitis. Ulcers on cornea. Orbital cellulitis, especially following operations for strabismus. Amblyopia, with lung or heart affections. Dark epistaxis in typhoid also in amenorrhœa. Coryza. Hay asthma. Chronic nasal catarrh. Facial neuralgia, especially left side. Facial erysipelas, dark, bluish hue, infiltration into cellular tissue. Gangrene of the mouth. Hæmorrhage from the gums. Syphilitic ulceration of mouth and throat. Lachesis is a very valuable remedy in tonsilitis, pharyngitis and other forms of sore throat. The left side is most often affected, or beginning on right side and going to left. The throat symptoms are well defined and have been fully detailed under their appropriate head, and need not be repeated.

According to Hering, there is no remedy so often effective in breaking up an attack of quinsy at its inception, nor in promoting resolution in the later stages. A most valuable remedy in malignant diphtheria, and malignant ulcerations of the throat, the fauces and pharynx presenting a purplish appearance, great prostration and other characteristic symptoms. Gangrenous sore throat. Elongated uvula, constant inclination to hawk, hacking cough; chronic irritability of fauces. Lachesis is useful in a variety of affections of the lower air passages. Aphonia from paralysis or œdema of the vocal chords. Laryngitis, catarrhal, croupous or diphtheritic, with the sensitiveness of throat, suffocation and other symptoms already mentioned. Spasms of the glottis. Whooping cough. Subacute and chronic bronchial catarrh. Asthma, paroxysms awaken from sleep, intolerance of pressure about neck and chest, relief from expectoration. Hay asthma. Only useful in pneumonia when typhoid symptoms supervene, especially after abscesses have formed. The threatening paralysis of the lungs, greatest difficulty in breathing, with long lasting attacks of suffocation. Hydrothorax, suffocative fits, waking from sleep, cyanotic symptoms. Emphysema. Nervous cough of reflex origin, especially from uterine or ovarian disease.

Lachesis is an important remedy in the female sexual sphere. It is especially useful in ovarian disease, the left ovary being most often affected. Ovarian neuralgia. Ovaritis. Ovarian tumors. Pelvic cellulitis and peritonitis. Acute general peritonitis, pus formed, typhoid symptoms. Puerperal metritis, metro-peritonitis, offensive lochial discharge. Endo-metritis. Dysmenorrhœa. Hot flashes. Metrorrhagia and other troubles during the climaxis. Cancer of the uterus. Displacements of the uterus. In all uterine and ovarian diseases the chief symptom is an intolerance of clothing or bed clothes about the abdomen, which, with other characteristics of the drug, may indicate its use in any disease of the pelvic viscera. Mastitis, bluish appearance. Cancer of the breast. Extreme sensitiveness of the nipples. Phlegmasia alba dolens. Syphilitic ulceration, especially of external genitals. Vaginal fistulæ becoming gangrenous. Subacute or chronic cystitis, especially from uterine disease. Post-scarlatinal nephritis. Sometimes useful in dyspepsia and gastralgia. Gastritis in drunkards or after Mercury. Hepatitis, liver swollen, painful and sensitive, throbbing, intolerance of clothing, abscess forming, typhoid symptoms supervening. Gall-stones. Jaundice. A valuable remedy in typhlitis. Fistula in ano. Hæmorrhoids, with stitches in tumors from every cough or sneeze; strangulated from constriction of sphincter. Chronic diarrhœa, watery offensive stools; in drunkards; during hot or relaxing spring weather: reflex from uterine irritation; in the course of adynamic diseases. Often useful in cardiac troubles. Pericarditis. Rheumatism of the heart. Hypertrophy. Angina pectoris. Reflex functional disturbances, especially from ovarian or uterine disease. Atheromatous arteries, chronic aortitis. Threatened heart failure after exhausting diseases. Cyanosis neonatorum. In all cardiac troubles the terrible dyspnœa is a prominent indication. Intermittent fever recurring every spring, or after suppression in the previous fall by quinine.

LACHNANTHES.

Synonym.—Lachnanthes Tinctoria. *Natural order.*—Hæmodoraceæ. *Common names.*—Red Root. Spirit Weed. *Habitat.*—A plant growing in sandy swamps from Rhode Island to New Jersey southward, near the coast. *Preparation.*—Tincture from the fresh plant.

GENERAL ANALYSIS.

Acts upon the cerebro-spinal system, affecting particularly the sensorium and muscular system, its tendency being to the production of an active congestion and inflammation.

CHARACTERISTIC SYMPTOMS.

Mind.—Became much excited over a trifle. Delirium, with brilliant eyes (Bell., Stram.).
Head.—Dull headache, particularly frontal. Tearing in forehead from left to right side. Scalp painful to the touch. Vertex feels enlarged and extended upward.
Eyes.—Yellow spots before the eyes. Bright, sparkling eyes with delirium (Bell., Stram.). Pressing as from dust in the eyes, with secretion of white mucus. Twitching of upper eyelids (Agar.); worse on closing them tightly. Sight became obscured.

Ears.—Itching or tingling in ears; relieved by boring with the finger, but again returns. Singing in the ear.

Face.—Circumscribed redness of the face (Sang.), with delirium and brilliant eyes (Bell.).

Mouth.—Pain in all the teeth, aggravated by warmth.

Throat.—Sore throat, with short cough. Sensation of swelling in pharynx, with stiffness of neck, and head drawn to one side, diphtheria. Dryness of throat; afterward soreness.

Stomach.—Aversion to meat (Arn., Carb. v., Graph., Puls.).

Abdomen.—Continuous rumbling and rolling in abdomen, as of gas (Aloe, Lyc.).

Stool and Anus.—Frequent stool; passes much wind.

Respiratory Organs.—Cough dry as from larynx, with sore throat. Stitches in chest under right breast and under the clavicle. Heat in chest (Acon., Ars., Sang.).

Heart and Pulse.—Pulse slow, irregular (Digit.). Sensation of heat in region of heart.

Neck and Back.—*Stiffness of the neck (Rhus tox.).* Pain in nape of neck as if from dislocation. Burning in the sacral and lumbar region.

Generalities.—Very restless; throws herself about (Acon., Ars.); feels weak (Cinch., Coccul.).

Skin.—Pimples appear here and there, containing a watery fluid (Graph.). Stinging, itching and tingling on thighs, legs, feet, arms, etc. (Acon., Apis, Urt. ur.).

Sleep.—*Sleepless,* or restless sleep, with distressing dreams. Cannot go to sleep easily.

Fever.—Flashes of heat alternating with chilliness. Burning in palms of hands and soles of feet (Sulph.). Heat with redness of face; after heat *circumscribed redness of both cheeks;* worse on right side (Sang.). Perspires freely, especially after midnight. *During cold sensation the skin is moist and sticky.*

Compare.—Agar., Bell., Camph., Cic., Cimic., Gels., Hyos., Lach., Rhus tox., Sang., Stram.

THERAPEUTICS.

Has been used principally for wry-neck (Lyc.). Also in diphtheria, scarlatina and cerebro-spinal meningitis, when there is a stiff neck, the head being drawn to one side. Pneumonia, especially typhoid pneumonia.

LACTIC ACID.

Preparation.—Dilutions of pure Lactic Acid made with alcohol.

GENERAL ANALYSIS.

Acts especially upon the mucous surfaces and upon the joints, producing inflammatory conditions, which, in the latter, partake of a rheumatic character.

CHARACTERISTIC SYMPTOMS.

Head.—Vertigo when turning the head (Kali c., Sang.), with heat, on rising (Bry.); at night. Congestion of head; painless, with strong pulsation of vessels of neck (Glon.). Headache, with sensation of fullness in vertex. Dull pain in forehead, just over the eyes, and extending into the eyes. °Pain in head and back all night. Pain in occiput, and alternating between there and forehead.

Eyes.—Sensation of fullness in the eyes, with headache. Eyes feel as if they would burst. Photophobia. Jerking of the left upper lid. Pupils dilated (Bell., Hyos., Stram.). °Hyperæsthesia of retina, steady aching in and behind eye ball.

Nose.—°Great sensitiveness of smell. °Nosebleed every morning.

Face.—Face flushed or congested from headache (*Bell.*).

Mouth.—Tongue coated thick white (Ant. crud., Bry., Nux v., Sulph.). Tongue raw and red; °dry, parched, sticky. Mouth and fauces very dry and hot. °Very sore mouth; canker sores. Much saliva in mouth, tasting salty (Merc.). Bad taste in mouth. Sour, coppery taste (Merc.).

Throat.—Sensation of a plug in the throat. Sense of constriction in throat; rough and dry (Lach.). Fauces hot, dry and swollen (Bell.). Difficulty of swallowing solids, liquids (Bell.).

Stomach—Appetite impaired. °Voracious appetite. *Eructations of hot, acrid fluid, which burns from the stomach to the throat. Food sours. Eructations of burning, hot gas from the stomach, causing a profuse secretion of* *tenacious mucus, which must be constantly hawked up;* aggravated by smoking tobacco. Constant nausea. Nausea on rising in the morning. Nausea after breakfast; not severe, but very persistent. Nausea, with water brash or vomiting. Sensation as if all food was lodged under upper end of sternum, which oppresses and distresses her for hours.

Stool and Anus.—Aching pain in anus. Soft, mushy stool; diarrhœa.

Urinary Organs.—*Frequent desire to urinate large quantities. Urinates frequently day and night; the attempt to retain it causes pain.*

Female Organs.—°Aching pain in region of right ovary, worse by rapid walking or exercise. °Leucorrhœa; staining linen yellow; when checked nasal catarrh ensues.

Respiratory Organs.—Dryness and rawness, extending to larynx. Aphonia. After rising the voice was *entirely without control,* whispering and squeaking when expecting to speak aloud. Spasmodic, ringing cough, caused by irritation in the throat. Hoarse, hard dry cough, with dryness of glottis. Left side of chest sore and painful. Cutting or sticking pain in upper third of right side.

Neck and Back.—Pain in small of back, extending into shoulders. Sore aching in lower part of back; worse when walking.

Limbs.—Severe, sharp pains in the joints.

Upper Limbs.—Rheumatic pain in shoulders. Rheumatic swelling and pain in wrists and elbows and small joints of the hands (Act. spic., Caul.).

Lower Limbs.—Knees and other joints stiff and painful. Rheumatic pain in the knee joints.

Generalities.—Weakness as if from exercise, with rheumatic pains in the bones. °Debility, weariness of the limbs. Aversion to exercise.

Skin.—°Skin harsh and dry, no sweat. Red spots or blotches on various parts of the body particularly the thighs and lower extremities. Itching and burning, aggravated by cold.

Sleep.—Restless all night. Does not sleep well.

Fever.—Cold and chilly at times. Flashes of heat. °Chilly.

mostly on limbs. Copious perspiration. *Unusual perspiration of feet.*
Compare.—Acon., Act. spic., Bell., Caul., Cimic., Ipec., Nux v., Puls., Rhus tox.

THERAPEUTICS.

Lactic acid has been used successfully in rheumatism, both articular and muscular, with symptoms above mentioned, worse at night, and from motion, acrid and profuse sweat. A valuable remedy in diabetes mellitus. Dyspepsia, food sours, hot, acrid eructations, which burn from the stomach to the mouth, water brash, nausea and vomiting. Valuable in morning sickness of pregnancy, especially in pale anæmic women, who have had menorrhagia. Epistaxis. Croup.

LACTUCA VIROSA.

Synonym.—Lactuca Fœtida. *Natural order.*—Compositæ. *Common names.*—Poisonous Lettuce. Lettuce Opium. *Habitat.*—A biennial herb, native of Europe. *Preparation.*—Tincture from the fresh plant.

GENERAL ANALYSIS.

The physiological action of this drug is chiefly upon the brain and nervous system, diminishing the force and frequency of the pulse, and disposing to sleep; unlike Opium, producing no excitement either of brain or circulation. Secondarily, it affects the vegetative sphere, and the respiratory mucous membrane, as is shown by its symptoms, very few of which, however, have been verified by practice.

CHARACTERISTIC SYMPTOMS.

Mind.—Ill-humored; fretful; peevish. Disinclination to mental labor; mind confused; power of thought diminished (Gels., *Nux v., Phos. ac.*).
Head.—Confusion of the head; vertigo. Dull headache.
Eyes.—*Pupils very much dilated (Bell., Hyos., Stram.).*

Stomach.—Pit of stomach retracted, with slight pain in stomach; aggravated by pressure. Feeling of warmth in stomach, accompanied by nausea rising into the throat, and flat taste at root of tongue, soon changing to icy coldness of stomach and throat. Tightness in pit of stomach, followed by true præcordial anxiety.

Abdomen.—Feeling of fullness in abdomen, especially in right side, which impedes respiration; relieved by discharge of flatulence upward or downward.

Urinary Organs.—Increased secretion of urine (Ambr., Phos. ac.).

Respiratory Organs.—*Incessant spasmodic cough, which threatens to burst the chest;* always caused by a peculiar tickling in fauces, which, in turn. seems to be produced by a sensation of suffocation in the throat; °followed by copious expectoration. Dry cough in short paroxysms, with shaking of the chest and occiput. Tightness of chest wakens from sleep, with anxiety (*Acon.*). Cramping, pressive pains in various parts of the chest. Pinching, dull, sticking pain in upper left side of chest. Sharp stitches beneath short ribs of left side of chest. Sharp stitches beneath short ribs of left side.

Generalities.—Great weariness and exhaustion. Unusual feeling of tightness of the body. Slight shivering.

Sleep.—Sleeplessness; sound refreshing sleep. Stupid sleep at night. Restless sleep at night.

Compare.—Coff., Dros., Op.

THERAPEUTICS.

Has been used but little in homœopathic practice. According to Hughes, it seems indicated in some forms of hepatic and pulmonary congestion, of clavus, and of cerebral weakness, with somnolence. Has been found useful in catarrhal laryngitis and bronchitis with the symptoms above mentioned. Whooping cough. Hydrothorax. Angina pectoris.

LAUROCERASUS.

Synonym.—Prunus Laurocerasus. *Natural order.*—Rosaceæ. *Common name.*—Cherry Laurel. *Habitat.*—A handsome evergreen shrub, native of the Caucasus, of Northwestern Asia Minor and of Northern Persia. *Preparation.*—Tincture from the fresh mature leaves.

GENERAL ANALYSIS.

Acts upon the brain and spinal cord, paralyzing the nerve centers in a manner resembling the poison of Hydrocyanic acid.

CHARACTERISTIC SYMPTOMS.

Mind.—Insensibility and complete loss of sensation (*Op.*).

Head.—Stupefaction with vertigo. Stupefying pain in the whole head. Sensation of coldness in forehead (Arn.) and vertex (Calc. c., Phos.), as if a cold wind were blowing on it, descending through the neck to the back. Feeling as if ice lay on the vertex.

Eyes.—Obscuration of vision, as if a veil were before the eyes (Caust., Hyos., Phos., Merc., Petrol., *Sulph.*). Eyes open and staring; distorted (*Bell.*, Hyos., *Stram.*).

Face.—Sunken face, with livid, gray-yellow complexion. Twitching and convulsions of the facial muscles (Cic.).

Mouth.—Lock jaw (*Bell.*, Cic., Hyos., Ign., *Nux v.*, Œnan.). Foam at mouth (Cic., Coccul., Cupr., Hyos., Naja). Loss of speech (Dulc., Gels., Caust., Naja).

Throat.—Impeded deglutition (Bell., *Hyos., Stram.*). Spasmodic contraction of the throat and œsophagus (*Bell., Hyos., Stram.*). °*Drink rolls audibly through œsophagus and intestines.*

Stomach.—Vomiting of food, with cough. Hiccough.

Abdomen.—Sensation like the falling of a heavy lump from just above the umbilicus to the small of back; produced by talking or over-exertion. Distension in hepatic region, with pain as if suppurating, and as if an ulcer would burst. Stitches and pain in the liver extending toward the back;

with burning and pain on touch. Paralytic bruised pain in liver on inspiration, extending to shoulder (Chel.). Burning in liver.

Stool and Anus.—Diarrhœa; with tenesmus; stools frequent, thin greenish mucus; °with suffocative spells about the heart.

Respiratory Organs.—Spasmodic oppression of the chest (Ign.). Dyspnœa, with sensation as if the lungs would not be sufficiently expanded (*Asaf., Crot. tig.*). Gasping for breath; suffocating spells. Cough, with a whistling sound, as if the membranes were too dry; from tickling in the throat; *in paroxysms;* frequent, short; coughing up blood; dry cough, with feeling as if mucus were hanging in throat, and could not be loosened. Stitches in the region of the heart (*Kalm., Kali carb.*).

Heart and Pulse.—Irregular beating of the heart, with slow pulse (Dig., Lachn.). ᶜFluttering in region of heart and gasping for breath with cough.

Generalities.—Want of energy of the vital powers, and want of reaction (Caps., Carb. v.). Painlessness with the ailments. Rapid sinking of the forces (*Ars.*, Camph., Sec. c.).

Sleep.—Deep, snoring sleep; soporous condition (Ars., *Op.,* Sulph.).

Compare.—Baryt. c., *Bell.,* Bry., Calc. c., Hydroc. ac., Hyos., Kalmia, Lyc., Nux v., Op., *Phos.,* Puls., Rhus tox., Sep., Sulph., Verat. alb.

Antidotes.—Camph., *Coff.,* Ipec., Op. Too large doses: Amm. Strong Coffee, Cold Effusions.

THERAPEUTICS.

Laurocerasus is chiefly used in nervous and organic affections of the lungs and heart, characterized by spasmodic contraction of the throat and chest, causing suffocative attacks, extreme dyspnœa, slow irregular pulse, and great nervous excitement. Apoplexia. Cyanosis. Cyanosis neonatorum, face blue with gasping. Chorea. Trismus. Tetanus. Epilepsy. Hiccough. Whooping cough; nervous spasmodic cough. Dry cough during phthisis or heart disease, very harassing, especially when lying down (Hyos.). Threatened paralysis of the lungs. Neuralgic dysmenorrhœa. Induration and inflammation of the liver. Abscess threatening. Diarrhœa, green mucous stools, with suffocative spells about the heart. Cholera. Cholera infantum.

LEDUM.

Synonym.—Ledum Palustre. *Natural order.*—Ericaceæ. **Common names.**—Marsh Tea. Wild Rosemary. *Habitat.*—An evergreen shrub growing in moist, swampy grounds in Europe, France, Asia and British America. *Preparation.*—Tincture from the fresh herb.

GENERAL ANALYSIS.

Acts upon the serous, fibrous and mucous tissues, upon the periosteum, and upon the skin, producing inflammatory symptoms of an arthritic or rheumatic character, increasing and thickening secretions, and causing a deposit of solid, earthy masses in the tissues.

CHARACTERISTIC SYMPTOMS.

Mind.—Discontented; morose; peevish (*Bry., Nux v.*).
Head.—Vertigo as from intoxication (Nux m., Coccul.), especially when walking in the open air (Agar., Calc. c., Glon., Sep., *Sulph.*); the head tends to sink back. Stupefying headache. Raging, pulsating headache (*Bell., Glon.*).
Eyes.—Photophobia; dilated pupils (Bell.). Burning, corrosive lachrymation (Ars., Euphr.).
Ears.—Roaring in ears, as from a storm of wind (Gels.). Hardness of hearing.
Face.—Pimples like those of drunkards, on face and forehead. Boils on the forehead (Hep. s.).
Mouth.—Sudden running of water, with colic, waterbrash.
Throat.—Sore throat, with fine, stinging pain.
Stomach.—Pressure in stomach after a light meal (Cinch., Lyc.).
Respiratory Organs.—Cough, preceded by suffocative arrest of breathing (Ars.). Hollow, racking cough, with purulent expectoration, or of bright-red and foaming blood. Constrictive oppression of the chest (Ars., Lob.); aggravated

by moving and walking. Respiration painfully impeded. Eruption like varicella on the chest and upper arms.

Heart.—Pushing or pressing inward at left edge of sternum; palpitation; °also in hæmorrhage.

Neck and Back.—Painful stiffness of the back and loins, on rising from a seat (*Berb., Rhus tox.*); and in scapulæ.

Limbs.—*Painful hard nodes,* and calcareous concretions on the joints (Calc. c., Merc., Phos.). Pressive pains in the knees and wrists. Rheumatism of the small joints (*Act. spic., Caul.*). °Rheumatism begins in lower limbs and ascends. Paralytic pain in all joints on moving body at night in bed. The limbs are numb and fall asleep. Drawing pain in various parts and joints, worse from wine.

Upper Limbs.—Rheumatic, tearing pains in the joints (Bry., Puls., Rhus tox., Spig.); worse from movement. Great trembling of hands, as from old age, on moving them, or on seizing anything. Boring pain in first joint of thumb. *Periosteum of phalanges, painful on pressure.*

Lower Limbs.—Sprained pain toward posterior part of left hip, as if muscles were not in proper position, worse from walking or touch. Swelling and tensive, sticking pains in knee, when walking (*Bry.*). Cracking in knee. Swelling extending above calves, with tensive pain, worse evenings. Stiffness of the legs in the morning. Weakness and tremor of the knees when walking. Tearing, and sore pains in knees. *Pain in the ankles, as from a sprain or a false step; worse on motion* (Arn., Bry.). Swelling of the feet, and up to the knees (Ars., Digit.). Feet heavy, weary; stiff and rigid. Pains in soles of the feet, as if bruised, when walking. *Ball of great toe swollen, soft and painful on stepping.* Stitches in great toes.

Generalities.—The limbs and whole body are painful, as if bruised or beaten (*Arn.*, Merc.). *Heat of bed intolerable, on account of heat and burning of limbs, wants to uncover. Pains change location suddenly* (Benz. ac., Kali bi., Puls.). °*Emaciation of suffering parts* (Graph.). Œdematous swellings (Apis, Ars., Rhus tox.). *Pains sticking, tearing, throbbing.*

Skin.—Red, pimply eruptions, especially on face and forehead. Excessive corrosive itching of the skin; worse from scratching, and from the heat of the bed (*Merc.*). *Eruptions which burn and sting like the bites or stings of insects* (*Ant. crud., Apis, Arn.*).

Sleep.—Sleeplessness, with restlessness and tossing about. Uneasy dreams, in which he changes from place to place, and from one subject to another.

Fever.—*Coldness; want of animal heat* (Sep., Sil.). Shaking chill over back, with cold hands, hot cheeks and hot forehead. Burning heat in limbs, hands and feet, *making heat of bed intolerable* (*Sulph.*). Perspiration from least exertion (Ambr., *Calc. c.*, Hep. s., Phos., Sep., Sil.), principally on forehead. Warm sweat on hands and feet. Sweat, waking from sleep, with itching over whole body. Night sweats, with inclination to uncover.

Aggravation.—Towards evening. From heat, especially heat of bed; when sitting; during rest; cold; wet weather.

Amelioration.—Of pains at night. After Camphor.

Conditions.—Rheumatic, gouty diathesis. Constitutions abused by Alcohol.

Compare.—Arn., Ars., Bell., Bry., Calc. c., Cinch., Crot. tig., Dulc., Kalmia, Lyc., Merc. cor., *Puls.*, Rhus tox., Ruta, Sep., Sulph.

Antidote.—Camph.

Ledum Antidotes.——Alcohol, Apis, Cinch.

THERAPEUTICS.

A valuable remedy in rheumatic and arthritic affections. The smaller joints are most affected. Generally worse from the heat of the bed; usually a great deal of bruised soreness in the muscles, with stitching, tearing pains, rapidly shifting; rarely useful if joints are hot and swollen. Synovitis of the knee, especially strumous. Sciatica. Sprains of the ankles and feet. Used locally for punctured or penetrating wounds, produced by sharp-pointed instruments; also for the stings of insects, especially mosquitoes. Papular and eczematous eruptions in habitual drunkards, especially on face and forehead. Urticaria and other chronic eruptions with violent itching, worse from warmth of bed. Ecchymoses. Hæmorrhages, especially of bright-red blood. Hæmoptysis; blood frothy; alternating with attacks of rheumatism. Uterine hæmorrhage. Phthisical symptoms, alternating with coxalgia or rheumatism. Whooping cough. Chronic cough, usually hollow, racking. spasmodic, characterized by coldness and deficiency of animal heat. Bronchitis. Suppuration of lungs; purulent, greenish expectoration; after neglected pneumonia. Rheumatic ophthalmia. Ecchymoses of the conjunctiva. Intra-occular hæmorrhages. Asthenopia. Rheumatic otitis, from getting cold, having hair cut, or exposure to a damp, cold wind. Ascites. Ailments from abuse of alcoholic drinks.

LEPTANDRA.

Synonyms.—Leptandra Virginica. Veronica Virginica. *Natural order.*—Scrofulariceæ. *Common names.*—Culver's Physic. Black Root. *Habitat.*—A perennial herbaceous plant growing throughout the United States east of the Mississippi. *Preparation.*—Tincture from the fresh root.

GENERAL ANALYSIS.

Acts especially upon the liver and the intestinal canal, arousing their secretory functions. Its chief characteristic is a *profuse black, tar-like, very fœtid stool (Ars.)*.

CHARACTERISTIC SYMPTOMS.

Head.—Constant dull frontal headache; dizziness; pain in bowels.

Mouth.—Tongue coated yellow mornings. Flat, unpleasant taste in the morning.

Stomach.—° *Vomiting of bile, yellow tongue, shooting pains about liver, black stools.*

Abdomen.—*Aching in liver, extending to spine, worse in region of gall-bladder.* Aching in umbilical region, rumbling in abdomen and urging to stool, relieved by passing a profuse dark, fœtid stool. Rumbling in hypogastrium in the morning, with distress, followed by characteristic stool.

Stool.—*Profuse, black, fœtid stool, running out in a stream.* Stool first hard, black and lumpy, then mushy.

Compare.—Ars., Bry., Cinch., Iris, Podo.

THERAPEUTICS.

Its therapeutic range is confined to bilious conditions, and hepatic diseases in general, especially when the characteristic blackish stools are present. Sick-headache from hepatic derangement. Bilious headache, constipation, bitter taste. Jaundice with clay-colored stools. Dysentery or typhoid, with black, tar-like stools. Bilious fever. Chronic congestion and other chronic disorders of the liver. Chronic abdominal complaints caused by derangement of portal system, even ascites and anasarca.

LILIUM TIGRINUM.

Natural order.—Liliaceæ. *Common name.*—Tiger Lily. *Habitat.*—A plant, native of China and Japan; cultivated in gardens. *Preparation.*—Tincture from the fresh plant.

GENERAL ANALYSIS.

Acts profoundly upon the female generative organs, and upon the heart; in the former producing irritation, congestion and subacute inflammation, together with the various forms of uterine displacement. Through reflex action it depresses the action of the heart, and produces symptoms of cardiac irritability, palpitation, etc. The chief characteristic of Lilium is a bearing down sensation in the uterine region, as if everything would press out of the vagina.

CHARACTERISTIC SYMPTOMS.

Mind.—*Depression of spirits;* inclination to weep, timidity, apprehensiveness (*Nux m., Puls., Phos.*). °Tormented about her salvation, with uterine complaints. Constant hurried feeling, as of imperative duties and utter inability to perform them; during sexual excitement. °Disposed to curse, to strike, to think of obscene things; as these mental states came, uterine irritation abated.

Head.—°Headache, especially if depending on uterine disorders (*Caul., Cimic.*). Dull pain in forehead over the eyes.

Eyes.—Hypermetropia; presbyopia. Vision dim; and etc.

fused, with disposition to cover eyes and press upon them. Blurred vision with heat in eyes and lids.

Stomach.—Nausea, with hawking of mucus. Loss of appetite (Alum., Ars., Calc. c., *Cinch.*, Nux m.). Craving for meat. Hollow, empty sensation in stomach and bowels (Ign., Hydras., Sep.).

Abdomen.—Distension of the abdomen (*Calc. c.*, Cinch., Lyc., Nux v.). Dragging down of whole abdominal contents, extending even to organs of chest: must support the abdomen (*Bell., Plat., Sep.*). *Sensation as if diarrhœa would come on* (Aloe); *also passing off by urinating.*

Stool and Anus.—*Pressure in rectum with almost constant desire to go to stool.* Morning diarrhœa (Aloe, Rumex. Sulph.); stools loose, bilious (Podo.); dark, offensive, very urgent, can't wait a moment; stool preceded by griping pains or great urging, with pressure in the rectum; followed by smarting, burning of the anus and rectum (*Ars., Canth.*). Constipation.

Urinary Organs.—*Frequent urination during the day, with smarting in the urethra* (Canth., Can. sat.). *Continuous pressure in the bladder. Constant desire to urinate, with scanty discharge; burning and smarting in urethra after* (Acon., Canth.).

Female Organs.—*Bearing down, with sensation of heavy weight and pressure in uterine region, as if the whole contents would press out through the vagina* (Bell., Nux m., Plat., Sep.); *relieved by pressure of the hand against the vulva. Sharp pains in the ovarian region* (Bell., Cimic.). Pains in right ovary and back. Ovaries sore on pressure, worse right side. Gnawing and dragging in right ovary, worse from walking. Severe neuralgic pains in uterus; could not bear touch; not even weight of bedclothes or slightest jar; anteversion. Fundus of uterus low down, tilted against bladder, the os pressing upon rectum. Bearing down in uterus, with pains in left ovary and mamma. Voluptuous itching in vagina, with feeling of fullness of parts; stinging in left ovarian region. Sexual desire increased; ending in orgasm. °Leucorrhœa; bright-yellow, acrid excoriating (Alum., Ars., Kreos.); leaving a brown stain.

LILIUM TIGRINUM.

Chest and Heart.—*Dull, pressive pain in region of heart* (Iod., Cact.). *Pain in heart* worse when lying down at night. Constant feeling of a load or weight in left chest. *Sharp and quick pain in left side of chest* (Kreos.), *with fluttering of the heart* (Spig.). Heart feels as if squeezed in a vise (Arn., Cact.); or alternately grasped and relaxed. Fluttering or palpitation of the heart (Natr. mur.).

Back.—Dull pain in sacrum (Æsc.). Sensation of pulling upward from tip of coccyx.

Limbs.—Limbs cold, clammy; more when excited or nervous. Burning in palms and soles. Pain in right hip, extending down the thighs. Paralytic pricking in fingers and hands.

Generalities.—Weak, trembling, nervous. Faintness, worse in a warm room or after being on the feet a long time. Worse walking, yet pains so much worse after ceasing to walk that he must walk again. Pains in small spots; shifting pains (*Puls.*). Throbbing as if in all the blood vessels.

Aggravation.—In evening; at night, from loss of self-control.

Amelioration.—During the day; from fresh air; from keeping busy; in warm room.

Compare.—Aloe, Apis, Bell., Cact., Canth., Cimic., Helon., Ign., Nux v., Plat., Podo., Puls., Sep., Spig., Sulph.

Antidotes.—Helon. (anteversion), Nux v. (colic).

THERAPEUTICS.

The therapeutic, like the pathogenetic, range of Lilium centers in the female sexual system, from which source seems to arise all the disturbances for which it has proved curative. It is a valuable remedy in all forms of uterine displacement, especially versions, with pressure against the rectum and bladder (especially rectum), and consequent constipation and cystic irritation; the uterus is usually more or less congested and sensitive, and there are shooting pains, in which it differs from Sepia, which also has the heaviness and pressing down and relief from pressing against the vulva, so characteristic of Lilium. Often indicated and of great value in chronic metritis and subinvolution. Leucorrhœa. Ovaritis. Ovarian neuralgia. An important characteristic of Lilium is that the ovarian symptoms have usually associated with them reflex heart symptoms, pain, fluttering, palpitation, sensation as if alternately grasped and relaxed, etc. A valuable remedy in nervous affections of the heart dependent upon uterine or ovarian disease. Pruritus of the vagina and vulva. The mental symptoms of Lilium are also dependent on uterine disease; hysteria; melancholia; religious melancholia; mania; useful in certain forms of asthenopia, especially for astigmatism. Disturbed vision from uterine or ovarian diseases.

LITHIUM.

Synonym.—Lithium Carbonicum. *Preparation.*—Triturations of pure Carbonate of Lithium.

GENERAL ANALYSIS.

The sphere of action of this drug is not well defined. It evidently acts most prominently upon mucous surfaces and muscular tissues. Its local action upon the heart, kidneys and eyes seems most pronounced, and it is in diseases of these organs that its curative virtues have mainly been displayed.

CHARACTERISTIC SYMPTOMS.

Mind.—Difficulty in remembering names. Anxiety and hopelessness at night.

Head.—Heaviness in sinciput; worse in frontal eminences. Confusion of the head. Headache ceases while eating, but returns and remains un il food is again taken. Headache, like a stitch, superiorly in the vertex, on right side, sensitive when touched. Sunlight blinds him.

Eyes.—°Black motes before eyes; eyes sensitive after using them by candle light; asthenopia. *Vision uncertain; entire vanishing of the right half of objects; if two short words occur in succession, that on right hand is invisible* (Calc. c., Lyc. Lower half, Aur.). Eyes pain as if sore; pain as from grains of sand; feel dry and pain after reading.

Nose.—Swollen, red; worse right side; internally sore and dry; shining crusts form. Coryza; dropping from nose.

Throat.—Sore throat, extending into the ear, and from **ear to**

LITHIUM.

throat (*Hep. s.,* Kali bi.). Hawking up mucus in large quantities.

Stomach.—Acidity of stomach. Appetite decreased, satisfied on beginning to eat (Lyc.). Nausea, with gnawing in stomach, fullness in temples, headache. Fullness in stomach; cannot endure slightest pressure of clothes (Calc. c., *Lyc., Nux v.*). Sticking burning extending upwards in epigastrium.

Abdomen.—Pressure in hepatic region. Violent pain in hepatic region, between ilium and ribs. Feels swollen as if distended with wind.

Stool.—Diarrhœa; stools light-yellow (Chel.); offensive (Ars., Asaf.).

Urinary Organs.—Pain in bladder extending into spermatic cord (*Clem., Puls., Spong.*), after urinating. Tenesmus of bladder while and after urinating (*Canth.*). On rising to urinate a pressing in the region of the heart, which did not cease until after urination. Urine scanty, dark, acrid; pain when passed; emission difficult, with dark, reddish-brown deposit; turbid, with mucous deposit; profuse, with uric acid deposit.

Respiratory Organs.—°On inspiring the air feels cold, even in the lungs (Hydras.).

Heart and Pulse.—Violent pain in region of heart (Acon., Cact., Digit.), when bending over bed in morning. Pressive pain in heart (Cact., Lil. tig., Digit.). °Valvular deficiencies, worse from mental agitation, which causes a fluttering and trembling of the heart. Sudden shocks in cardiac region. Rheumatic soreness in region of heart. Pains in heart before and at time of urinating; also before and at time of menses (Lil. tig.).

Back.—Pressure as with a dull point, here and there, internally, as if near the sacral bone, in evening; most on left side.

Limbs.—Occasional rheumatic pains in the limbs. *Pain in right shoulder joint near insertion of pectoralis major, at margin of muscle.* Rheumatic pains in the fingers and thumb. Gouty pain in ankles and bones of feet.

Generalities.—Pains burning sticking in jerks outward, and ending in burning itching. Paralytic stiffness of whole body. Prostration of whole body, especially knee joints and sacrum. Bones, joints, muscles of whole body sore, as if beaten. Before menses, symptoms more violent on *left* side; after menses on *right* side. All symptoms worse on right side.

Compare.—Cact., Digit., Lach., Lyc., Graph., Mag. c.

THERAPEUTICS.

Lithium is of great value in the treatment of rheumatism and gout, especially acute arthritic inflammation of the small joints, occurring occasionally in gouty subjects. It is a valuable remedy in rheumatism of the heart, chronic rheumatic endocarditis, with soreness about the heart, and pain, especially before and at the time of urinating; usually associated with chronic arthritis of the finger joints. Valvular insufficiency. Useful in asthenopia, anæmia of the retina, ophthalmia and other eye affections, the symptoms agreeing. Acid dyspepsia in gouty subjects. Useful in irritation of the bladder, dysuria, and even albuminuria, where the urine is scanty and very acid; excess of uric acid deposit, gouty symptoms; acid dyspepsia. Inflammation of the prostate gland, with pink sediment in urine.

LOBELIA INFLATA.

Natural order.—Lobeliaceæ. *Common names.*—Indian Tobacco. Puke Root. *Habitat.*—An indigenous annual plant found growing on road-sides and in neglected fields. *Preparation.*—Tincture from the fresh plant.

GENERAL ANALYSIS.

Acts upon the cerebro-spinal system, especially on the pneumogastric nerve, producing profound prostration, a depressed relaxed condition of the system, oppression of the chest, impeded respiration and deglutition, together with epigastric oppression, nausea, and vomiting, finally paralyzing the pneumogastrics, and causing failure of the heart and respiration, collapse and death. In small doses it produces spasms of the larynx and bronchi, and hence is useful in spasmodic conditions of those parts, especially when accompanied by nausea.

LOBELIA INFLATA.

CHARACTERISTIC SYMPTOMS.

Head.—Vertigo with nausea (*Alum., Ant. crud., Cocc.*). Dull, heavy pain passing around the forehead from one temple to the other. Pressive pain on left side of occiput; worse at night and from motion.

Mouth.—Copious discharge of saliva (*Iodi., Iris, Merc.*). Sharp, disagreeable taste in the mouth, especially at tip of tongue and back of throat.

Throat.—Sensation as if the œsophagus were contracted from below upward. Sensation as of a lump in pit of throat (*Bell., Lach.*). Mucus in throat, causing frequent necessity to hawk.

Stomach.—Loss of appetite, with acrid, burning taste in the mouth (*Ars.*). Acidity of the stomach, with a contractive feeling in the pit of stomach. Flatulent eructations (*Carb. v., Cinch., Phos.*). Incessant, violent nausea (*Ant. tart., Ipec., Digit.*). *Nausea in the morning disappears after a swallow of water.* Nausea, with cold perspiration on the head (*Tabac., Verat. alb.*). Nausea, with indescribable pain, heat, oppression, and excessive uneasiness about the stomach. Heartburn and running of water from the mouth, and oppression (*Ars.*). Feeling of weakness at the epigastrium with qualmishness and oppression of the chest (*Ars.*). Oppression of epigastrium, as if too full. Burning in the stomach (*Ars., Calc. c., Canth., Mez.*).

Respiratory Organs.—*Extremely difficult breathing*, caused by constriction of the chest (*Ars., Phos.*). Oppression of breathing.

Pulse.—Pulse small; and weak.

Urinary Organs.—Urine deposits a rosy-red sediment, with crystals of uric acid.

Generalities.—Great prostration and weariness.

Aggravation.—From cold, especially cold washing.

Amelioration.—Toward evening.

Conditions.—Light hair, blue eyes, fair complexion; inclined to be fleshy.

Compare.—Ars., Ant. tart., Cocc., Digit., Ipec., Tabac., Verat. alb. after Ant. tart. and Ipec. fail in morning sickness.—*Hering*.

Antidote.—Ipec. (?)

THERAPEUTICS.

The chief use of Lobelia has been in the treatment of diseases of the respiratory tract when accompanied by nausea, vomiting, great prostration, oppression of the chest and dyspnœa; asthma; bronchitis; capillary bronchitis; spasmodic croup; whooping cough; emphysema; spasmodic cough, etc., during phthisis. Sometimes an efficient palliative in heart disease. Has been successfully used in gastralgia and dyspepsia characterized by heartburn, weakness at epigastrium, deathly nausea, oppression of chest, etc. Morning sickness of pregnancy. Intussusception of bowels. Incarcerated hernia. Has been used in quotidian type of intermittent fever with characteristic Lobelia symptoms. Rheumatism. "Lobelia is, to the bad effects from drunkenness in people with light hair, blue or gray eyes, florid complexion, fat or corpulent, what Nux vom. is to people of opposite temperament."

LYCOPODIUM.

Synonym.—Lycopodium Clavatum. *Natural order.*—Lycopodiaceæ. *Common names.*—Club Moss. Wolf's Foot. *Habitat.*—A moss growing in all parts of the world, especially in Northern countries. *Preparation.*—Triturations of the pollen of the plant (see special directions in Pharmacopœia).

GENERAL ANALYSIS.

Lycopodium acts powerfully upon the vegetative system, depressing its action, and causing a slowly advancing weakness of functional power and decay of tissue. It acts especially upon the mucous membranes of the respiratory, digestive and genito-urinary organs and upon the skin, but shows its most important local action upon the liver and the digestive tract, where it produces a disturbed digestion, hepatic congestion, constipation, etc., and upon the kidneys causing the "uric acid diathesis." The lymphatic system becomes weakened, the glands, especially of the neck, swollen and indurated, and the skin sluggish and unhealthy. The chief characteristic of this remedy is an excessive accumulation of flatulence in the abdomen.

CHARACTERISTIC SYMPTOMS.

Mind.—Depression of spirits; weeping; sad, melancholy, despondent (Natr. mur., Lob., *Puls.*); apprehensive. Great anxiety, as if in pit of stomach. Suspicious. Anthrophobia. Fretful, ill-humored, irritable (Anac., Bry., Cham., Nux v., Hep. s., Calc. c.), morose, peevish, vehement, angry, timid. Easily aroused to anger. *Weak memory* (Anac.); *confused thoughts; speaks or writes wrong words and syllables* (Dulc., Melil., Osm.). *Confusion about every-day things,* but rational talking on abstract subjects. Disinclined to talk. Inability to comprehend or remember what is read. Stupefaction. Dullness.

Head.—*Vertigo in the morning when and after rising* (Alum., Bry., Cham., Nitr. ac., Phos.), *so that he reels back and forth.* Rush of blood to the head in the morning on waking. Head shakes on stepping hard. Confusion and heaviness in the head. Headache, with ravenous hunger, better from eating. Pressing, stupefying headache; worse from 4 to 8 P.M. *Throbbing headache; on leaning head backward during the day; after coughing.* Pressing or tearing frontal headache, especially in right of head; worse on rising up better on lying down. Pressive headache in the vertex. Frontal headache after breakfast; afternoon when riding in carriage, with pressure in stomach. *Shattering pain in temples and chest during cough.* Stitches in temples during difficult stool. Hair becomes gray early (Phos. ac.); falling out of hair (*Graph.*, Natr. mur., *Nitr. ac.*, Phos., *Sep.*). Eruption beginning on the occiput; crusts thick, easily bleeding; oozing a fœtid moisture; worse after scratching, and from warmth (*Graph.*, Hep. s., *Merc.*, Nitr. ac.). Itching of the scalp.

Eyes.—Inflammation of the eyes, with itching in canthi, redness, and swelling of lids; *distressing pain as if they were dry, with nightly agglutination* (Alum., Calc. c., Merc., Puls., *Graph.*, Sil., *Sulph.*). Sticking, worse mornings, without redness. Must wipe mucus from eye in order to see clearly (Euph., Puls.). Purulent mucus. Dryness and smarting in the eyes, as if dust were in them; difficult to open, mornings; burning itching. *Styes on the lids,* more toward inner canthi (Graph., *Puls.,* Staph.). *Ulceration and redness of lids,* with acrid lachrymation (Merc., Sulph.). Photophobia; *evening light blinds very much; can see nothing on the table.* Sees only the left half of an object distinctly (Calc. c., Lith. Upper half, *Aur.*). Veil and flickering before the eyes; black spots before the eyes (*Cycl.,* Merc., *Phos.,* Sulph.).

Ears.—Hearing over-sensitive (*Acon., Bell.,* Mur. ac.). Roaring in the ears (Acon., Bell., Cinch.). Purulent, ichorous discharge from the ears (Aur., Graph., Hep. s., Merc., Nitr. ac.).

Nose.—*Violent catarrh, with swelling of the nose and acrid discharge* (Ars., Cepa, Merc. cor.). °The ichorous discharge from the nose begins in right nostril; scarlatina or diphtheria. *Nose stopped up;* at night; *cannot breathe through it* (Nux v.); with excessive dryness; evenings. Smell extremely sensitive (Acon., Agar., *Bell.,* Coff. c., Colch., Hep. s.). °Fan-like motion of the alæ nasi in pneumonia.

Face.—*Yellowish-gray color of the face* (Cinch.). Pale, sickly, puffy (Ars.). Flushes of heat in the face (Kreos., Sulph.). Tearing pains in the bones of the face. Ulcers on lips.

Mouth.—Humid suppurating eruption around the mouth; corners of mouth sore (Ant. crud., *Graph.,* Merc.). The lower jaw hangs down (Op.). *Teeth excessively painful to touch, and when chewing;* front teeth loose or too long (Carb. an., Merc., Nitr. ac.); drawing cramp-like pains, relieved by warm drinks; with swelling of gums. Gums bleed violently when cleaning the teeth (*Merc., Nitr.* ac., *Phos.*). Tongue coated white (*Ant. crud., Bry., Nux-v., Puls.*). Ulcers on and under the tongue. *Vesicles on the tip of the tongue* (Kali carb., Natr. mur., Mur. ac.). Dryness of the mouth and tongue, without thirst (*Nux m., Puls.*). Laxity and heaviness of the tongue. Accumulation of water in mouth. Saliva dries on palate and lips to a tenacious mucus. °Tongue is darted out and oscillates to and fro; in sore throat. °Tongue distended, giving patient silly expression; in angina or diphtheria. Sour or bitter **taste**

(Cinch. Nux v., Mag. carb.); in the morning; after eating. Food tastes sour.

Throat.—Accumulation of mucus in throat; hawking of bloody mucus; with inclination to swallow; small greenish yellow masses; granular. Choking provoking constant swallowing. Sticking; in region of right parotid. |Dryness in throat.| Soreness and pain on swallowing and coughing. °Pain and soreness beginning on right side of throat. *Feeling as if a ball rose from below up into the throat (Asaf., Physos.). Feeling of constriction in throat; nothing can be swallowed; food and drink regurgitate through the nose (Merc.).* °Swelling and suppuration of tonsils, going from right to left (Hep. s., Merc.). Sensitiveness of the submaxillary glands.

Stomach.—*Excessive appetite; the more he eats the more he wants (Bry., Cina, Ferr., Merc.).* Hunger, but a small quantity of food fills him up; constant feeling of satiety (Cinch.). Appetite lost; whatever she eats goes against her, even to vomiting. Aversion to coffee (Natr. mur., Phos. ac.), and tobacco. *Eructations acrid; incomplete and burning hiccough* (Bry., Cic., Hyos.). *Sour taste extending to stomach, causing acrid gnawings.* Heartburn; *waterbrash* (Led., Natr. carb., Nux v.). Nausea; in pharynx and stomach; in mornings, fasting. *Distension and cramp in stomach.* Vomiting of food and bile; vomiting after a meal with salivation; during menses; better in open air. *Pressure and heaviness in stomach, as if distended; in evening after eating a little* (Cinch., Led., Sulph.). Slow digestion. Pit of stomach swollen and sensitive to touch (Ant. crud., Ars., Bry.); anxiety in pit. Constriction and tightness in stomach and hypochondria.

Abdomen.—*Sore, pressive bruised pain in region of liver, on breathing; aggravated by touch. Sensation of something heavy lying on left side of abdomen. Excessive fullness and distension of the abdomen from flatulence* (Absinth., Cinch., Carb. veg., Kali carb., Phos.); *better from passing flatus. Much flatus accumulates here and there in the abdomen, in the hypochondria, in the back, in region of ribs and chest, causing tension and bubbling; relieved by empty eructations* (Carb. v.). Griping. *Tension and pain*

LYCOPODIUM.

in abdomen from incarcerated flatulence (Cinch., *Carb., v.*). Continuous rumbling and roaring in the abdomen (Agar., Aloe, Hep. s., *Sulph.*, Zinc.). °Brown spots on abdomen.

Stool and Anus.—*Rectum contracted and protrudes during hard stool.* Burning in the anus with frequent stools. Stitches and cramps in the rectum. Hæmorrhoids protruding, *very painful to the touch;* painful when sitting. Discharge of blood during stool. Constipation; stools dry and hard (*Bry., Sulph.*), or *first part lumpy, second soft;* feeling as if much remained unpassed (*Nux v.*).

Urinary Organs.—Severe backache; °relieved by passing urine. Passing only small quantities. Frequent desire to urinate. Burning during micturition. *Red, sandy sediment in the urine* (Arn., Cinch., Coccus, Natr. mur., Phos.). Turbid, milky urine, with an offensive purulent sediment; dull pressing in region of bladder and abdomen; disposition to calculi; cystitis. °Incontinence; no urine secreted. °Hæmaturia from gravel or chronic catarrh. °Before passing water child screams with pain; red sand on diaper.

Male Organs.—Impotence: penis, small, cold, relaxed. Desire diminished (Agn., Baryt. c., Berb., Caps., Sulph.). Itching on inner surface of prepuce; on scrotum.

Female Organs.—Menses too profuse, and long protracted. Suppression of menses: °also from fright (*Acon.*). °Sense of dryness in vagina. Burning in vagina (Sulph.), during and after coition. Leucorrhœa like milk (Calc. c., Coni., Kreos., *Puls.*, Sulph. ac., *Sep.*); bloody; corroding. Cutting across the hypogastrium; from right to left. °Discharge of wind from the vagina (Brom.).

Respiratory Organs.—Hoarseness. Itching and tickling in larynx, compelling forcible cough. *Shortness of breath, especially during sleep.* Difficult breathing, as if he had inhaled sulphur fumes (Ars., Cinch.). *Dyspnœa, as if the chest were constricted by cramp.* Cough, dry, day and night, with painfulness in region of stomach; in evening before going to sleep, from tickling in larynx as from a feather; as from sulphur fumes in larynx; from deep breathing. Cough at night, better before sunrise, affecting stomach and diaphragm. Violent cough with tightness of the chest (Phos.). Expectoration scanty; thick, yellow mucus; bloody; purulent; *gray* (Stan.); *salty* (Ambr., Calc., c., Carb. v., Phos., Sep.). Dull aching all over the lungs, with feeling of constriction of the chest. Violent oppression of the chest. Stitches in left chest; also during inspiration.

Heart.—Palpitation of the heart (Acon., *Ars., Spig., Sulph., Verat. alb.*); in evening in bed. Accelerated pulse, with cold face and feet.

Neck and Back.—Stiffness of the neck (*Chel.*, Rhus tox.). Drawing pain. Swelling of the cervical glands (*Baryt. c.*, Calc. c., Iodi., Merc., Sil.). Tensive pain in nape of neck and occiput. *Burning, as from glowing coals, between the scapulæ.* Pain in the small of the back (*Bell.*, Nux. v., *Puls.*). Pain in back and right side, from congestion of liver. Stitches in region of kidneys, worse from pressure; extending into rectum. Tearing pain in region of kidneys.

Limbs.—Drawing tearing pains in all the limbs (Bry., Coloc., Merc., *Sulph.*). Stiffness and painfulness of joints.

Upper Limbs.—Swelling of the axillary glands (Baryt. c., Sil.). Tearing pains in elbows and shoulder joints. Arms and fingers go to sleep easily (Cham.). Drawing pains in inner surface of arms. Finger joints inflamed, red and swollen.

Lower Limbs.—Swelling and stiffness of the knees. Soreness in inner side of left thigh, with biting itching, extending to the genitals. Brown spots on inner side of thighs, inflamed with burning pain. Tearing pain in middle of right thigh. Swelling of the feet. Cramps in the calves at night. Pain in the soles when walking (Sulph.). Smarting sore pain between the toes. Cold, *sweaty feet* (Calc. c., Sil.). Feet sweat until they become sore. One foot hot, the other cold.

Generalities.—Weariness; weakness after every exertion; in morning on rising, with heaviness. *Desire for the open air* (*Puls.*). Discomfort in every position at night. °Involuntary alternate extension and contraction of muscles. Emaciation and debility (*Ars.*, Ferr., Phos.). °Bones inflamed, mostly the ends; nocturnal bone pains. °Softening of bones; caries. *All symptoms aggravated from 4 to 8 P.M.; better after 8 P.M., but weak.*

Skin.—Humid suppurating eruptions (*Hep. s., Graph.*). Itching "liver spots." Boils on nates. Itching pimples. Intertrigo; raw places, bleeding easily (Graph., Hydras.). Chronic urticaria. Skin unhealthy, corrosive vesicles. °Nævus maternus. °Vascular tumors.

Sleep.—Yawning and sleepiness during the day (Nux m.). Restless, uneasy sleep; full of dreams (Ars.). Starting up on falling asleep. Soporous sleep in typhoid and exanthematous fevers (Arn., Op.). Crying or laughing in sleep. On awakening, cross, scolds, unrefreshed.

Fever.—Creeping chills over the back in the evening. Slight chill, followed by long-continued heat, weariness. and pains in the limbs. Chill, alternating with heat; and redness and heat of cheeks. Flushes of heat over the whole body, mostly evenings. Sweats from least exertion (*Calc. c., Hep. s., Phos.*, Sep., Sil.).

Compare.—Ars., Bell., Bry., *Calc. c.*, Carb., Chel., Cinch., *Cycl.*, Graph., Iod., Iris, Hep. s., Kali bi., Mag. c., Merc., Natr. mur., Nitr. ac., *Nux v.*, Petrol., Phos., *Puls.*, Rhus tox., Sep., Sil., *Sulph.*, Zinc.

Antidotes.—Acon., Camph., Caust., Cham., Graph., Op., Puls.; also a cup of coffee.

Lycopodium Antidotes.—Cinch.

THERAPEUTICS.

The clinical range of Lycopodium is wide, and seems to have its origin in the sphere of nutrition, which is profoundly affected. It is of most use in chronic forms of disease, but occasionally is indicated in acute diseases, especially as an intercurrent remedy, somewhat like Sulphur, the symptoms of Lyc. being present. In conditions of malnutrition, where the patient becomes emaciated in spite of an enormous appetite, Lyc. is especially useful. Also in children who become emaciated and look wrinkled and prematurely old. Probably the most important use of Lyc. is in the treatment of chronic indigestion and gastric diseases in general characterized by an excessive accumulation of flatulence and much rumbling and rolling in the stomach and abdomen. Remembering these prominent general features of the clinical action of the drug, we may best refer to its special uses in the usual anatomical order. Useful in hypochondriasis and melancholia resulting from indigestion and malnutrition; great mental weakness; loss of self-confidence; loss of memory, especially in old people. Has been used in chronic hydrocephalus, especially in delicate anæmic children, with indigestion and malnutrition. Chronic ophthalmia, catarrhal or scrofulous ulcers and pustules on lids. Polypus. Lachrymal fistula. Cataract. Hemiopia. Asthenopia. Hemeralopia; resulting from chronic disease of the retina; retinitis. Polypus of the ear. Otitis media. Otorrhœa, purulent, ichorous, with impaired hearing, especially after scarlet fever. Polypus of the nose. Chronic nasal catarrh, with stoppage of the nose. Violent acute coryza, with swelling of nose and acrid discharge. Diphtheria, with stoppage of the nose, great dryness of throat, ichorous discharges from nose; tongue protruding; begins on right side. Tonsilitis going from right to left. An excellent remedy for an inordinate appetite, especially for sweets, delicacies, pastry, etc., also for the ultimate consequences of such an appetite and diet. Chronic dyspepsia; acid dyspepsia; atonic dyspepsia; gastralgia; chronic gastritis, etc., with characteristic flatulence, constant satiety, etc., already mentioned. Said to be especially useful in gastralgia and chronic gastritis occurring in peasants who subsist on heavy bread, sour small-beer and adulterated coffee. Indigestion from eating onions; from liquors, especially wine; from smoking. Scirrhus of the stomach, with great flatulence. Diaphragmitis. (Gall stone colic. Jaundice with flatulence. Chronic hepatitis especially in children after Mercury. Fatty degeneration of liver. Atrophic nutmeg liver. Cirrhosis of liver. Ascites from liver disease, especially after abuse of Alcohol. Palliative in strangulated hernia with flatulence. Flatulent colic. Enteritis in children from milk and farinaceous diet. Hæmorrhoids, large, bleeding, do not mature, being hard, bluish, lumpy; chronic. Sometimes indicated in diarrhœa; but constipation usually accompanies Lyc. conditions, constriction of the anus and rectum with severe pain at stool being the chief characteristic. A valuable remedy in cystic and renal troubles, red sand in the urine (uric acid diathesis) being the chief indication. (Gravel; urinary calculi. Renal colic. Hæmaturia, from gravel.. Chronic cystitis. Chronic prostatitis. Diabetes. Bright's disease. An excellent remedy for impotence, sexual exhaustion and loss of sexual appetite in the male. Useful in a variety of female troubles, but is mostly indicated by the characteristic gastric symptoms. Ovaritis. Ovaralgia. Endometritis, with discharge of wind from the vagina; physometra. Cancer of the uterus. Leucorrhœa, milky, corroding. Menorrhagia. Chronic dryness of vagina. Varicose veins of pudenda. Sore nipples. Hard burning nodosities in mammæ. Chronic bronchitis, especially in old people with dyspnœa; threatened paralysis of lungs. Subacute pneumonia, dyspnœa as from sulphur fumes, worse when lying on back, fan-like motion of alæ nasi. Neglected pneumonia; threatening phthisis. Typhoid pneumonia. Phthisis, with gastric symptoms, oppressed breathing etc. Chronic cough. Hydrothorax. Hydropericardium. Angina pectoris. Carotid aneurism. Torticollis (Lachn.). Lumbago, especially after Bry.; backache relieved by passing urine. Chronic rheumatism. Chronic gout, with calcarea deposits in joints. Hip disease, suppurative stage. Varicose veins on legs. Old ulcers on legs, with nightly tearing burning pains. Mercurial ulcers Fissures on hands. Useful in a variety of ulcers, which are usually humid and suppurating, vesicular; eczema; herpes; psoriasis; impetigo; lupus; urticaria; intertrigo; nævus; boils; carbuncles. Liver spots. Glandular swellings. Caries. Useful in old broken down cases of malarial fever; sour vomiting between chill and heat; thirst after the sweating stage; paroxysms at 4 P.M.; red sand in urine; also with typhoid tendency. Lyc. may be useful in typhoid fever if the indications for its use are present. Also in hectic fever during tuberculosis or other chronic suppurating diseases.

LYCOPUS VIRGINICUS.

Natural order.—Labiatæ. *Common names.*—Bugle Weed. Virginia Hoarhound. *Habitat.*—An indigenous perennial herb found in bogs and wet soils. *Preparation.*—Tincture from the fresh whole plant.

GENERAL ANALYSIS.

Chief action is upon the heart, where it much resembles the action of Digitalis, without, however, the cumulative effects of

LYCOPUS VIRGINICUS.

the latter. Primarily it weakens the power and vitality of the heart, decreasing the blood pressure in the arteries, and consequently the tension everywhere, and thus producing a condition of cardiac irritability, with depressed force. Secondarily, it gives rise to cardiac erethism, and if pushed far enough would result in hypertrophy with dilatation. As a result of the primary action upon the heart, a general venous stasis occurs in all the organs of the body, notably the liver, lungs and kidneys.

CHARACTERISTIC SYMPTOMS.

Eyes.—°Protrusion of the eyes, with tumultous action of the heart; exophthalmus from cardiac disease. Dull pain in left supra-orbital region. Painful pressure in eyeballs (Aloe, Bapt., Cimic.).

Stomach—Circumscribed pain and compression in region of stomach. Indigestion, with pain and distress in epigastric region.

Stool.—Diarrhœa, with griping and rumbling. °Diarrhœa in jaundice, from weakened heart. Constipation.

Urinary Organs.—Urine scanty, thick and muddy, with œdema of the feet. Urine contains excess of mucus, epithelial cells, and oxalate of lime, 1012-1020 sp. gr. °Diabetes mellitus.

Respiratory Organs.—Dyspnœa; sense of constriction in larynx. Cough, with slight pale expectoration. Intercostal pains (Cimic., Ranunc., Rhod., Rhus tox.). Pains in chest, with oppressed respiration.

Heart and Pulse.—Constricting pain and tenderness around the heart. Rheumatoid aching pains, and acute darting pains in region of heart (Acon., Kalm., Rhus tox., Spig.). First sound of the heart displaced by a blowing sound of mitral regurgitations. Beats of heart more distinct on right side of sternum. Cardiac oppression and distress. Cardiac pulsation scarcely perceptible to touch (Digit.). Cardiac depression, with intermittent pulse and faintness (Digit.); also on quickly ascending (Ars.). Heart sounds indistinct; systolic running into diastolic. On waking, labored cardiac action, with frequent intermissions. Feeble, quick, irregular action of the heart (Digit.). °Action tumultous and forcible (Spig., Verat. vir.); could be heard several feet from the bed; eyes protruding. Pulse quick, intermittent; feeble, irregular, intermittent; quickened at each inspiration; scarcely perceptible; extremely variable; irregular in rhythm; extremely compressible.

Back.—Acute rheumatoid pains in neck, back and loins (Rhus tox.).

Limbs.—Acute rheumatoid pains in all the limbs (Rhus tox.).

Generalities.—°Rheumatoid pains, passing from left to right; returning to left side; chiefly affecting muscles and articulations; increased by movement, by cold air, and by concentrating the thought upon them.

Aggravation.—On alternate days.

Compare.—Acon Cact., *Digit.*, Kalm., Spig., Verat. alb.

THERAPEUTICS.

Lycopus is especially useful in cardiac irritability and weakness, whether from over-strain of the heart, from rheumatic disease, constitutional debility, or from the use of drugs or stimulants affecting the heart, such as tobacco, etc. It renders the beats of the heart slower, fuller and more regular. Palpitation from nervous irritation or organic cardiac disease. An excellent substitute for Digitalis in such affections, it quiets cough and irritation of the lungs; lessens arterial action in fevers and plethora. Hæmoptysis in phthisis with palpitation, pains in chest and cardiac weakness. An excellent remedy for exophthalmia from cardiac disease, relieving the protrusion of the eyes and tumultous action of the heart. Dysentery and diarrhœa. Pleurodynia. Rheumatism. Neuralgia, or rather, neuraloid pains.

MAGNESIA CARBONICA.

Common name.—Carbonate of Magnesia. *Preparation.*—Triturations.

GENERAL ANALYSIS.

Acts on the mucous membranes of the intestinal canal, and upon the female generative organs, producing irritation and catarrhal inflammation, and in the latter deranged menstruation.

MAGNESIA CARBONICA.

CHARACTERISTIC SYMPTOMS.

Head.—Pressive headache. Rush of blood to the head. Falling out of the hair (*Graph.*, Merc., *Nitr. ac.*, Natr. mur., Phos., *Sep.*). Tetter on the scalp, itching during wet, rainy weather.

Eyes.—Agglutination of the lids in the morning (Calc. c., *Lyc.*, Merc., *Puls.*, *Sulph.*).

Ears.—Hardness of hearing.

Face.—Nightly tearing, digging, boring in the cheek bones; insupportable during rest, and driving from one place to another.

Mouth.—Toothache at night, compelling one to rise and walk about; pain insupportable while at rest; worse in cold; during pregnancy. Bloody saliva. Bitter or sour taste in the mouth (Cinch., Lyc., Nux v.).

Stomach.—Desire for fruit and acid things (Ant. crud., Ant. tart., Cinch., *Hep. s.*, Phos., Phos. ac., Verat. alb.); *for meat* (*Abies can.*); aversion to green food. Violent thirst, especially toward evening. Constrictive pain in the stomach.

Abdomen.—Distension of the abdomen, with profuse emission of flatulence, with relief (Aloe, Lyc.). *Griping, cutting and rumbling in the whole abdomen, followed by thin, green stools, without tenesmus.*

Stool and Anus.—Piercing pain in rectum, as from needles (*Aloe*). *Stools green and frothy, like the scum of a frog pond,* or °with white floating lumps, like tallow; always preceded by griping, worse on right side. Constipation (Amm. mur., *Alum.*, *Bry.*, *Nux v.*, *Op.*).

Female Organs.—Menses too late and scanty (Puls.). *Menstrual flow more profuse during the night than during the day,* with dragging pains, better from pressure on abdomen and stooping. No menstrual discharge during the pains, only after them. Menstrual discharge glutinous, thick, acrid, black, pitch-like.

Generalities.—Rheumatic pains in shoulders, and limbs in general. °Neuralgic lightning-like pains. °Epileptic attacks; frequently falls down suddenly, with consciousness. Weakness, especially in the morning. °Weary and tired, especially in the feet, and when sitting. Restlessness in the limbs in the evening, after sitting long.

Sleep.—Cannot sleep after 2 or 3 A.M. °Unrefreshing sleep, more tired in the morning than when going to bed.
Skin.—Violent itching over the whole body.
Fever.—Great internal heat at night, with night sweats and aversion to uncovering, with dread of exposure.
Amelioration.—From motion (Rhus tox.); in the open air.
Conditions.—Persons, especially children of irritable disposition, nervous temperament; lax fibre; sour smell.
Compare.—Ars., Aloe, Calc. c., Cham., Graph., Lyc., Nitr. ac., Nux m., *Phos.*, Sep., Sil. Complementary to Cham.
Antidotes.—Cham., Puls., Merc., Nux v., Rheum.

THERAPEUTICS.

Magnesia carb. is a useful remedy in acid dyspepsia. Dyspepsia from milk which sours; also from cabbage, potatoes and other gross food. Diarrhœa, especially of children with characteristic stools, and usually more or less colic, which is relieved by bending over, sour eructations, etc. Apthæ. With this drug there is, especially with dyspepsia, a marked disposition to neuralgia, especially of the face, in which it is an excellent remedy; the pains are lightning-like, are usually worse at night, and are accompanied by great restlessness, must get up and walk about. Neuralgic toothache, especially during pregnancy, worse at night from warmth of bed and better from cold drinks. Lenticular cataract. Warts on lids. Styes. Chronic blepharitis. Nausea and sour vomiting during pregnancy. Dysmenorrhœa with symptoms mentioned in pathogenesis. Leucorrhœa, white, acrid, with colic, relieved by bending over. Epileptiform spasms.

MAGNESIA MURIATICA.

Synonym.—Magnesia Chloride. *Common name.*—Muriate of Magnesia. *Preparation.*—Triturations.

GENERAL ANALYSIS.

Acts upon the ganglionic nervous system, and exerts its most important local influence upon the mucous surfaces.

CHARACTERISTIC SYMPTOMS.

Mind.—Fretful, morose, peevish.

Head.—Heaviness in the head, with reeling as if one would fall down. Tightness and pressure in the forehead. Squeezing, griping pain in both temples, with sensation as if vertigo and loss of consciousnes were about to ensue, in the evening after lying down; *better on strong pressure with the hands.* Tearing and stitches in right temple, extending to the eye; necessity to press eyes together. Headache, relieved by wrapping up the head (Sil.).

Eyes.—Eyes inflamed, with violent burning and redness of scleroticæ. Nocturnal agglutination of the eyelids (*Calc. c., Lyc., Merc., Puls., Rhus tox., Sulph.*).

Ears.—Pulsation in the ears.

Nose.—Violent coryza, at one time stopped, at another fluent, with dullness of the head, and complete loss of taste and smell. Tickling with sneezing and sensation of coryza. Discharge of offensive purulent mucus. Redness and swelling of the nose, or of the alæ; painful to touch. Sore pain and burning in the nostrils. Scurf in the nostrils, painful to touch; ulcerated nostrils.

Face.—Pale, yellowish complexion. Eruption on the face (Viola tric.), itching, burning vesicles.

Mouth.—Sensation as if the upper incisors were elongated. Painful swelling and easy bleeding of the gums. Continual rising of white froth in the mouth.

Throat.—Dryness and rawness in the throat, with a hoarse voice. Hawking of clammy, thick mucus, often mixed with blood.

Stomach.—Hunger, but knows not for what. Violent thirst (*Acon., Ars., Bell., Bry., Rhus tox.*). Acidity after dinner. Water rises from the stomach into the mouth, with nausea. Nausea in the morning after rising (Calad., Nux v., *Petrol.,* Puls.). Rising, as of a ball, from the stomach into the œsophagus (*Asaf.*); relieved by eructations. Pain in the stomach as from ulceration, or from a bruise. Epigastric region sensitive to pressure.

Abdomen.—*Sharp drawing and tensive burning stitches in region of liver; worse from pressure.* Pressive pains in liver, when walking, or touching it; worse when lying on the right side; liver hard and enlarged. Drawing pains in the abdomen at night. Cramp-like pains in the abdomen. Rumbling. Incarcerated flatus. Incessant emission of flatus.

Stool and Anus.—Hæmorrhoids pain during normal stool. Burning and smarting in anus during and after stool. *Hard, difficult, slow and insufficient evacuations. Stools knotty, like sheep's dung* (Alum., Kali carb., Op.); crumbling as if burnt: hard, covered with mucus and streaks of blood. Stool crumbles at the verge of anus. °Chronic recurrence of diarrhœa

Urinary Organs.—*Urine can only be passed by bearing down with the abdominal muscles.* Urine passes only by drops, always some seeming to remain behind.

Female Organs.—Catamenia too early and too copious (Calc. c., Nux v.); blood passes in black clots, more when sitting than when walking. During menses face is pale, with pain in loins and mental depression. Uterine cramps, extending to the thighs. Leucorrhœa, with cramps in abdomen.

Respiratory Organs.—Dry cough evening and night, with burning and soreness in chest. Spasmodic cough at night, with tickling in the throat (Hyos.). Tension and constriction of the chest.

Heart.—Palpitation of the heart on sitting, disappearing on motion.

Generalities.—°Attacks of spasms and hysterical weakness (Asaf.). Uneasiness in evening in bed, on closing the eyes. Weakness of the body, as if coming from the stomach.

Sleep.—Sleepiness during the day. Goes to sleep late; sleeplessness on account of heat and thirst. Restlessness on closing the eyes. Sleep unrefreshing; tired in the morning.

Fever.—Chilliness every evening; disappears after going to bed.

Aggravation.—Most symptoms appear while sitting, and are relieved on motion and by exercise, and in the open air.

Conditions.—Women, especially hysterical, with uterine troubles. Children, especially during dentition.

Compare.—Baryt. c., Bry., *Calc. c.,* Cham., Con., *Graph., Kali carb., Lyc.,* Mag. c., Mur. ac., Natr. c., Natr. mur., Nitr. ac., Nux v., Puls., Sil., Sulph.

Antidote.—Cham.

THERAPEUTICS.

A valuable remedy in certain forms of neuralgia, especially of the head and face, usually associated with the characteristic constipation of this drug. The headache is better from wrapping up the head, the amelioration coming from the pressure of the bandage and not from the warmth as in Silicia. Nasal catarrh. Ozœna, with ulcerated, scurfy nostrils. Often a valuable remedy in chronic gastralgia. An excellent remedy for the indigestion of children during dentition; milk causes pain in stomach and passes undigested. Enlargement and congestion of the liver, with symptoms already given and characteristic constipation. Hepatic derangements in general with symptoms of the drug as given. Hepatic affections with tendency to hæmorrhages from various organs. In all hepatic disorders there is pain and sensitiveness in region of liver, coated tongue, flatulence, distended abdomen, weak pulse and constipation; often the face is yellow; the breath offensive, the extremities swollen, urine high-colored, etc. Cirrhosis of liver. Ascites from hepatic disease. Hæmorrhoids. A valuable remedy for constipation when the stools are hard, knotty like sheep's dung, or crumbling as if burnt. Constipation of puny, rachitic children with enlarged abdomen, etc.; infants during dentition, A valuable remedy in uterine complaints, with flatulence, characteristic constipation, and attended with hysterical and spasmodic affections. Usually the menses are black and clotted, and more profuse when sitting than walking. Metrorrhagia. Leucorrhœa, with abdominal cramps. Uterine fibroids and scirrhus.

MANGANUM.

Preparation.—Triturations of the Carbonate or Acetate of Manganese.

GENERAL ANALYSIS.

Acts powerfully upon the motor nervous system, producing paralysis, beginning with paraplegia. It differs from Mercury in first affecting the lower extremities, and in not exciting tremors, and from Lead in not causing colic and constipation.

MANGANUM.

Through its nervous influence, Manganum produces irritation of various organs, even extending to inflammation.

CHARACTERISTIC SYMPTOMS.

Mind.—Moping mood (*Puls.*); fretful; ill-humored.

Head.—Head feels heavy, with sensation as if it were larger, could hardly hold it up. Congestion of blood to the head, with throbbing in the head (*Acon., Bell., Glon.*); better in open air. Drawing, stinging or tensive headache, in the open air; better indoors. Jarring of the brain from motion of the head. Contractive, stitching pain in forepart of head, especially in temples; worse in open air. Frequent rising of heat in the head, with thirst. Headaches arising in the room; better in open air, and *vice versa*.

Eyes.—Burning heat and dryness of the eyes. Eyelids pain on moving, and become dry on looking at bright light. Pupils much dilated or contracted.

Ears.—Dull shooting pain in ears when speaking. Deafness, as if the ears were stopped (Coccus). Loud cracking noise in ears, when blowing the nose or swallowing (Graph.). Swelling in left parotid, with a reddish hue, in typhus.

Nose.—Dry coryza, with obstruction of the nostrils (Nux v.); in evening, with red, sore, painful nose and upper lip. Sometimes dry, and sometimes fluent coryza.

Face.—*Suffering expression; face pale and sunken.* Eruptions and ulcers at the corners of the mouth (Ant. crud., Graph., Lyc.).

Mouth.—Violent pains in the teeth, which pass rapidly to other parts.

Throat.—Throat dry; scratching feeling, as if the trachea were closed with a leaf. Sore throat, with cutting pain, as from excoriation, when not swallowing.

Stomach.—Absence of thirst (Apis, Puls.). Heat and burning in the stomach, ascending to the chest (Ars.), with nausea.

Abdomen.—Cutting in umbilical region during deep inspiration.

Stool and Anus.—Constrictive pain in the anus while sitting. Constipation; difficult, dry, knotty evacuations (*Plumb., Mag. m.*).

Urinary Organs—Frequent desire to urinate (Acon., Apis, Apoc.); during the day.

Male Organs.—Sensation of weakness in the genitals, with burning and drawing in the spermatic cord, extending to the glands.

Female Organs.—*Menses too early and too scanty;* lasting two days.

Respiratory Organs.—Dry cough from loud reading or talking, with painful dryness, roughness and constriction of larynx, causing sensation to cough, with which mucus was loosened after long hawking. Inclination to cough mornings. *Deep cough, without expectoration; ceasing on lying down. Obstinate hoarseness and roughness, especially in the morning* (Caust., Nux v.), and in the open air; better from smoking. Warm constriction, extending from the middle of the abdomen to the chest, with nausea.

Heart.—Sudden shocks at the heart and in the left side of the chest, from above downward. Pulse irregular, sometimes rapid, sometimes slow, but constantly weak and soft.

Limbs.—Tensive pain in the joints of the arms and hands. Rheumatic, tearing pains, extending from the shoulders to the fingers. Tension and drawing stitches in the thigh.

Generalities.—Weakness. Paraplegia. Paralysis, first of the lower limbs (Ars.). Tension or cramp-like drawing and tearing in various parts. °Arthritic pains in the joints; worse at night (Merc.). Insupportable digging pains in bones and periosteum; worse at night (Merc., Phos. ac.). °All bones, particularly in lower limbs, sensitive to touch; in typhus.

Skin.—Excoriations and fissures in the bends of the joints (Graph., Squilla). Voluptuous itching; relieved by scratching (Sulph.). Itching in the hollow of the knee and on the shin.

Sleep.—Vivid, anxious dreams, which are well remembered.

Aggravation.—*At night;* from changes of weather (Ranunc.), which sometimes also ameliorate; symptoms coming on indoors are better in the open air, and *vice versa*.

Compare.—Amm. carb., Ars., Coff. c., Coni., Ferr., *Lyc.*, Plat., Puls., Thuja, Verat. alb.

Antidote.—Coff.

THERAPEUTICS.

Manganum has been mostly used in laryngeal affections; laryngeal catarrh with symptoms above given, and especially in anæmic persons with tubercular deposits in lungs. Said to be very useful in boys and girls when the voice is changing, and remains harsh and hoarse, with continual catarrh and clearing of the throat. Hoarseness and cough from reading aloud, with dryness and rawness of the larynx, and efforts to detach mucus from the throat. Laryngeal phthisis, with rawness and hoarseness. General anæmia, especially in tuberculous patients with profuse menstruation and metrorrhagia. Chronic nasal catarrh with obstructed and sore nostrils. Chronic rheumatism shifting from place to place. Otalgia. Earache with cracking in ears when blowing the nose, ears stopped up, worse from change of weather. Periostitis. Has been used in psoriasis and other skin diseases.

MELILOTUS.

Synonym.—Melilotus Officinalis. *Natural order.*—Leguminosæ. *Common names.*—Yellow Melilot (not White Melilot). Sweet Clover. *Habitat.*—A plant indigenous to Europe, naturalized in the United States. *Preparation.*—Tincture from the fresh flowers.

GENERAL ANALYSIS.

This plant is especially noted for its action upon the nervous system, producing a *very severe headache* with congestion of blood to the head, flushed face, and even sometimes epistaxis (*Bell.*). It rapidly relieves headaches of nervous origin, or resulting from cerebral oppression, and is quite useful in so-called "sick headache." Its chief constituent "cumarin," in large doses, causes nausea, vertigo, vomiting and great oppression, with sleepiness, confusion, severe pain in head, depression of heart's action and cold extremities.

CHARACTERISTIC SYMPTOMS.

Mind.—Irascible, impatient, discontented, fault-finding. Indolent, unable to fix mind, stupid, indifferent. Unable to study, memory will not retain anything. Omit words and letters in writing. (Lyc.).

Head.—Vertigo; on moving. Swaying sensation in the brain with tired pain. Headache, better from nosebleed. Headache with red face, bloodshot eyes, and finally epistaxis, which affords relief. Sick headache better from epistaxis or menstrual flow. Periodical nervous headache every week, or once in four weeks, more frequent in winter. *Violent congestion of the head,* with heaviness, *fullness and throbbing* as if the blood would burst through the nose, eyes and ears, with dizzy sick feeling that is worse from motion. Throbbing frontal headache preceded by great prostration. Intense frontal headache preceded by hot, flushed face and feverish sensation. Throbbing headache in right eminence from 9 A.M. till noon.

Eyes—Eyelids very heavy.

Nose.—Excessive dryness of nose. *Profuse and frequent epistaxis with general relief.*

Face.—Redness of face and head, with throbbing in carotids (*Amyl nit., Bell.*). Face almost livid.

Urinary Organs.—Frequent and profuse urination. Urine profuse watery, and relieving the dull, congestive headache (Gels.).

Female Sexual Organs.—Frequent momentary stitches in external genitals.

Respiratory Organs.—Cough from fullness in chest. Hæmoptysis, blood bright red. Smothering sensations; cannot get air enough. Breathing difficult from weight on chest; fullness of chest and head; violent congestion of the lungs.

Amelioration.—Better in the open air; from walking and change of position.

Compare.—Amyl nit., Bell., Cact., Glon., Ferr., Sang.

THERAPEUTICS.

Has been used chiefly in neuralgic and congestive headaches with foregoing symptoms. Considered invaluable in so-called "sick headache." Nosebleed relieving the headache is very characteristic. Has cured religious melancholia, with very red face, etc. Hypochondriasis. Congestion and inflammation of the lungs. Infantile spasms during dentition with great congestion of the head; especially in nervous children. Puerperal eclampsia.

MENYANTHES.

Synonym.—Menyanthes Trifoliata. *Natural order.*—Gentianaceæ. *Common names.*—Buck Bean. Bitterworm. *Habitat.*—A perennial plant growing in North America, Europe and Asia, in swamps, etc. *Preparation.*—Tincture from the fresh plant.

GENERAL ANALYSIS.

Acts upon the mucous surfaces, producing some irritation and congestion. It likewise acts primarily upon the brain and optic nerve, resulting in headache and obscuration of sight, and upon the ganglionic system, developing symptoms which simulate certain forms of fever and ague. Teste claims that it is closely analogous to Drosera, except that the effects of the latter are more intense. He also claims that there are few diseases where Menyanthes is indicated which could not be cured much better with Drosera—a statement that is not generally accepted.

CHARACTERISTIC SYMPTOMS.

Head.—Confusion and heaviness of the head. *Pressure in head from above downward, relieved during hard pressure with the hand; on ascending steps as if at every step a weight pressed upon the brain.* Pressive stupefying headache, mostly in forehead. Stitch-like tearing pain in right side of forehead, near temporal region. Stitches in left side of brain extending toward vertex.
Eyes.—Obscuration of sight; mist and flickerings before the eyes (*Agar., Cycl., Merc., Phos., Sulph.*).
Face.—Visible, though not painful, twitching of the facial muscles (*Agar., Ign., Nux v.*); especially on right side (*Bell.*); worse during rest.
Stomach.—Sensation of coldness extending up the œsophagus,

with great nausea, following pressure in stomach. Empty eructations.

Abdomen.—Distension and fullness of abdomen, as if overloaded by food, with undiminished appetite, together with a sensation as of incarcerated flatulence, and frequent ineffectual efforts to emit flatus (*Carb v., Cinch., Lyc.*); fullness much increased by smoking tobacco (Ign.).

Stool.—Constipation.

Urinary Organs.—Frequent desire to urinate with scanty discharge.

Respiratory Organs.—Hoarseness; dyspnœa. Pressure on both sides of chest, with sharp stitches, greatly aggravated on inspiration.

Back.—Dull, boring sticking in left scapula, extending across the spine. Painful tearing pains between scapulæ, extending downward, especially on deep breathing. Pressive, bruised pain in small of back and sacral region.

Limbs.—Muscular twitches in right upper arm. Cramp-like pain in muscles of left forearm, extending to palm of hand, almost like paralysis. Cramp-like pain in muscles of right leg, extending from below upward, like paralysis. Cramp-like pains in all the limbs.

Sleep.—Vivid unremembered dreams.

Fever.—Sensation of chilliness, especially in fingers. Feet cold up to knees, as if in cold water. *Icy coldness of hands and feet* (Tabac.), *with warmth of rest of body.* Shivering over upper part of body, with yawning.

Compare.—Aranea, Cact., Dros., Natr. mur.

THERAPEUTICS.

Hahnemann recommends Menyanthes in some forms of ague when the chill predominates, and forms a very pronounced part of the paroxysm as above described. Catarrhal affections. Amaurosis. Neuralgic headaches with symptoms above described. Sciatica.

MEPHITIS.

Synonym.—Mephitis Americana. *Class.*—Mammalia. *Order.*—Carnivora. *Family.*—Mustelodæ. *Common names.*—Skunk. Pole Cat. *Preparation.*—A tincture is made by dissolving the liquid obtained from the anal glands in alcohol.

GENERAL ANALYSIS.

Acts prominently upon the cerebro-spinal system, especially the pneumogastrics, including spasmodic conditions of the respiratory organs, which has led to its use in the treatment of asthma and whooping cough.

CHARACTERISTIC SYMPTOMS.

Eyes.—Stitches, as if with needles in the eyes. Pain above the eyes. Conjunctivæ red and injected. Letters become blurred; unable to distinguish them; they run together; short-sighted.

Mouth.—Sudden jerks in roots of teeth.

Stomach.—No appetite in morning. Nausea, with emptiness in stomach, and sensation as if head were distended. Pressure in stomach, and colic.

Stool.—Stools infrequent, but thin.

Respiratory Organs.—When drinking, the fluid gets into the larynx. Asthma, as from inhaling vapor of sulphur; °of drunkards; during sleep. Inhalation difficult; exhalation almost impossible; or barking. Cough after drinking, talking or loud reading; spasmodic, hollow or deep, with rawness, hoarseness and pain through chest, with suffocative feeling when inhaling; cannot exhale; vomits food some hours after eating; worse at night and after lying down; in morning loose, with some expectoration.

Limbs.—Uneasiness in arms and legs. Rheumatic pains in limbs. Burning and pain in corns.

Generalities.—Convulsions; restlessness. Inclination to stretch; disinclination to work. Paralyzed sensation, especially with the pains. Very fine nervous vibrations, causing great uneasiness, as if extending into the interior of the bone.

Sleep.—Asthma during sleep. Awakens early, and feels refreshed. Sleepy in the morning. Vivid remembered dreams.

Fever.—Increased warmth, especially in the morning. Less chilly in cold air; cold water agreeable.

Compare.—Ambr., Ars., Coccus, Coral. rub., Dros.

THERAPEUTICS.

Has been found useful in asthma, whooping cough and prosopalgia, with symptoms above described.

MERCURIUS.

Synonym.—Mercurius Vivus. *Common names.*—Quicksilver. Mercury. *Mercurius Solubilis Hahnemanni.*—Precipitated black oxide of Mercury, with Nitric Acid and Ammonia.*
Preparation.—Triturations of either of the above preparations are employed.

GENERAL ANALYSIS.

Mercurius acts profoundly upon the entire organism, affecting both the functions and the substance of every organ and tissue of the body. Pre-eminently it operates upon the vegetative system, altering its functional power, both quantitatively and qualitatively, and decomposing and destroying its organic constituents. The red blood corpuscles are destroyed, the albumen and fibrin of the blood are lost, and consequently the

---

*I have, in accordance with the usual custom, embraced both these preparations under the one head—their similarity being so great that no distinction is usually made in practice. Most of the symptoms are obtained from the solubilis; and, in order to facilitate the student's knowledge, I have as far as possible designated those obtained from the vivus by an asterisk, those obtained from both preparations by a double asterisk. On account of the varying and doubtful composition of the solubilis, the vivus is usually considered the more reliable remedy, and has replaced the former to a great extent since Hahnemann's time, and even by Hahnemann himself in the latter years of his practice.

coagulability of the blood is diminished. Secretion and absorption are both increased, and the secretions, loosing their plasticity, become thinner and more fluid, and at the same time acrid and excoriating.

On the organic system Mercury acts more especially upon the mucous and serous membranes, the glandular system, the parenchymatous organs, the fibrous and osseous tissues and the skin. The first condition produced is one of excitation, swelling and inflammation, soon followed by reaction and subsequent weakness and exhaustion, which betokens commencing organic decomposition. The tissues above mentioned become the seat of destructive ulcerative processes, suppurations and puriform collections, while there is at the same time a tendency to the deposition of new products, according to the character of the tissue involved Thus we see that Mercury penetrates the entire organism, and permeates every tissue, acting upon these tissues by virtue of its presence in them. In some instances the inflammatory and ulcerative processes mentioned are lacking, and there occurs instead nervous phenomena such as paralysis agitans, epilepsy, chorea, neuralgia and melancholia. Its special action upon each we may clearly comprehend by a careful study of the characteristic effects as given below. The most essential feature of the action of Mercury is its remarkable resemblance to the effects of the syphilitic poison, though it should be noted that Mercury attacks the long bones, while in syphilis the flat bones are attacked. The chief characteristic of Mercury is an aggravation of all the symptoms at night, and from the warmth of the bed.

CHARACTERISTIC SYMPTOMS.

Mind.—*Weakness of memory* (Agn., Ambr., *Anac.*, Kreos., Lach., Natr. mur., *Nux m.*, Phos ac.); and will-power lost. **Great anxiety, restlessness* (Ars.), and apprehension, especially in evening and at night (Acon., Ars., Calc. c., Rhus tox.). *Answers questions slowly* (Phos., Phos. ac.).   Intellect weak; imbecile. Imaginary fears of dying, or of losing reason (Can. ind.).   *Low muttering delirium (Agar., Alianth., Bell., Hyos.). Delirium like that of delirium tremens. Wretchedness, and dejection of spirits. Inclined to sopor, coma. Morose and suspicious. Irritability and ill-humor. *Hurried and rapid talking* (Bell., Hyos., Lach., Stram.).

Head.—Vertigo. Confusion in morning on awaking. Weakness in head like a dullness, as if there was a vibration in forehead and turning about in a circle. Head feels as if bound around with a cord (Gels., Merc. bin., Natr. mur., Nitr. ac., Puls., Sulph.). Head feels as if it would burst with fullness of the brain (*Acon., Bry., Cinch., Natr. mur.*). Aching just beneath scalp, as if heavy and tight. Pressive pain in left temple. Pressure outward in forehead, and pain in bone beneath eyebrow, worse on touch. Tearing or drawing pains or stinging on one side of head, extending to the ears, teeth and neck. *Constant rotary motion of the head, even when lying. *The scalp is painful to touch* (Cinch., Natr. mur., Nitr. ac.); worse when scratching, which is followed by bleeding. Itching of the scalp day and night. Moist eruption on the scalp (Hep. s., *Graph.*, Lyc., Merc., Nitr. ac.), which eats away the hair; yellow running scabs and excoriation, *Falling out of the hair (*Graph., Nitr. ac.*, Phos., Sep.). Tearing and stinging in the bones of the skull. °Sutures open; large head; precocious mental development. °Exostoses on hairy scalp, with feeling of soreness when touched; worse at night in bed.

Eyes.—*Eyes inflamed, with swollen inverted tarsi (Borax), and very sensitive to the light. Heat, biting as from horseradish, burning, redness, and pressure in the eyes (Acon., Ars., Sulph.). Pupils dilated. Lachrymation profuse, burning excoriating. Chronic conjunctivitis, with fine injection around cornea. *Lids spasmodically closed* (Hep. s.), red, inflamed, swollen; agglutinated in the morning (Alum., Calc. c., *Lyc., Puls.*, Sil., *Sulph.*). Sensation as if a cutting substance were beneath left upper lid. *Eyes forcibly drawn together on attempting to look at anything; cannot see distinctly.* Inability to open the eyes well, as if agglutinated to balls. *Dimness of vision; fog before the eyes* (Kali carb., Lach.); also black points, flies, etc. (Agar., Cycl., Phos., Sulph.). *Intolerance of light and fire-light* (*Acon., Bell., Sulph.*).

Ears.—*Inflammation of internal and external ear, with stinging, tearing, and cramp-like pains* (*Bell.*, Puls.);

bloody, offensive discharge (Calc. c., Hep. s., Graph., Lyc.). Stitches deep in ears with burning. Ringing and roaring in the ears (Cinch., *Sulph.*, Sil.). Stoppage. Soreness and excoriation of the ears. Hardness of hearing, with obstruction; sounds vibrate in the ears; obstruction momentarily, better after swallowing, or blowing the nose.

Nose.—*Nosebleed during sleep;* during cough. *Coryza; fluent, corrosive, with much sneezing; offensive odor;* nostrils bleeding, scurfy; nose red, swollen, shining (Ars., Arum., Puls.). *Nasal bones swollen and painful to touch* (Alum., *Aur.*, Bry., Hep. s.).

Face.—**Paleness of face. Sallow. Swollen. **Face earthy colored, puffy* (Ars., Puls.). Coldness. Internal swelling of the upper lip (Bell.). *Corners of the mouth ulcerated and painfully sore* (Ant. crud., *Graph.*). Fissures. Lips dry, cracked and ulcerated (Ars.); painful to touch. Masseter muscles contracted so that speech was difficult. Periostitis of lower jaw. Necrosis (Phos.). Caries. Atrophy and exfoliation of alveolar processes. Tearing in lower jaw towards evening. ***Spasm and immobility of the jaws.*

Mouth.—***Teeth feel loose, fall out* (*Merc. cor.*), **become black; carious* (Staph.); *denuded of gum; painful on touch of tongue.* Dirty-gray discoloration.' *Pulsating jerking toothache, extending into ear and head; worse at night* (Ant. crud., Bell.), *and from warmth of bed* (Clem.). *Aching at night, then general chilliness, with swelling of gums and salivary glands.* ***Gums painful to touch and on chewing; swollen, spongy, receding from the teeth* (Carb. v., Nitr. ac.); *edges whitish; bleeding; fœtid odor from the mouth* (*Arn.*, Hep. s., Iodi., Kali nit., *Nitr. ac.*, Kreos.); *ulcerated; suppurating.* Tongue *red and swollen (Bell.); **ulcerated; **black, with red edges* (Ars.); ***swollen, coated white* (*Ant. crud., Bry.*, Nux v.); **moist with intense thirst;* ***swollen, flabby* (Natr. ars.); *showing impress of teeth on margin;* ***movement difficult; speech difficult* on account of trembling of mouth and tongue; *stammering* (Caust., *Hyos., Stram.*). Gray patches on edges, dirty-yellow coat on upper surface. *Apthæ in the mouth* (Borax, Hell., Hydras., Iodi.); *bluish-red and spongy; ulcers spread without penetrating the* flesh. Stomatitis. *Inflammation and superficial ulceration of the mucous membranes of the mouth (*Nitr. ac.*). Salivary glands swollen and painful. **Profuse salivation (Acon., Cinch., Euc., Iod., *Nitr. ac.*); *saliva foetid or tastes coppery*. Taste *sweetish* (Ars., Bry., *Coccus*, Sulph.); *especially bread;* salty (Natr. mur.); *metallic (*Æsc., Coccul.,* Coccus, Naja, Osm., *Sulph.*); slimy or putrid (Arn., Rhus tox.).

Throat.—*Uvula swollen and elongated. Syphilitic ulcers in throat and mouth. *Painful dryness of the throat, with mouth full of saliva; pressure on swallowing.* Suppuration of the tonsils, with sharp, sticking pain in fauces when swallowing (Hep. s., *Nitr. ac.*). *Angina, throat and fauces of a coppery-red color and swollen. Sensation as if something (an apple-core) were sticking in the throat. *Throat constantly dry; pain as if tight posteriorly; with pressure on swallowing, yet constantly obliged to swallow, because the mouth is always full of saliva.* Inability to swallow liquids, which return through the nose (*Lyc.*). *Glands swollen (Arum., Aur., Baryt. c., Calc. c., Sil.).

Stomach.—Excessive hunger or complete loss of appetite; *appetite only for bread and butter;* aversion to butter. Violent empty eructations (Ipec., Phos., Verat. alb.). *Extremely violent thirst (Acon., Ars., Bry.).* Hiccough. Nausea when coughing. Water collects in mouth, causing nausea and vomiting of a bitter substance. Pit of stomach burns; swollen and sensitive to touch. Weak digestion, with continuous hunger. The stomach feels replete and constricted.

Abdomen.—Stitches in hepatic region, interfering with breathing and eructations (Acon., Ars., Bry., Chel., Cinch., Kali carb., Nux v.). Region of liver swollen, sensitive, cannot lie on right side (Bry., Chel.). *Abdomen hard, distended and painful (Ars., Calc. c.,* Cinch., Lach.). *Chronic atrophy of the liver, with emaciation and desiccation of the body. Complete icterus (Chel., Nux v.). Pressive pain in abdomen, as from a stone (Ars., Bry.). Bruised feeling of intestines (Ferr., Nux. v.); cannot lie on right side. Violent colic, with cutting and stinging pains, as if caused by knives (Coni.), principally at night or in cool of evening; colic from cold (*Dulc.*, Nux v.). Boring pain in right groin. *Inguinal glands swollen or suppurating* (Calc. c., Nitr. ac., Thuja): *circumscribed redness.* Bubo.

Stool and Anus.—*Ineffectual urging to stool every moment, with tenesmus in the rectum;* with protruding, painful sore hæmorrhoids. *Prolapsus ani. Burning pain in anus with soft stool. Weakness after stool.* Griping in abdomen with constant desire for stool, but little is evacuated (Nux v.). Colic; burning cutting and tenesmus before, during, and after stool; chilliness between stools (*Rheum*). Colic and diarrhœa caused by evening air. Stools *green or green mucus* (*Arg. nit.*, Ars., Bell., Ipec., Sulph.); **bloody; mucous and bloody (Canth., Nitr. ac.); slimy; brownish; whitish-gray; acrid and burning fæcal matter (*Ars., Sulph.*); excoriating anus. Discharge of ascarides and lumbrici (Ferr., Spig., Sep.).

Urinary Organs.—*Burning in the urethra* (Acon., Ars., Canth., Coni.). *Frequent desire to urinate, with scanty discharge* (Apis, *Coloc.*, Digit.), *worse at night.* Sudden irresistible urging to urinate, passing large quantities (*Kreos.*). Urine dark-red, turbid; deposits a sediment; acrid; dark-yellow, albuminous, mixed with blood. °*Gonorrhœa; with phymosis; chancroids; green painless discharge; worse at night* (Merc. cor.).

Male Organs.—*Total loss of sexual power (*Agn.*, Arg. nit., Camph.). Emissions at night mixed with blood. °Ulcers on the glans with cheesy base (Hep. s., *Nitr. ac.*), *like raw meat, caseous coat on bases,* margins everted. Painful inflammation and swelling of the glans and prepuce. Dragging pains in testes and spermatic cord (Berb.). Feeling of coldness in the testicles (Berb., Caps., Sulph.). Testicles swollen, hard and shinning.

Female Organs.—Menses too profuse, with anxiety and conc. *Leucorrhœa always worse at night; greenish discharge; smarting, corroding, itching, burning after scratching* (Alum., Coni., Phos., *Puls.*). Inflammation of the vagina, and still more of the external genitals, with rawness, smarting and excoriated spots (Carb. v.). Itching of the genitals (Canth., Coni.), worse from the contact of the urine. Prolapsus of the vagina. Mammæ swollen, hard with ulcerative pains; suppuration (Coni., Hep. s., Phytol., Sil.).

Respiratory Organs.—Hoarse, rough voice; burning rawness in larynx; fluent coryza and sore throat. Shortness of breath, on ascending or walking (Acon., Amm. c., *Ars.*, Calc. c.); with suffocation. Asthma. Short, dry, fatiguing cough, principally in bed, in the evening or at night; caused by tickling in upper part of chest (Hyos., Phos.). Cough which sounds and feels as if everything in the chest were dry; with pain in chest and small of back (Bell., Bry., Phcs.). *Stitches in the chest* (Acon., Bry., Kali carb., Phos.); *right side, extending through to the back on sneezing and coughing* (*Sulph.*); *on stooping constricts the chest.* °Bloody sputum in tuberculosis. Burning in chest extending to throat. Rush of blood to the chest. Sensation of dryness in the chest. ᶜSuppuration of the lungs after hæmorrhages, or after pneumonia. **Constriction of the chest. *Emphysema of the lungs.

Heart.—*Palpitation on slightest exertion (Staph.).

Neck and Back.—*Swelling and inflammation of the glands (*Baryt. c.*, Bell., Calc., Iodi.). Indurated lymphatics. Bruised pain in back and small of back. *Sticking in small of back on breathing.*

Limbs.—*Trembling of all the limbs (Coccul., Coni., Gels., Stram.), *especially of hands and feet.* **Involuntary jerking in the limbs. ** *Weakness and weariness in all the limbs;* unusual heaviness. Drawing and tearing in all the limbs (Bry., Coloc., Led., Lyc., *Sulph.*), worse at night, in the warm bed; with profuse sweat, which gives no relief. *Cold hands and feet.*

Upper Limbs.—*Tremor of the hands,* with weakness; could neither feed nor dress himself. Cramp-like contraction of the hands and fingers. Scaling off and exfoliation of the finger nails. Moist itch-like eruption of the hands, with nightly itching; bleeding rhagades.

Lower Limbs.—Burning in the nates. Soreness between the thighs and genitals (Graph.). Swelling of the backs of the feet. Tearing in hip-joint and knee, worse at night; beginning suppuration. Heaviness. Weakness and giving way in knees, could scarcely stand. Boring in periosteum of tibæ. Drawing pain in tibia.

Generalities.—***Great weariness and prostration; *trembling.* **Involuntary trembling of the voluntary muscles, hands, tongue, etc.* Hastiness in all motions. *Breath and whole body smell foul (Iod.). Paralysis agitans. All discharges acrid. Œdema of face, hands and feet, with anæmia. Whole body feels bruised, with soreness in all the bones (Arn.). Peritonitis, then necrosis. *Pains return in evening on going to bed and banish sleep* (Colch., Iod., Nitr. ac., Plumb.). Restlessness and anxiety towards evening, could not remain sitting or in any one posture. **Boring pains in the exostosis at night; bone pains* (Aran.). Excitability and sensibility of all the organs (*Cinch.*). *Glandular swellings with or without suppuration (Hep. s., Graph., Nitr. ac.). Cannot lie on the right side (Reverse, *Phos.*).

Skin.—Skin dirty-yellow (Ferr., Iod.); jaundice (*Cinch.*). Itching all over, worse at night when warm in bed (Alum., Clem., Mez., *Puls.*, Psor., *Sulph.*). **Eruption of watery vesicles. *Ulcers bleeding readily* (*Asaf., Hep. s., Mez., Sulph.*), *base lardaceous; margins everted like raw meat.* Ulceration very superficial and widespread. Flat, painless ulcers, pale, covered with phlegm-like pus; on the scalp, skin of penis, etc. °Primary and secondary syphilis (Nitr. ac.); round, coppery, red spots shining through the skin. Herpetic and pustular eruptions, forming dry, scaly spots, or yellow crusts and acrid discharges.

Sleep.—Excessive sleepiness day and night. **Sleeplessness (Cimic., Cinch., Coff.).

Fever.—Chilliness in open air; between diarrhœic stools; in morning or in evening after lying down, as from cold water poured over one; not relieved by warmth of stove. Alternations of chilliness and heat (Calc. c., Coccul.). Attacks of heat at night (Cinch., Phos.).

Sweat **profuse at night (*Cinch., Phos., Sulph.*) *on every motion* (*Calc. c., Phos., Hep. s.,* Sil.); *cold and clammy* (*Ars., Camph.*); *fatty and oily* (Bry.); **offensive (Arn., Ars., Carb. an., Sil.); stains linen yellow (Carls.). Sweat with all complaints, but giving no relief.

MERCURIUS. 499

Aggravation.—In the evening and at *night; from heat of bed; during perspiration;* in wet weather; in cold evening air; in fall, with warm days and damp, cold nights; during exercise; from lying on right side.

Conditions.—Young people affected more than old.

Compare.—Amm. mur., Ant. tart., Ant. crud., Arg. met., Arg. nit., Ars., *Aur.,* Bell., Calc. c., Cinch., Coni., Graph., *Hep. s., Iodi.,* Lach., Lyc., Mez., Natr. mur., *Nitr. ac.,* Phos., *Puls.,* Sil., Staph., *Sulph.,* Tellur., Thuja. Merc. follows well after Bell., Hep. s., Sulph., Lach.; after Merc. follows Bell., Cinch., Dulc., Hep. s., Nitr. ac., Sulph. Merc. and Sil. do not follow each other well.—*Hering.*

Antidotes.—Asaf., *Aur.,* Bell., Carb. v., Cinch., *Hep. s.,* Iodi., Kali. Lach., Lyc., Mez., *Nitr. ac.,* Staph., Sulph., Electricity.

Mercurius Antidotes.—Ant. crud., Ars., Aur., Calc. c., Cinch., Cupr., Mez., Sulph.

THERAPEUTICS.

The therapeutic range of Mercury is so great, including, as it does, to a greater or less degree, almost every diseased condition to which flesh is heir, it would be impossible to give a complete list of the individual pathological states in which it may be useful. Its most important uses are quite clearly outlined in the foregoing pathogenesis. It is a valuable remedy in syphilitic affections. Primary syphilis for the so-called soft chancre or chancroid, the ulceration is superficial, with raw everted edges and a lardaceous or cheesy base. The drug may also be used in secondary syphilis, providing its use has not been abused in the primary stage. In this connection it should be remembered that Mercury affects only the long bones, and as syphilis affects only the flat bones, the drug is rarely useful in syphilitic bone diseases, though it is an excellent remedy for the nightly bone pains. Valuable in syphilitic rheumatism. Chronic and subacute rheumatism, of non-syphilitic origin when the pains are aggravated at night from the warmth of the bed and sweat which affords no relief. Rheumatoid arthritis. Diseases of bones, especially periostitis of the long bones. Exostoses. An extremely valuable remedy in glandular swellings, with or without suppuration, but especially if suppuration is profuse (Sil.); in the former case dissipating the swelling and preventing suppuration, in the latter checking the suppurative process. Cold swellings; slowly suppurating abscesses. Inflammations. Valuable in the first stage of suppurative conditions in general after Bell. has failed to dissipate the local inflammation and pus is about to form; it may absorb the products of inflammation and bring about resolution. Dropsical conditions, with emaciation; from organic diseases of the liver (ascites); after scarlatina. Anæmia. General tremors. Paralysis agitans. Convulsions. Chorea. In all neuroses, especially chorea, Merc. may be indicated by the general cachexia and constitutional symptoms rather than by the nervous condition. Neuralgia, especially of the face, from cold, tearing pains, worse at night. Rheumatic catarrhal inflammations with disposition to sweat. Often useful in catarrhal conditions of the respiratory tract. Acute coryza, with much sneezing, fluent corrosive discharge, etc. Chronic nasal catarrh, acrid, offensive discharge of green mucus, bones of nose swollen and painful. Syphilitic ozœna. A valuable remedy in catarrhal or follicular tonsilitis or pharyngitis. Ulcerated throat. Syphilitic sore throat. Seldom useful in diphtheria. Chronic hoarseness. Aphonia, catarrhal or syphilitic. Chronic laryngitis. Laryngeo-tracheitis. Chronic bronchitis. Pneumonia, especially with hepatic symptoms. Lobular pneumonia of infants. Phthisis. Asthma. Valuable in many forms of eye disease. Catarrhal or scrofulous ophthalmia. Purulent ophthalmia. Ophthalmia neonatorum. The pains are always worse at night, and the discharge excoriating. Ulcers of the cornea, vascular and surrounded by grayish opacity; tendency to slough; pus between the corneal layers, or in the anterior chamber. Ciliary blepharitis or retinitis caused by working over fires or forges. Blepharitis. According to Allen (*op. cit. p. 701*), the drug "is rarely useful in syphilitic inflammation of the eyes, as it has no power whatever to affect the iris," but it has been recommended by Hering and others for syphilitic iritis. Choroiditis. Keratitis. Episcleritis. Sclerotitis. Inflammation and ulceration of meibomian glands. An invaluable remedy in catarrhal inflammation of the ear, both internal and external; also of the tympanum, involving the Eustachian tube; discharges offensive, purulent, excoriating; deafness; ringing, roaring and buzzing sounds in the ear; pain worse at night, etc. Catarrh of the ear from cold, moment-

MERCURIUS. 501

ary obstruction, better after swallowing or blowing the nose. Inflammation of the auditory canal, herpetic suppuration or ulceration, violent pain, worse at night. Polypus in external meatus; also furuncles. Especially valuable for parotitis. Mercurius is an important remedy in diseases of the digestive sphere. It is the chief remedy in dental periostitis; teeth feel sore and elongated, pain worse at night, carious teeth; they turn black, become loose, the gums become soft and recede from the teeth, nightly pains. Unhealthy. Swollen, spongy, suppurating gums; gums bleed easily. Ulcers on gums; scorbutis. Glossitis. The most often used remedy in aphthous stomatitis; especially indicated when there is salivation and fœtid odor from the mouth. Pain, swelling and ulceration of salivary glands. Ptyalism. Chronic gastritis, with burning pain, swollen and sensitive to touch. Exceptionally valuable in diseases of the liver. Acute and chronic hepatitis. Chronic atrophy of the liver. Jaundice from gall-stones or duodenal catarrh. Enlarged liver. Bilious colic. In most liver diseases the region is painful and sore, worse when lying on the right side, and frequently the characteristic tongue and other symptoms of Merc. are present. Gastro-enteritis. Catarrhal enteritis, with characteristic symptoms. Peri-typhlitis. Subacute colitis. Catarrhal diarrhœa from taking cold with colic, tenesmus, and acrid green mucous stools (green mucous stools without tenesmus, Merc. dulc.). Green stools in teething children with colic and straining. Bilious diarrhœa. Dysentery, stools green or bloody mucus, violent tenesmus and burning pain, chilliness between the stools. Autumnal dysentery. Worms. A valuable remedy in nephritis; urine albuminous, mixed with blood, bruised pain in small of back, worse at night. Albuminuria of pregnancy with other Merc. symptoms. Chronic cystitis. Gonorrhœa, green, painless discharge, worse at night. Nocturnal enuresis. Impotence. Spermatorrhœa. Orchitis. Buboes. Venereal ulcers, having the peculiar Merc. characteristic. Herpes præputialis. Vaginal catarrh, rawness and smarting, green, corrosive leucorrhœa, worse at night. Ulcers, especially venereal, on external and internal genitals. Prolapsus of vagina. Pruritus of vulva. Menorrhagia. Subacute ovaritis. Pelvic peritonitis and pelvic cellulitis, after Bell., pus about to form. Morning sickness of pregnancy. Mastitis, breasts hard, swollen with ulcerative pains; suppuration; favors evacuation of pus. Cancer of mammæ, raw, sore feeling. Useful in a variety of skin diseases. Moist eczema. Vesicular eruptions. Herpes. Herpes zoster. Moist intertrigo. Impetigo. Prurigo. Ulcers superficial and widespread, readily bleeding, cheesy base, everted edges like raw meat. Varicose ulcers. Erysipelas, simple and phlegmonous; of new-born, scrofulous or syphilitic children. Variola, stage of maturation, with dysenteric symptoms. May be useful in scarlatina or measles with general Merc. symptoms. Catarrhal and bilious fevers. Yellow fever. Intermittent and remittent fevers. Hectic fever, especially of children; irritative fevers. An important characteristic of Merc. in fevers as well as in other diseases is that there is usually free perspiration, but it affords the patient no relief; rather aggravates. According to Hering, Merc. is "contra-indicated in typhoid fever, except for marked icteroid or scorbutic symptoms."

MERCURIUS CORROSIVUS.

Synonym.—Mercurius Sublimatus Corrosivus. Bi-Chloride of Mercury. Mercuric Chloride. *Common name.*—Corrosive Sublimate. *Preparation.*—Corrosive sublimate is dissolved in Alcohol, one to ninety-nine, making the 2x dilution. Subsequent dilutions with Alcohol. Triturations from the Salt.

GENERAL ANALYSIS.

The general action of Merc. cor. is essentially the same as of other Mercurial preparations, yet it offers peculiarities of its own, which are found in no other. It is, as the name indicates, a highly corrosive, irritating poison, acting pre-eminently upon mucous membranes with destructive energy, producing an intensely acute inflammation, rapidly tending to softening and gangrenous disorganization. Its irritant influence also extends to the serous membranes, especially to the peritoneum. The most essential feature of Merc. cor. is the phagedenic tendency of all inflammatory conditions.

CHARACTERISTIC SYMPTOMS.

Mind.—Depressed; low spirited (Ign., Puls.). Ill-humored (*Bry., Cham., Nux v.*). Weakness of the intellect; stares at persons who talk to him, and does not understand them. Stupor and delirium. Coma (Bell., *Op.*).

Head.—Congestion to the head and face, with burning of the cheeks (Acon., *Bell.*). Violent frontal headache (*Puls., Sang.*). Pain, like a drawing in the periosteum of the skull.

Eyes.—Pupils contracted (*Physos.*) and insensible (*Op.*). Excessive photophobia and acrid lachrymation (*Ars., Euphr., Led.*). Redness of the conjunctiva. Pains behind the eyeballs, as if they would be forced out. Lids everted, swollen, red, excoriated, burning, and smarting; edges covered with thick crusts or pustules (Merc., *Sulph.*). Tearing pain in bone and over left eye, near root of nose, and in other parts of bone.

Ears.—Violent pulsation in the ears.

Nose.—Swelling and redness of the nose (Bell., Merc.). *Fluent coryza;* rawness and smarting in the nostrils (*Amm. mur., Cepa,* Hydras.). Frequent nosebleed.

Face.—Countenance pale; anxious; as if exhausted. Face flushed; red; swollen; puffy. *Lips black; excessively swollen and tender;* dry and cracked (Ars.); incrusted with a dry secretion. Stiffness of the jaws; soreness. °Œdematous swelling of the face; paleness; albuminuria.

Mouth.—*Teeth loose;* pain and fall out (Merc.). Sordes. Soreness in teeth and gums; aching at night. *Gums swollen and spongy; bleed easily;* detached from teeth (Carb. v., Cistus, *Merc., Nitr. ac.*); ulcerated. Tongue coated with thick white mucus (*Ant. crud.*), or dry and red (Bell., Rhus tox.); excessively swollen and inflamed (Bell.); red with black coat; covered with a grayish white crust; moist edges, red; pale dirty-yellow posteriorly and edges. Mouth inflamed; dry, burning and parched, as if scalded (Apis). Exudations and ulcers on the mucous membranes of mouth and throat. Accumulation of tenacious saliva, expectorated with difficulty (Kali bi.). *Ptyalism. Salty* (Ant. crud., Sulph.), *or very bitter taste.* Swallowing not so painful as depressing the tongue.

Throat.—*Throat intensely inflamed and swollen, preventing swallowing and threatening suffocation* (Bell.). *Violent burning pain in throat and œsophagus* (Ars., Canth., Caps.); *aggravated by slightest external pressure.* Dryness of fauces. Dark-red color. Constriction. Difficult painful swallowing, even of fluids. *Uvula swollen, elongated* (Merc.) *dark-red.* External throat and glands of throat enormously swollen. Spasms of œsophagus and stomach on attempting to swallow a drop of liquid. Burning in œsophagus.

Stomach.—Violent unquenchable thirst for cold water (Acon., Ars., Bry.). Drink frequently regurgitates through the nose. Painful retching and vomiting. *Incessant green bilious vomiting* (Iris). Streaks of blood in matter vomited. Burning in stomach. Great distension and *sensitiveness in the epigastric region* (Ars., Bell., *Bry.*, Nux v., Lyc.) to the slightest touch or pressure.

Abdomen.—Stitches in the hepatic region (Acon., Ars., Calc. c., Chel., Cinch., Coni., Kali c., Merc., Natr. mur., Nux v., Sep., Sulph.). Abdomen distended and very painful to least touch (Acon., Bell., Cupr.). *Bruised pain in abdomen* (Ferr., Merc.), *especially in cœcal region and over transverse colon.*

Stool and Anus.—Constant burning in rectum and anus (Ars., Canth.); during stool. Corrosive ichor oozes from anus, excoriating the parts (Carb. v.). *Very distressing, persistent tenesmus and cutting colicky pains; after stool burning and tenesmus of rectum and bladder; stools frequent, scanty, nothing but mucus tinged with blood* (Canth.). Stool pasty, dark-green, bilious, blackish, offensive (Ars.). Constipation; tenacious fæces.

Urinary Organs.—*Tenesmus of the bladder* (Canth., Caps., Colch.); urine suppressed (Acon., Hyos., Stram.). Frequent urination; *passed in drops with much pain* (Acon., Bell., Canth.). Urine scanty, bloody; *albuminous* (Osm., Phos., Phyt., *Plumb.*) containing filaments, flocks or dark flesh-like pieces of mucus; *epithelial cells of the tubuli uriniferi* in a state of fatty degeneration. Gonorrhœa, at first thin, afterward thick, greenish, worse at night (*Merc.*), burning, smarting urination (Can. sat.).

Male Organs.—Penis and testes enormously swollen (Ars.). °Chancres assuming a phagedenic appearance, and secreting a thin, ichorous pus.

Female Organs.—Intense inflammation of the vulva. *Painful glandular swellings about the nipple.*

Respiratory Organs.—Hoarseness or aphonia, burning, cutting and stinging in the trachea; tightness across the chest; influenza (Osm.). Difficult respiration. Spasm of the glottis when swallowing. Cough, with expectoration of mucus tinged with blood. *Stitches shoot through the thorax* (right side).

Pulse.—Small, *intermittent*, irregular (Kali c., *Natr. mur.*); rapid.

Limbs.—Lassitude in all the limbs; trembling. Stitches in hip-joint, better on motion.

Generalities.—*Lies on the back with knees bent up. Great debility;* trembling (Calc. c., Cinch.). Convulsive twitchings and contractions (Cic., Ign.). Glandular swellings Baryt., c., Calc. c., Graph., Iod.). Drawing pains in periosteum (Nitr. ac.). General anasarca (Ars., Apis, Apoc.).

Sleep.—Frequent yawning and stretching. *Sleepless at night;* starting from sleep (Ars., *Bell., Hyos.,* Stram.).

Fever.—Chilliness from slightest exertion (*Calc. c., Hep. s., Lyc., Phos.,* Sil.). Surface cold and *covered with profuse perspiration, especially on forehead* (*Camph., Verat. alb.*). Great heat of the skin (*Acon., Ars., Bell., Bry.*); at night with anxiety, preventing rest. Clammy, cold perspiration (Ars., Camph., Merc.); offensive, toward morning.

Aggravation—In evening and at night; in open air; from fat food; from motion.

Amelioration.—While at rest.

Compare.—Acon., Ars., Bell., Bry., Canth., Cepa, Lach., Natr. mur., Nitr. ac., Sulph.

Antidotes.—Hep. s., Nitr. ac., Sil. To large doses: white of an egg.

THERAPEUTICS.

Merc. cor. is mostly used in the treatment of acute inflammations, especially of mucous membranes, characterized by great violence. It is invaluable in inflammatory conditions of the eye and lids. Ophthalmia, catarrhal, scrofulous, syphilitic or gonorrhœal, characterized by intense inflammation and swelling, extreme pain and photophobia and acrid lachrymation. Ophthalmia neonatorum, with acrid discharges; caused by syphilitic or gonorrhœal leucorrhœa. Blepharitis scrofulosa. Phlyctenulæ; deep ulcers on the cornea. Iritis, especially if syphilitic; pains severe; worse at night. Kerato-iritis. Episcleritis. Retinitis albuminurica; also with tearing in the eyebrow; bones tender. Retinitis hæmorrhagica. Choroiditis. Sclerotitis. Hypopyon occurring in abscess of cornea or iritis. Fluent coryza with excessive rawness, smarting and burning, acrid mucous discharges, nose swollen and very sore. Ozœna, gluey discharge; drying up in posterior nares; much burning; ulceration; perforation of septum. Facial neuralgia. Inflammation of the gums, purple color, spongy, ulcerated, gangrenous tendency. Violent glossitis, tongue excessively swollen, so that it cannot be protruded. Stomatitis with intense burning pain. Pharyngitis, intense, throat dry, swollen, dark red, violent burning pains, difficult swallowing, constriction, suffocation. Œsophagitis, burning pains. Diphtheria, intense, rapid, destructive. Inflammation of uvula and arch of palate, swollen, dark-red, burning. Chronic dyspepsia, with distension and soreness of epigastrium, burning pains. Hepatitis. Useful in various forms of partial peritonitis, with tendency to the formation of an abscess, sore, burning pains, etc. Colonitis, especially of transverse and descending colon, burning pains. Typhlitis. Proctitis. Periproctitis, abscess about to form. Merc. cor. is the remedy oftenest indicated and most useful in what might be termed a typical dysentery, characterized by scanty stools of pure mucus tinged or streaked with blood, and extreme persistent tenesmus and burning pains, and frequently also great tenesmus of the bladder. The drug may also be useful when the stools are of a different character, as noted in the pathogenesis, if the violent tenesmus is present, which is the chief indication. A very useful remedy in severe cases of cystitis with violent tenesmus and burning, resembling Canth. Acute nephritis, urine scanty and albuminous; with violent cystic symptoms. Albuminuria; after diphtheria or in Bright's disease; acute early stages. Gonorrhœa, with thick, greenish discharge, and intolerable burning and smarting during urination. Venereal ulcers in both sexes, assuming a phagedenic appearance, and secreting a thin, ichorous pus. Intense inflammation of the vulva, with violent burning, destructive tendency. Pelvic peritonitis, especially pelvic cellulitis, abscess about to form. A very useful remedy in catarrhal hoarseness and aphonia. Violent influenza, with burning, stinging, cutting pains in larynx and trachea, tightness across the chest. Bronchitis. General dropsy especially from kidney disease. Glandular swellings. May be useful in diseases of bones, characterized by rapid destruction of tissue forming abscesses, with the usual symptoms indicating the drug. Condylomata. Ulcers which perforate and become phagedenic.

MERCURIUS IODATUS FLAVUS.

Synonyms.—Protoiodide of Mercury. Mercurius Iodide. *Common name.*—Yellow Iodide of Mercury. *Preparation.*—Triturations, which should be protected from the light.

GENERAL ANALYSIS.

The Iodide of Mercury acts especially upon the glands and mucous membranes of the throat, after the manner of other Mercuries, though partaking somewhat of the action of Iodine. In the Biniodide this latter action preponderates, while the action of the Protoiodide more closely resembles that of Mercury.

CHARACTERISTIC SYMPTOMS.

Head.—Headache on the top of the head, or on the right side. Dull headache on awaking in the morning. Dull frontal headache, with pain in the root of the nose (*Kali bi.*, Natr. ars.). Itching of the scalp (*Graph.*, Nitr. ac., *Sulph.*).
Nose.—Shooting pain at root of nose.
Face.—Dull aching and soreness in the bones of the face.
Mouth.—Tongue coated bright-yellow; tip and edges red. *Base of tongue covered with a thick, dirty-yellow coating* (Chin. sulph.), especially on rising in the morning.

Throat.—Much tenacious mucus in throat; hawking causes gagging. Burning in the throat (*Ars.*, Caps., *Canth.*, *Merc. cor.*). Fauces and pharynx red and inflamed; tonsils swollen; *especially the right; pain on swallowing; sensation of a lump as if swollen* (*Bell.*). Posterior wall of pharynx dotted with patches of mucus and *small spots, which look ulcerated.*

Stool.—Tough, almost like putty, with much straining. Stools thin, light-yellowish brown, frothy; soft, copious, dark.

Generalities.—Faintness, wants to lie down (Nux m.). Has troublesome itching over the whole body; worse at night, especially while in bed. Glands swollen and indurated (Merc.). °Milk crust in children of a syphilitic taint.

Aggravation.—Most symptoms appear at night in bed. From passive motion; during rest on right side.

Amelioration.—During the day; in the open air; from active motion.

Compare.—Bell., Iod., Kali bi., Lach., Merc., Nitr. ac., Sulph.

THERAPEUTICS.

Mostly useful in sore throat, especially in the so-called diphtheritic sore throat or follicular tonsilitis, usually worse on the right side, or beginning on the right side, glands not greatly swollen. May be useful in mild cases of diphtheria with little glandular swelling (glands much swollen the biniodide of Merc. is better), but is never useful in malignant forms of the disease. Sometimes useful in chronic nasal catarrh, the posterior nares being most affected. Catarrh with shooting pains at root of nose and along frontal sinuses. Ulcers on cornea, sometimes commence at margin and extend over whole cornea. Syphilitic iritis. Pustular conjunctivitis. Ciliary blepharitis, especially syphilitic. Hard chancres, given at once may prevent secondary symptoms. Painless chancres, with swelling of inguinal glands; not disposed to suppurate. Yellow leucorrhœa, especially of young girls and children.

MERCURIUS IODATUS RUBER.

Synonyms.—Biniodide of Mercury. Mercuric Iodide. *Common name.*—Red Iodide of Mercury. *Preparation.*—Triturations.

CHARACTERISTIC SYMPTOMS.

Mind.—Low-spirited; disposed to cry (*Ign., Natr. mur., Nux m., Puls., Rhus tox.*). Ill-humored in the morning.

Head.—Vertigo. Sensation as if bound by a tight cord in frontal region (Iod., Merc.). *Heat and pulsation in vertex*, especially in evening. Aching in the bones of the head, chiefly occipital.

Eyes.—Inflammation, with burning. Albuginea inflamed and painful.

Ears.—Itching in both ears (Baryt. c., Hep. s., Sulph.). Swelling of parotid and neighboring glands (Iodi.).

Nose.—Coryza, nose hot, swollen; much sneezing and running from the head (Acon., Merc., Sang.); hoarseness. Whitish-yellow or bloody discharge; affection of posterior nares, with raw sensation; nasal bones diseased; turbinated bones swollen. Hawks mucus from posterior nares. Crusty eruption on wings of nose.

Mouth.—*Lips slimy and sticky on waking.* Profuse flow of saliva, and aching of teeth in lower jaw (Merc.). Taste bitter.

Throat.—Much phlegm in the throat and nose; hawks it out. Sensation of a lump in the throat (*Bell.*), with disposition to hawk it out; hawks up a hard, greenish lump. *Inflammation and swelling of left tonsil,* velum elongated causing cough, next day both tonsils involved. Painful swellings of tonsils and submaxillary glands. °Diphtheritic patches, and superficial ulcers in the throat (*Nitr. ac.*).

Stomach.—Pain in the epigastrium on pressure.

Urinary Organs.—Increased flow of urine (Apis, Apoc.). °Hard, red swelling in front of prepuce, and painless hard chancre in the center. °Sarcocele of left testicle; syphilis. °Bubo, discharging for years; indolent chancre.

Respiratory Organs.—Constriction across the chest. Catching pain under right breast. Sticking pain in heart.

Skin.—Pustules, with inflamed base, sore to touch; itching slightly scab over, but pus oozes.

Sleep.—Frightful dreams.

Fever.—Shivering, then feverishness, copious sweat at night. °Fever with grippe.

Compare.—Bell., Lach., Merc., Mez., Nitr. ac., Kali bi., Iodi. Bell. follows well in scarlet fever.

Antidotes.—See Merc. and Iodi.

THERAPEUTICS.

This drug is a valuable remedy in sore throats, its action resembling the protoiodide. It differs in that the inflammation is worse on the left side, or, at least, begins on the left side, there is more glandular swelling and more fever and headache. Not so often useful in follicular tonsilitis as the protoiodide, but more often useful in true diphtheria, especially with great glandular swelling. During course of malignant scarlatina, swelling of parotids and neighboring glands; fauces and tonsils covered with large fœtid ulcers, etc. Scrofulous ophthalmia; granulated lids; ulceration of cornea. Diphtheritic conjunctivitis. Old cases of granular lids and pannus. Colds in the head, acute coryza. Nasal polypus. A valuable remedy in syphilitic ulcers. Bubo. Hunterian chancre. Old cases of syphilis, particularly in persons of lax fibre, scrofulous, and in those who have taken much Mercury. Sarcocele. Inflammations, erosions and ulceration of the os and cervix, especially of syphilitic origin. Yellow corrosive leucorrhœa. Chronic metritis. Laryngitis. Laryngeal phthisis. Goitre. Grippe, with fever, headache, giddiness, furred tongue. Bronchial catarrh.

MEZEREUM.

Synonym.—Daphne Mezereum. *Natural order.*—Thymelaceæ. *Common name.*—Spurge Olive. *Habitat.*—A small shrub, native of Northern and Central Europe. *Preparation.*—Tincture from the fresh bark.

MEZEREUM. 511

GENERAL ANALYSIS.

Acts especially upon the skin and the mucous membranes of the genito-urinary organs, and the alimentary tract, producing a high degree of irritation, which results in inflammation of the mucous membranes, and in characteristic eruptions of the skin. It also acts in a similar manner upon the long bones and the periosteum of the jaw, resembling the action of Mercury and also the syphilitic poison.

CHARACTERISTIC SYMPTOMS.

Mind.—*Hypochondriac and despondent* (Natr. carb., Nux v.); everything seems dead and nothing makes a vivid impression on his mind. Inclination to weep (*Natr. mur., Puls., Ign.*). Vexed and angry at trifles (Bry., Cham.). Mental dullness and distraction; thinking difficult; unable to recollect (Natr. mur.).

Head.—Dullness of head, as if intoxicated, and as if he had been up all night (Coccul., Nux m., Puls.). Pain in bones of skull; aggravated by touch. Headache in temples and sides of head after exertion and from talking much. Violent headache; *head painful on slightest touch after vexation.* pressive headache from root of nose into forehead (Kali bi.). Stupefying pain through right hemisphere of brain to forehead. Pressive pain, from within outward, in left temple. Boring in the bones of the occiput. *Head covered with a thick leathery crust, under which pus collects and mats the hair* (Graph., Psor.). Itching of the scalp, better from scratching. Elevated, white, chalk-like scabs, with ichor beneath, breeding vermin. Dry scurf on the scalp; dandruff (Bad., Canth.).

Eyes.—Eyes hot, inflamed; conjunctiva injected, dirty-red; pressive pain and a *sensation of dryness.* Pressing and tearing pain in eyes. Smarting, compelling rubbing. *Obstinate twitching of the muscles of the left upper lid.* Lachrymation, with smarting in the eyes (Ars., Euphr.) Inclination to wink (Croc., Euph.); to close the eyes (Caust., Gels.). Itching of margins of lids and skin near the nose.

Ears.—*Sensation as though air were distending the right* *external meatus;* afterward in left; as if roaring would occur; with stopped sensation. Itching behind the ears.

Nose.—Catarrh, with discharge of yellow, thin at times, bloody mucus, making the nostrils sore; soreness and burning of upper lip. Pressing asunder pain in root of nose, in morning, with pain in temples on touch. Dryness of the nose and diminished smell. Frequent sneezing, with fluent coryza.

Face.—Violent tearing pains in the face, especially on left side. Cramp-like and stunning pressure in zygomatic process. Violent, frequent jerking and twitching of the muscles of the right cheek. Lips swollen, dry; scaly externally; painful, sore and burning (*Ars.*). Dryness of the tongue. *Inflammatory redness of face, with fat, moist eruption. Child scratches the face continually, which becomes covered with blood; itching worse at night (Merc.); tears off scab, leaving raw spots, on which fat pustules form.* The ichor from scratched face excoriates other parts.

Mouth.—Pains in carious teeth (*Merc.*). Hollow teeth decay very rapidly. Boring toothache, extending into bones of jaw, malar bones and temples. *Teeth feel blunt and elongated;* on biting on them and from fresh air. *Violent burning in tongue and mouth, extending to the stomach* (*Ars.*, Canth., Caps.).

Throat.—*Burning in the throat, pharynx and œsophagus* (*Ars., Canth., Caps., Merc. cor.*). Irritation in fauces causing dry fatiguing cough. Sensation as if the throat were full of mucus. Dryness, *heat, scraping* and rawness in the fauces (Arg. met., Arg. nit., *Arum., Nux v.*).

Stomach.—Great hunger or loss of appetite. Hunger at noon or in evening. Frequent empty and tasteless eructations. Nausea in the throat: *bitter* vomiting. Burning in pit of stomach (*Ars.,* Camph., Canth., Lob.), on pressure, with pain. Pain in epigastric region, evening and night, worse by paroxysms. Burning pressure extending transversely at intervals, worse from pressure.

Abdomen.—Dull pain in region of spleen. Stitches in left hypochondrium. Loud flatulence; much offensive flatus passing (Aloe, *Bry., Graph.*). Burning and heat in the abdomen (Acon., *Ars.,* Canth.).

Stool and Anus.—Stitches in the rectum. Biting sore pain in anus on walking, and burning in rectum. Itching in the anus (Alum., Ars., *Cina, Cham., Sulph.*). Constipation (Alum., Calc. c., *Bry. Nux v., Op., Sulph.*). Stool soft, brown, sour, fermented; containing small, white shining grains.

Urinary Organs.—Discharge of a few drops of blood after urinating. Sore pain in urethra, on touch, when urinating. Biting burning in forepart of urethra at close of micturition. Urine hot, with reddish sediment (Bell., Kreos.); bloody.

Male Organs.—Itching of the glans penis (Sulph.). Heat and swelling of the penis. Fine, pricking stitches in the penis and tip of glans penis. Swelling of scrotum and testicles.

Female Organs.—Menses too soon, profuse and long-lasting. Leucorrhœa like the white of an egg (Amm. mur., Calc. phos., *Borax*, Bovis.).

Respiratory Organs.—Hoarseness, with cough and rawness of the chest (*Caust., Nux m., Phos.*). After eating, must cough till he vomits. Violent cough when lying down (*Coni., Puls.*). Violent inclination to cough, low down in the trachea; cannot loosen anything by the cough. Constriction and contracting pains transversely across the chest. Stitches in the chest (*Bry., Kali carb.*).

Pulse.—Pulse intermittent (Coni., *Digit., Natr. mur.*); full tense, hard.

Neck and Back.—Pain from stiffness of nape and external cervical muscles; in right side of neck and throat, worse on motion. Rheumatic pains in scapular muscles; they feel tense and swollen, preventing motion.

Limbs.—Trembling of the limbs (Coccul., Coni., Gels.). Pains in periosteum of long bones, especially the tibiæ, worse at night and in bed; least touch intolerable; worse in damp weather; °syphilis (*Merc.*).

Upper Limbs.—Tearing pain in right shoulder joint, as if it would be torn asunder. Sore sensation in right axillæ. Finger ends powerless, cannot hold anything. Paralysis of flexors.

Lower Limbs.—Jerking pain in hip-joint, also in knee. Pains in bones of thigh and leg. Sudden sprained pain below right nates when walking. Violent pains in bones of feet;

in bones of instep, worse when walking. Pain in ball of little toe. *Burning pain in left tibia.* Pain in tibia as if periosteum would be torn off after midnight.

Generalities.—Feeling of great lightness of the body (Asar.). General sick feeling. Hot, jerking stitches in various parts of the body. Joints feel bruised and weary, as if they would give way. °Bones inflamed, swollen (Asaf., Hep. s., Kali bi., Staph.). especially shafts of cylindrical bones; caries, after abuse of Mercury. Sensitiveness to cold air.

Skin.—Usual liver spots on chest and arms become dark and desquamate. Red rash, itching violently; worse in bed, from touch; burning and change of place after scratching (Alum., Merc., *Sulph.*). Cutaneous ulcers form over bony protuberances. *Ulcers, easily bleeding* (Asaf., *Hep. s., Sulph.*), *sensitive, painful at night (Merc.); thick whitish yellow scabs, under which thick, yellow pus collects; burning, itching vesicles around the ulcers (Hep. s., Merc.).* Skin covered with elevated white scabs.

Sleep.—Irresistible sleepiness *(Ant. tart., Apis, Nux m.).* Yawning and stretching.

Fever.—Constant chilliness over the whole body (Puls.). Cold, with no desire for warmth; nor dread of open air; great thirst. Violent hot fever.

Conditions.—One side of the body generally affected. Phlegmatic temperament.

Compare.—*Anac.,* Ars., Bell., Bry., Calc. c., Ign., Iodi., Lyc., *Merc.,* Nitr. ac., Nux v., Phos., *Puls., Phyt., Rhus tox.,* Sep., Sulph., Zinc.

Antidotes.—Acet. ac., Bry., Calc. c., Camph., Nux v., *Merc.,* Rhus tox., Mucilaginous Drinks, Milk, etc.

Mezereum Antidotes.—Merc., Nitr. ac., Phos., Spirituous Liquors.

THERAPEUTICS.

The chief use of Mezereum is in the treatment of syphilitic (especially after the abuse of Mercury) and scrofulous affections, especially diseases of the periosteum and bones, and of the skin. Periosteal inflammation of the shafts of long bones, particularly of the tibiæ, soreness and swelling, burning pains worse at night, worse in damp weather; syphilitic. Periostitis

MEZEREUM.

of the lower jaw. Periosteal rheumatism. Rheumatic neuralgia, flying stitching pains along bones, worse at night. Exostoses. The skin symptoms of Mezereum are important. It is a valuable remedy in herpetic and eczematous eruptions of the nature described in the above pathogenesis. The chief characteristics is the moist vesicular eruption with the exudation of much thick purulent matter, over which thick scabs form, the intolerable itching and burning worse from scratching, and the aggravation at night and from heat. This eruption may occur on any part of the body, but more especially upon the face and chin and on the scalp. Tinea capitis. Pityriasis. Ulcers of a nature already described. Herpes zoster, with severe neuralgia and burning pains, worse at night and from warmth of bed. Mezereum is a valuable remedy in neuralgia, especially following eruptions or after the abuse of Mercury. Neuralgia, especially intercostal, after zona. Ciliary neuralgia, the pains radiate and shoot downwards, cold feeling, as though cold air were blowing in the eye, bones diseased; also after operations, especially removal of the eyeball. Facial neuralgia, involving the eye, cheek and teeth, intolerable tearing pains, worse at night and from heat, bones of face sore, parts feel numb after the pain. Aching in carious teeth, they feel blunt and elongated (see symptoms). Chronic inflammation of the ear, after suppressed eruption, abuse of Mercury, or in cases where Merc. was indicated, but did no good. Catarrh, scrofulous (see symptoms). Syphilitic ozœna. Syphilitic sore throat, burning sensation and raw pain extending from pharynx halfway down œsophagus, also involving the larynx, with hoarseness, etc., sometimes ulceration. Gastric catarrh with burning and pressure. Ulcer of the stomach, with burning corroding pains as if the stomach were raw. Chronic diarrhœa, with or following characteristic eruption, psoric diathesis. Has cured constipation, stools large and hard as a stone, feel as if they would split the anus, sometimes with prolapsus. Gonorrhœa. Gleet, with watery mucous discharge, sometimes with bloody urine, and other symptoms already given. Uterine ulcers, with albuminous, corrosive leucorrhœa and other symptoms of the drug.

MILLEFOLIUM.

Synonym.—Achillea Millefolium. *Natural order.*—Compositæ. *Common names.*—Yarrow. Milfoil. *Habitat.*—A common perennial herb found growing in old fields, etc., in North America and Europe. *Preparation.*—Tincture from the fresh leaves.

GENERAL ANALYSIS.

Through the spinal nerves, Millefolium exerts its action upon the venous capillaries, especially within the pelvis, where it gives rise to hæmorrhages from the organs therein contained, and from the nose, and has proved curative not only in hæmorrhages from the pelvic viscera, but also in hæmorrhages from the nose and lungs, the flow in each instance being of a more active character than in Hamamelis. It also affects mucous membranes, causing irritation and slight congestion, gastric and abdominal pain, diarrhœa and enuresis.

CHARACTERISTIC SYMPTOMS.

Head.—Congestion to the head (Acon., Bell.). Confused, dull headache. Slight throbbing in arteries of head and face. Dull pain in vertex. Sensation in right side of head, as if screwed together.

Eyes.—Sensation of too much blood in the eyes. Inward piercing pressing in eyes, to root of nose and sides of forehead.

Ears.—Sensation of stoppage in the ears.

Nose.—*Nosebleed* (*Acon., Bell., Bry., Ham.*); also in congestions to head and chest.

Face.—Sensation of heat, as if blood were rising to the head. Tearing pains in lower jaw.

Mouth.—Rheumatic toothache, with diseased gums. Thirst; mouth dry.

Stomach.—Eructations. Painful gnawing and digging in stomach, as from hunger (Ign., *Puls., Sulph.*). Sensation of fullness in stomach. Burning in stomach (Ars., Canth., Sulph.).

Abdomen.—Pain in region of liver. Pain as from incarcerated flatulence: abdomen distended; emission of offensive flatus.

MILLEFOLIUM. 517

Stool.—°Bloody discharges from the bowels; tenesmus. Diarrhœic stools; violent colic. °Hæmorrhoids; profuse flow of blood (*Erig., Euc., Ham.*).

Urinary Organs.—*Bloody urine* (*Ars., Canth.*, Phos.). Frequent desire to urinate; involuntary. °Catarrh of bladder from atony.

Female Organs.—Menses suppressed or too profuse. °Uterine hæmorrhages (Acon., *Bell.*, Erig., *Ham.*, Sec.); after great exertion; with congestive headache. Leucorrhœa. °Lochia suppressed or too copious.

Respiratory Organs.—°Cough with frequent spitting of bright blood (Ferr., Ham.); oppression of chest; palpitation (*Acon.*) in phthisis; suppressed hæmorrhoids; suppressed menses (Bry., Ham., *Puls.*). Excessive accumulation of mucus in bronchi. In lungs, piercing pains; stinging, bruised feelings.

Heart and Pulse.—°Excessive palpitation and bloody sputum. °Ebullitions from coughing blood. Pulse accelerated and contracted.

Generalities.—Piercing, drawing, tearing pains in the limbs. Congestions; *hæmorrhages;* mucous discharges from atony (Helon.). °Wounds bleed profusely, especially from a fall. °Effects of over-lifting or over-exertion. Worse in evening and night; better during the day.

Sleep.—Yawning without any weariness.

Compare.—Arnica, Carb. v., Erig., Ham., Ipec., Sen. aur., Tril.

Millefolium Antidotes.—Arum. mur. Coffee drank after Mille. causes congestion to head.

THERAPEUTICS.

Especially useful in active (Ham., passive) bright-red hæmorrhages from the nose, lungs and bowels, and from the sexual organs of women, especially when resulting from atony, or from violent exertion. Resembles Aconite in hæmorrhages, only lacking the anxiety of the latter. Bleeding hæmorrhoids. Phthisis pulmonalis. Catarrh from atony. Painful varicose veins during pregnancy.

MURIATICUM ACIDUM.

Synonyms.—Hydrochloric Acid. Hydrogen Chloride. *Common name.*—Muriatic Acid. *Preparation.*—A solution in distilled water (1-2) is called the 1x dilution. The 2x dilution is made with distilled water, the 3x with dilute Alcohol and subsequent dilutions with Alcohol.

GENERAL ANALYSIS.

Acts upon the ganglionic nervous system, and through it upon the blood, the skin and the alimentary tract, especially the mouth and anus. Causes a morbid condition of the blood, increases its coagulability and renders it prone to disorganization. In the gastro-intestinal mucous membrane it produces inflammation, ulceration and causes grayish-white deposits. Its most essential feature is a low, adynamic condition, similar to that of low, putrid fevers.

CHARACTERISTIC SYMPTOMS.

Mind.—Unconsciousness (*Arn., Bell., Op.*); moaning. Irritable, peevish, fretful; disposed to anger (*Bry., Cham., Nux v.*).

Head.—Vertigo in the open air and unsteadiness while walking. Headache as if the brain were torn or bruised (Coff.). Heaviness in the occiput. Feeling of falling aslep and deadness. Tearing in right parietal bone.

Ears.—Hardness of hearing. Over-sensitive to noise (Acon., *Bell., Lyc.*).

Nose.—Coryza, with itching, tickling and sneezing. Nosebleed.

Face.—Pimples forming scabs on face, forehead and temples; whole face red; °every summer. Margins of lips raw, and the skin dry and cracked. Burning in the lips (Acon., Ars.). Lower jaw hangs down.

Mouth.—Tongue thick, bluish and covered with grayish-white membrane; or containing deep ulcers; with black bases; vesicles (Lyc., Natr. mur.), with burning. Tongue heavy as lead, hinders speech (Lach.). °Tongue dwindles. Mucous lining of the lips and mouth inflamed, red, raw, painful, dotted with whitish points; fœtid breath; stomatitis (*Hydras.*).

Throat.—Mucous lining of throat and fauces deep, dark-red, swollen and burning; rawness and smarting; covered with grayish-white diphtheritic-like deposits (Merc. iod., *Nitr. ac.*, Phyt.). Swelling of uvula; of tonsils. Much saliva that must be swallowed. Attempting to swallow produces violent spasms and choking.

Stomach.—Appetite lost. Sensation of emptiness in the stomach and œsophagus not relieved by eating.

Abdomen.—Fullness and distension of the abdomen (Cinch., *Hep. s.*). Cramp-like pains in the abdomen.

Stool and Anus.—Prolapsus ani while urinating. Hæmorrhoids protruding (Calc. c., Lach., *Puls.*); like a bunch of grapes (*Aloe*), swollen, blue, with burning soreness. Smarting in rectum and anus with soft stool. Stool difficult, as from inactivity of the bowels (Alum.); thin, watery, involuntary while urinating (Hyos.); followed by smarting and burning in the anus.

Urinary Organs.—Frequent and profuse urination (Apis, Apoc., Arg. met.).

Male Organs.—Impotence (Agn., Cinch., Camph.).

Female Organs.—Menses too early and too profuse (Calc. c.). °Ulcers in genitals, with putrid discharge, much sensitiveness and general weakness.

Respiratory Organs.—Deep respiration, sighing and groaning.

Pulse.—Pulse rapid and *very feeble;* and small.

Generalities.—Tearing pains in the limbs during rest, better from motion. Weakness of the thighs, causing a tottering gait. All joints feel as if bruised. *Excessive prostration.* °Great debility, as soon as he sits down his eyes close; *the lower jaw hangs down; slides down in bed;* typhus fever. Coldness of the extremities. Great sensitiveness to damp weather. Paralysis of tongue and sphincter ani.

Sleep.—Frequent waking at night; anxious dreams.

Skin.—Scabby or scurfy eruptions. Painful putrid ulcers (lower legs), with burning in their circumference. Ulcers painful, deep, putrid; covered with scurf.

MURIATICUM ACIDUM.

Conditions.—Black hair and dark eyes.
Compare.—Amm. carb., Ars., Arum tri., *Bapt.,* Calc. c., Carbol. ac., Lyc., *Nitr. ac.,* Phos., *Puls., Rhus tox.,* Sep., Sulph. It follows well after Rhus and Bry.
Antidotes.—Bry., Camph. To large doses: Carbonate of Soda, Lime or Magnesia; Sapo Medicinalis.
Muriaticum Acidum Antidotes.—Op.

THERAPEUTICS.

Muriatic acid is especially adapted to low adynamic conditions, typhoid states with involuntary discharges, sliding down in bed, sordès on teeth, etc., low, putrid fevers, typhus, malignant diphtheria, malignant scarlatina (compare Bapt., Rhus tox.). Low types of remittent fever. Great debility following low fevers, as soon as he sits down his eyes close; lower jaw hangs down; slides down in bed. A valuable remedy in apthous sore mouth of infants; also after long-continued debilitating diseases. Ulceration of the tongue and mouth, deep ulcers with black bases, bleeding easily, tendency to slough. Malignant ulcer of the tongue (epithelioma), has a bluish color, also surrounding parts. Ulcers in throat of similar character. Gangrenous angina. Useful in diphtheria, fauces dark-red, swollen, thin excoriating discharge from the nose, tough, fœtid phlegm in throat, great prostration and typhoid symptoms before mentioned. Cirrhosis of the liver. Hernia. Hæmorrhoids protruding, blue or dark-purple, especially in pregnant women or in feeble children who are suffering from gastric atony, muscular debility and threatened marasmus. Diarrhœa, thin, watery offensive, especially in debilitated and typhoid states. Dysentery, with typhoid symptoms. Involuntary stools while urinating (Hyos.). Scorbutic affections. Papular and vesicular eruptions. Carbuncles with low states of the system. Putrid offensive ulcers, with burning at their circumference, covered with scurf, especially on lower extremities.

MYRICA CERIFERA.

Natural order.—Myricaceæ. *Common names.*—Bayberry. Wax Myrtle. *Habitat.*—An indigenous plant growing in great abundance along the sea shore and also near Lake Erie. *Preparation.*—Tincture from the fresh bark of the root.

GENERAL ANALYSIS.

Acts prominently upon mucous surfaces, more especially of the digestive tract, giving rise to catarrhal disorders of these parts. Its most notable action is upon the liver, where it causes a suspension of the biliary secretions, resulting in jaundice and its usual consequent phenomena.

CHARACTERISTIC SYMPTOMS.

Mind.—Great despondency; dejected; irritable. Cannot concentrate the mind on any subject. Dull, drowsy state.

Head.—Vertigo, with dullness and drowsiness; with rush of blood to the head and face, on stooping; with nausea. Awakens with pain in forehead, temples and small of back; better in the open air. Dull, heavy feeling over and in the eyes.

Eyes.—Congested and yellow. Feel dull and heavy; also on awaking. Burn and tire easily when reading (Phos., Ruta, Sepia); lids heavy (Coni., Gels.).

Face.—Yellow color of the face; jaundice (Chel., Cinch.). Fullness, with heat and throbbing, especially after being out in open air.

Mouth.—Thick, yellowish, dark, dry and crusty coating on tongue, rendering it almost immovable. Foul, bad taste; cannot eat because of it; bitter, nauseous taste. Adhesive coating over buccal membrane; dry, scaly crusts on roof of mouth, that water scarcely moistens or dissolves. Mouth dry; thirst; water relieves only partially for awhile.

Throat.—Stringy mucus in throat; detached with difficulty. Throat and nasal organs filled with an offensive, tenacious mucus, detached with difficulty (Amm. carb., Nitr. ac.,

Phyt.). Pharynx dry; sore, as if it would crack, impeding and finally obstructing, deglutition. Slimy, glutinous, frothy mucus in pharynx; even gargling scarcely detaches it; causes disgusting taste, prevents eating.

Stomach.—Hunger, yet full feeling, as after a hasty meal (*Cinch.*, Lyc.). Loss of appetite; loathing of food. Fullness and pressure, or weak, sinking feeling in stomach.

Abdomen.—Dull pain in region of liver; fullness; drowsiness; debility; mushy, clay-colored stools; *jaundice*. Griping pains; rumbling; urging to stool; passing only flatus. Weak, faint feeling, as if diarrhœa would ensue.

Stool.—Passing of much offensive flatus. Loose stools, mushy, with tenesmus and cramp-like sensation in umbilical region (Coloc.). Stools light-yellow, mushy, clay-colored (Calc. c., Dol., Hep. s., Podo.); jaundice.

Urine.—Beer-colored, with yellowish froth; pinkish-brown sediment, scanty.

Heart and Pulse.—Heart's impulse increased, but pulse sixty; pulse feeble, irregular.

Neck and Back.—Dull aching, dragging, lassitude, headache.

Generalities.—Slight nervous excitement and restlessness; soon followed by a sick, debilitated sensation. General muscular lameness and soreness; lassitude; depression of spirits.

Sleep.—Drowsiness; vertigo; semi-stupor. Restless, or sleeps soundly until toward morning; awakens generally feeling worse.

Fever.—Chilliness on going out of doors; slight aching in lumbar region. Excited, feverish feeling, alternating with chilliness; warm sensation along spine, then chill and gentle sweat. Face hot and flushed.

Skin.—Yellow jaundiced appearance; itching as from flea-bites.

Aggravation.—From warmth of bed at night.

Amelioration.—After breakfast; in the open air.

Compare.—Chel., Digit., Podo.

THERAPEUTICS.

Useful in catarrhal conditions of mucous membranes, mouth, pharynx, bile ducts, etc.; hepatic disturbances; jaundice; with symptoms already described. "Seems to affect the system profoundly, and has proved curative in low states, with or without jaundice, when, with necessary debility, there is a viscous state of the mucous membranes, characterized by scanty tenacious, crust-forming secretions on tongue, and in mouth and pharynx."—*Farrington.*

NAJA.

Synonym.—Naja Tripudians. *Class.*—Reptilia. *Order.*—Squamata. *Family.*—Elapidæ. *Common name.*—Cobra. *Preparation.*—The poison obtained by compressing the gland which secretes it, is triturated in the usual manner.

GENERAL ANALYSIS.

Naja, like Lachesis and other serpent poisons, affects profoundly the cerebro-spinal system, the pneumogastric and glosso-pharyngeal nerves being most affected. Hence we have difficult respiration, cardiac oppression and the usual decomposition and fluidity of the blood, resulting in ecchymoses, hæmorrhages and other general effects which result alike from all the serpent poisons.

CHARACTERISTIC SYMPTOMS.

Mind.—°Suicidal insanity (Aur., Nux v.). Wandering of the mind. Sad and serious; irresolute; melancholia; makes himself wretched brooding over imaginary wrongs and misfortunes (Nux v., Ign.). Very forgetful; absent-minded (Anac., Apis, Carls., Nux m., Phos. ac.). Insensible; loss of consciousness.

Head.—Confusion and dullness in head. Dull frontal headache. Severe throbbing and aching in temples. Heat and congestion in head.

Eyes.—Eyes fixed and staring (*Bell., Stram.*); wide open and insensible to light (*Op., Hyos., Stram.*). Heaviness in eyelids (Coni., Gels., Natr. carb.). Loss of the sense of vision.

Nose.—Severe coryza, thin, acrid secretion; nose sore, hot and swollen.

Face.—Pale, thin, haggard; greenish-yellow color; *livid*. Neuralgic pains in face, sometimes shooting to eye and temple. Lips dry, parched and cracked (Ars., Lach.), hot and sore. Jaws firmly clenched (Cic., Ign., Hyos., Laur., Nux v.).

Mouth.—Mouth wide open; tongue cold (Camph.). Gnawing toothache; gums hot, swollen and painful to touch. Tongue coated thick, yellow; white, dry, no thirst (Nux m.). Ulcers on frænum. Great dryness of the mouth (Ars., Bry., Nux m.). Foaming at the mouth (Cic., Coccul., Cupr., Laur.). Taste insipid, bitter, sour, metallic (Coccul., Æsc., Merc.). Loss of speech (Dulc., Caust., Gels., Hyos., Laur.).

Throat.—Much mucus in throat. Pressure and gagging in throat. Roughness and scraping in throat. Grasping at throat, with sense of choking (Acon., Iod.). Dryness and constriction of throat and fauces. Soreness and pricking in left side of throat. Stricture of the œsophagus; deglutition difficult or impossible. Dark-red color of the fauces (*Alianth.*, Bapt., Phyt.).

Stomach.—Loss of appetite. Craving for stimulants, which aggravate the sufferings. Eructations; heartburn. Nausea, with faint feeling; vomiting. Uneasy, disagreeable feeling in stomach, as from indigestion; pressure as from stones, after a meal (*Ars., Bry., Nux v., Puls.*).

Abdomen.—Cutting, twisting, griping pains. Much flatulence, with rumbling and colicky pains.

Stool.—Sudden urging to stool. Bilious diarrhœa. Constipation.

Urinary Organs.—Uneasiness and pressure in bladder. Urine deposits red sediment, mixed with mucus.

Male Organs.—Increased sexual desire. Nocturnal emissions.

Female Organs—Crampy pain in left ovary. Thin, whitish leucorrhœa. Secretion of milk decreased.

Respiratory Organs.—Cough, with tightness and fullness in larynx. Irritation and tickling in larynx and trachea. Hoarseness; short, hoarse cough. Dry, hacking cough; blood spitting (Acon., Ferr., Ham.). Respiration very slow, shallow and scarcely perceptible; labored and difficult; gasping for breath. Uneasiness and dull, heavy pain in chest. Lancinating pains, worse on deep inspiration

(*Bry.*). Asthmatic constriction of chest; followed by mucous expectoration.

Heart and Pulse.—Feeling of depression and uneasiness about the heart. Severe pain in region of heart. Fluttering and palpitation of the heart. Audible beating of the heart (*Spig.*). Pulse slow and irregular in rhythm and force (*Digit.*); weak and thready; scarcely perceptible (Acon., Ars.).

Neck and Back.—Rheumatic pains in neck and back. Pain between the shoulders. Aching in loins. Acute pain in small of back; gnawing pain.

Limbs.—Sudden prostration of strength in limbs. Rheumatic pains in limbs.

Generalities.—Languor; fatigue, torpor. °Organs seem to be drawn together, especially ovary and heart. Depression of both mental and physical powers. Symptoms worse from stimulants; better when walking in open air.

Skin.—Creeping, itching, and tingling sensation in skin. Skin swelled, mottled, and of dark-purple livid color. Large pimples on inflamed base. Small white blisters on inflamed base, with much itching. °Gangrene.

Sleep.—Yawning; great sleepiness. Restless, disturbed sleep. Vivid dreams.

Fever.—Body cold and collapsed (Carb. v., Camph.). Extremities very cold; icy coldness of feet (Tabac.). Burning heat in face. Feels very uncomfortable, hot and feverish. Free perspiration.

Compare.—*Apis, Ars.*, Cact., Crot. tig., Hep. s., *Lach.*, Merc., Nitr. ac., Phos., Rhus tox., Sulph., Spig.

Antidotes.—Heat, Alcohol, Salt.

THERAPEUTICS.

Naja is useful in similar conditions with Lachesis, but not so generally employed: asthma; spasmodic croup; jaundice; angina pectoris; pericarditis; rheumatic carditis; neuralgia; neuralgia of left ovary, with palpitation and pain about the heart; organic disease of the heart; chronic nervous palpitation of the heart; sympathetic, irritative cough, with organic diseases of the heart; diphtheria, with symptoms similar to Lach., larynx invaded, threatening paralysis of the heart; ulcers; hay fever, with asthmatic symptoms, after first stage has commenced to subside, parts feel dry, suffocative attacks, especially when lying down or after sleeping (Lach.); hydrophobia; purpura.

NATRUM ARSENICATUM.

Synonym.—Sodium Arsenate. *Common name.*—Arsenate of Soda. *Preparation.*—Triturations.

GENERAL ANALYSIS.

The action of Natr. ars. is especially upon mucous surfaces, where it causes irritation, congestion and subacute catarrhal inflammation. It also acts upon the blood to a limited degree, and interferes with nutrition, the patient becoming weak and emaciated. In its general action the drug resembles Natrum mur. more than it does Arsenic.

CHARACTERISTIC SYMPTOMS.

Mind.—Nervous restlessness (*Acon., Ars., Camph.*). Cannot concentrate mind; dull, listless (Gels., *Nux v., Phos. ac.*); forgetful (Anac., Apis).

Head.—Confused feeling; head heavy, dull. Feeling of heat and fullness in whole head. Dull aching in frontal region and root of nose; on awaking in morning; severe during day; indisposed to study or speak. Aching across brow over orbits and eyeballs. Fullness in forehead, with throbbing in top of head (Bry.). Every motion jars the head (Bell.).

Eyes.—Vision weakened; objects blur when he looks at them for a short time; eyes sensitive to light (Acon., *Bell., Merc., Sulph.*). °Eyes soon tire and pain when reading or writing (Myrica. Natr. mur., Phos., *Ruta,* Sep.). Feels as though he must close lids to protect the weak eyes. Lids disposed to close; cannot open them as wide as usual (Caust., Coni., Gels., Natr. carb.). Blood vessels of balls and lids much congested, whole orbital region swollen; œdema of orbital region (*Ars., Rhus tox.,* Phos.), especially of supraorbital region (*Apis, Kali c.*). °Congestion of conjunctiva from least exposure to cold or wind (Acon.); conjunctiva dry and painful. Eyes smart as from wood smoke; smarting and lachrymation on going into open air. Inner surface of (lower) lids granulated. Edges chronically inflamed; morning agglutination. Aching through and over brows and orbits, and in temples on awaking. Eye symptoms worse in the morning, better towards evening.

Nose.—Smell defective or lost. Patient feels stuffed up in nose and chest. Nose constantly stopped up, worse at night and in morning (Nux v.); must breathe at night with mouth open (Amm. carb.). Nasal discharge yellow, tough; also hawked up from posterior nares; mucus drops from posterior nares (Hydras., Kali bi.). Pieces of hardened bluish mucus flow from nose, after which mucus membrane feels raw. Dry crust in nose; when removed blood follows. Nasal mucous membrane thickened, can inhale air, but difficult to exhale. Compressive pain at root of nose and in forehead; catarrh (Acon., *Kali bi.*, Merc. iod.).

Face.—Face flushed and hot (Bapt., Bell.); feels puffed. Malar bones feel large, as if swollen. Swollen, œdematous; more orbital region (Ars., Apis, Rhus tox.); worse mornings on awaking.

Mouth.—Corners fissured; also indurated. Muscles of mastication stiff, painful to move jaw. Tongue furred; coated yellow; deep-red, corrugated, anterior part fissured; large, moist, fissured, flabby (*Merc.*).

Throat.—Fauces dry on swallowing and on inspiration, worse in morning and after a cold. Fauces and pharynx red and glossy. Tonsils, fauces and pharynx purplish and œdematous; patched with yellow mucus (Merc. iod.); °diphtheria. Uvula, tonsils and pharynx thickened; surface irregular, swollen, purplish-red, covered with yellowish-gray mucus, which is hawked out.

Stomach.—Drinks often, but little at a time (Ars., Hyos.); very thirsty, made worse by drinking. Belching and sour eructations. Nausea, worse from cold drink of water. Vomits large quantities of sour water, worse after eating. Stomach feels sore; warm things cause a sensation of burning, and can be felt entering stomach. Moderate dinner lies

NATRUM ARSENICATUM.

heavy (*Lyc.*, *Nux v.*); Feeling of fullness. Epigastrium tender, also sinking sensation.

Abdomen.—Gas forms rapidly (Carb. v., Lyc.), worse only when bowels move; colic from flatus and before stool.

Stool.—Alternate diarrhœa and constipation (*Ant. crud.*, Cimic., Card. m., Nux v., Pod.). Stool thin, soft, dark, followed by burning at anus (*Sulph.*). Yellowish, watery; copious, painless, hurries out of bed in morning (Sulph.); preceded by colic, relived after (Coloc.).

Urinary Organs.—Dull aching in kidneys, with profuse urine. Sore feeling in region of bladder, worse while urinating. Urine copious, frequent, clear; heat precipitates phosphates; contains some epithelial scales, casts and fat globules.

Respiratory Organs.—Dark slate-colored, scanty mucus in larynx, detached with difficulty. Oppressed or stuffed sensation all day from larynx to bottom of sternum. Roughness and irritation in bronchi mornings, with slight cough. Lungs feel dry, as though smoke had been inhaled (Baryt. c., Brom.). Dry cough, with feeling of tightness and opression in middle and upper third of chest. Chest feels full and oppressed; worse during exertion and on full inspiration. Sharp, quick pain below seventh rib anteriorly. Supraclavicular regions sore on pressure.

Heart and Pulse.—Oppression about heart on least exertion. Pulse irregular, variable in volume, slower than usual (Digit., Can. ind., Op.).

Neck and Back.—Neck stiff and sore. Pain and soreness in back, between scapulæ; in lumbar region.

Limbs.—Neuralgic pains recur frequently. Joints feel stiff (*Rhus tox.*); pains erratic, worse in joints and on left side. Lower limbs feel heavy; weary, bruised feelings. Aching anteriorly down legs, until restless, uneasy feeling is produced.

Generalities.—Restless, nervous, cannot sit still without great effort (*Rhus tox.*). Feels tired all over; desire to remain quiet. More susceptible to cold air, takes cold easily (Calc., c., Kali c., Sil.). Pains show preference for left leg. Œdema (*Apis*, Ars., Rhus tox.). Marked emaciation (*Iodi.*, Natr. mur.); after previous increase in flesh.

Sleep.—Drowsy, heavy, restless; wakes as if frightened.

Skin.—Squamous eruption, scales thin, white, and when removed leave skin slightly reddened; if scales remain they cause itching, worse when warm from exercise.

Fever.—Chilly, disposed to wrap up or get near a fire. Chilly at night, then burning, dry heat. Skin hot and dry. Surface cool, covered with cold, clammy sweat (*Ars.*, Camph., *Verat. alb.*).

Aggravation.—In the morning. After eating.

Amelioration.—When walking in the open air.

Compare.—Ars., Lyc., Kali bi., Hydras., Nux v., Natr. mur., Natr. carb.

THERAPEUTICS.

Natrum ars. is especially useful in chronic catarrhal conditions—nasal, pharyngeal, bronchial, gastric, cystic or intestinal; conjunctivitis; granular lids; rheumatism; neuralgia; sciatica; œdema. The symptoms have already been described, and need not be repeated. Often a valuable remedy in diphtheria where there is great prostration, dark, purplish hue of the throat, great swelling, not much pain, uvula hangs down like a sac of water, feeble intermittent pulse, surface cool, covered with a cold, clammy sweat. Intermittent fever. Hectic fever, night sweats, emaciation, in phthisis pulmonalis.

NATRUM CARBONICUM.

Common name.—Carbonate of Soda. *Preparation.*—Triturations.

GENERAL ANALYSIS.

Natr. carb. acts through the ganglionic nervous system, upon the mucous membranes, especially of the nasal cavity, the eyes and the digestive tract, including the liver, producing symptoms of catarrhal inflammation.

CHARACTERISTIC SYMPTOMS.

Mind.—*Depressed, extremely despondent mood; intolerable melancholy and apprehension* (Ign., Puls.). Peevish and irritable (Bry., Cham., Nux v.); indifferent; fretful; timid.

°Restlessness and anxiety. especially during a thunder storm. Makes mistakes in writing. Forgetful. Stupefaction in morning on waking. Aversion to man and society (Carb. an., Hyos., Ign.).

Head.—Vertigo from drinking wine, or from mental exertion (Nux v.). Dullness and confusion of the head. Headache from the sun (Bell., Glon., Lach.). Frontal headache when turning the head rapidly.

Eyes.—Black spots before the eyes when writing (*Merc., Phos., Sulph.*). Dazzling flashing before the eyes on awaking (Bell.). Inflammation of the eyes and eyelids, with photophobia (Acon., Bell., Merc.). Dimness of vision, must wipe his eyes constantly. Inability to read small print. Ulcers on the cornea (Calc. c., Sil.), with stinging pains. Ulcerative keratitis. Needle-like stitches in both eyes, after dinner. Burning in the eyes, worse from reading and writing, with dryness. Difficult opening, then closed involuntarily. Heaviness of the eyelids (Caust., Coni., Gels., Natr. ars.).

Ears.—Otalgia, with sharp, piercing stitches in the ears (Kali c., Puls.). Hardness of hearing. Stopped sensation. Dryness and heat.

Nose.—Coryza, fluent; violent sneezing; nose obstructed; yellow, offensive, thin mucous, or thick, green mucous discharge. Intermittent coryza, with burning in eyes. Hard, fœtid pieces from one nostril. Ulceration high up in the nostrils. Bleeding of the nose. *Much nasal mucus passes through the mouth* (Hydras.). Nose red, with white pimples on it.

Face.—Face pale, puffy, with blue rings around the eyes; swollen lids (Phos.). Swelling of both cheeks with glowing redness (*Bell.*). Freckles on the face (Nitr. ac.). Yellow blotches on forehead and upper lip. Burning crack in lower lip (Graph.).

Mouth.—Toothache during or after a meal, especially after sweet things. Sensitiveness of the teeth (Carb. an., Merc., *Nitr. ac.*). Pimples on tip of tongue. Burning on tip of tongue, as if full of cracks (Calc. c., Carb. an., Kali bi.). Dry tongue, and heavy, rendering speech difficult (Mur. ac., Lach.). Constant dryness of the mouth and lips. Superficial ulcers inside of the mouth, with burning pain when touched. Taste bitter (Ars., Bry., Nux v., Puls.); metallic (Merc., Sulph.); sour. Tongue coated.

Throat.—*Violent hawking up of thick mucus, which constantly collects again.* Swelling of the submaxillary glands (Baryt. c., Calc. c., Iodi., *Rhus tox.*).

Stomach.—Incessant hunger (Bry., Cina, Ferr., Iodi.). Violent thirst, and uneasiness after drinking anything cold; in afternoon. °Bad effects from a cold drink while overheated (Ars.). Frequent empty or *sour* eructations (Carb. v., Nux v.). Waterbrash (Nux v., Lyc., Led., Sulph.). Scraping heartburn after fat food (Puls.). Violent retching in the morning, without actual vomiting. Stomach weak and easily disordered (Ars., Cinch., Carb. v., *Puls.*). Violent pressure in stomach after meals. Fullness in stomach evenings. Pit of stomach sensitive to touch (Hyos., *Kali c.*): swollen feeling.

Abdomen.—Violent stitches in the hepatic and splenic regions (*Natr. mur., Sulph.*). Distension of the abdomen, especially after eating (*Cinch.*, Lyc., Nux. m., *Nux v.*). Griping in the abdomen, like colic, immediately after eating (Coloc.). Incarcerated flatus. Swelling of the glands of groin and axilla; generally painful.

Stool and Anus.—Frequent ineffectual urging to stool (Ambr., *Nux v., Coni.*). Itching in the anus (Sil., Sep., Sulph.). Burning in rectum after stool. Difficult evacuation of stool that was hard (Carb. v.). Hurried urging, thin stool *forcibly spurting from him* (*Crot. tig., Grat., Thuja*). Stool *spotted with blood.* Stool like sheep's dung, with great straining; balls of mucus like peas.

Urinary Organs.—Frequent desire to urinate, with copious discharge; with scanty discharge. Urine smells like horse urine (Benz. ac., Nitr. ac.). Involuntary urination at night (Ars., *Caust.*, Sulph., *Puls.*, Graph.). Burning in urethra during urination (Ant. tart., Ars.).

Male Organs.—Incomplete coition; erections weak; emissions speedy (Calc. c.). Emissions without erections. Glans penis easily become sore. Soreness between scrotum and thighs (*Hep. s.*).

Female Organs.—Pressure in the hypogastrium, as if everything would come out, and the menses would come on

(*Bell.*, Sep.). Leucorrhœa, thick, yellow (*Hydras.*, Kali bi.), putrid, ceasing after urination.

Respiratory Organs.—Hoarseness. Violent dry cough; worse when entering a warm room (*Bry.*, Verat. alb. Reverse, Phos.). Cough, with salty, purulent, greenish sputa, and rawness in chest. Short breath, with difficult respiration.

Heart.—Violent palpitation of the heart, especially on going up stairs or at night, when lying on left side (Natur.,mur., Phos.).

Neck and Back.—Cracking of the cervical vertebræ on moving the head. Backache; violent pain in small of back after walking.

Limbs.—Tearing pain in the limbs (*Bry.*, Coloc., Lyc.). Excessive soreness and lassitude of the limbs. Weakness, unsteadiness, and heaviness of lower extremities, and heaviness of the arms. Drawing pain in the elbows. °Coldness between the scapulæ. Jerking sensation in the finger joints.

Lower Limbs.—Jerking in lower extremities, and in parts of lower portion of the body. Heaviness and bruised sensation. Hollow of knees painful on motion. Needle-like stitches on sole of right foot. Swelling of soles. Throbbing and crawling in both heels. Easy dislocation and spraining of the ankle. Ulcer on the heel, arising from spreading blisters. Blisters on points of toes, as if scalded.

Generalities.—Restlessness. Great prostration and heaviness of the whole body. It hurts to lie on the left side. Whole body relaxed and limber, in morning. Swelling and induration of glands (Baryt. c., Calc. c., Graph., Iodi.).

Skin.—Skin dry, rough and chapped. Itching over the whole body, as from fleas. Herpes, with yellow rings or suppurating.

Sleep.—Sleepiness and much yawning during the day (Natr. mur.). Falls asleep late at night. Sleep full of dreams at night.

Fever.—Cold hands *and feet*, head hot, or hands and feet hot, with cold cheeks. Heat and burning thirst (*Acon., Ars., Bell., Bry.*). Burning in feet, especially soles, on walking. Cold, anxious perspiration, with trembling from the pains. Sweats in the morning.

NATRUM CARBONICUM.

Aggravation.—*During a thunder storm;* after slightest exertion after meals; while sitting; from talking.
Amelioration.—On motion; on pressure; from rubbing.
Compare.—Alum., Ars., Calc. c., Carb. v., Lyc., Mag. m., Merc., Natr. mur., Nat. sulph., Nux v., Phos., *Puls.*, Sil., *Sep., Sulph.*).
Antidotes.—*Camph.*, Nitr. sp. d.
Natrum Carbonicum Antidotes.—Cinchona.

THERAPEUTICS.

The chief use of Natr. carb. is in the treatment of catarrhal conditions. It is a valuable remedy in some forms of mental weakness, loss of memory, melancholia, especially from overstudy or a previous sunstroke, also headache, vertigo, etc., from exposure to the sun's rays, or in hot weather after a previous sunstroke. Headache from working under gas-light. The nervous symptoms of the drug are important, great prostration, weakness of extremities, especially with headache, etc., coming on in hot weather. Hysteria. All the nervous symptoms, especially nervousness and anxiety, are much worse during a thunder storm, not from timidity, but from the electric changes in the atmosphere. Small corneal ulcers or phyctenules, with great photophobia and stinging pains, particularly in scrofulous children. Lachrymal abscess. Dry catarrh of conjunctiva (Alum.). Chronic inflammation of the middle ear, with deafness and roaring in ears. Otalgia. Chronic nasal catarrh or ozœna, thick, yellowish-green discharge, thick, fœtid, lumpy, worse from slightest draught of air, better from free perspiration. May also be useful in fluent coryza, very profuse, violent sneezing, worse from draught, better after sweat. Weak digestion. Acid dyspepsia, especially marked after vegetable diet, starchy food, with hypochondriasis, palpitation of the heart and other symptoms already described (see symptoms). Sometimes useful in diarrhœa with forcible, spurting stools, but more often in constipation, the stools being difficult to expel, though not very hard. Impotence. Has cured indurated cervix, resembling scirrhus, with the symptoms of pressure across the hypogastrium, as if everything would come out of the vagina. Leucorrhœa, thick, yellow, offensive. Swelling and induration of glands. Dry, rough chapped skin, especially dorsi of hands and feet. Vesicles, with shooting pains and aching ulcers. Herpetic eruptions.

NATRUM MURIATICUM.

Synonym.—Chloride of Sodium. *Common names.*—Common Salt. Table Salt. *Preparation.*—Triturations.

GENERAL ANALYSIS.

Acts upon the blood, the lymphatic system, the mucous lining of the digestive tract and upon the liver and spleen. It causes a deterioration of the blood, which, with a high degree of irritation, results in inflammation, partaking of a scorbutic nature, and from which arise various ulcers and eruptions on the skin, as well as destructive inflammations of mucous and glandular tissues and conditions generally pointing to a distinct dyscrasia of a scorbutic character. Aside from this dyscrasia the most essential feature of Salt is its power to produce a condition of system or a cachexia simulating that which results from long-lasting or badly treated cases of ague, and it is in this sphere of therapeutics that Salt has achieved its greatest victory.

CHARACTERISTIC SYMPTOMS.

Mind.—*Melancholia depressed, sad and weeping (Ign., Nux m., Puls., Rhus tox.); consolation aggravates; prefers to be alone.* Very irritable and ill-humored; easily provoked to anger (Bry., Cham., Nux v.). *Excitement.* Laughs immoderately and cannot be quieted. Despair depriving him of all power. Disinclination to mental work. Difficult thinking; absence of mind; weakness of memory (Agn., Ambr., Anac., Kreos., Lach., *Merc.*, Nux m., Phos. ac.). Distraction when talking. Easily makes mistakes in writing.
Head.—Vertigo; in morning on rising, better on lying down again; and great dullness of the head; with flickering before the eyes (Bell.). Involuntary nodding the head

forward. *Dullness* and heaviness of the head (*Caps.*, Cinch.); in morning after thinking. *Headache as if the head would burst* (*Bry.*, Merc., Puls.). Headache in the morning on awaking (Kali bi., Nitr. ac., Nux v.); lasts till noon; sick headache. Headache from sneezing and coughing, disappearing on pressure. Dull, pressing stupefying headache. Rush of blood to the head. Throbbing or stitches in head, extending to neck or chest. Throbbing and heat in the head, with redness in the face, nausea and vomiting. *Heavy pressive pain in forehead over both eyes;* as if the eyes would be pressed out, better from pressure on the eyes. Falling out of the hair (*Graph.*, Merc., *Nitr. ac.*, Petrol., Phos., *Sep.*, *Sulph.*); sensitiveness of the scalp (Cinch., *Merc.*, *Mez.*, Nitr. ac.). *Itching eruption of margins of hair at nape of neck.*

Eyes.—Dimness of vision, as if looking through a mist or veil (Caust., Croc., Petrol., Phos., Sil., Sulph.). *Objects become confused; letters and stitches run together* (Sil.). Small fiery points constantly before the eyes (*Cycl.*, *Merc.*, *Sulph.*). *Eyes give out on using them* (Phos., Ruta, Sep.). *Inflammation, redness and lachrymation* (Acon., Bell.); *feeling as if balls were too large* and compressed. Pressure in the eyes on looking intently at anything. *Sensation of sand in the eyes mornings* (Ars., *Caust.*, Ign., *Sulph.*). Burning and smarting in the eyes (Nux v.). Sensitive to light. Margins of lids red, inflamed, burning, agglutinated in morning (Alum., Graph., *Lyc.*, *Puls.*, *Sulph.*). Spasmodic closure of lids. *Irritability of margins of lids and of their conjunctivæ.* Itching of inner canthi, with lachrymation.

Ears.—Hardness of hearing. Cracking in ears when chewing. Discharge of pus from ears (Graph., Hep. s., Merc.).

Nose.—Inflammation and swelling of left side of nose; painful to touch, itching. Internal soreness and swelling. Liable to catch cold; coryza, fluent; discharge of thick mucus; or nose dry and stopped up; sneezing. Epistaxis, blood clotted. Painful burning pustules below septum of nose, afterward confluent and covered with a scab.

Face.—Yellow color of face (*Chel.*, Hep. s., Sep.). Face shines as if greasy. *Redness of the left cheek.* Lips dry, chapped

Pain in ring when coughing, extending into testicles, as if spermatic cords would be torn to pieces.

Stool and Anus.—*Constipation, with sensation of contraction of the anus; difficult expulsion of hard, dry and crumbling stool (Amm. mur.), fissuring the anus (Nitr. ac.), so that it bleeds and pains as if sore.* Itching stitches in the rectum; evening in bed. Protrusion of the rectum. Burning in anus after hard stool. Alternate constipation and diarrhœa (*Ant. crud.*, Cimic., Nux v., Podo.), irregular, unsatisfactory stools. Painless watery diarrhœa (*Ars., Cinch., Podo.*).

Urinary Organs.—Discharge of mucus from the urethra during and after urination (Mer. cor.), causing itching and biting. *Cutting and burning in urethra after urination* (*Canth*). Urethra painfully sore to pressure. Frequent desire to urinate, with copious flow of *light watery urine*. Urine dark and turbid. Clear, pale. Urine passes involuntarily while walking, coughing or laughing (*Caust., Puls., Zinc.*). Brick-dust sediment in urine (Arn., Cinch., Lyc., Phos.).

Male Organs.—Phymosis. Excessive irritability of the sexual instinct, but with physical weakness. Emissions; every night; soon after coition. Violent itching on and under the scrotum.

Female Organs.—°Pressing and bearing down in the genitals every morning; has to sit down to prevent prolapsus (*Bell., Plat., Lil., Sep.*). Menses too early and too profuse; last too long. Suppression of the menses (Acon., Cimic., Puls.). Itching of the genital organs (Canth., Coni., Merc.). Leucorrhœa, profuse, of a greenish color, worse while walking.

Respiratory Organs.—Hoarseness in the morning; accumulation of mucus in the larynx. Cough in the morning; in evening after lying down in bed; from empty swallowing; from tickling in the throat; *with bursting pain in forehead* (*Bry., Nux v.*); with shortness of breath; with vomiting of food; with tearing pains in spermatic cords. *Dry cough with expectoration of blood;* tickling cough, worse mornings, with hawking of mucus. Hacking cough. Stitches (*Bry., Kali c.*) or sore pain in chest (Arn., Baryt.

c., *Nux v., Phos., Stan.*). Dyspnœa, on ascending stairs; breath short.

Heart and Pulse.—*Fluttering motion of the heart* (Lil. tig.). *Palpitation of the heart;* on going up stairs; when lying on left side (Natr. carb., Phos.); with anxiety. *Coldness about the heart.* Painful stitches in region of heart (*Bry., Cact., Kali c.*); after reading aloud. Constriction of the heart with intermittent pulse and oppression in lower part of chest, as if lungs had not room enough to expand. *Intermission in the beating of the heart and pulse* (Coni., *Digit.*, Kali c.). Pulse rapid.

Neck and Back.—Pain in small of back as if broken (Aloe, *Bell.*, Cimic., Nux v.). Swelling of lymphatic glands. °Pain in back relieved by lying on something hard (*Rhus tox.*). °Throat and neck emaciate rapidly, especially during summer complaint. Stitches in the neck and back part of the head. Paralytic feeling in small of back, in morning on rising; paralytic weakness nearly all day, better from lying, worse from eating. Violent pulsation in small of back.

Upper Limbs.—Weakness and paralytic heaviness in the arms. Trembling of the hands when writing (Zinc.). Skin of hands, especially about the nails, dry, cracked; hangnails (*Sulph.*, Thuja); whitish hives on arms and hands. Bruised pain in upper arm. Cold hands.

Lower Limbs.—Weakness and trembling of the lower extremities, on rising from a seat, better from continued walking. Red tetter in hollow of knees. Stitches in the hip-joint; in left knee. Drawing pains in thighs, knees and legs. Swelling from middle of leg downward in evening and next morning, with feeling as if feet were filled with lead. Great heaviness of the legs and feet. Tension in the calves while walking. Tension in hollow of knees, as if tendons were too short (Amm. mur.). Paralytic feeling in ankle-joint, while sitting or walking. Restlessness in legs and feet: must move them constantly (Zinc.). Heaviness in feet; in evening on walking. Cramp-like stitching pain in left foot. Cold feet.

Generalities.—*Great emaciation* (Acet. ac., Ars., Ferr., Graph., Iodi., Phos.); more of body than face; trembling of the whole body; caused by tobacco smoking (Ars.). *Easily* *fatigued;* mental and physical exhaustion, and weakness; *great prostration* (Ars., Cinch., Phos.). Takes cold easily (Calc. c., Kali c., Phos., Sil.). Dread of open air. Muscles, especially of thighs and arms, painful on motion, as if flesh were loose. Pulsation in whole body, even during rest.

Skin.—Itching and pricking in the skin. Itching over the whole body. Large red blotches, like hives, itching violently. Itching nettle rash after bodily exertion. Herpes circinnatus (Sep.). Tettery eruptions, oozing an acrid fluid; crusts with deep cracks.

Sleep.—Sleepiness during the day, with frequent yawning (Natr. carb.). Sleepy at night, but cannot sleep. Sleepless. Waking from fright, *thought there were thieves in the house.* Talking in sleep. Uneasy, anxious sleep; weeping in sleep (Nitr. ac.). Vivid, anxious dreams.

Fever.—Chill predominates (*Bry.*), mostly internal; hands and feet icy-cold (Gels.). Chilliness over whole body, with heat in the forehead, pressure in root of nose, and violent thirst. Chill 10 to 11 A.M., beginning in feet or small of back; blue nails; thirst; bursting headache; nausea and vomiting. *Heat, with violent headache and thirst,* chilliness over the back, and sweat in axillæ and soles of feet. Profuse perspiration, too easily excited by motion (*Calc. c., Hep. s., Phos.*); at night. °During apyrexia; stitches about the liver; languor; emaciation; sallow complexion; loss of appetite; fever blisters on the lips.

Aggravation.—While lying down, especially in morning or evening; at 10 A.M.; after exertion; in heat of sun; heat in general.

Amelioration.—In open air; while fasting; after dinner; from sitting up.

Compare.—*Alum.*, Ars., Bry., Calc. c., Carb. v., Cinch., *Graph.*, Ign., *Lyc.*, Merc., Mur. ac., Nitr. ac., Nux v., Phos., *Plumb., Puls.*, Rhus tox., *Sep., Sil., Sulph., Zinc.* Natr. mur. is followed well by Sep.

Antidotes.—Apis, Ars., Camph., Phos., Nitr. sp. d.

Natrum Muriaticum Antidotes.—Apis, Arg. nit., Quin.

THERAPEUTICS.

The chief clinical use of Natrum mur. is in the treatment of scorbutic affections, and in diseases resulting from malnutrition. It is also a valuable remedy in intermittent fever, especially inveterate or badly treated cases; after Quinine; in damp regions, or near newly turned ground; chill 10–11 A.M. Fever blisters on lips, and other symptoms as mentioned above. Cases are reported as cured with distinctly different symptoms, but the above only are characteristic Cachexia from ague plus Quinine. Is also recommended in rheumatic fever with chilliness. Typhus fever with much stupor and chilliness, gastric symptoms; after typhus suppuration of parotids. A valuable remedy in infantile marasmus from malnutrition; also in children and adults who lose flesh through living well; emaciation most about neck. General anæmia, emaciation, complete prostration of vital forces, depression of spirits, palpitation, etc.; anæmia from loss of vital fluids, blood or semen. Useful in hæmorrhages, especially cachectic subjects, blood red, thin, watery, not coagulable. Dropsical affections; after scarlatina caused by heart, liver or kidney disease. Collection of serum in joints and in closed sacs. Chronic swelling of lymphatic and sebaceous glands, chronic inflammation of salivary glands, excess of saliva. Fistulous, phagedenic ulcers. Varices. Tendency to dryness or erosion of mucous membranes; secretions acrid, scanty; smarting, burning at edges of mucous surfaces.

A valuable remedy in catarrhs of all mucous membranes, with secretions of transparent, watery, coarse, frothy mucus; white mucus full of bubbles, color of white of egg or like boiled starch. Nasal catarrh, thick yellow mucous discharge, loss of taste and smell. Takes cold in head easily; is constantly obliged to wrap it up; if remains uncovered the nose stops up. Fluent coryza, alternate with stoppage; discharge as above described. Chronic naso-pharyngeal catarrh. Chronic nasal and pharyngeal catarrhs which have been abused by local applications, douches, etc., especially Nitrate of Silver. There is no doubt but that Natr. mur. is one of our most valuable remedies in catarrhal conditions of the head and pharynx, and should be more often used. A simple solution of salt and water could in many cases, at least, advantageously supplant the many local applications already employed, and which usually do more

NATRUM MURIATICUM. 541

harm than good. Hay fever, watery discharge from eyes and nose. Chronic catarrh of the ear. Bronchitis, acute or chronic, with symptoms given under respiratory organs. Chronic bronchial catarrh. Catarrhal pneumonia, with characteristic cough and expectoration. Pleurisy, after exudation. Asthma, with profuse watery or frothy mucus. Emphysema. Œdema of the lungs; spasmodic cough; suffocation; serous, frothy expectoration. Palpitation of the heart in anæmic persons. Organic disease of the heart, especially hypertrophy; dyspnœa and palpitation, worse on ascending, or when lying down, especially on left side. Natrum mur. is useful in many affections of the eye. Asthenopia, particularly muscular; drawing, stiff sensation in muscles of eyes when moving them; often caused by general muscular weakness or spinal irritation. Amblyopia and amaurosis; pupils contracted, dependent on menstrual disorders in the chlorotic; from debilitating nervous losses. Blepharitis; ulcers on cornea; smarting and burning; acrid, excoriating tears; photophobia, marked by spasmodic closure of the lids. Follicular conjunctivitis. Granular lids. Keratitis pustulosa. Iritis. Ciliary neuralgia, coming and going with the sun. Stricture of lachrymal duct, fistula and blenorrhœa of lachrymal sac. Affections of the eyes and lids maltreated with lunar caustic, especially entropium and pannus. Insufficiency of the internal recti muscles, even to strabismus. Styes. Morbus Basedowii. A valuable remedy in headaches; morning headaches; sick headache. Nervous headache, from shocks. Malarial headache. Neuralgic headache. Headaches of school girls, during menses (consult symptoms.). Dandruff. Humid eruption of scalp, with gluey discharge, matting the hair, especially on margins of hair at nape of neck and behind the ears. Neuralgia especially malarial; after checked ague; periodical: often in place of ague paroxysms; supra-orbital; face sallow and waxy. Natrum symptoms. Barber's itch. Acne punctata. Anæmic condition of the jaws and buccal cavity. Apthæ. Fissura dentalis. Dyspepsia, with other Natrum conditions. Enlarged liver and spleen, in old, badly treated agues. (Intestinal mucus catarrh. Often a valuable remedy in constipation (see symptoms). Hæmorrhoids. Ascarides. Chronic diarrhœa. Summer complaint of children when the throat and neck emaciate rapidly, cachectic condition, etc. Diabetes insipidus. Polyuria.

Gleet, with soreness of urethra, clear mucous discharge and other symptoms especially after injections of Nitrate of Silver. Impotence. Spermatorrhœa. Hydrocele. Menorrhagia. Delayed or checked menstruation. Often valuable in chlorosis, with profuse or delayed menses, leucorrhœa, cachexia, palpitation, etc. Prolapsus uteri, with pressure and bearing down, backache, relieved by lying on something hard, or by having a pillow under the back. Subinvolution. Sterility. Vaginitis, great dryness and soreness of the parts. Vulvitis. Pruritus of vulva. Spinal irritation; sensitiveness between vertebræ; general weariness, backache, better from pressure or lying on something hard; from grief, anger, and especially from sexual excesses. Paralytic condition of lower extremities, after fever, diphtheria or excesses. Useful in many skin diseases some of which have already been mentioned. Eczema. Urticaria. Intertrigo. Herpes. Herpes circinnatus. Herpes zoster. Purpura hæmorrhagica, with cachectic symptoms.

NATRUM SULFURICUM.

Synonym.—Sodium Sulphate. *Common names.*—Glauber's Salts. Sulphate of Soda. *Preparation.*—Triturations.

GENERAL ANALYSIS.

The physiological effects of this drug are not well understood. Its action is undoubtedly directly upon the blood, through which it produces an irritating and disturbing influence upon nearly every tissue of the body, more especially upon the mucous and fibrous tissues, which are involved, respectively, in catarrhal and rheumatic inflammations. Dr. Von Grauvogl considered it especially useful in patients who were hydræmic, and whose symptoms were always aggravated by damp influences, it thus being a remedy for the "hydrogenoid constitution," according to his classification. He also looked upon it as representing that condition known as sycosis, and held that a gonorrhœal taint could also be discovered when it was indicated.

NATRUM SULFURICUM.

CHARACTERISTIC SYMPTOMS.

Mind.—Depressed; tearful; music makes her sad (Natr. carb., Sab.). Very irritable, ill-humored; worse mornings.

Head.—Vertigo; confusion and dullness. Vertigo at 6 P.M., then vomiting of sour mucus. Pressure in forehead, particularly after meals, as if forehead would burst (Bry.). Heaviness in the head. Boring pain in forehead and left temple. °Irritation of brain after lesions of the head.

Eyes.—Sight dim; eyes weak, watering. Pain in evening when reading by artificial light, with heaviness of the lids. Sensitiveness of eyes to light, with headache. Burning in right eye; lachrymation; dim sight; worse near fire; burning of edges of lids. Agglutination in morning with photophobia (Calc. c., Graph., Sulph.). Itching on edges of lids mornings.

Ears.—Ringing in the ears, as of bells. Piercing pain in right ear inward; lightning-like stitches in the ear; worse going from cold air into warm room; worse in damp weather, living on wet ground, etc.

Nose.—Nosebleed during menses (Bry., Ham.); stops and returns often. Nose stopped up; sneezing with fluent coryza.

Face.—Face pale and wan. Tearing pain in left zygoma.

Mouth.—Blisters with burning pain on tip of tongue. °Toothache, better from holding cold water in the mouth (Puls., Coff.). Burning in mouth as from pepper, or highly seasoned food; mouth dry; thirst; gums red. °Dirty grayish-green coat at root of tongue. Blisters on palate; sensitive, can hardly eat; better from cold things. Much saliva after meals.

Throat.—Dryness of throat; no thirst (Nux. m., Puls.). Hawking of mucus mornings; salt mucus. Tonsils and uvula inflamed and swollen; °ulcers on tonsils.

Stomach.—Great thirst in the evening for ice or ice-cold water. Squeamishness in stomach before meals. Constant rising of sour water. Waterbrash with stitches in right groin. Nausea not relieved by vomiting, salty, sour water.

Abdomen.—Stitches in region of liver and sensitiveness, when walking in open air; also with tension, as if hepatic region would burst open. Region of liver sensitive to touch, stepping, deep breathing, or sudden jar. Tearing pain around umbilicus, *with flatulence,* before breakfast; relieved by eating. Great flatulence; much rolling and rumbling; incarcerated, especially on right side, causing great pain; relieved by emission of flatus (Aloe, Lyc.). Inflammation of right groin; °typhlitis. Piercing pain in right flank, with nausea.

Stool.—Diarrhœa; worse in wet weather; in morning; after vegetables and farinaceous food; also in cold evening air. Stools fluid, yellow, with flatulence. Hard, knotty stools, streaked with blood, accompanied and preceded by smarting in the anus; often with scanty menses. Emission of fœtid flatus in large quantities. °Knotty, wart-like eruption on the anus and between the thighs; sycosis.

Urinary Organs.—Urine scanty; burns while passing; brick-red sediment; dark and passed more frequently, had to get up several times at night.

Male Organs.—Desire excited in evening; also in morning, with erections. Itching of genitals. °Gonorrhœa. °Sycosis.

Female Organs.—Scanty menses too late; knotty stools. Nosebleed before the menses.

Respiratory Organs.—Short breath when walking; gradually relieved by rest. Frequent cough with some expectoration, if he coughs while standing he feels a sharp stitch in left side of chest, with shortness of breath. Dry cough, worse morning after rising; worse at night; *relief from sitting up and holding chest with both hands.* Pressure on chest, as of a heavy load. Pressure in left side of chest, near lumbar region; worse from motion and pressure. Stitches in left side of chest.

Neck and Back.—Soreness up and down spine and neck. Bruised pain in small of back.

Limbs.—Drawing, tearing pains in limbs and joints

Upper Limbs.—Tingling in arms and hands; they feel as if paralyzed. Symptoms like those of panaritium.

Lower Limbs.—Pain in right hip-joint; worse from stooping, rising from a seat, or moving in bed. Suddenly, when walking, unbearable stitch in left hip; cannot walk.

Generalities.—Prostration: tired, weary, especially knees. Attacks come on suddenly. Sore across abdomen, sides and back.

NATRUM SULFURICUM. 545

Skin.—Eczema, moist and oozing profusely. Itching while undressing. Wart-like, raised, red lumps all over the body.
Fever.—Chilliness, with shuddering, evenings. Internal coldness, with stretching and yawning. Sudden flashes of heat, toward evening.
Aggravation.—°From dampness; °damp change of weather; from lying on the left side.
Amelioration.—In open air; after dinner; from motion; at night.
Conditions.—"Hydrogenoid" constitution; sycosis.
Compare.—Bry., Dulc., Kali c., Natr. mur., Puls., Rhus tox., Staph., Thuja.

THERAPEUTICS.

The remarks as to the hydrogenoid constitution of this remedy in the "General Analysis" should not be overlooked, and consequently its usefulness not only in sycotic and gonorrhœal diseases, but in all other conditions where there is a decided aggravation from dampness, other symptoms agreeing. Catarrhal and rheumatic affections in general, in sycotic and hydrogenoid patients. Granular conjunctivitis, sycotic subjects; dim sight, lachrymation, photophobia. Earache, with lightning-like piercing pains, from exposure to damp. Nasal catarrh, bloody. offensive discharges. Ozœna syphilitica, beginning with ulcers in fauces; no fœtor (with fœtor, Aur.). Inflammation of tonsils; of uvula; of pharynx; hawking of much thick. salty mucus. Acid dyspepsia, with heartburn and flatulence. Chronic hepatitis and other liver complaints with sensitiveness of hepatic region, worse when lying on left side. Jaundice. Lead colic. Typhlitis. Sometimes useful in a diarrhœa of fluid, yellow stools, coming on in damp weather and after vegetable and farinaceous food. always worse in the morning after moving about, with great flatulence, soreness of the liver, etc. Constipation, hard knotty stools, especially with scanty menses. A general remedy in lithæmia. Uric acid deposits. Enlarged prostate. Chronic bronchitis, with symptoms already given. Asthma with young people, from a general bronchial catarrh; worse after every change to damp weather, and other symptoms. Non-tubercular phthisis in sycotic constitutions; muco-purulent expectoration, loud râles, lower lobe of left lung mostly affected. Panaritium, pain better out of doors; patient pale and sickly from living in damp region, damp houses, etc. Neuralgia and other affections of hip-joint, with symptoms already given.

NITRICUM ACIDUM.

Synonyms.—Hydrogen Nitrate. Aqua Fortis. *Common name.*—Nitric Acid. *Preparation.*—One part of Nitric Acid, sp. gr. 1.42, to nine parts of water makes the 1x dilution. The 2x dilution is made with distilled water; the 3x dilution with dilute Alcohol; subsequent dilutions with Alcohol.

GENERAL ANALYSIS.

Acts upon the blood, the mucous membranes, the glands, the bones and the skin, its special action being upon the muco-cutaneous outlets of the body, the mouth, the rectum and anus, and the vagina. Intense irritation is produced, resulting in inflammation and destructive ulceration of the parts, even to gangrene. The whole action of Nitric Acid points to a violent dyscrasia or poison, resembling either the syphilitic, scrofulous, or mercurial miasms.

CHARACTERISTIC SYMPTOMS.

Mind.—Nervous, *excitable, easily startled and frightened* (Kali carb.). *Irritable, peevish, vexed at trifles* (Acon.). Anxiety about his disease, with fear of death (*Ars., Acon., Cimic.*); *depressed, despondent mood;* discontented; inclined to weep (Ign., Natr. mur., Puls., Rhus tox.). Weakness of memory (Anac., Lach., Nux. m., Phos.); aversion to mental exercise (Phos. ac., Nux v.).

Head.—Vertigo in the morning, on rising (Alum., Bry., Phos., Lyc.), with weakness, must sit down. Congestion to the head, with much heat in it. Headache in the morning on waking (Natr. mur.), disappearing on rising. Tension. *Headache as if the head were tightly bound up; as if in a vise* (Gels., Kali Iod., Merc., Nitr. ac., Sulph.). Feeling of fullness and pressure in the head, especially forehead and over the eyes on vertex. Drawing and stitching pains in the temples; pressive and drawing bone-pains in left temple, even in teeth and meatus auditorius. *Profuse falling off of the hair* (*Graph.*, Hep. s., Merc., Lach., Natr. mur., Lyc., Petrol., Phos., *Sep.,* Sulph.). Scabby, moist, itching eruption on scalp (*Graph.*). Offensive scurf on the scalp. Tension of skin on forehead. Painful sensitiveness of the scalp (Acon., Baryt. c., Cinch., *Merc.,* Natr. mur.), even to the pressure of the hat (*Carb. v., Sil.*).

Eyes.—*Double vision of horizontal objects* (Aur., Bell., Cyc., Stram.). *Obscuration of sight while reading;* shortsighted. °Iritis, which continually relapses; also old cases spoiled by Mercury. °Inflammation of the eyes, after syphilis, or the abuse of Mercury. Pressure and stinging in the eyes. Spots on the cornea (Euphr., Sil., Sulph.). Paralysis of upper lids (Caust., Gels., Plumb.); especially mornings. Biting and stitches in the eyes. Lachrymation.

Ears.—Hardness of hearing after the abuse of Mercury (Staph.). Swelling of the glands beneath and behind the left ear, with stitches and tearing extending through the ear. Offensive purulent discharge from the ear (Aur., Graph., Hep. s., Merc.). Stitches in the ears (Coni., Graph., Kali c.). Roaring. Cracking in the ears when chewing (Natr. mur.).

Nose.—*Violent coryza, with soreness and bleeding of the nose* (Brom.); *at same time stopped,* with difficult breathing. Tip of nose red (Bell., Rhus tox.); nostrils ulcerated and *sore* (Alum. *Ant. crud.,* Aur., Graph., Kali bi., *Puls.*). *Dry coryza, nose obstructed, throat dry.* Itching in nostrils. Offensive yellow matter is blown from the nose (*Puls.*). Nosebleed; morning; at night. *Stitches, as from a splinter in the nose, on touch.* °Large, soft protuberances on alæ, covered with crusts; syphilis.

Face.—Yellowness of the face (Hep. s., Natr. mur., Sep.), about the eyes, with red cheeks. °Suppurating pustules, with broad red circumferences, forming crusts; syphilis. Bones of the face painful (Carb. v., Hep. s., Kali bi.). *Cracking of jaws when chewing and eating.* Lips are swollen and itch. Eruption of pimples on the face. Dark freckles on the face (Natr. carb.).

Mouth.—The teeth become yellow or loose; pain on chewing (Carb. an., *Merc.*). Stitching, tearing, or boring pains in teeth, when touched by anything cold or warm. Gums white, swollen, bleeding (Carb. v., Kali nit., Merc., Phos.). *Blisters and ulcers on the tongue* (Borax, Nux v., Sep., Thuja); *and on its margins, with burning pain when touched* (*Merc.*). He bites the tongue when chewing; and cheeks (Ign.). Tongue sensitive, even to soft food, which causes smarting (Carb. v.). *Ulcerated spots on inner surface of cheeks, with sticking pains, as from a splinter. Corners of mouth ulcerated* (Ant. crud , *Graph.*, Lyc.); *with stitches. Foul odor from the mouth* (Arn., Aur., Iodi.). Dryness and intense burning in mouth and fauces (*Ars., Canth.,* Caps., *Merc. cor.*). Mucous membrane of the mouth and throat swollen and ulcerated; with pricking pains; °after abuse of Mercury. *Profuse flow of saliva* (Iodi., Ign., Kali iod., *Merc.*). Saliva bloody in morning (Sulph.). *Saliva has foul odor.* Sour taste in the mouth (Calc. c., Cinch. Mag., carb.). °Tongue coated; yellow, sometimes white in the mornings; green, with ptyalism.

Throat.—Heat and dryness in the throat. Much mucus in the throat posteriorly. Sore throat on swallowing, as if swollen; raw and ulcerated. Swelling and inflammation of tonsils, uvula and fauces. *Pricking as from a splinter in the throat* (*Alum., Arg. nit., Hep. s.*), worse when swallowing. *Stitches in throat and fauces. Cracking in maxillary articulation when chewing. Diphtheritic patches on tonsils and fauces, extending to mouth, lips, nose* (Merc. iod., Phyt.). *Swallowing very difficult, as from constriction of the pharynx* (*Bell.*). Submaxillary glands swollen and painful.

Stomach.—Loss of appetite (Ars., Calc. c., *Cinch.*, Natr. mur., Sulph.). Great hunger; with weariness of life. Violent thirst (*Acon., Ars., Bry., Sulph.*). Stomach and abdomen tense after a moderate meal, clothes seem too tight (Lyc.). Eructations before and after eating; sour, empty. Nausea and vomiting of mucus and food; of tenacious, purulent and bloody mucus (Phos.). Nausea after eating with heaviness and dullness of the head. Stomach and abdomen tense

NITRICUM ACIDUM.

after a moderate meal, clothes seem too tight (Lyc.). Stitches in pit of stomach.

Abdomen.—Abdomen distended, with flatulence (Carb. v., Cinch.), very tender. Stitches in hepatic region, worse from motion. Pressure in left side of abdomen. Rumbling and uneasiness. Cutting and pinching pains in abdomen (Coloc.); in morning; in bed; at night; before stool. Incarcerated flatulence, worse mornings and evenings. Inguinal hernia; also of children (Alum., *Nux v.*). Swelling and suppuration of inguinal glands (*Calc. c.*, Merc., Thuja).

Stool and Anus.—Hæmorrhoids; protruding; swollen; bleeding; painless or burning. *Itching in the anus and rectum* (*Sulph., Sil.*). Moisture and soreness about anus. *Burning sensation in rectum and anus* (*Ars.*, Canth.). *Sticking in rectum, and spasmodic constriction in anus during stool; fissures* (*Natr. mur.*, Phyt.). *Pain as if rectum would be torn asunder during stool.* Inactivity and inability to evacuate fæces. Constant ineffectual desire, not relieved by stool. Stools dysenteric; bloody, with tenesmus (Merc.); black offensive blood (Ars.); mucous: pseudomembranes, with straining and burning in rectum. *Painful constipation; stool evacuated in hard masses* (*Alum., Bry., Sulph.*).

Urinary Organs.—Cutting, smarting and burning in the urethra during and after urination (Acon., *Ars., Canth.*, Coni.). Discharge of bloody mucus and pus from the urethra (Natr. mur., Merc. cor.), of prostatic fluid after a difficult stool. Orifice of urethra swollen and dark-red. *Needle-like stitches in the orifice of the urethra.* Frequent urging to urinate, with scanty discharge (Apis, Coloc., Hell., Merc.); at night. Urine is cold when passed. Micturition in a thin stream, as from stricture. Urine scanty, dark-brown; smelling intolerably strong (*Benz. ac.*), like horse's urine (Absinth., Natr. carb.); turbid, offensive.

Male Organs.—*Superficial ulcers, like chancres, on the glans and prepuce* (Hep. s., Phyt.), *looking clean, but exuding an offensive moisture* (Merc.). *Ulcers deep, fistulous, irregular, ragged; edges often raised, lead-colored; bleed easily when touched;* °syphilis. °Chancres after Mercury, especially with exuberant granulations. Secondary syphilis; condylomata: phymosis. Sycotic excrescences on the glans (Staph., *Thuja*); *bleeding when touched*: exuding an offensive moisture. Vesicles on the prepuce: becoming covered with small, dry scabs. Sharp stitches in the prepuce. Itching of the prepuce: of scrotum. Violent erections at night (Graph.). Sexual desire too strong or absent.

Female Organs.—Itching on the pudenda (Merc., Natr. mur., Sulph.). Ulcers in the vagina, burning and itching (Coni., Sulph.); covered with yellow pus. Leucorrhœa offensive: green mucus; cherry-colored; flesh-colored: after menstruation. °Excrescences on cervix uteri.

Respiratory Organs.—Hoarseness (*Acon., Hep. s., Phos.*). Loss of breath, palpitation and anxiety on ascending steps. °Empyema with considerable muco-purulent sputum. Cough more during the night, or when lying down during the day. Cough causing anxiety and vomiting of mucus and food. Rough, dry cough before midnight. Whistling inspiration with râles. Stitches in the right side of chest (Bry., *Kali carb.*). Purulent, yellowish expectoration with the cough. Congestion to upper part of chest. Oppression, tightness and fullness in chest. Catching at every attempt to breathe.

Neck and Back.—Stitches in and between the shoulder blades. Stiffness of the nape of the neck. Drawing in lumbar region, as if stiff. Pain in back, and small of back. Swelling of the glands of the neck and axillæ (Baryt. c Calc. c., Iod., Staph.). Pain between the scapulæ.

Upper Limbs.—Drawing pain in both arms. Bruised pain in arm. Pressive pain in the shoulders. Cold hands. Offensive sweat in axillæ. Falling asleep of the hands.

Lower Limbs.—Bruised pain, as from excessive fatigue (Cinch., Calc. c.). Digging, gnawing pains in the flesh and bones. Tensive pain in right hip-joint. *Tearing in lower extremities, especially at night.* Violent cramp in calf at night (Calc. c., Nux v., *Sulph.*). Chilblains on the toes (Agar., Puls., Zinc.). *Offensive, profuse perspiration on feet* (Baryt. c., Sep., Sil.), *causing soreness, with sticking pains, as if he were walking on pins.* Constant coldness of feet. Stiffness and stitches in the knees. Cracking in the ankles while walking.

Generalities.—*Excessive emaciation* (Ars., Ferr., Graph., *Iod.*, *Phos.*, *Natr. mur.*). Much inclined to take cold. Jaundice, with constipation. Pains in bones. *So weak almost constantly obliged to lie down* (*Sil.*). Frequent drawing pains in almost all parts of the body, *suddenly appearing and disappearing*. Epileptic attacks after midnight, beginning like a mouse moving up and down left side, then loss of consciousness. *Stitches and sticking pains as from splinters, especially on touch,* in all parts of the body. Glands inflamed, swollen, suppurating (Hep. s., Graph.).

Skin.—Skin dry and scaly (*Ars.*); yellowness of the skin. Rhagades, deep, bleeding. Dark freckles. Comedones. Ulcers, with stinging and pricking pains, as of splinters; edges irregular; exuberant granulations; °after Mercury, or in secondary syphilis. Condylomata moist, like cauliflower, hard, rhagadic, or in thin pedicles.

Sleep.—Difficulty of going to sleep in evening; wakens too early in morning, or difficult waking. Sleepiness during the day. Restless, disturbed sleep, and frequent waking with a start. Anxious sleep, with throbbing. Anxious dreams.

Fever.—Chill afternoon and evening, on lying down (Nux v.). Flushes of heat, with perspiration on the hands. *Dry heat, especially at night,* with excessive thirst. Frequent heat in face and hands. Profuse, offensive night sweats, *every other night. Perspiration in the morning* (Calc. c., Cinch., Rhus tox.).

Aggravation.—In evening and at night; from change of temperature or weather; while walking; on rising from a seat; on lying down.

Amelioration.—Most symptoms disappear when riding in a carriage (Graph.; reverse, Coccul.).

Conditions.—Especially useful in dark-complexioned persons; old people.

Compare.—Aur., Calc. c., Graph., Hep. s., Iod., Kali bi., Kali iod., Lyc., *Merc.*, Mez., *Mur. ac.*, Sil., *Thuja*. Nitric Acid follows well after Calc. c., Hep. s., Kali c., Natr. carb., Puls., Sulph., Thuja. After Nitric Acid are often indicated Calc. c., Puls., Sulph.

Antidotes.—Calc. c., Camph., *Hep. s.*, Merc., Mez., Sulph. To large doses: Alkalies, Soap, Magnesia, etc.

Nitricum Acidum Antidotes.—Calc. c., Digit., Merc.

THERAPEUTICS.

Nitric Acid is a valuable remedy in syphilitic and sycotic diseases and in Mercurio-syphilitic affections, in which latter it is the chief remedy, and only second to Hep. s. in the abuse of Mercury in non-syphilitic subjects. A valuable remedy in catarrhal and other conditions of mucous membranes, especially of the muco-cutaneous outlets of the body, mouth, lips, eyelids, nostrils, vulva and anus. It should be remembered that all the secretions and exudations under Nitric Acid are offensive and corrosive, frequently purulent, dirty, yellowish-green, not laudable. The characteristic pains are like splinters sticking into the parts. Nitric Acid is a valuable remedy in skin diseases, especially when resulting from syphilis or sycosis. Eczema. Deep, bleeding rhagades. Crusta lactea. Ulcers, with sticking pains, exuberant granulations, readily bleeding, etc. Condylomata on muco-cutaneous outlets. Warts on hands. Bleeding warts. Carbuncles. Urticaria. Said to remove freckles. A valuable remedy in affection of bones and glands, especially of syphilitic or mercurial origin. Noting the more special affections in which Nitric Acid is useful in the usual order: Syphilitic iritis; old cases spoiled by Mercury; frequent relapses; syphilitic ophthalmia; ulcers of the cornea; opacities of the cornea. Herpetic pannus. Fistula lachrymalis. Chronic inflammation of the middle ear. Eustachian tubes obstructed, auditory canal nearly closed, especially after abuse of Mercury. Caries of the mastoid process, and of the bones of the face, especially of the malar bones, syphilitic or mercurial. Syphilitic ozœna, nostrils ulcerated. Nasal catarrh. Especially useful in diseased conditions of the gums, teeth, tongue and mouth in general, resulting from the abuse of Mercury; characteristic ulcers, etc., as described in pathogenesis. Tonsilitis or pharyngitis with splinter-like pains. Syphilitic ulceration of throat, diphtheria, also involving the nose with very offensive excoriating discharge; terrible fœtor; intermittent pulse; swollen parotids. Dyspepsia. Chronic enlargement of liver, clay-colored stools; jaundice. Frequently a valuable remedy in dysentery with symptoms noted in pathogenesis. Diphtheritic dysentery. Ulceration of rectum with sticking pains; also after dysentery, from irritating local treatment. Hæmorrhoids, old pendulous. Fissures in rectum. Ulcers in urethra, bloody, mucous or purulent discharge. Oxaluria. Cystitis. The urine usually has a very strong odor (Benz. ac.). Hæmaturia. Syphilitic ulceration of the genitals of both sexes; superficial chancre-like, or deep and ragged; bleeding easily; chancres after Mercury, with exuberant granulations. Condylomata, exuding an offensive moisture. Phymosis. Herpes of the prepuce. Inflammation and ulceration of vulva and vagina. Cervicitis. Erosions and ulcerations of cervix. Watery excrescences in cervix. Tendency to uterine hæmorrhages. Cancer of uterus, profuse, brown, offensive discharge. Cough from secondary syphilis. Empyema with profuse muco-purulent expectoration. Laryngeal phthisis, with extensive ulceration, in syphilitic subjects. Pneumonia of old people, pain suddenly abates, but pulse becomes smaller and quicker. Phthisis, hectic fever, bright-red hæmorrhages; dyspnœa; exhausting diarrhœa; offensive, purulent, expectoration. May be useful in typhoid fever, with offensive, purulent, bloody stools; ulceration; great prostration; intermittent pulse; sometimes threatened paralysis of the lungs. Chronic intermittent fever, liver diseased, patient anæmic; general cachectic condition.

NUPHAR LUTEUM.

Synonym.—Nymphæa Lutea. *Common name.*—Small Yellow Pond Lily. *Habitat.*—Native of Europe, also found near Philadelphia. *Preparation.*—Tincture from the fresh root.

GENERAL ANALYSIS.

Acts most prominently upon the lower portion of the intestinal canal and upon the male generative organs.

CHARACTERISTIC SYMPTOMS.

Head.—Pressive headache in forehead and temples, ceasing in the open air. Dull, deep, lancinating pains behind the left frontal eminence. Painful, bruising shocks in the brain at every step.

Eyes.—Dull pain and sensation of weight in orbit. Brilliant sparks before the eyes, especially after hard coughing.

Stool.—Soft stools, preceded by colic; more mornings. Yellow diarrhœa in the morning. Smarting and burning in anus after stool (*Ars., Sulph.*). Stitches, as from needles. in rectum. *Painless morning diarrhœa (Podo.).*

Urinary Organs.—Urine deposits a copious reddish sand (Cinch., Natr. mur., Lyc., Phos.), which adheres to vessel.

Male Organs.—Complete absence of sexual desire (Agn.); voluptuous thoughts do not cause erections (Agar., *Agn.*, Coni.); penis retracted; scrotum relaxed. Severe lancinations in both testicles, with pains in end of penis. Impotency, with involuntary emissions (Agar., Agn., Coni., Phos., Phos. ac.); during sleep, at stool, and when urinating.

Skin.—Sensation like flea-bites in different spots. Itching eruption, resembling psoriasis.

Compare.—Agn., Ars., Baryt. c., Coni., Gels., Podo., Rumex, Sulph.).

THERAPEUTICS.

Has been found useful in the following conditions: morning diarrhœa; entero-colitis, chronic; sexual debility; impotence; spermatorrhœa.

NUX MOSCHATA.

Synonym.—Myristica Moschata. *Common name.*—Nutmeg. *Habitat.*—The nutmeg is a native of the Molucca Islands, and is cultivated in other tropical and semi-tropical countries. *Preparation.*—Tincture from the dried, coarsely powdered nutmeg.

GENERAL ANALYSIS.

Through the nervous system Nux mosch. affects particularly the digestive tract, the ovaries and the uterus, the symptoms it produces being of a purely nervous character, and indicative of no change whatever in organic substance, save the

NUX MOSCHATA. 555

slight congestion which the nervous irritation may produce; but death may result from heart failure. Its chief characteristic is a sleepy, drowsy condition, with all complaints.

CHARACTERISTIC SYMPTOMS.

Mind.—*Changeable mood; one moment laughing; the next crying* (*Acon.*, Coca, *Ign.*). Disposition to laugh or jest at everything; feels lively and bright. Weeping, gloomy mood (Cact., *Ign.*, *Natr. mur.*, Plat., *Puls.*, *Rhus tox.*). *Absence of mind, cannot think* (Anac., Kreos., Lach., Natr. mur., Merc.); has to collect his thoughts slowly before speaking or answering (Ambr., Phos. ac., Sep.); thoughts vanish while reading, with tendency to sleep. Ideas confused; incoherent expression, either in speaking or writing (Cham., Lyc.). *Loss of memory* (Ambr., *Anac.*, Kreos., Lach., Merc.). Soporous condition, as if intoxicated (*Op.*); with loss of motion and sensation. Momentary unconsciousness.

Head.—Vertigo, as if intoxicated (Coccul., Led., Mez.). Head drops forward while sitting. Head feels full and as if expanding, but without pain; seems bulky, and rolls around without control; has to support with the hands. Painless pulsation in the head (Glon., Puls.), with fear to go to sleep. Pain, especially in the temples, with a sensation as if the brain were loose, with wobbling on motion, as if it struck the sides of the skull (Cinch., Hyos., Rhus tox.). *Pressive headache in a small spot* over left frontal eminence. °Headache after eating, as from overeating (Nux v.).

Eyes.—*Sensation of dryness in the eyes;* in evening, is difficult to read by artificial light; can move eyelids only with difficulty. Blindness, then fainting. *Objects appear too large* (*Hyos.*), or °too distant, too small (*Plat.*).

Nose.—Dryness, stopped up.

Face.—Face pale; blue rings around the eyes,

Mouth.—Taste like chalk in the mouth; in morning, fasting. Painfulness of the teeth while eating (Carb. an., Merc.). Toothache; °during pregnancy; from damp, cold, evening air. *Dryness of the mouth, tongue and lips* (Ars., Bry.), *but without thirst* (Apis, Puls.). Saliva seems like cotton. Accumulation of saliva and thick mucus in the mouth.

Paralysis of the tongue; speech difficult (Caust., Dulc., Gels., Hyos,); indistinct.

Throat.—Great dryness in the throat, without thirst (Apis, Lach., Puls.). Difficult swallowing, from paralysis of the muscles of deglutition (Op.). Scraping in the throat.

Stomach.—Very great hunger; not thirst (Apis, Puls.). Thirst. Deathly nausea if her head were raised from the pillow. Nausea and vomiting, with inclination to sleep (*Ant. tart.*); °during pregnancy (Kali carb., Puls.. Sep.); °while riding in a carriage (*Coccul.*); °from irritation of pessaries. Fullness in stomach impeding breathing. °Irritation of stomach from overtaxed mental powers.

Abdomen.—Pressure in the liver, as from something sharp, or as if stones were cutting and tearing their way out; weight about the liver. Abdomen enormously distended; after meals (Cinch., Natr. carb.. *Nux v.*). Rumbling in the abdomen; feeling as though colic would occur.

Stool.—*Stools soft, but expelled with difficulty* (Carb. v., Cinch.); rectum inactive (Alum., Camph.). °Diarrhœa, undigested, or like chopped eggs, with loss of appetite and great sleepiness; in summer with children.

Male Organs.—Inclined to coitus, but erections weak and of short duration.

Female Organs.—Menses irregular in time and quantity; flow generally dark and thick. °Flatulent distension of uterus. °Leucorrhœa in place of menses. During menses great pressure in the back from within outward; abdominal bearing down and drawing in the limbs. Spasmodic labor-like pains.

Respiratory Organs.—Hoarseness; °sudden, from walking against the wind. Dry cough, with sudden loss of breath. °Cough when becoming warm in bed. Oppression of the chest; short breath after eating.

Heart and Pulse.—Feeling of rush of blood to the heart, and thence to head and all over the body. Palpitation with fainting, followed by sleep. Pulse small, slow and weak (Digit.).

Back.—Pain in small of back, as if broken (Aloe, *Bell.*, Cimic., Natr. mur., Kali carb., Nux v.), when riding in a carriage. Bruised pain at side of lumbar vertebræ.

Limbs.—Numbness in all the limbs. °Pain in all the limbs

NUX MOSCHATA.

and joints in cold, damp weather (Rhod.). Tingling in toes, as if frozen (Agar.).

Generalities.—Great weakness and fatigue; feels as though he must lie down after the least exertion, *with sleepiness.* Jactitation of muscles. Disposition to faint; also, from the pains when slight (Hep. s.); sickly sensation. Intermittent, wandering, digging pain in small spots. °Convulsions; hysterical, epileptic, with consciousness; children, with diarrhœa; catalepsy. Skin cold over the whole body, and sensitive to cold air (Coccul., Hep. s.). °Anæmia. Marasmus of children.

Sleep.—*Sleepiness, with all complaints,* particularly with pains; lies in stupid slumber. *Almost irresistible desire for sleep (Ant. tart., Apis).* Starting in sleep, but does not always awake.

Aggravation.—From cold, damp weather; from washing or getting wet; from riding in a carriage; after eating or drinking; from spirituous liquors.

Amelioration.—In the room; in open air.

Conditions.—Especially suitable for women and children; for nervous people; also for the aged.

Compare.—*Ambr., Asaf.,* Bell., Can. ind., Coccul., Coni., Dig., Hyos., Ign., Lyc., Mosch., *Nux v.,* Op., Phos., *Puls., Rhus tox.,* Sep., Sil., Sulph., Stram.

Antidotes.—Camph., Gels., Nux v.

Nux Moschata Antidotes.—Ars., Rhod., Laur.

THERAPEUTICS.

The peculiar nervous and mental phenomena of this drug already described have led to its successful use in hysteria, and in functional disturbances of the mind and sensorium from overtaxing the mind and from gastric ailments. Hysteria during pregnancy, with attacks of faintness, or momentary unconsciousness. The latter is a prominent feature of the drug. Hysteria with enormous bloating of the abdomen, excessive dryness of the mouth, sudden oppression of the heart with choking sensation, unconsciousness or fainting. The least emotional excitement renews the symptoms. Tonic followed by clonic spasms. Epileptiform spasms with consciousness. Spasms of children, with diarrhœa. Catalepsy. Paralysis of tongue, eyelids, œsophagus. Anæmia. Marasmus of children. Headache from overeating; before menses, in nervous subjects; during pregnancy. Supra-orbital neuralgia with pulsation in the head, every day. Ptosis. Toothache during pregnancy; from damp, cold, evening air. Nausea and vomiting of pregnancy; from riding in a carriage; from irritation of pessaries. Dyspepsia from overtaxing the mind, enormous distension of the stomach and abdomen after meals; can only digest highly seasoned foods; worse from any motion. Summer complaint of children, with undigested stools, like beaten eggs, loss of appetite and great sleepiness. Suppression of menses with fainting, and other nervous symptoms of the drug. Various nervous phenomena from uterine displacement, ovarian irritation or during pregnancy, with flatulent distension of the abdomen, etc. Sterility. Leucorrhœa in place of the menses. Menorrhagia, thick, dark blood, tendency to syncope. Nervous aphonia. Hoarseness from walking against the wind. Nervous palpitation of the heart, with fainting, followed by sleep. Neuralgia of the sacrum and coccyx, worse from riding in a carriage.

NUX VOMICA.

Synonym.—Strychnos Nux Vomica. *Natural order.*—Loganiaceæ. *Common name.*—Poison Nut. *Habitat.*—A tree indigenous to most of India, also found in Burmah, Siam, Cochin-China and Northern Australia. *Preparation.*—Tincture or trituration from the finely pulverized seeds.

GENERAL ANALYSIS.

Nux vom. acts pre-eminently upon the spinal cord, including the motory and sensory centers at the base of the brain, affecting chiefly that portion of the spinal tract which presides over reflex functions. The condition produced is one of excessive irritation and excitability, giving rise to incoherent muscular action, which, in the extreme, constitutes violent tetanic contractions, and which, finally, may end in entire cessation of muscular movement, or paralysis. These tetanic convulsions affect particularly the limbs and trunk; the former being rig-

NUX VOMICA.

idly flexed, and the body arched as in opisthotonos, the respiratory muscles rigidly contracted, rendering breathing laborious, even to asphyxia, while at the same time there are present spasmodic conditions of the face, jaws, throat, œsophagus and of the intestinal and urinary tracts. The entire condition thus presents a horrible aspect; but, through it all, the mind is unaffected, though it is probable that little pain is experienced. The paroxysms are usually interrupted "by periods of calm, from which, however, the least noise, a breath of air or the lightest touch may act with the suddenness of lightning to renew the scene" (Stram.). Death finally results, either from asthenia or asphyxia.

In addition to this remarkable action upon the muscular system, Nux vom. affects profoundly the organs and functions of nutrition, the secretions being altered, the functions perverted and the organic substance changed, giving rise to a long train of symptoms, presenting accurate pictures of gastric, hepatic and intestinal affections, which may only be appreciated and understood by a careful study of the pathogenesis of the drug.

The same character of irritation which, in the mucous membrane of the alimentary tract, gives rise to dyspeptic symptoms and aids in the production of constipation, produces in the respiratory sphere a dry catarrhal condition, giving obstruction in the nasal passages, and dry cough. Nux vom. also affects prominently the genito-urinary sphere, producing at first an increased activity of these organs, followed by depression and relaxation.

The chief peculiarity of Nux vom. is its adaptation to disorders of digestion, especially when resulting from long-continued errors of diet, from highly seasoned foods, stimulating drinks, hot medicines, and drug mixtures in general, and especially when occurring in persons of sedentary habits.

CHARACTERISTIC SYMPTOMS.

Mind.—*Quarrelsome, even to violence; ill-humored;* finds fault and scolds; irritable; morose; stubborn (Agar., Alum., Borax, Caps., *Bry., Cham.*). °Careful, zealous persons inclined to get excited and angry, or of a spiteful, malicious disposition. *Over-sensitiveness to external impres-*

sions; *cannot tolerate noise, music, talking, strong odors or bright light* (Bell., Colch., *Stram.*). Over-sensitiveness, every harmless word offends (Caps., Staph.); every little noise frightens (Op.); anxious and beside themselves; cannot bear the least, even suitable medicine. *Hypochondriac mood, worse after eating;* °especially in persons of sedentary habits, or in those who dissipate, with abdominal sufferings and constipation. The time passes too slowly (Alum.). Great anxiety, with inclination to commit suicide (Aur., Naja), but is afraid to die; much lamentation and weeping. Anxiety in the morning on waking, better on rising, with orgasm of blood, and ill-humor. *Great dread of, and incapacity for, literary work* (Aloe); cannot think correctly (Æth., Cimic., *Gels., Phos., ac.*). Disinclination to bodily labor (Cinch., *Phos.,* Phos. ac.).

Head.—*Intoxicated confusion in the head* (Cinch., Graph.); stupefaction (Op.). *Vertigo after dinner,* as if the brain were turning in a circle (Alum., Arn., Bell., *Bry.,* Coni.), with momentary loss of consciousness; dizzy, reeling while walking, as if he would fall to one side or backward (Bell.). *Intoxicated, dizzy heaviness in the head in the morning* (Kreos.). *Headache in the morning in bed* (Kali bi., Natr. mur., Nitr. ac.); in the middle of the brain, *felt before opening the eyes; in forehead;* in occiput, as if the skull would burst (*Bry., Natr. mur.*); *as if the head had been beaten with an ax; as if he had not slept; makes him stupid; disappears after rising.* Pressive boring pains in the head commencing in the morning; *worse after eating, with nausea and sour vomiting,* toward evening, after lying down. Drawing, tearing, jerking, burning or pinching pains in the head, especially in morning and after eating. *Heaviness and pressure in the head after dinner, especially on moving the eyes.* Pressing as if something heavy were sinking forward in the head, on stooping. Headache, as if the brain were bruised or beaten (Mur. ac.). Pressing pain, as if a nail were being driven deeply into the side of the brain (Arn., Coff., Ign.). Violent jerking or dull stitches in left side of brain, from orbit to parietal bone or occiput. *Tension in the forehead,* as if it were pressed in, at night and in the morning; worse on exposing head to

NUX VOMICA. 561

cold air. Sensation as from a bruise in back part of head. *Small painful swelling on the forehead.* Scalp sensitive to the touch (Acon., Baryt. c., Cinch., Merc., Mez., Natr. mur., Natr. carb., Nitr. ac.), °or to wind; better from being warmly covered. *Head symptoms worse in the morning, from mental exertion, exercising in the open air after eating, and from wine (Zinc.) and coffee; better in the warm room and from sitting quietly or lying down.*

Eyes.—*Photophobia; much worse in the morning.* Vision cloudy (Caust., *Gels.*); sensitive. Inflammation, with swelling, red streaks in the whites, and pressive, tensive pain. Painless injection of the whites of the eyes; ecchymoses (Arn.). Burning and smarting, as from salt, with lachrymation (Natr. mur.); worse in external canthus. Margins of lids and canthi itch and burn, as if rubbed sore, *especially in the morning. Itching better from rubbing. Smarting, dry sensation in inner canthi, in the morning in bed.* Movement of lids difficult on account of stiffness of muscles.

Ears.—*Itching in the ear* and through the Eustachian tube, which compels frequent swallowing. Ringing, roaring and hissing in the ears (Bell., *Cinch.*, Merc., *Sulph.*). Tearing, sticking pains in the ears (*Puls.*); worse in the morning in bed.

Nose.—*Profuse discharge of acrid mucus from the obstructed nostrils. Coryza; fluent in the morning; fluent during the day, and stopped at night* (Amm. carb., Natr. ars.); *in the morning and after dinner; with scraping and crawling in the nose and throat, with frequent sneezing especially in morning in bed; with headache, heat in the face, chilliness* (Acon.). Coryza, worse in the warm room, better in the cool air (*Puls.*). Nostrils internally painful, as if ulcerated; also margins.

Face.—Paleness of the face. Twitching and spasmodic distortion of the facial muscles (Agar., *Bell.*, Cic., Ign.). Tearing and drawing pains in the face, extending into the ear. Drawing in masseter muscles, with stiffness. *Tetanic contraction of the jaws; trismus* (Absinth., Cic., Hyos., Laur.). Itching pimples on chin. °Pimples on the face, from excessive use of spirituous liquors. Ulcer on inside of lower lip, painful to touch. Painful desquamation of the lips. Inter-

36

mittent neuralgia; worse in infra-orbital branch of trifacial; always worse in morning; better sometimes when lying in bed, especially after abuse of coffee or liquors.

Mouth.—Drawing, tearing toothache; worse from mental exertion, from cold or cold things, after eating (Ant. crud., Lach., Staph.); from coffee or wine; relieved by warmth (Bry.). Stinging in decayed teeth; in whole row of teeth. Tongue coated thick white (Acon., Ant. crud., Bry., Puls.). Painful blisters on tongue (Borax, Merc., Nitr. ac.). Heaviness of the tongue, with difficult speech (Caust., Gels., Lach.). Internal mouth, tongue and palate are slimy, and feel raw and sore. Dryness of the mouth, without much thirst (Apis, *Nux m.*, Puls.) but *with much accumulation of saliva (Merc.) in the fauces.* Bad taste in the mouth in the morning (Puls.), *though food and drink taste natural; taste sour* (Calc. c., Cinch., Mag., Nitr. ac.); *bitter* (Bry., Coloc., Cinch., Puls., Sulph.). Offensive odor from the mouth (Arn., Aur., Iodi., Kreos., *Nitr. ac.*); mornings; after dinner; sour. °Small apthous ulcers in the mouth and throat, with putrid smell; bloody saliva runs out at night; gums scorbutic; spits coagulated blood.

Throat.—*Throat raw* (*Arum.*, Sang.), *sore, rough, as if scraped* (Arg.), principally when swallowing, and when inhaling cold air. *Scraping, as after heartburn.* Pharynx constricted; swallowing, as from a plug in throat (Natr. mur.). Spasmodic pain from pharynx to pit of stomach in morning. Stitches in ear when swallowing.

Stomach.—*Hunger, with aversion to food, especially bread* (Lyc., Natr. mur.), *water, coffee and tobacco.* Thirst for milk; for beer. *Bitter, sour eructations* (Alum., Carb. v., Phos., Sulph.). Violent hiccough (Cic., Hyos., Lyc.). *Heartburn* (Lyc., Natr. mur.); as from overloading stomach with rancid fats (Puls.); waterbrash (Led.); after eating. *Nausea in morning* (Calc. c., Puls., Sulph.); *after eating or drinking* (*Ars.*); *from smoking tobacco* (Ign.), with faintness (Ant. tart.); *after dinner.* *Vomiting of sour mucus;* of food and drink (Ipec., Phos., Podo.); of bile (Grat., Iris, Podo.); of blood (Ham., Op., Podo., Stan.). *Retching as if to vomit, while hawking mucus from fauces.* Region of stomach sensitive to pressure. Clawing,

NUX VOMICA. 563

cramping pains in the stomach (Bell., Coccul.). *Tension and fullness in the epigastrium.* Sensation as if something in epigastric region turned over. Discomfort in pit of stomach, ascending to throat, choking and impeding breathing. Fluttering in the epigastrium. *Pressure in the stomach an hour or two after a meal (Puls.), with dullness of the head and hypochondriacal mood Bloatedness, and pressure as from a stone in the stomach (Ars., Bry., Puls.); especially after eating.* °Disordered stomach from overeating; from debauchery; from high living; from drugs; from sedentary habits. *Scraped sensation in pit of stomach (Puls.).*

Abdomen.—Stitches in the region of the liver; worse from contact or motion (*Bry.*, Cinch.). Throbbing pain as from hepatic abscesses. Jaundice (Chel., Merc.); aversion to food; fainting turns; gall-stones (Cinch.). Loud rumbling and gurgling in the abdomen (*Lyc.*) in the morning. *Flatulent distension of the abdomen after eating* (Cinch., Lyc., Nux m., Rhus tox.). Colic; flatulent; from indigestion; from overeating; as from a cold (Dulc., Merc.); cutting pains as from stones (*Coloc.*); griping, pinching; periodical after breakfast or after meals; evening after lying down; making hemi bend together (Aloe, Caust., *Coloc.*, Iris, Rheum). *Pain as before diarrhœa from taking cold.* Constriction. Weight. Sensation as if everything would fall, obliging him to walk carefully. Pressure under short ribs as from incarcerated flatulence (Carb. v.). Bruised, sore pain in the intestines (Merc.). Stitches in abdomen. Griping, tearing pains, extending into the chest. *Development of a tendency to inguinal hernia. Sensation of weakness in inguinal ring, as if hernia would occur; or pain as if a hernia would become incarcerated.* (Alum., Nitr. ac.). Jerking and twitching in the abdominal muscles.

Stool and Anus.—*Blind hæmhorrhoids; with sticking, beating or pressive pain in rectum and anus; after stool, after a meal, and after exerting the mind. Constipation, with frequent and ineffectual desire for stool* (Ambr., Coni., Nitr. ac., Sil., Sulph.), *and a sensation of constriction in rectum. After stool, sensation as if more remained* (*Aloe*, Lyc.), *but could not be evacuated.* Alternate constipation and diarrhœa (*Ant. crud.*, Card. m., Cimic., Natr. ars., Podo.). *Discharge of bright-red blood with fæces, with sensation of constriction and contraction in rectum. Frequent and ineffectual urging, with griping and soft stool.* Jerking in anus when not at stool. Itching in anus with sore pain, as from hæmorrhoids. *Diarrhœa, especially in the morning, of a dark color* (*Rumex, Sulph.*); *after dinner.* Small stools, of a slimy, bloody mucus, with much urging, ceasing after stool: scanty, corrosive, in morning.

Urinary Organs.—*Painful, ineffectual urging to urinate* (*Canth.*). *Urine passes in drops* (Acon., Bell., Canth.), with burning and tearing in urethra and neck of bladder (Apis, Canth., Can. sat., Caps.). Constriction in fore part of urethra extending backward. Urine pale, later thick, whitish, purulent; reddish, with brick-dust sediment; turbid, with dirty-yellow sediment in morning and when thinking. Tenacious mucus passes with the urine, without pain.

Male Organs.—Easily excited desire (Coni.), painful erections, especially in the morning; after mid-day nap. Nightly emissions, with lascivious dreams; from high living, etc.; bad effects of sexual excesses. Prepuce sore on margin; biting, itching on inner surface. Itching of scrotum. Stitches in testicles.

Female Organs.—*Menses too early and too profuse* (Alum., Ambr., Amm. carb., Bell., Calc. c.); *flow dark; with cramps. During menses, nausea in morning, with chilliness and attacks of faintness. Pressure toward the genitals, especially in the morning.* Contractive uterine spasms; colic, with discharge of coagula (Caul., Sec.). Internal swelling of vagina like prolapsus, with burning pain, worse on touch. Burning in pudenda.

Respiratory Organs.—*Hoarseness, with roughness and scraping in the throat* (*Caust.*); *provoking a cough.* Accumulation of tenacious mucus in upper part of trachea (Bry., Rumex). Itching and tickling in the trachea, exciting a cough (Baryt. c.). Oppressed breathing; tightness of breathing from spasmodic constriction of lower part of thorax (Ign., Laur.); especially when walking and ascending. *Dry, fatiguing cough* (*Rumex*), *from midnight till day-break;* in the evening after lying down (*Coni.*, Hyos., Mez., *Puls.*), or *very early in the morning.* Violent cough before rising in the morning, with expectoration of clotted blood (Puls.), *and soreness in the chest* (Arn.). Cough, causing bruised pain in abdominal walls; headache, as if skull would burst (*Bry.*, *Natr. mur.*). °Cough worse after eating or drinking (Cinch.); after mental or physical exertion; when lying on the back; from cold; from tobacco. Pressing in the chest, as from a heavy load (*Ferr.*, *Phos.*); in open air; at night in bed. °Intercostal neuralgia, better when lying on the well side. *Roughness, rawness and scraping in the chest* (Cham.). Congestion in the chest, with heat and burning.

Heart and Pulse.—Palpitation; on lying down after dinner; after eating; °from coffee; °from protracted study.

Back and Neck.—Heaviness and stiffness in the neck. Drawing pain in muscles of neck. Paroxysmal tearing pain in nape of neck and in back. Pain in back and small of back as if bruised or broken (Aloe, *Bell.*, Cimic., Kali c., Natr. mur., Plat.). Back spasmodically curved like an arch (*Cic.*, Op.). °Cervico-brachial neuralgia, neck stiff, worse in the morning, or after eating, and from touch.

Limbs.—Bruised pain in the limbs and joints, worse in the morning in bed; better on rising. Spasmodic pain in joints after yawning and stretching, with chilliness and internal beating. Trembling of the limbs, and jerking of the heart. Great weariness and relaxation in all the limbs, after taking the open air. *Chilliness of back and limbs in morning, with pain of skin as from freezing cold, and falling asleep of limbs.* Sensation of sudden loss of power in the extremities, in the morning. Falling asleep of arms, hands and soles of feet

Lower Limbs.—Tottering and unsteadiness of the lower extremities; knocking under of the knees; drags the feet. Paralytic drawing of the muscles of thighs and calves, painful on walking. Painful swelling of the knees. Stiffness and tension in hollows of knees, especially after standing; sensation as if tendons were too short, on arising from a seat. Numbness and deadness of the legs. Cramps in the calves at night (Calc. c., Nitr. ac., Sulph.).

Generalities.—*Great debility, with over-sensitiveness of all the senses* (Cinch.). *Everything makes too strong an impression.* Emaciation (Ars., Ferr., Graph., Natr. mur., Phos., Iodi.). Stitches in jerks through the whole body, causing shuddering. Trembling all over: mostly of hands, especially in morning; in drunkards. *Violent contractive painful sensation through the whole body.* Greater weariness in the morning after rising than in the evening on going to bed. Sensitiveness and aversion to open air (Amm. carb., Aur., Coccul., Phos., Rumex, Sep., Sil.). *Takes cold in the slightest draught of air.* Fainting fits after walking in the open air. Wants to sit or lie down. Convulsions, with tetanic rigidity of nearly all the muscles of the body, with interruptions of a few minutes, during which muscles are relaxed. Opisthotonos. *Spasms renewed by the slightest touch* (Stram.). °Paralysis, with numbness and coldness of the paralyzed parts, caused by apoplexia, alcohol, sexual excesses, etc.

Sleep.—Much yawning and sleepiness during the day (Nux m.); irresistible sleepiness after eating, for several hours (Kali carb., Sil.). Sleepy in the early evening, but sleepless at night. *Awakens at 3 A. M., lies awake for hours, with a rush of thoughts, falls into a dreamy sleep at day-break, from which it is hard to arouse, and then feels tired, weak and averse to rising.* Sleeps mostly lying on the back. Loud, snoring respiration during sleep (Laur., Op.). Dreams, with frightful visions, causing fear.

Fever.—Chilliness and shivering over the whole body, with blueness of the skin, *especially the hands and nails.* Chill in evening on lying down (Nitr. ac.), followed by heat in head and face. Chill not relieved by heat; aggravated by motion. Dry heat, which does not tolerate covering, or else desires it, yet chilly on being uncovered. Heat precedes the chill, and is renewed after the chill. Sweat after midnight and in the morning; sour, offensive (Arn., Ars., Carb. an., Hep. s., Sil.); cold, clammy on face (Camph., Verat. alb.).

Aggravation.—*From mental exertion; in the morning; after eating, especially after dinner; from motion; from slight touch; in open air; in dry weather.*

Amelioration.—From frequent stretching; after dinner; of all pains by cold sweat.

Conditions.—Fiery, excitable temperaments. Suits thin, irritable, choleric persons, with dark hair, and persons who make great mental exertion, or lead a sedentary life; debauchers who are irritable and thin.

Compare.—Amm. mur., Am. carb., Ars., Bell., Bry., Calc. c., Carb. v., Cham., Cedron, *Cic. v.,* Cinch., *Coccul., Coff.,* Cupr., *Ign.,* Ipec., *Lyc.,* Merc., Op., Phos., *Puls.,* Rhus tox., Sec. c., Sep., *Sulph.* Its relations are: Ars., Ipec., Phos., Sulph. precede Nux v. well, while Bry., Puls. and Sulph. follow it well. Intensifies the action of Sepia. Inimical to Zinc.

Antidotes.—Acon., Bell., Camph., Cham., Coff., Coccul., Ign., Puls. To large doses: Wine, Coffee, Camph., Op.

Nux Vomica Antidotes.—Ars., Cham., Cinch., Coccul., Coff., Op., Phos., Puls. It is also an antidote to aromatics, drastics, "hot medicines," narcotics, Coffee and Alcohol.

THERAPEUTICS.

Nux vom., while not having so wide a range of action as Mercurius and possibly other remedies, is nevertheless more often prescribed than any other drug in the Materia Medica, owing to the fact that its pathogenesis covers a class of ailments, both acute and chronic, such as are very commonly met with in practice. This is also largely due to the fact that Nux vom. is more often indicated for indigestion and the various consequences arising from errors in diet and digestive habits, than any other remedy, and is therefore often required for certain persons who are so engrossed in business that they pay little attention to their physical requirements. Especially useful in persons having a Nux temperament as above described under the head of "Conditions." It is the remedy preëminently for the bad effects from highly seasoned foods, coffee, tobacco and spirituous liquors; from all kinds of drug mixtures, hot medicines and nostrums; from over-exertion of the mind, sedentary habits, over-eating, loss of sleep; from debauchery. Dyspepsia from above causes, with pain, nausea and other

NUX VOMICA.

symptoms noted in pathogenesis. Atonic dyspepsia, with slow and imperfect digestion. Gastralgia, with clawing, cramping pains, worse after eating; worse in morning before breakfast; better from hot drinks. A valuable remedy in nausea and vomiting from above named causes. Vomiting of drunkards; of pregnancy. Valuable in cases where the stomach has been ruined by allopathic medicines and nostrums. Gastro-duodenal catarrh, with coated tongue, nausea, soreness, pain, etc. Nux is invaluable in functional derangements as well as organic diseases of the liver arising from the causes above named, especially from habitual use of alcoholic liquors, and particularly where there is associated indigestion, constipation and hæmorrhoids. Liver engorged, swollen, indurated, sensitive. Hepatitis from above causes: gall-stones; constipation nearly always present. Useful in hernia; has cured incarcerated hernia, apparently irreducible, as well as more recent cases. Infantile hernia, caused by crying, or by straining in obstinate constipation. Colic from indigestion, with other Nux symptoms; from suppressed hæmorrhoidal flow. An extremely valuable remedy in hæmorrhoids, especially when associated with gastric and hepatic derangements above mentioned, and from causes named. Particularly useful in blind, painful hæmorrhoids with constipation, much itching, and frequent urging to stool. Sometimes useful in diarrhœa or dysentery, with backache, nausea and ineffectual urging and other symptoms described under "Stool and Anus;" but the chief sphere of usefulness of the drug is in constipation, which is usually associated with most of the digestive troubles in which Nux vom. is indicated. The constipation seems not to arise from inactivity of the bowels as in Alumina, Opium, etc., but rather from an inharmonious peristalsis, there being usually an almost constant ineffectual urging to stool throughout the whole abdomen, the difficulty arising not from any local trouble in the rectum, but from a general derangement of the digestive system, interfering with the portal circulation. The mental and head symptoms of Nux vom. are extremely important, and, arising as they do in most instances from derangements of digestion, should be considered in this connection.

The characteristic Nux temperament has already been referred to, and should be continually borne in mind. Hypochondriasis is an important element in the action of the drug, and for which it is most often useful, occurring as it usually does from the class of troubles already mentioned, and with which it is very frequently associated. Hypochondriasis from mental strain and in persons of sedentary habits, or those who dissipate and who suffer with gastric and abdominal complaints, constipation and hæmorrhoids. Other mental symptoms mentioned in the pathogenesis usually arise from similar causes, and should be remembered as very important in indicating the use of the drug. The vertigo and headaches of Nux are in the same line, rarely occurring from other causes, and present too many individual phases to be repeated. Vertigo, dull headache, coated tongue, nausea, etc., following a debauch; especially worse in the morning; also from indigestion brought on by over-eating or by mental exertion. Headache from drinking coffee. Supra-orbital neuralgia, recurring early every morning. The sleep symptoms are important, and usually associated with the above-named conditions. The patient is usually very sleepy after meals, but sleepless at night, goes to sleep late, then wakens about 2 or 3 A.M., and lies awake a long time with a rush of thoughts, then falling into a dreamy sleep and waking in the morning unrefreshed, tired and weary, with dull headache, bad taste in the mouth, etc.

The action of Nux vom. upon the spinal nerves has been pretty fully described in the foregoing analysis and pathogenesis. Clinically it is of great value where similar conditions are present. Convulsions, epileptiform, with tetanic rigidity, opisthotonos, with intervals of relaxation, renewed by the slightest touch; with consciousness; from indigestion; from emotions. Chorea. Paralysis; from apoplexia in high livers; partial paralysis with gastric symptoms, in drunkards; usually numbness and coldness of paralyzed parts; general Nux symptoms. Spinal irritation, partial paralysis of extremities, numbness, etc. Sometimes useful as an intercurrent in locomotor ataxia; also multiple sclerosis. Torticollis in spinal disease, from cold. Cervico-bronchial neuralgia, neck stiff, worse mornings, etc. Lumbago, pain as if bruised or broken, worse at night in bed, cannot turn over, the longer he lies the worse it gets. Rheumatism, especially the large muscles of the back or the large joints; muscles palpitate and are cramped;

parts feel torpid. paralytic; gastric symptoms. Nux is indicated in many diseases of the eyes. Catarrh. Conjunctivitis, with photophobia, worse mornings. Keratitis, with excessive photophobia, worse mornings. Scrofulous ophthalmia. Spasms of the lids. Atrophy of the retina; of the optic nerve. Hyperæsthesia of the retina, any attempt to use the eyes accompanied by intense pain and lachrymation. Ecchymoses of sclerotica, especially after debauchery. Infraorbital neuralgia from indigestion, from abuse of coffee or alcoholic liquors, relieved by warmth. Ciliary neuralgia. Amaurosis from tobacco or alcohol. Eustachian catarrh, with itching along the tube and frequent desire to swallow. Otalgia, worse in the morning in bed. Often useful in nasal catarrh more often acute than chronic; useful in beginning of a severe cold caused by exposure to dry, cold weather, or sitting in a cold room, or on cold steps. The discharge may be fluent, at the same time the nose seems dry and obstructed, with frequent sneezing especially mornings, fluent during day, stopped at night; worse in warm room, better in open air. Coryza of nursing infants, preventing nursing. Epistaxis from suppressed hæmorrhoidal flow. Sometimes useful in facial neuralgia and toothache (see symptoms). Acne of the face, especially in high livers and drunkards. Small, putrid apthous ulcers in mouth and throat. Catarrhal sore throat, often with coryza, rough, scraping sensation; allays irritation caused by topical applications, especially if rawness and scraping are present. Useful in reflex coughs of nervous origin, from gastric troubles or mental exertion. Violent, dry cough, worse early in morning (see symptoms). Bronchial catarrh with roughness, rawness and scraping in the chest. Asthma from gastric troubles, worse after eating, relieved by eructations, etc. Whooping cough, with characteristic aggravations. Intercostal neuralgia from usual causes before mentioned. Angina pectoris from indigestion, suppressed hæmorrhoids, coffee, tobacco or alcohol. Cardiac complaints from suppressed hæmorrhoids (Collin.). Palpitation after eating, from coffee or mental over-exertion.

Nux vom. is frequently a valuable remedy in diseases of the genito-urinary organs. Renal colic, more right side, backache, pains into genital organs and down the limbs. Hæmaturia after suppressed hæmorrhoids or menses; after debauchery. Irritable bladder, not inflammation, with strangury, discharge only of a few drops, high colored, burning urine; from gastric or hepatic disturbances. Paralysis of bladder with dribbling of urine, in old dyspeptics, especially drunkards. Bad effects from sexual excesses or masturbation; nocturnal emissions; also from high living. Menorrhagia, flow dark, with cramps, fainting. Dysmenorrhœa with characteristic Nux symptoms. Nausea during menses or pregnancy especially with constipation, etc. Prolapsus uteri, of recent origin, from a sprain or wrench, with general Nux symptoms. In such cases Sepia follows well. Sometimes useful during labor with reflex symptoms of rectum and bladder (not from pressure of the head) constant urging, rigid os; pains seem to run down the thighs. Often useful in intermittent fever, chill accompanied by blueness especially of the finger nails; yawning; aching in the back and limbs; followed by fever, and then light sweat; during apyrexia, gastric and bilious symptoms. During fever wants to be covered, feels chilly if uncovered. Nux may be useful in typhoid and other types of fever when its characteristic, gastric and bilious symptoms are present.

ŒNANTHE CROCATA.

Natural order.—Umbelliferæ. *Common names.*—Drop Water. Water Hemlock. *Habitat.*—A plant growing in moist and swampy places in England, Sweden, France and Spain. *Preparation.*—Tincture from the fresh root.

GENERAL ANALYSIS.

Acts powerfully upon the cerebro-spinal nervous system, producing epileptiform spasms, and causing inflammation and softening of the medulla oblongata and contiguous nerve tissue. It is the most powerful and energetic poison of its family, which includes Æthusa, Cicuta and Conium, though it has been used but little clinically.

CHARACTERISTIC SYMPTOMS.

Mind.—Furious delirium (*Bell., Canth., Stram.*), as if drunk (*Op.*): insanity. Sudden and complete loss of consciousness (*Bell., Op.*).

ŒNANTHE CROCATA.

Head.—Violent vertigo, with falling; with nausea, vomiting, syncope and convulsions. Violent pain in the head. Apoplectic conditions; speechless; insensible; face puffed and livid; pupils dilated; respiration laborious; limbs contracted; trismus (*Bell.*). Coma after the convulsions.

Eyes.—*Pupils dilated* (*Bell., Hyos.,* Op., *Stram.*); eyes turned upward and inward.

Nose.—Bleeding from the nose.

Face.—*Rapid convulsive twitching of muscles of the face* (*Agar., Bell.,* Cic., Nux v., Ign.). Face livid and turgid, pale and cold; ghastly; anxious. Trismus; jaws rigidly closed (Absinth., Cic., Ign., Hyos., Laur., Naja, *Nux v.*). Rose-colored spots on face.

Mouth.—Tongue swollen and protruded; slightly furred. Foaming at the mouth (Cic., Cupr., Hyos., Laur.); bloody mucus. Mouth dry and parched; speechless.

Throat.—Violent constriction and burning in throat.

Stomach.—Hiccough; cardialgia. Nausea and vomiting.

Abdomen.—Much distended, with colic pains.

Stool.—Involuntary; diarrhœa.

Respiratory Organs.—Convulsive respiration; breathing labored, hurried, stertorous, short; interrupted by constant sighing and convulsive cough; hardly perceptible.

Heart and Pulse.—Pain in region of heart. Pulse small, feeble, irregular, scarcely perceptible.

Generalities.—*Epileptiform convulsions. Terrible convulsions*, followed by coma or deep sleep. *Convulsions*, with vertigo, madness, nausea, vomiting, unconscious, risus sardonicus, eyeballs turned up, pupils dilated (Absinth., Bell., Cic.). *Sudden convulsions, trismus, biting of tongue; followed by total unconsciousness.* Convulsions, with swollen, livid face; bloody froth from mouth and nostrils; convulsive respirations; insensibility; feeble pulse; prostration.

Fever.—Extreme coldness: loss of animal heat. Profuse sweat; offensive.

Aggravation.—All symptoms worse from water.

Compare.—Agar., *Cic.,* Stram., Hydroc. ac.

THERAPEUTICS.

Has cured epileptiform convulsions. One case in a woman at seven months' pregnancy; another in a child apparently preceding an outbreak of exanthema; another case of epilepsy, worse during menstruation. Also reported to have cured a tickling cough, with rattling in lower part of chest, and thick, frothy expectoration.—*Allen.*

ŒNOTHERA.

Synonym.—Œnothera Biennis. *Natural order.*—Onagraceæ. *Common names.*—Large Evening Primrose. Tree Primrose. *Habitat.*—An indigenous plant commonly found in fields and waste places. *Preparation.*—Tincture from the fresh plant.

GENERAL ANALYSIS AND THERAPEUTICS.

The physiological action of this remedy has not been ascertained. It is claimed to be especially useful in the treatment of chronic diarrhœa, *cholera infantum,* and the *summer diarrhœa of children,* with exhausting watery almost involuntary discharges, which the single proving we have would seem to verify.

OLEANDER.

Synonym.—Nerium Oleander. *Natural order.*—Apocynaceæ. *Common name.*—Rose Laurel. *Habitat.*—A shrub native of Southern Europe, Arabia and Northern Africa. Cultivated elsewhere as an ornamental plant. *Preparation.*—Tincture from the fresh leaves.

GENERAL ANALYSIS.

Acts upon the cerebro-spinal system, producing paralytic conditions with a weak, irregular pulse; but its most important action as regards therapeutics is upon the skin, especially the scalp.

OLEANDER.

CHARACTERISTIC SYMPTOMS.

Mind.—Absence of mind and inattention; confusion when reading. Difficulty of grasping the connection when reading a long sentence. Loss of memory. Dullness of intellect, slow perception. Peevish, fretful, out of humor with everything. Indolence, aversion to doing anything.

Head.—Vertigo, with tottering of the limbs; °on looking fixedly, or on rising in bed or on looking down. Heaviness and pressure in the head. Pressive headache in forehead, from within outward. Pain in forehead as if it woud split. °Headache better from forcible squinting. *Violent gnawing itching on the scalp as from vermin; better when first scratching; after scratching, smarting and soreness as if raw. Desquamation of the epidermis of the scalp. Humid scaly biting, itching eruption, especially on back part of the head.*

Eyes.—Burning and tension in eyelids when reading.

Ears.—Cramp-like drawing in the outer ear.

Mouth.—Toothache only when masticating. Loss of speech. Food has a flat, insipid taste in evening.

Stomach.—*Ravenous hunger,* with trembling of the hands while eating. °Vomiting of food and greenish water, followed by renewed hunger and great weakness over the whole body. Much thirst, especially for cold water. Violent, empty eructations. °Pulsation in pit of stomach, as of beating of the heart.

Abdomen.—Rolling and rumbling in the intestines, with emission of a great quantity of fœtid flatus, smelling like rotten eggs (Arn.).

Stool and Anus.—Burning at the anus before and after stool; when not at stool. *Passes food undigested in the morning which he has eaten the day before.* Liquid, soft, yellow fæces. Involuntary stools; °in children when passing flatus.

Respiratory Organs.—Stitches in sternum and left side of chest, during inspiration and expiration.

Heart.—Dull, drawing pain over the heart, worse when stooping, and at last during expiration. Anxious palpitation of the heart; chest feels expanded.

Upper Limbs.—Cramp-like drawing in arms and fingers. Dull pressure in forearms, hands and fingers.

Lower Limbs.—Weakness of the lower limbs when walking, with sensation as if "asleep" in fore part of feet, worse in soles. Paralysis of the legs and feet.

Skin.—Violent itching of various parts of the body; eruption, bleeding, oozing out of fluid, forming scabs. Biting, itching on undressing.

Sleep.—Voluptuous dreams with seminal emissions.

Fever.—Febrile chilliness over the body, without thirst or subsequent heat.

Compare.—Anac., Cinch., Coccul., Clem., Nux v., Staph., Sil.

Antidote.—Camph.

THERAPEUTICS.

Has been used chiefly in Crusta lactea, with symptoms above described, especially on occiput and behind the ears. Has also been used in paralysis, especially hemiplegia, preceded by vertigo. Very weak digestion. Diarrhœa with above-symptoms. Diarrhœa of phthisis.

OPIUM.

Synonym.—Papaver Somniferum. *Natural order.*—Papaveraceæ. *Common names.*—Opium. White Poppy. *Habitat.*—A plant native of Asia, extensively cultivated. *Preparation.*—Tincture from inspissated juice.

GENERAL ANALYSIS.

Acts upon the cerebro-spinal and the sympathetic nervous system, producing brief excitation, rapidly followed by depression and paralysis of all functional activity. As a result there is a general torpidity of the entire system. The cerebral powers are overcome and stupor ensues; motion and sensation are destroyed; the secretions of the mucous membranes are diminished, and the mucous surfaces become dry and congested; the breathing becomes slow, sighing and irregular; the heart's action is retarded, and these evidences of cerebro-spinal paralysis continuing, death results; or, passing off, leave deranged digestion, headache, sleeplessness and constipation.

OPIUM.

The leading feature of Opium is its depression of the cerebral functions, indicated by great drowsiness and stupor, with stertorous breathing, in which condition it is the true homœopathic remedy. Its universal use as a palliative to diminish reflex irritability and destroy the consciousness of suffering pain cannot be too strongly condemned. Such palliation is only admissible in hopelessly fatal cases, or possibly under other very exceptional circumstances, but is not in any sense homœopathic.

CHARACTERISTIC SYMPTOMS

Mind.—*Complete loss of consciousness* (*Bell.*, *Hyos.*, Laur.), *with slow stertorous breathing; insensibility to external impressions*. *Delirious; eyes wide open; glistening, face red, puffed up;* sees **frightful** and **distressing** visions (Absinth., Bell., Hyos., Stram.). *Drunkenness with stupor, as from smoke in the brain; eyes burning, hot and dry* (Bell.). *Dull and stupid, as if drunk* (Nux m.). Imbecility. Confusion. Fear of *impending* death. Anxiety. Vivid imaginations, exaltation of the mind (Can. ind.). Fretful, nervous and irritable; easily frightened (Nux v.).

Head.—Great confusion, dullness and heaviness of the head, making thought and writing difficult (Nux v.). Sensation like that following a debauch. *Vertigo, as from intoxication* (Cinch., Coccul., Nux m., Nux v., Puls.). Congestion of blood to the head, with pulsation in it (Bell.). Aching above right frontal eminence when reading, with heat, then pinching in right temple. Pressing pains in the temples. *Cold sweat on forehead* (Verat. alb.).

Eyes.—Pupils dilated and insensible to light (*Bell.*). Pupils contracted (*Merc. cor.*, Phos., Phyt., Physos.). Eyes glassy, protruded, immovable (Amyl., Bell., Hyos., Stram.). Eyes half-closed, red, burning, hot and dry (Bell.). Sensation of dust in the eyes. Lids hang down as if paralyzed (*Caust.*, Coni., Gels.).

Ears.—Violent roaring in the ears (Acon., Bell., Cinch.). Acuteness of hearing (Coff., Coca).

Face.—*Face bloated, dark-red and hot* (Acon., Bell., Hyos., Stram.); *flushed; pale; earthy*. The face of a suckling was like that of an old man. Features distorted (Cic.,

OPIUM. 577

Cupr.). The lower lip and jaw hang down (Lyc.). Twitching in the corners of the mouth (Ign.).

Tongue.—Paralysis of the tongue, and difficult articulation (Caust., Dulc., Nux m., Nux v., Hyos., Gels.). Tongue: purple; black (Phos.); white (Ars., Bry., *Nux v.*, Puls., Sulph.). Dryness of the mouth (Ars., Bry., Dulc., Nux m., *Puls.*). Constriction in pharynx.

Throat.—Dryness of the throat (Apis, Ars., Nux m.). Inability to swallow from paralysis (Nux m.).

Stomach.—Loss of appetite (Alum., Ars., Cinch., Natr. mur., Phos., *Sulph.*). *Violent thirst* (*Acon., Ars., Bry.,* Nitr. ac., *Sulph.*). Hiccough; vomiting of food; of green substance (Iris, Podo.); of blood (Ham., Nux v., Podo., Stan.); of fæcal matter; with violent cutting colic and convulsions. Heaviness and pressure in the stomach (Ars., Bry.). Violent pain in the stomach; increased by pressure. Constriction in stomach; with constipation.

Abdomen.—Inactivity of the digestive organs (*Alum.*). Intestines sluggish, strongest purgatives lose their power. Abdomen hard, distended and sensitive to touch (*Acon., Bell.*). *Distension, but no power to expel contents.* Accumulation of much flatus, with rumbling in abdomen (Carb. v., *Lyc.*). Tension in hypogastrium, with pain on touch. °Incarcerated umbilical and inguinal hernia; fæcal vomit. *Violent griping and cutting in the abdomen* (*Coloc.*). *Pressive pain in the abdomen, as if the intestines would be cut to pieces.*

Stool and Anus.—Anus spasmodically closed during the colic, with difficult emission of flatus. Involuntary stool (*Arn.,* Carb. v., *Hyos.,* Rhus tox.); offensive (Ars.); °after fright (Gels.). Diarrhœic stools, whitish pasty, frothy, causing burning in anus (*Aloe, Ars., Sulph.*); black, fœtid (*Ars., Lept.*). *Constipation from inactivity of the bowels* (Alum., Camph., Plumb.); from spasmodic retention in small intestines. *Stool composed of hard, round, black balls* (*Alum.,* Kali carb., *Plumb.*); gray; crumbling. °Cholera infantum, with stupor, snoring, convulsions.

Urinary Organs.—Involuntary micturition (Bell., Hyos.). *Retention of urine from paralysis of fundus of bladder;* from spasm of sphincter; °from nursing after

37

passion of nurse. Desire to urinate, but inability; only after long exertion. Urine scanty, red, dark-brown, cloudy (Canth.).

Male Organs.—Increased sexual desire, with frequent erections and pollutions (*Phos.,* Nux v.).

Respiratory Organs.—Dry cough, with tickling and scraping in the larynx (*Rumex*); better from drink of water, with gaping, drowsiness (*Ant. tart.*), yet cannot sleep. *Deep snoring respiration, with open mouth. Frequent involuntary deep breathing; long and sighing respiration* Respiration irregular, slow and stertorous. °Laryngismus stridulus. Cough, with scanty, tenacious expectoration and rattling in the chest. Cough, with dyspnœa and blue face. °Cough, with profuse sweat on whole body.

Pulse.—*Full and slow* (*Digit.*), *with snoring;* slow and soft; small and weak (Ferr.); beat of heart and pulse cannot be felt; irregular.

Back.—Spasmodically curved, like an arch (Cic.).

Limbs.—Trembling of all the limbs, especially arms and hands °after fright. Numbness and sensation of swelling in hands and forearms. Spasmodic jerkings and numbness of limbs. Convulsive movements of limbs (Cic., Bell., Hyos.). *Coldness of the extremities* (Camph., Verat. alb.).

Generalities.—Twitching, trembling of head, arms and hands; now and then jerks of flexors; body cold; inclination to stupor; motion of body and uncovering of head relieves. Tetanic spasms; opisthotonos; begin with loud screams, foam at mouth, trembling of limbs, eyes half open, pupils dilated and insensible to light; face dark-red and hot (Hyos.); °from fright, anger, etc. *General insensibility of the nervous system; no reaction* (Carb. v.). Sensation diminished; afterwards reflex irritability. °Paralysis after apoplexia; in drunkards; in old people. °*Bed feels so hot she cannot lie on it.* Emaciation and debility.

Sleep.—*Great drowsiness, can hardly keep awake* (*Nux m.*). *Unrefreshing, soporous sleep* (Arn., Laur., Physos.), *with eyes half open and snoring* (Sulph.). *Sleepy, but cannot go to sleep* (Cham., Bell., Lach.). Restless, uneasy sleep; full of visions and imaginations. Whining in sleep. °Sleeplessness (Cimic., Coff.), with acuteness of hearing; clocks

OPIUM. 579

striking and cocks crowing at a great distance keep her awake.

Fever.—Body cool, head warm. *Cold limbs. Head hot,* cheeks red and burning. Whole body burning, even when bathed in sweat; wants to uncover; complains that bed is too hot. Cold perspiration over whole body, especially on the head and *forehead*.

Aggravation.—From heat; from brandy, wine; while perspiring; during and after sleep.

Amelioration.—From vomiting; from coffee, all symptoms except trembling, but they soon return.

Conditions.—Especially suitable for children and old persons; for drunkards.

Compare.—Acon., Ars., *Bell.*, Bry., Camph., *Can. ind.*, Carb. v., Coff., Digit., *Gels.*, Hyos., Lyc., Merc., *Nux v.*, Puls., Rhus tox., Sec. c., Stram., Sulph., Verat. alb.

Antidotes.—Bell., Coff., Coni., Camph., *Ipec.*, Merc., Nux v., Plumb., Vinum. To large doses: very strong Coffee; Camph., Bell., emetics; warm baths.

Opium Antidotes.—Ant. tart., Bell., Digit., Lach., Merc., Nux v., Strych., Plumb., Stram., Charcoal Vapors.

THERAPEUTICS.

A valuable remedy for ailments from fright (Acon., Gels.), or emotion after fright, fear of the fright still remaining—after-effects. An extremely valuable remedy in apoplexia, the symptoms agreeing, especially in drunkards. Paralysis of the brain. Cerebral hæmorrhage. Delirium tremens, especially old and oft-repeated cases, worse from the least quantity of liquor. Convulsions, as described in symptoms; especially from fright or anger; particularly in infants, especially after nurse has been frightened or very angry. Epilepsy. Lock jaw. Puerperal convulsions with coma, etc. Paralysis of tongue. Paralysis of pharynx. Colic, with great tympanitis, belching without relief, constipation. Intestinal obstruction, colicky pains, fæcal vomiting. A most valuable remedy in constipation resulting from inertia of the rectum and the entire intestinal tract; no inclination for stool; impacted fæces and incarcerated flatus; often after long-lasting and debilitating diseases from long-continued and habitual use of enemas. Ailments from lead in paints, pipes and otherwise; lead colic. According to Allen, Opium "has cured chronic catarrh and ulceration of the ileocæcal region, with persistent discharge of enormous quantities of flakes of mucus, constipation, fæcal stools completely enveloped in mucus, the indication being complete atony of the lower bowels and the accumulation of hard balls of fæces." Cholera infantum, especially after discharges have been suppressed, with stupor, snoring and convulsions. Has been found useful for retention of urine, especially when resulting from fright, or after parturition. Aphonia from fright. Laryngismus stridulus. Threatening paralysis of lungs. Bronchial catarrh. Hæmoptysis, especially in drunkards, chest hot, limbs cold, drowsy, with cough. Suppuration of the lungs, especially in drunkards; rattling and snoring respiration, blue face, etc. Amenorrhœa from fright. Threatening abortion from fright. Suppressed lochia from fright. Has been used in diphtheria, with characteristic respiration, etc. Sometimes indicated in typhoid types of fever, stupor, can scarcely be aroused; speechless; eyes half open; mild delirium or loud talking, fury, singing, desire to escape; the darker-red the face, the more it is indicated; impending cerebral paralysis from profound congestion. Puerperal fever, with stupor, etc.; offensive discharges. Intermittent fever, cold stage predominates; fever, with heat of the head and great drowsiness, the body burning hot even with a profuse sweat, which does not relieve the heat or drowsiness. Congestive chills with characteristic stupor, snoring respiration, hot sweat without relief, etc. Said to be useful in ailments from charcoal vapors.

ORIGANUM.

Synonyms.—Origanum Majorana. Origanum Vulgare. *Habitat.*—An indigenous perennial plant found growing in poor soils, along road-sides and in fields. *Preparation.*—Tincture from the fresh plant.

GENERAL ANALYSIS AND THERAPEUTICS.

Acts especially upon the generative organs, particularly of women, stimulating the seat of erotic impulses, and affecting the brain and nervous system just as excessive sexual excitement does. Its chief symptom is an *increased sexual desire, lascivious ideas and dreams*. It is used successfully for troubles arising from sexual irritation and onanism, especially in girls; leucorrhœa, with sexual irritation.

OSMIUM.

Synonym.—Osmium Tetroxide. An element. *Common name.*—Osmic Acid. *Preparation.* Triturations.

GENERAL ANALYSIS.

Through the cerebro-spinal system Osmium exerts its chief action on the respiratory tract and upon the kidneys, producing violent irritation and inflammation.

CHARACTERISTIC SYMPTOMS.

Mind.—Morose, irritable, impatient. Consciousness of mental weakness. Misplacement of words (Dulc., Plumb.). Disinclination for work.

Head.—Dull, heavy headache.

Eyes.—Sharp pain in orbit; lids spasmodically closed. Dimness of sight; letters run together, as from a fog (*Cycl.*, Phos., *Gels.*). Burning pain in eyes, with profuse lachrymation. Flame of candle surrounded by a bluish-green or yellow circle (*Phos.*); or a rainbow ring; at a distance the flame seems enveloped by dust or smoke.

Ears.—Ringing in right ear. Earache evenings; first right, then left ear.

Nose.—Coryza, with sneezing (Acon., Arg., Euphorb.). Burning irritation in nose. Nostrils sensitive to cold air (Hydras., Psor.). Sense of smell diminished.

Mouth.—Aching in jaws; pain in muscles of mastication. Tongue coated; edges rough; red stripe in middle. Copious salivation. Taste of blood; metallic (*Æsc., Coccul., Merc., Naja*).

Stomach.—Eructations; nausea; vomiting. Qualmishness and extreme discomfort, with dull pain and heaviness in pit of stomach.

Abdomen.—Distended and sensitive; much rumbling.
Stool and Anus.—Burning in anus during and after stool (Ars., Canth., *Iris*, Merc.). Diarrhœa. Constipation.
Urinary Organs.—Urine albuminous (*Merc. cor.*, Phos., Phyt., *Plumb.*). Strong-scented; dark-brown and scanty (Plumb.). Deposits bright-red sediment. °Bright's disease.
Male Organs.—Pain in testicles and spermatic cords (*Clem.*, Spong.). Violent erections.
Respiratory Organs.—Larynx, tickling, irritation to hawk and cough; sore pain; burning; rawness and scraping (Rhus tox., *Rumex*). Profuse secretion of mucus in air passages (*Ant. tart., Ipec., Phos., Stan.*). Stringy mucus, very difficult to loosen, has to swallow it (Kali bi.). Burning irritation in trachea. Hoarseness and pain in larynx; with cough and coryza. Hoarseness, worse from singing, and worse entering the house. Paroxysms of convulsive coughing (Coral. rub., Dros.). Dry, hacking cough. Bronchitis. Difficult respiration; tightness and oppression of the chest (Merc. cor., Phos.). Pain under sternum when coughing, extending to both sides of chest, with burning soreness, as if everything were raw; after long coughing, expectorates lumps of yellow, tenacious mucus.
Back.—Pressive pain in back and loins.
Generalities.—Great weakness and prostration. Cutting and pinching pains in limbs.
Skin.—Red spots on dorsum of hand. Copious exanthema on forearms, hands and cheeks. Red-brown papules, with desquamation, on arms. Small, pointed vesicles, surrounded by red areola. Itching, as from crawling of insects.
Compare.—Ars., Mang., Selen.

THERAPEUTICS.

Has been used but little clinically. Has been of benefit in acute laryngitis, bronchitis and pneumonia and in whooping cough with characteristic irritation in air passages, spasmodic cough, stringy mucus, with great and futile efforts to expectorate, etc. Has been used in supra and infra-orbital neuralgia, with lachrymation. Has actually cured glaucoma (Allen); is indicated by iridescent vision and severe pain around the eyes.

OXALICUM ACIDUM.

Synonym.—Hydrogen Oxalate. *Common name.*—Oxalic Acid. *Preparation.*—Triturations.

GENERAL ANALYSIS.

Acts powerfully upon the brain and spinal cord, exerting its special influence upon the motor nerve centers, paralyzing them and sometimes annihilating the functional power of the cerebro-spinal axis and destroying life very suddenly. It produces violent spasmodic conditions, especially of the muscles of the chest, and stiffness of the limbs, and also anæsthesia, neuralgia and paralytic symptoms. It also affects the respiratory mucous membrane, producing an inflammatory condition, and in large doses, by its irritating presence, causes violent inflammation of the mucous lining of the alimentary tract.

CHARACTERISTIC SYMPTOMS.

Mind.—Diminished power to concentrate ideas. Very much exhilarated; quicker thought and action (Coff.). As soon as she thinks about the pains they return (Baryt. c.).

Head.—Vertigo; swimming sensation on lying down. Sensation of emptiness in head; faint feeling, as if all the blood had left the brain. Dull, heavy headache in forehead and vertex. Compression in head, as if from a screw behind each ear.

Eyes.—Type blurs when reading. Vanishing of sight, with giddiness and sweat. Pains in both orbits; worse in left.

Nose.—Sneezing; watery coryza. °Red, shining swelling of right side of nose, beginning at the tip (Bell.); with pimples in nose.

Face.—Face pale and and livid. Feeling of heat in face. Feeling of fullness in face; face redder. Face covered with cold sweat (Tabac., Verat. alb.).

Mouth.—Gums bleed and are painful in spots. Small ulcers on gums. Tongue swollen, sensitive, red, dry, burning; swollen, with thick, white coating. Sour taste in mouth (Calc.

c., Mag. carb., Nux v.). Profuse secretion of saliva (*Iodi., Merc., Nitr. ac.*).

Throat.—Burning in throat and stomach. Rawness and scraping in throat; thick mucus accumulates. Difficult, painful swallowing.

Stomach.—Appetite increased; absent, with loss of taste. Thirst, with vertigo, loss of appetite, nausea, colic. Heartburn; worse, evenings. Empty or sour eructations; of tasteless wind, after each meal. Frequent hiccough (Ign., Hyos.). Nausea and frequent vomiting. Empty feeling, compelling one to eat. Violent pressive pain at pit of stomach. Burning at pit of stomach (Ars., *Colch.*, Merc. cor.). Stomach sensitive; slightest touch causes excruciating pain.

Abdomen.—Stitches in liver; relieved by a deep breath. Continuous pain in left hypochondrium, as if bruised; stitches. Colic about the navel (Coloc.); difficult emission of flatus. Burning and pain in abdomen.

Stool.—Constant involuntary stools. Stools: dark, muddy, copious; mucus and blood. °Diarrhœa as soon as one drinks coffee. °Lying down causes return of diarrhœa. Pressing and straining in rectum; tenesmus. Constipation.

Urinary Organs.—Pain in region of kidneys. Frequent and copious urination, which is clear, straw-colored; oxaluria. Burning in urethra, as from acrid drops. Pain in glans penis when urinating.

Male Organs.—Great increase of sexual desire. Emissions at night with lascivious dreams. Testicles feel heavy and contused; shooting along cords (Clem., Spong.).

Respiratory Organs.—Hoarseness and sensation of mucus in larynx during talking. Constant dry cough on violent exertion. Difficulty of breathing, with constrictive pain in larynx, and wheezing; oppression more toward right side; °angina pectoris. Spasmodic breathing. Paroxysms of short, hurried breathing, with intervals of ease. Sharp, shooting pains in left lung and heart, extending down to epigastrium; °angina pectoris. Dull, heavy, sore pain in chest.

Heart and Pulse.—Shooting pains about the heart. Heart in a continual fluttering palpitation. Pulse increased in frequency, almost imperceptible; with coldness, clammy sweat, etc. (*Tabac., Verat. alb.*).

Neck and Back.—Pain under point of scapula, between shoulders, extending to loins; bruised sensation, worse beneath tip of left scapula, with stiffness. Stitches from chest into scapulæ. Acute pain in back, gradually extending down the thighs, with great torture; seeks relief in change of posture. Weakness in loins and hips, extending down to lower extremities; back feels too weak to support the body.

Limbs.—Strange sensation of numbness in limbs. °Pains in rheumatic gout worse from sweets.

Upper Limbs.—Numbness of shoulders to tips of fingers. Sharp, lancinating pains in arms; °angina pectoris. Right wrist pains as if sprained; wants to stretch it; cannot hold anything. Hands feel heavy; cold, as if dead; fingers and nails livid; fingers twitching.

Lower Limbs.—Blueness, coldness, and almost complete immobility of the lower limbs. Numbness and tickling or pricking in thighs. Lameness and stiffness in lower limbs. Numbness and weariness in lower limbs, making it difficult to ascend stairs. Violent contracting pain in external tendon of left knee.

Generalities.—Peculiar numbness, approaching to palsy. Symptoms recur in paroxysms; intermit for hours or a day. *Pain in small circumscribed spots.* Jerking pains, like short stitches, *confined to small spots,* lasting only a few seconds.

Skin.—Sensation during shaving, as from chafing. Skin mottled in circular patches.

Sleep.—Yawning; sleepy during the day. awakens at night with palpitation.

Fever.—Chilliness, with sneezing. Shaking chill, with red face. Creeping chill up the spine. Heat from every exertion. Flushes of heat, with perspiration. Cold, clammy perspiration.

Aggravation.—All symptoms and pains reappear when thinking about them (Baryt. c.); from sugar, coffee, wine. Better in the open air (*Puls.*).

Compare.—Ars., Merc. cor.

Antidotes.—Chalk or Lime; Carbonate of Magnesia; Potash and Soda not available, since their oxalates are exceedingly poisonous. Sugar, Coffee and Wine disagree.

THERAPEUTICS.

Has been used chiefly in spinal diseases. Softening of the spine, with weakness and numbness about the loins and hips, extending down the legs, and numbness in the back. Spinal meningitis, intense inflammatory pains all through the back. Locomotor ataxia, with violent shooting pains down the limbs, dyspnœa and numbness, with symptoms of the drug. Paralysis from inflammation of the spinal cord, stiffness of limbs; paroxysms of dyspnœa. Acute spinal symptoms of this drug are characteristic and important. Spinal neuralgia from under joint of scapula to loins, sharp, lancinating pains. Has proved useful in angina pectoris, sharp, shooting pains about left lung and heart, dyspnœa, with forced expiration; back numb and weak, legs cold and powerless, etc. Palpitation after lying down at night. Congestion and inflammation localized at base of left lung. Neuralgia of spermatic cords, shooting pains. Sometimes useful in amenorrhœa, with spinal symptoms. Oxaluria, with characteristic symptoms of extremities. Rheumatic gout, pains worse from sweets. Diarrhœa immediately after drinking coffee. Dysentery. Gastro-enteritis. Gastralgia.

PAREIRA BRAVA.

Synonym.—Chondodendron. Tomentosum. *Natural order.*—Menispermaceæ. *Habitat.*—A plant supposed to be native of West Indies and South America. *Preparation.*—Tincture from the dried roots.

GENERAL ANALYSIS AND THERAPEUTICS.

Acts specifically upon the mucous lining of the genito-urinary passages, producing irritation and catarrhal inflammation, which has led to its successful use in the treatment of gonorrhœa, leucorrhœa and chronic inflammation of the bladder.

Its chief symptoms are *constant urging to urinate; violent pain in glans penis; straining; pain extorts screams; must get down on all fours to urinate; urine contains much viscid, thick, white mucus, or deposits a red sand.* The urine has a strong ammoniacal odor. Frequently there are pains down the thighs, during the efforts to urinate.

Compare.—Acon., Berb., Can. sat., Chim., Canth., Hydrangea arb., Urva ursi.

PARIS QUADRIFOLIA.

Natural order.—Liliaceæ. *Common names.*—Herb Paris. Fox Grape. True Love. *Habitat.*—A plant growing in Europe, in wet woods and thickets. *Preparation.*—Tincture from the entire fresh plant.

GENERAL ANALYSIS.

Acts upon the cerebro-spinal system, causing neuralgic pains and other symptoms of nerve irritation. Its chief local action is upon the respiratory tract.

CHARACTERISTIC SYMPTOMS.

Mind.—Loquacious mania (*Lach.*); foolish talk and silly actions.

Head.—Vertigo and dullness in the head. Piercing and single stitches in the head; in temples; then weight on forehead, worse from stooping. Constrictive pressure in forehead and temples; brain, eyes and skin feel tense, and the bones scraped sore; worse from motion, excitement or using the eyes; worse in evening. Pressive pain in right temporal region, relieved by pressure of the hand. Bruised pain in left parietal bone on touch.

Eyes.—Feel too large or swollen, and orbits too large (Carls., Phos. ac., Plumb.). °*Eyes feel as if projecting with a sensation as if a thread were tightly drawn through the eyeball, and backward, into the middle of the brain, very painful;* sight weak; stitches through middle of eye. Jerking and twitching of right upper lid (Agar.).

Ears.—Sudden pain in ears, as if forced apart by a wedge. Ringing in left ear.

PARIS QUADRIFOLIA.

Nose.—Red and greenish mucus blown from the nose. Alternate fluent and stopped coryza (Amm. carb., Natr. ars., *Nux v.*).

Face.—Tetter around the mouth. Vesicles on surface of lower lip.

Mouth.—Tongue dry, rough, and coated white; feels too large. Dryness of mouth in morning. Profuse tart saliva.

Throat.—Sore throat, as if a ball were lodged in it. Much mucus in fauces, causes hawking.

Stomach.—Hiccough, after eating (Bry., Ign., Hyos.); eructations. Heaviness in stomach, as from a stone (*Ars., Bry., Nux v., Puls.*); better from eructations. Weak, slow digestion.

Abdomen.—Rumbling and rolling in abdomen (Aloe, *Carb. v.*, Cinch., *Lyc.*); cutting, griping pains.

Stool.—Diarrhœa; stools smell like putrid meat.

Urinary Organs.—Burning and stinging in urethra when sitting. Sticking in forepart of urethra. Frequent micturition, with burning. Dark-red urine, with red sediment, and a greasy-looking pellicle on surface; acrid, excoriating.

Respiratory Organs.—Periodical, painless hoarseness. Hoarseness, voice feeble, continuous hawking of mucus and burning in larynx. Expectoration of greenish, viscid mucus. Oppression, with desire to draw a long breath. Constant hawking and gagging from tenacious mucus in larynx and trachea. Stitches in the chest (*Bry., Kali c.*).

Heart and Pulse.—Palpitation during rest and motion; in evening. Pulse full but slow.

Neck and Back.—*Nape of neck weary, as if a great weight were lying on it.* Neck feels stiff and swollen on turning it. Stitches between the scapulæ.

Limbs.—Stinging pains in limbs. All joints painful on motion. Icy-cold feet (Sil., Verat. alb.); at night in bed. Paralytic pain in limbs. Fingers feel asleep. Stitches in all the limbs. Heaviness in all the limbs. Contractive pressure in joints.

Skin.—Papular eruptions, especially face and lips. Skin sore; crawling sensations.

Sleep.—Restless, broken sleep, with many dreams. Yawning and sleepiness

PETROLEUM.

Fever.—Chilliness, mostly toward evening. Coldness of right side; left side natural. Chilliness and goose-flesh, yawning and cold feet. Heat descending back from neck (reverse, Phos.). Heat and sweat of upper part of body. Sweat in morning, on waking, attended with frequent biting itching.
Compare.—Led., Lyc., Rhus tox.
Antidote.—Coff.

THERAPEUTICS.

Perhaps the most common use of this not commonly used drug is in neuralgic headache when the eyes feel as if projecting, and a painful sensation, as if a thread were drawing through the eye backwards into the middle of the brain. Facial neuralgia, hot stitches in left malar bone, which is very sore. Neuralgia in left chest extending into arm, which becomes stiff; nape of neck weary, as if a great weight were lying on it. Has also been successfully used in spinal neuralgia. Neuralgia of coccyx. Catarrhal laryngitis, green viscid mucus, painless hoarseness. Laryngo-tracheitis, much tenacious mucus, causing constant hawking and gagging.

PETROLEUM.

Synonyms.—Oleum Petræ. Naptha Montana. *Common names.*—Rock Oil. Coal Oil. *Preparation.*—A tincture is prepared by dissolving one part of the crude oil in ninety-nine parts of Alcohol, which corresponds to the 2x dilution.

GENERAL ANALYSIS.

Acts especially upon the skin and mucous membranes, producing irritation and the usual secondary conditions, as indicated in the following pathogenesis. Allen says the action is "very complex and not easily defined."

CHARACTERISTIC SYMPTOMS.

Mind.—Violent, excitable, irritable, easily offended (Nux v.). Quarrelsome. Great fearfulness; easily frightened (Nux v., Op.). Loss of consciousness. Very forgetful; disinclined to think. *Delirium, thinks another person is* *alongside of him,* °or that he is double, or one limb is double.

Head.—Vertigo on stooping or on rising (Bell.) Confusion after eating a little. Dullness and heaviness of the head; as if enveloped in a fog. Headache from anger, or after fasting in the morning. Dull, pressive frontal headache. Heavy headache in the morning. °Neuralgic headache, beginning in occiput and extending forward. °Occipital headache extending to vertex, with vertigo. Stiffness of neck, swelling of muscles; rapid motion of the hands seems to relieve. °Vertigo in the occiput, with general feeling of numbness, stiffness and nausea. °Occipital headache, with nausea, especially in seasickness. *Pressure and heaviness, like lead, in occiput.* Dull, pulsating pain in the occiput. Pinching in occiput. Falling off of the hair (*Graph., Nitr. ac., Phos., Sep.*). Moist eczema, worse on occiput (Lyc., Sep.). Moist, itching eczema; sore after scratching (*Graph., Lyc., Merc.*).

Eyes.—Burning and pressure in the eyes and on exerting them dimness. Conjunctivitis and blepharadenitis. Inflamed swelling in inner canthus, like an incipient lachrymal fistula, with dryness of right side of nose. Inflammation, with itching and stitches in the eyes. Weakness of vision; veil before the eyes (Caust., *Puls*). Itching of the lids; he is obliged to rub them.

Ears.—Inflammation and painful swelling of meatus auditorius. Hardness of hearing. Roaring, ringing and cracking in the ears (Bell., Cinch.). Redness behind the ears, with rawness, soreness and moisture. Eruption on outer ear.

Nose.—Bleeding of the nose (Acon., Bell., Bry., Ham.). Ulcerated nostrils; and stopped catarrh. Much mucus in nose. Itching on tip of nose.

Face.—Pale. Papular eruption at corners of mouth.

Mouth.—Swelling of the gums. Pustule above a hollow tooth, like a fistula. Painful soreness on chewing. Tongue coated white (*Ant. crud., Bry., Nux v., Puls.*). Bad odor from the mouth (Hep. s., Iodi., *Nitr. ac., Merc., Nux v.*). Taste slimy, sour, bitter (*Ars., Bry., Puls.*). Accumulation of mucus in the mouth (Iodi., *Merc.*).

Throat.—Swelling of the submaxillary glands (Baryt. c., Calc. c.,

Natr. carb., Rhus tox.). Rawness in pharynx on swallowing. Tickling on swallowing extending to the ear. Dryness and burning in pharynx.

Stomach.—Ravenous hunger, but speedily satisfied after a stool. Violent thirst for beer (Coccul., Puls.). Hot, sharp, sour eructations, tasting like bad eggs (Arn.). Heartburn toward evening. *Incessant nausea and qualmishness in the morning, with accumulation of water in the mouth;* °from motion of carriage or boat (*Coccul.*, Nux m.). Violent vomiting (*Ant. tart., Ipec.*). Feeling of great emptiness in stomach (Hydras., *Ign., Sep.*, Sulph.). Heaviness and pressure in stomach (Nux m.).

Abdomen.—Distension. Violent, cutting colic, with nausea, retching and diarrhœa; as from taking cold; evenings: °colic better from bending double (Coloc.).

Stool and Anus.—In anus burning itching; pressure. Weakness of rectum. Diarrhœa, preceded by colic, only during the day. Stools difficult and hard; slimy, profuse mucus; bloody mucus; violent, involuntary.

Urinary Organs.—Constant dribbling of urine after micturition (Caust., Stram.). Involuntary micturition. Frequent, scanty urination. Discharge of mucus with the urine. Burning pain in the urethra. Urine bloody and turbid; offensive; it deposits a red, slimy sand that adheres tightly to vessel; urine contains albumen, hyalin and granular casts; covered with a glistening film and with red sediment.

Male Organs.—Reddish eruption on glans, with itching. Itching and moisture on scrotum (Sil.).

Female Organs.—Itching, soreness and moisture of external parts. Menses too early; the discharge causes itching. The nipples itch, and have a mealy coating.

Respiratory Organs.—Hoarseness (*Carb. v., Caust., Phos., Sulph.*). Dry cough at night (*Coni., Hyos., Puls., Sulph.*). Oppression of the chest at night.

Heart.—°Feeling of coldness about the heart (Graph., Kali nit., Natr. m.).

Neck and Back.—Heaviness and pain in nape of neck. Pain in the back and loins. Painful drawing extending from nape to occiput. Coccyx painful on sitting.

Upper Limbs.—Great weakness in the arms. Bruised pain in finger nails when touched. *Tips of fingers rough, cracked, fissured, with sticking, cutting pains.* Hands cracked and rough. °Salt-rheum, red, raw, burning; moist or covered with thick crusts.

Lower Limbs.—Itching, burning, moist eruption on legs. Stiffness in thighs on walking, with heaviness. Stiffness in knees, legs and ankles. Heel painfully swollen and red, with stitches; blisters; chilblains (Agar., Nitr. ac., Zinc.). Burning and stitching in corns. Eruption between the toes (Calc. c., Camph., Nux v., Nitr. ac., Sep.). Profuse perspiration on feet (Sil.). °Fœtid perspiration of the feet with tenderness. Cramp in calves, thighs and feet all day. Cramp in the soles at night (Sulph.).

Generalities.—Limbs go to sleep and become stiff. Cracking and arthritic stiffness in joints. Aversion to open air (Aur., Coccul., Nux v., Sep., Sil.). Takes cold easily. Weakness in morning in bed.

Skin.—Unhealthy skin; small wounds ulcerate and spread (Borax, Cham., *Hep. s.*, Graph., *Sil.*, *Sulph.*). Chronic moist eczema; parts seem excoriated (Graph.). Painful sensitiveness of skin of whole body; clothing painful (Bell.). Ulcers, with stinging pain and proud flesh (Carb. v., Nitr., ac.); often deep ulcers, with raised edges.

Aggravation.—°Before or during a thunder storm; °from riding in a carriage or ship.

Amelioration.—At noon; °in the open air.

Compare.—Bell., Bry., Calc. c., Cham., Coccul., Colch., *Graph.*, Ign., *Lyc.*, Nux v., Phos., *Puls.*, Rhus tox., *Sep.*, Sil., *Sulph.*, Tabac.

Antidotes.—Coccul., Nux v.

Petroleum Antidote.—Lead Poisoning.

THERAPEUTICS.

The chief use of Petroleum is in the treatment of diseases of the skin, especially eczema and herpes, upon any part of the body, but more especially in and about the ears, on the occiput and on the hands. In eczema there is a raw, moist surface over which thick scabs form, or the eczema may first appear as a vesicular eruption, forming a thick crust and oozing pus.

PETROLEUM. 593

The herpetic conditions calling for Petroleum are very important and often met with. The affected part becomes fiery-red and almost entirely raw and oozing a thick gelatinous fluid, with violent itching and burning. This is most liable to attack the perineum and scrotum. Herpes zoster. An important condition of the skin indicating Petroleum, and which is often present with eczematous eruptions, is where the skin is dry, rough and chapped, and frequently, especially on the tips of the fingers, bleeding fissures form which are very sore, always worse in cold weather. The skin is unhealthy, slight wounds ulcerate and spread. Ulcers with stinging pains and proud flesh. Intertrigo. Psoriasis of the hands. Has been found useful in the eruption of secondary syphilis. Blepharitis marginalis. Inflammation of the lachrymal canal when suppuration has commenced and a fistula has formed. Catarrh of the middle ear. Often valuable in chronic nasal catarrh and ozœna where scabs and purulent mucus are discharged, and the posterior nares obstructed, nose sore and nostrils cracked. Tendency to the formation of dental fistula. Catarrhal pharyngitis, rawness on swallowing, with pain and tickling which extends along the Eustachian tube to the ears. Has been found useful in the morning sickness of pregnancy. Sea-sickness. Acid dyspepsia with nausea and attacks of vertigo, better after eating. Gastralgia, with sharp, cutting pains and feeling of great emptiness in stomach. Hæmorrhoids and fissures in anus. Diarrhœa, containing undigested food; also with other symptoms described in pathogenesis; from taking cold; from eating cabbage or saur-kraut, with offensive stools, nausea and offensive eructations. Catarrh of the bladder. Atony of the bladder, dribbling after urination. Hæmaturia. Chronic Bright's disease. Sprains of joints, especially in old rheumatic patients. Rheumatism with great stiffness of the joints, especially knees and neck; cracking sounds when moving the head, due to roughness of the muscular fiber. A popular domestic remedy in rheumatism (externally), in which it undoubtedly possesses curative virtues not yet understood. Has cured intermittent fever with the characteristic occipital headache. Is given in typhoid fever and other low fevers, when the patient imagines that another person lies alongside of her, or that she is double, or that one limb is double (Bapt.). In childbed the patient imagined that there were two sick babies in bed with her, and that she could not take care of both.

PETROSELINUM.

Synonym.—Apium Petroselinum. Petroselinum Salivum. *Natural order.*—Umbelliferæ. *Common name.*—Parsely. *Habitat.*—A plant native of Southern Europe, cultivated as a house-plant. *Preparation.*—Tincture from the fresh plant.

GENERAL ANALYSIS.

Acts decidedly upon the urethral mucous membrane, producing a considerable degree of irritation and inflammation, and has been used accordingly in subacute gonorrhœa and gleet.

CHARACTERISTIC SYMPTOMS.

Urinary and Sexual Organs.—Discharge of a milky fluid from the urethra. Orifice of urethra agglutinated with mucus. Yellow discharge from the urethra (*Hydras., Puls.*). Burning in navicular fossa while urinating. *Drawing and sticking in navicular fossa, changing to a cutting biting after urination* (Can. sat.). Creeping and crawling throughout whole length of urethra. Pressure just behind navicular fossa. Frequent voluptuous tickling in navicular fossa. Frequent desire to urinate, caused by crawling stitch behind navicular fossa. Priapismus, with curvature of penis. Profuse emission toward morning.

Compare.—Canth., Can. sat., Copaib.

THERAPEUTICS.

Subacute gonorrhœa and gleet, especially with the characteristic localization of the sensations in the navicular fossa.

PHOSPHORICUM ACIDUM.

Common name.—Glacial Phosphoric Acid. *Preparation.*—
One part of the purified Glacial Phosphoric Acid is dissolved in ninety parts of distilled water, and then ten parts of Alcohol are added to make the 2x dilution. The 3x dilution is prepared with dilute Alcohol. Subsequent dilutions with Alcohol.

GENERAL ANALYSIS.

The chief sphere of action of Phosphoric Acid is upon the nervous system, in which, from waste of nerve tissue or from depression, it produces debility without erethism (with erethism, Cinchona), giving rise to conditions simulating those which result from continued grief, over-exertion of mind or body, sexual excess, etc. Through this influence its chief local effects are upon the kidneys and male sexual organs, and next upon the bones and skin, as indicated by its pathogenesis.

CHARACTERISTIC SYMPTOMS.

Mind.—Weakness of memory (*Anac.*, Agn., Ambr., Kreos., Lach., *Merc.*, Natr. mur., Nux m.). *Quiet; perfectly indifferent* (Berb., Selen., Sep.); difficult comprehension; imbecility. Ideas lost and mind weak. *Incapacity for thought* (Æth., Cimic., Gels., *Nux v.*). *Disinclination to talk; answers questions reluctantly* (Agar., Phos.). Cannot find the right word when talking. Homesickness (Caps., Hell.), with inclination to weep. Quiet delirium, with stupefaction and dullness of the head (Bell., Rhus tox., Phos.).

Head.—Vertigo; in the morning; towards evening, when standing and walking; and head sinks backward and forward. Confusion and dullness of the head. Pressure as from a weight in the head, or as if the vertex had been beaten. Aching with tingling in the head. Violent pressure in the forehead, in the morning on waking. Headache forces one to lie down, and is insupportably aggravated by least shaking or noise (*Bell.*). *Bones in the skull feel as if some one had scraped the swollen and tender periosteum with a* knife. °Hair turns gray early (Lyc.), or flaxen; *falls off, especially after grief or sorrow.* Itching of the scalp (Calc. c., Carb. an., Sulph.).

Eyes.—Pressure in the eyes, as if the eyeballs were too large (Carls., Paris, Plumb., *Spig.*). Agglutination, mornings. Yellow spots on the white of the eyes. Dilated pupils (Bell., *Hyos., Stram.*).

Ears.—Every sound re-echoes loudly in the ears (*Caust.*, Merc., Phos.). Intolerance of noise, especially music (Acon., Ambr.). *Roaring in the ears, with difficult hearing* (Calc. c., Merc., Sec., *Sulph.*). Spasmodic drawing pain in the ear.

Nose.—Bleeding of the nose, dark blood (Croc., Ham.).

Face.—Paleness of the face. Large pimples on the face.

Mouth.—°Red streak in middle of tongue, widens in front. °Teeth become yellow. °Degeneration of the gums, which bleed easily. °Speech difficult, tongue swollen. Dryness of tongue, palate and whole mouth, without thirst (Apis, *Nux m.*, Puls.). °Lips dry and cracked, with brownish crusts, in fever. °*Bites side of tongue involuntarily; also at night.*

Throat.—Sticking in throat on swallowing food.

Stomach.—Loss of appetite (Alum., Ars., *Cinch.*, Natr. mur., *Sulph.*). Unquenchable thirst (Acon., *Ars., Bry.*, Nitr. ac.). Longs for something refreshing and juicy (Phos.). Sour or acrid eructations (*Carb. v.*, Nux v., *Phos., Puls., Sulph.*). Aversion to coffee (Lyc.); desire for milk and beer (Coccul., Puls.). °Sensitiveness in lower cæcal region. Pressure in the stomach, as from a weight, after every meal (Acon., Ars., *Bry., Nux v.*, Puls., Sep.). Pressive pain in stomach, from touching pit of stomach.

Abdomen.—*Meteoristic distension of the abdomen* (*Acon.*); rumbling and gurgling. °General tympanitis with enlarged spleen. Pressure in the hypogastrium.

Stool.—*Diarrhœa not debilitating* (*Puls.*), though of long continuance (reverse, Ars., Cinch., Phos., Sec.). *Involuntary stools*, with the emission of flatus (*Aloe*). *Stool thin, whitish-gray* (Phos.); yellowish and very offensive (Asaf.); pasty, *involuntary*, bright-yellow.

Urinary Organs.—°*Urine like milk* (Stil.), even coagulating. Urine passed in large quantities (Acet. ac., Ascl. c., Eupat.

purp., Physos.), especially at night (Ambr., Amm. mur.), profuse, watery, pale, flowing freely; deposits a sediment.

Male Organs.—Erections in the morning in bed; in morning when standing. *Frequent, profuse and debilitating emissions* (Cinch.). Emissions when pressing at stool. Emissions at night without erections. Weakness of sexual organs (Agar., Agn., Baryt. c., Coni., Phos., Sulph.), with onanism and little sexual desire. Exhaustion after coition; also after pollutions (Agar., *Cinch.*, Kali c., *Staph.*). Swelling of left testicle.

Female Organs—.°Menses too early and too long; too copious: blood dark. °*Pain in the liver during menstruation.* Profuse, yellow leucorrhœa, mostly after the menses, with itching. °*Meteoristic distension of the uterus.*

Respiratory Organs.—Hoarseness and roughness in the throat (*Phos.*, *Carb. v.*, *Nux v.*). Capillary bronchitis, worse evenings, with fever, dyspnœa, pain under sternum, then violent sneezing, thirst and coryza, profuse purulent secretions. *Dry cough, caused by tickling low down in the chest;* worse evenings after lying down. Cough in morning, with yellow expectoration. Cough, with copious expectoration; with expectoration of herby taste and odor. Salty expectoration in the morning. Oppressed, difficult respiration. *Pain in the chest, as from weakness* (*Stan.*).

Heart.—°Palpitation in young persons growing too fast; after onanism. Pulse irregular, intermittent.

Back.—Boring pain between the scapulæ. Burning pain in a spot above small of back.

Limbs.—Bruised pain in all the joints in the morning, and in the arms and legs. Burning, gnawing, tearing pains in the bones of the extremities. °Weakness of extremities after loss of fluids (Calc. c., *Cinch.*, Phos.).

Generalities.—*Great weakness and prostration, especially in the morning.* Disinclination to do anything (Cinch., Nux v.). °Swelling and sponginess of the bones (Asaf., Hep. s.). °Painless swellings of glands (Iodi.). Periosteal inflammation (Staph.), with burning, gnawing, tearing pains. Bruised sensation in all joints in morning; in hips, arms, thighs and nape, as from growing pains. Pains at night, as if bones were being scraped with a knife (Cinch.); °after contusions. Constant disposition to move (**Acon., Rhus tox.**).

Skin.—Formication of the whole body. Herpes dry or humid, squamous; °variola.

Sleep.—Great drowsiness and apathy. Sleeps in the evening. Sleeplessness after midnight. Cannot arouse in the morning. *Lascivious dreams* (**Sil.**), *with emissions*.

Fever.—Chills with shuddering and shaking, always in the evening; more internal shivering than external coldness (*Eupat.*); with coldness in hands and tips of fingers. Heat over the whole body in the evening. Internal heat, without being hot to the touch. Profuse sweat during the night and in the morning (**Calc. c., Cinch., Merc., Sil.,** Sulph. ac.). Fever heat, almost depriving one of consciousness.

Aggravation.—At rest, at night; from uncovering; from warm food; from coffee.

Amelioration.—General relief of pains by motion, sometimes by pressure.

Conditions.—Especially suitable for young people who are growing too fast.

Compare.—*The Mineral acids.* Fluoric acid, Picric acid Asaf., Anac., Ars., Bell., Calc. c., *Cinch.,* Coni., *Ign.,* Lyc., Merc., *Phos.,* Puls., Rhus tox., *Sep., Sil.,* Staph., Sulph., Verat. alb., *Phos. ac.* follows Cinch. (sweat, diarrhœa and debility), Nux v. in fainting after a meal, while after it comes Ferr., Rhus tox., Verat. alb

Antidotes.—Camph., Coff.

THERAPEUTICS.

Phosphoric acid represents a mental and physical weakness and torpidity of a nature found in no other drug. It is especially useful in neurasthenia, or nervous debility. This may have resulted in young people, in whom the drug is most often useful, from growing too rapidly, the physical system developing at the expense of the nervous and mental, or it may result as a remote effect from depressing emotional causes, such as grief, sorrow, homesickness or disappointed love, but more often the neurasthenia is of sexual origin, and results from long-continued sexual excesses or onanism. The patient has involuntary emissions during sleep, or after urinating or straining at stool

Is greatly exhausted therefrom, and has vertigo, weakness of the back and limbs, mental torpidity, brain fag, etc. The sexual powers are so weakened that erections are deficient; during an embrace emissions take place too soon, and after coition the patient is greatly exhausted, with symptoms as above stated, and burning in the spine. It is unquestionably the chief remedy in spermatorrhœa and sexual neurasthenia. It has also been used for swollen and tender testicles. Herpes preputialis with tingling. Sycotic excrescences. Fig warts complicated with chancre. In women it has been useful for menorrhagia of dark blood, with great weakness; debility from long-continued nursing; leucorrhœa; meteoristic distension of the uterus. In all nervous diseases the urine is loaded with phosphates, and there is generally aching in the small of the back. Frequently the hair turns gray early, and falls out after the emotional causes above named. The drug causes polyuria, and is the chief remedy in diabetes insipidus, and is unquestionably curative in diabetes mellitus, as the experience of the author and many others abundantly testify. Catarrh of the bladder. The drug may be useful in chorea and hysteria, with characteristic weakness and mental symptoms. The peculiar mental apathy of Phos. ac. with its prostration, involuntary stools, nosebleed, etc., has led to its frequent use in typhoid and other low forms of fever. A clinical symptom is a red streak in the center of the tongue, which widens in front, the urine often looks milky, contains albumen, and decomposes rapidly, and the abdomen is tympanitic. It does not reach the very profound low types of fever, such as call for Ars. or Lach. or even Rhus tox. Has often proved useful in intermittent fever, probably not of malarial origin. Acid dyspepsia (see stomach symptoms). Chronic diarrhœa, painless, not debilitating. Painless diarrhœa during cholera time (Phos.). Sometimes useful in laryngitis, tracheitis and bronchitis; cough arising from tickling low down in the chest, worse in the evening after lying down; expectoration, mostly in the morning, tasting salty. Capillary bronchitis (see symptoms). Phthisis, with great weakness in chest (Stan.). Nervous palpitation of the heart, from causes previously named. Spinal anæmia from sexual excesses or onanism. Has proved palliative in caries of the lumbar vertebræ. Swelling and sponginess of bones. Caries (not necrosis). Periostitis.

oppression. Heaviness in the chest, as if a weight were lying on it (*Ferr.*, Nux v.). Stitches in the chest (*Acon., Bry., Kali c.*), especially on left side (Sep., Stram.). Stitches through lungs, worse on deep inspiration, in various parts. *Suffocative constriction of the chest;* at night. Burning, soreness and tension in chest. *Inflammation of the lungs; hepatization; especially of lower half of right lung,* later part of period of deposit, and early part of that of absorption. Suppuration. Cavities. Tubercles, with hectic fever. *All symptoms worse when lying on left side.* Yellow spots on chest (brown spots, Sep.).

Heart and Pulse.—*Violent palpitation,* with anxiety, evenings and mornings in bed; while lying on left side (Natr. carb., Natr. mur.); on slight motion. Blowing sounds of the heart. Pressure in middle of sternum and about the heart. Pulse rapid, full and hard; small, weak, easily compressed.

Neck and Back.—Stiffness in nape of neck (Kali c., Lach., Rhus tox.). Weakness in back, as if crushed, then weakness in limbs, and trembling on least exertion. *Sensitiveness of spinous processes of dorsal vertebræ to pressure* (Agar.). Softening of the spine. *Burning pain between the scapulæ.* Throbbing pain in a small spot between shoulder blades. Pain in lumbar region.

Limbs.—*Weakness in all the limbs, as if paralyzed;* especially in joints, trembling from every exertion. Swelling of hands and feet. Bruised pain in limbs. Extremities, especially hands and feet, heavy as lead.

Upper Limbs.—Tearing pain in left shoulder, worse at night in bed. Stiffness in morning on washing, with pressure. *Arms and hands become numb;* fall asleep. Trembling of the hands (Agar., Calc. c.). Fingers drawn bent at times, as from cramp. Fingers, especially tips, feel numb and insensible. Motor paralysis of fingers.

Lower Limbs.—Uneasiness, weakness, worse on ascending steps, with heaviness. Pain in right hip-joint. Suppurative pain in nates on sitting long. Bruised pain in periosteum of tibia. *Gangrenous periostitis of tibia, with fever; the periosteum peeled off as far as the knee, leaving the bone rough.* Weariness and heaviness of the legs and feet. Paralytic feeling in feet. Pain in knee drawing to feet.

PHOSPHORUS. 601

tracts. The special action of Phosphorus on each of the separate tissues and organs of the body may only be studied in the careful provings which Hahnemann and his immediate followers have left us.

CHARACTERISTIC SYMPTOMS.

Mind.—*Stupor, low muttering delirium* (Phos. ac., Rhus tox.); grasping at flocks (Bell., *Hyos., Stram.*); loquacious (Hyos.). Thinks he is several pieces, and cannot adjust the fragments (Bapt., Petrol.). *Stupor from which he could be aroused for a moment only to lapse back into a muttering lethargy; and forgetfulness. Great apathy; very sluggish; dislike to talk; answers slowly or not at all* (*Merc., Phos. ac.*). Great indifference to everything (Berb., Carb. v., Cinch., Phos. ac., Selen.). Alternations of hysterical laughing and weeping (Acon., Ign., Nux m.). Tender mood, weary of life. Sad, apprehensive, depressed; filled with gloomy forebodings (Ign., Natr. mur., Plat., *Puls.*). *Anxious, apprehensive. Great anxiety* and restlessness (Acon., Ars., Bell.), especially when alone or during a thunder storm. Nervous, fearful (Acon., Cinch., Ign.), especially in the evening (Calc. c., Rhus tox.). Very irritable and fretful mood (Bry., Nux v.). *Great indisposition to mental or physical exertion* (Nux v., Sep., Sulph.). *Inability to think; ideas slow; cannot keep the mind on any particular subject* (Gels., Nux v., Phos. ac.).

Head.—*Vertigo, with heaviness and pain in head, as if he had been lying with the head too low.* Staggers while walking (Nux m.); *after rising from bed* (*Bry.*, Cham., Lyc., Picr. ac.); or from a seat (*Bry.*, Kali bi.); worse mornings (Alum., Nitr. ac.). *Great dullness of the head;* confused and heavy, with some vertigo. Weakness in head, could not endure sound of a piano. Congestion to the head (Acon., Bell., Glon.). Dull, pressive, frontal headache, extending to the eyes and root of nose (Acon., Bapt., Kali bi., Merc. iod.). Throbbing pain in the temples. Stupefying pain in the vertex. °Sensation of coldness in cerebellum, with sensation of stiffness in the brain. Pulsations, sticking and burning in the brain: the heat enters the head from the spine (reverse, Paris). °Sensation of heavy pressure on the top of the head. *The brain always feels tired, as if he could not get it rested. *Shocks in the head following a mental strain. Sensation, as if the skin of the forehead were too tight (Caust.). Violent itching of the scalp (Caust.): with copious dandruff (Canth., Mez.). Falling out of the hair (*Graph., Nitr. ac., Sep., Sulph.*): the roots seem dry; in large bunches: bald spots above the ear.

Eyes—Pupils contracted (Merc. cor., Op., Phyt., *Physos.*): dilated. Eyes give out while reading (Myrica, *Ruta, Sep.*). Distant objects appear to be covered by a smoke or mist (*Gels., Lyc., Natr. mur., Sil.*). Sees better in the morning, in twilight, *or by shading the eyes with the hand.* As if a black veil were before the eyes. *Green halo around the candle* (Osm.: red halo, Bell.). *Black floating points;* sparks, spots and flickering before the eyes (Agar., Bell., Cycl., Merc., Sep., *Sulph.*). Œdema of the lids and about the eyes (*Ars., Apis,* Natr. ars., Rhus tox.). Twitching of left lids and external canthus. Frequent itching in the eyes.

Ears.—*Difficult hearing, especially of the human voice* (Sil.). Sounds re-echo in the ears (*Caust.,* Merc., Phos. ac.). Feeling as if something were in front of the ears. Roaring ringing in the ears. Aching. Tickling. Itching.

Nose.—*Nose swollen and painful to touch* (Alum., *Nitr. ac.,* Rhus tox.). *Internal nose swollen, dry,* and stopped up; ulcerated: scabs on margins of nostrils (Alum., Calc. c., Graph., Lyc., Merc., Sulph.). *Polypus of the nose* (Calc. c., Mar. ver.): bleeding easily. Frequent sneezing (Acon., Gels., Sang.). Greenish-yellow discharge from the nose (Kali bi.): bloody, purulent mucus. *Frequent blowing of blood from the nose;* profuse nosebleed (Acon., Ham.). *Nose bleeding.* Coryza; with inflammation of the throat (Merc.), and dullness of the head; fluent and dry alternating (Alum., Nux v., Sil.). Over-sensitive smell (Acon., Agar., Bell., Colch., *Graph.,* Hep. s., Lyc., Sulph.): especially with headache.

Face.—Face red, pale, sunken, earthy (Natr. carb.; sickly yellow (Sep.); icteric (Chel.); swollen, puffy (Rhus tox.). Eyes sunken with blue rings around (Cinch., Kali iod., Sec., Sulph.). Cheeks hot; one or the other. (Œdema of the lids and around the eyes (*Apis*). Tension of the skin of the face. Tearing, darting pains in bones of the face, temples and jaw. Lips dry and parched, swollen (Bry.). Crack in middle of lower lip. Necrosis of the lower jaw, rarely of the upper.

Mouth.—Tearing, stinging pains in teeth. Gums separated from the teeth, and bleed easily (Arg. nit., Carb. an., Carb. v.), especially from touch (*Merc., Nitr. ac.*); painfully sensitive (Carb. an., Merc.). °Toothache from having the hands in cold water. Tongue swollen, dry and black (*Op.*, Verat. alb.), chalky white; dry and white; dry and red (Rhus tox.); dry and brown center (Bapt., Plumb.); coated yellow (*Chel.*, Cinch.). Dryness of the mouth and throat (*Ars., Bry., Nux m., Puls.*). Bitter taste in the mouth, sour, after milk. Bloody erosions on inner surface of cheeks. Saliva increased, *watery*, tasting saltish (Ant. crud., *Merc. cor.*, Sulph.); or sweetish (*Plumb., Puls.*). Difficult articulation (*Bell., Gels.*, Stram.); speech slow.

Throat.—Dryness of the throat day and night. Tonsils swollen. Hawking of cool mucus in the morning. Roughness and scraping in the throat; worse toward evening (Amm. carb., *Carb. v., Caust., Puls.*, Rumex).

Stomach.—Ravenous hunger, especially at night; feels faint. Loss of appetite (Alum., Ars., *Cinch.*, Natr. mur., Op.). Longing for acids and spicy things (Ant. crud., Ant. tart., Hep. s., Verat. alb.). Thirst: unquenchable; longs for something refreshing (Phos. ac.). *Regurgitations of food* (Podo.); *also in mouthfuls* (Alum., Carb. v., Nux v., Sulph.). Eructations, empty, sour, of food; tasting *of the food* (Ant. crud., Calc. c., Carb. an., Cinch., *Graph.*); ineffectual. Much belching of wind after eating (*Carb. v.*, Cinch.). Constant nausea (*Ant. tart.*, Digit., Ipec., Lob.). As soon as the water becomes warm in the stomach it is thrown up (Bism.). *Vomiting of food* (Ipec., Kreos., Plumb., Verat. alb.); *of blood*, mingled with bile and mucus (Nitr. ac.); of black substances (Plumb.); like coffee grounds. Great fullness in stomach, and painfulness to touch and pressure (Ars., Bell., *Bry.*, Lyc.). Cardialgia. *Pressure, as from a hard substance above pit of stomach.* Pressure in pit of stomach, as from a heavy weight, after eating (*Bry.*, *Nux v.*). Oppression and burning in epigastrium (*Æsc.*, *Ars.*, Canth., Iris, Verat. alb.). Drawing pain in pit of stomach, extending to chest. Spasmodic drawing pains in stomach (*Puls.*).

Abdomen.—Enlargement and induration of the liver (Cinch., Sulph.); with pain. Pain in hepatic region on pressure. Enlargement of the spleen (Cinch.). Sensitiveness in hepatic region, worse when lying on right side, with pain on touch. Painful pulsation in right hypochondrium. Abdomen distended and tympanitic; painful to touch (*Bell.*, Cinch.). Incarcerated flatus; loud rumbling in abdomen (*Lyc.*); *emission of much flatus* (*Aloe, Cinch., Lyc.*). *Sensation of great weakness and emptiness in abdomen* (*Sep.*, Stan); must lie down. *Sensation of coldness in the abdomen* (Caps.).

Stool and Anus.—Stitches or smarting in rectum. °Paralysis of the sphincter ani, anus always open. Violent burning in anus and rectum, with great exhaustion, after stool (*Ars., Cinch.*). Urging in rectum; on rising; stitches and itching in anus. Painless, debilitating diarrhœa (*Cinch., Podo.*; *not debilitating*, Phos. ac.); worse mornings (Aloe, Apis, Rumex, *Sulph.*). Chronic, painless diarrhœa of undigested food (Calc. c., *Cinch.*, Podo.). °Desire for stool whenever she lies on left side. Intestinal hæmorrhage. *Diarrhœa; stools involuntary* (*Arn., Ars.*, Carb. v., *Hyos.*); at least motion, *gray or whitish-gray* (*Phos. ac.*); bloody; green; watery, with flakes of mucus and clots of blood; watery, *with whitish-yellow and cheesy masses; lumps of white mucus;* copious, like water from a hydrant. *Constipation;* fæces slender, long, dry, tough and hard, like a dog's; voided with difficulty (Caust.); *small, dark, difficult, clay-colored.*

Urinary Organs.—Frequent micturition at night; scanty discharge. Urine turbid and high-colored; brown, with red, sandy sediment (Arn., Cinch., Lyc., Natr. mur., Nuph.); deposits white, cloudy sediment (Calc. c., Sep.); variegated cuticle appears on surface; albuminous (*Merc. cor.*, Osm., Phyt., *Plumb.*); bloody, milky-white. *Hæmaturia* (Arn., Canth., Colch., Ham., Tereb.); with acute pain in region of kidneys and liver, and jaundice.

PHOSPHORUS. 605

Male Organs.—Sexual excitement; frequent erections and emissions, *or irresistible desire for coitus* (Canth.); with feeble erections or none at all. Emissions soon after coition. Impotence after excessive excitement and onanism (Cinch., Phos. ac., Staph.).

Female Ogans.—*Menses too early and too scanty,* or too profuse; pale, with colic, nausea and diarrhœa. Frequent and profuse metrorrhagia (Acon., Ham.). Acrid, excoriating leucorrhœa (Alum., Coni., *Kreos., Merc., Puls.*).

Respiratory Organs.—*Hoarseness, cannot speak above a whisper* (Acon., Carb. v., Caust., *Spong., Sulph.*); *mornings. Voice husky, rough. Aphonia;* from prolonged loud talking (Arg. met., Arg. nit., *Arum. triph.*). Irritability in lower part of trachea, with *suffocative pressure in upper part of chest.* °Cannot talk on account of pain in the larynx (*Bell.*). *Rawness in larynx* (Acon., Ambr., Lach., Plumb., Sulph.) *and trachea, with frequent hacking cough and hawking. Cough dry; tickling, with tightness across chest* (August., Merc. cor.); hollow spasmodic; loose, without expectoration; *with soreness of chest* (Arn., Caust., *Nux v., Stram.*); loose rattling; hacking; hollow, mornings in bed, with trembling of whole body; *dry on reading aloud; from tickling in throat* (Hep. s., *Rumex, Sang., Sep.*); *with violent oppression of the chest and difficult respiration,* causing pain in the abdomen. Expectoration *difficult,* frothy; *bloody;* rust-colored; *tenacious, purulent mucus* (*Kali bi.*); *mucus streaked with blood* (Digit.); purulent, white and tough; cold mucus, tasting salty (Ambr., Calc. c., Carb. v., Lyc., Sep.); *transparent mucus,* in morning after rising. Cough worse evening and night (Nux v., Puls.); change from warm to cold air (Ars.; reverse, Bry.); from reading, laughing or loud talking (Cinch., Dros.); from lying on left side or back; drinking; exercise. Pains in chest, with coughing, relieved by external pressure. *Respiration short, labored, anxious, panting, with tightness and oppression of the chest.* Loud mucous râles during respiration (*Ant. tart., Ipec.*), *especially in lower lobes. Tightness; of upper part; worse lying on left side. Sensation as if everything about the chest were too tight. Congestion of the chest, with anxiety and*

Cramp in the calves. Sprained pain in ankles on walking. Heaviness in the hollow of the knees. Feet swollen in the evening, or when walking.

Generalities.—*Great emaciation* (Ars., Ferr., Graph., *Iodi*.). *Can lie only on the right side* (reverse, Merc.). Hæmorrhages from various organs and parts of the body (Croc., Ham.); *blood fluid, non-coagulable. Small wounds bleed much. Great weakness and prostration of the whole system* (*Ars., Cinch.*, Ferr.). *Nervous exhaustion, with general heaviness and dread of motion. Mucous membrane pale. Muscular system lax.* Ataxia and adynamia. Trembling. Motions involuntary and uncertain, as in palsy. Paralyzed feeling. *Painful heaviness of the whole body. Lying on the left side at night causes anxiety.* Numbness of the whole body, accompanied by pricking sensations. Takes cold easily in open air (Calc. c., Kali c., Sil.). Pains tearing, drawing, tensive, excited by slightest chill; body feels bruised, with sensation of coldness. Epilepsy, with consciousness. Spasms of the paralyzed side. Paralysis, formication and tearing in the limbs; anæsthesia; increased heat. Exostosis, especially of the skull. Hip-joint disease, oozing a watery pus.

Skin.—Jaundice (Chel., *Cinch.*, Merc.). Pale. Ecchymosis (Arn., Sec.). Petechia (Arn., Ars., Sec.). Purpura hæmorrhagica spots. Anæsthesia. Formication. Itching over the whole body. Tetter in round spots over whole body. *Ulcers bleed on appearance of menses.* Fistulous ulcers: erysipelatous; pus thin, ichorous, hectic.

Sleep.—*Constant sleepiness;* °*coma vigil.* *Sleepless and restless before midnight.* Unrefreshing sleep. Dreams anxious, lascivious; of fire; of biting animals; of restless work and business which he could not finish. Sleepy all day, restless at night.

Fever.—*Typhus fever, often with pneumonia and bronchitis, that developed into consumption. Chilliness every evening, with shivering, without thirst* (Ign., *Puls.*); not relieved by warmth. Coldness of limbs; *in knees at night in bed.* Chill at night, alternating with heat. *Heat,* with anxiety, burning in face and hands, *flushed cheeks, left more than right;* afternoon and evening. *Heat at night.*

Profuse perspiration; at night (*Cinch., Merc.*); *during sleep* (Cinch.); *in morning, in bed* (Calc. c., Chin. sulph., Nitr. ac.*); *on slight exertion* (Calc. c., Hep. s., Kali nit., Lyc., Sep., Sil.). *Exhausting sweat in morning.* Cold, clammy sweat (*Ars.*, Camph., Kali nit., *Merc.*).

Aggravation.—*Before midnight;* °*during a thunder storm;* when lying on back or *left side;* in warm room; from onanism and emissions.

Amelioration.—In cold, open air; after eating; from rest.

Conditions.—Tall, slender women.

Compare.—Acon., Ambr., Amm., Apis, Ars., Bell., Bry., Calc. c., Carb. v., Caust., Cinch., Crotal., Ipec., Kali c., Lyc., Merc., Nux v., Natr. sulph., Podo., Puls., Rhus tox., Sec. cor., Sep., Sil., Sulph. The remedies Calc. c., Cinch., Kali c., Lyc., Nux v., Pier. ac., Rhus tox., Sil. and Sulph. precede Phos. well, while Ars., Carb. v., Rhus tox. and Sulph. follow well.

Antidotes.—Camph., Coff. c., Nux v., Tereb., Vinum. To large doses: Emetics, Magnesia in water.

Phosphorus Antidotes.—Excessive use of Salt: Iodi., Camph., Tereb., Rhus ven.

THERAPEUTICS.

Phosphorus is the first remedy to be thought of in fatty degeneration of organs, especially of the liver and kidneys. It may also be useful when it is the lungs, heart, brain or spine that is affected. It is indicated in a hæmorrhagic diathesis—hæmorrhages from various organs and parts of the body, the blood being fluid and non-coagulable, hence the symptoms "small wounds bleed much," it being almost impossible to stop the bleeding from the prick of a pin, or from a small cut (compare Lach.). Persistent hæmorrhages after extraction of a tooth. Useful in diseases of bones—caries and necrosis, as will be hereafter noticed. Exostosis, especially of the skull. Rickets. Frequently indicated in marasmus. Fistulous ulcers, especially in glands. Polypi, erectile tumors, ulcers, etc., which bleed readily. Vascular growths. Fungus hæmatodes. Fungus excrescences. Ecchymoses. Petechia. Purpura hæmorrhagica. Cancerous ulcerations, burning, profuse bleeding. Psoriasis palmaris. The action of Phos. upon the nervous system is of special clinical importance. The mental symptoms are pe-

PHOSPHORUS.

culiar, and frequently indicate the drug in typhoid fever, especially with painless diarrhœa, and swollen liver and spleen. Especially useful when a typhoid state sets in with pneumonia or other respiratory diseases—typhoid-pneumonia, etc. The chief remedy in brain fag; sometimes with a feeling of coldness in the cerebellum and stiffness in the brain. Neuralgia of the brain. Apoplexia; grasps at the head; mouth drawn to the left. Impending paralysis of the brain and collapse; burning pain in brain. Very often required in softening of the brain, with persistent headache; slow answering questions; vertigo; feet drag; formication; numbness of the limbs. Acute atrophy of the brain and medulla oblongata, with uræmia.

Useful in many forms of paralysis. Paralysis of face and extremities, usually hemiplegic. Post-diphtheritic paralysis. Paralysis following exposure to wet. Pseudo-hypertrophic paralysis, with numbness, etc. Spinal irritation; spine sensitive to touch; weakness, the back soon gives out, the limbs tremble and totter, etc., especially from loss of animal fluids, hæmorrhages, sexual excess, etc. Locomotor ataxia, with burning along the spine, formication; may arise from causes last named. Chorea especially in children who are growing too fast; they are weak and walk as if paralyzed. General neuritis, with numbness, etc. Phosphorus is an invaluable remedy in diseases of the deeper tissues of the eye, especially when involving the nerve supply. Dim vision from nervous exhaustion, especially sexual neurasthenia, objects seem covered by a smoke or mist. Various disturbances of vision from lesion of the retina and optic nerve. An invaluable remedy in muscular asthenopia, the eyes pain and give out when reading. Myopia. Ambylopia after typhoid fever, sexual excess or loss of fluids. Blindness after a lightning stroke. Retinitis albuminurica. Retinal apoplexia. Glaucoma, and detachment of retina. Will arrest the growth of a cataract if the symptoms of vision, etc., are present. Lachrymal fistula. Deafness from neurasthenia. Polypus of the nose, bleeding easily. Nasal catarrh, nose swollen and sore; obstructed; ulcerated; greenish, yellow, bloody discharge. Caries of the nasal bones. Necrosis of the lower jaw, rarely of the upper. Retarded development of speech in children. Phosphorus is useful in a variety of diseases of the digestive system. Atonic dyspepsia, and regurgitation of food with vomiting.

Vomiting o. pregnancy. The vomiting of Phos. is temporarily relieved by a cold drink, but returns as soon as the water becomes warm in the stomach. Chronic gastritis. Perforating ulcer of the stomach. Cancer of the stomach. Gastralgia, with excruciating, cutting, burning pains, and heavy pressure. Hæmorrhage of the stomach, temporarily better by drinking cold water. Diseases of the pancreas (Iris), especially inflammation or fatty degeneration, with Phos. symptoms, stools oily or like cooked sage. A useful remedy in various diseases of the liver, especially fatty degeneration. Jaundice from organic changes in the liver, stools grayish-white. Malignant jaundice. Jaundice from anæmia; from brain disease; during pregnancy. Diffuse hepatitis. Cirrhosis of the liver. Hepatitis, being extremely valuable in the stage of suppuration, much swelling and soreness of the liver, hectic fever, night sweats. Acute yellow atrophy of the liver. Ascites. Chronic enteritis, stools pasty and yellow. Intestinal hæmorrhage; bleeding hæmorrhoids; chronic diarrhœa; painless, worse in hot weather; stools contain undigested food; or particles like grains of tallow, very debilitating. Cholerina. A valuable remedy in constipation, with the characteristic long, dry, hard stool. Very frequently useful in Bright's disease, the urine containing epithelial, fatty or waxy casts, especially with the characteristic degenerative heart changes, pulmonary engorgement and œdema. Hæmaturia. A valuable remedy in sexual weakness, with great desire and excitement, too rapid emissions, nocturnal pollutions. Impotence after excesses. Nymphomania. Sterility. Menorrhagia. Metrorrhagia, especially in nursing women. Amenorrhœa, with blood-spitting, or hæmorrhage from nose, anus or urethra (Bry., Ham., Puls.). Chronic metritis. Membranous dysmenorrhœa. Cancer of the uterus, sharp, lancinating pains, bleeding easily. Abscesses and ulceration of the mammæ, with hardness (Coni.); bluish color (Lach.); red streaks start from the openings in the abscess; fistulous openings with burning, stinging pains; thin, watery, ichorous, offensive discharges (Silic.). Phosphorus is an exceedingly valuable remedy in respiratory diseases, in which it is more often prescribed than in any other form of disease. Laryngitis, with hoarseness and aphonia, larynx extremely sore, so that it causes pain to talk or cough. Aphonia from prolonged loud talking. Not useful in the first stages of croup, but may be later in the disease, when collapse threatens, rattling breathing, weak, thready pulse. Said to act as a prophylactic and prevent the return of the disease. Tracheitis and bronchitis, with dry cough; worse in going from warm to cold air, from lying on the left side, caused by tickling in trachea, frothy, mucous expectoration, with soreness, oppression and constriction in chest. Occasionally useful in capillary bronchitis. Phosphorus is indicated in a great variety of coughs, the character of which is mostly outlined in the foregoing pathogenesis. It is often a useful remedy for reflex coughs, brought on by excitement, strong odors, or any nervous disturbance; also reflex from stomach and hepatic derangement. Phosphorus is an invaluable remedy in pneumonia after exudation has taken place. It is never indicated in the inflammatory stage of this or any other disease, but follows after the symptoms usually indicating Acon. and Bry. (not in alternation) have subsided, and the patient has a dry cough with bloody mucus, or rust-colored expectoration, violent oppression or tightness of the chest, difficult breathing, as if a heavy weight lay on the chest, worse when lying on the left side. May be useful when any part of the lungs are involved, but more often the lower lobe of the right lung. There is complete solidification of lung tissue, with dullness on percussion and an absence of vesicular murmur. In purulent infiltration and abscesses of lungs in the third stage of pneumonia. May be indicated in any stage of pneumonia when typhoid symptoms supervene, as has already been mentioned. Chronic solidification of the lung after typhoid fever. Equally valuable in broncho-pneumonia and pleuro-pneumonia. Broncho-pulmonary catarrh, with dilitation, or fatty degeneration of the heart. In pulmonary tuberculosis Phos. is valuable in the stage of tubercular deposit, especially of miliary tubercles, attended with afternoon fever, flushed cheeks, dry, short cough, rapid respiration and progressive emaciation. Said to be especially useful in tuberculosis occurring in tall, slender persons, or in the young who are rapidly growing; great debility; frequent attacks of bronchitis; hoarseness and aphonia; dry, tormenting cough; hectic fever. Phthisis florida. Hæmoptysis. Fatty degeneration of the heart. Endo-carditis; myocarditis, especially when occurring in the course of pneumonia or acute rheumatism.

PHYSOSTIGMA.

Synonym.—Physostigma Venenosum. *Natural order.*—Leguminosæ. *Common name.*—Calabar Bean. *Habitat.*—A perennial plant growing near the mouths of the Niger and Old Calabar river on the Gulf of Guinea. *Preparation.*—Tincture from the pulverized bean.

GENERAL ANALYSIS.

Through the spinal cord, Physostigma produces general paralysis and loss of sensibility, death resulting from paralysis of respiration, or from diminished heart's action, due to paralysis of the exciting ganglia of the heart, in all cases the sense of touch and consciousness remaining unimpaired to the last. It first causes contraction of the smaller blood vessels, and afterward dilitation of the same, and both internally and externally applied, produces strongly contracted pupils, due to its convulsive action upon the muscular substance of the iris, which it causes to contract by small, rapid jerks or twitches. It also in a like manner acts on the accommodation in the approximation of both the far and near point of vision. Fibrillary muscular twitching occurs very persistently, due to local irritation caused by paralysis of the motor nerve termini. The same cause produces a tetanic condition of the involuntary muscles, resulting in frequent discharges from the bladder, stomach and bowels, the latter often being twisted up in knots. All secretions are somewhat increased, especially the tears and saliva. The most important feature in the action of this drug is its effect upon the eye, in causing contraction of the pupil and disturbed accommodation, myosis being only caused by Physostigma and Opium.

CHARACTERISTIC SYMPTOMS

Mind.—Uncommon mental activity (Cinch., Coff. c.). Difficult thinking; cannot concentrate the mind (Gels.). Nothing right; too many things in the room; continually counting them.

Head.—Confusion and dizziness; dull, heavy, stupid feeling. Dull, heavy, oppressive headache. Intolerable pain over both eyes (Cinch., Chin. sulph.). Severe, dull frontal headache, especially in the morning (Kali bi., Natr. mur., Nux v.). Sensation of rush of blood to frontal and temporal regions (*Bell., Glon.*). Sharp, shooting pains in temples. Throbbing of temporal and carotid arteries (*Bell.*). Intense, painful pressure in vertex and both temples, the pressure in vertex extending over to occiput; must lie down.

Eyes.—Inflamed, first right, then left; sclerotic dry, red and swollen; eyeballs pain and smart; lids feel sore. Sharp, shooting pains, and drawing, twisting sensation in the eyes. Eyes sore and painful when moved from side to side (Bry., *Spig*.). Pain deep in over top of eyeball, running up from inner canthus to right frontal eminence, then down obliquely outward into temple. *The muscularis internus seems not to do its work rightly, and the axis of the eyes differs in each;* eyes feel weak, with lachrymation. Sight blurred, hazy or misty (*Caust.*, Phos., Merc.), film over eyes (*Puls.*); objects mixed; after which dull pain over the eyes and between the eyes. Muscæ volitantes (Agar.), both black and white. Aching in posterior part of orbit, extending back into the brain; worse on reading, causing nausea. Lids heavy (Coni., Caust.); cannot bear to raise them; twitching of the lids (Agar.). *Contraction of the pupil* (Merc. cor., *Op.*, Phos., Phyt.). Eyes sensitive to light (*Acon., Bell., Sulph.*). Disturbed accommodation; approximation of far point (myopia), and also of near point (the accommodation recovers before the pupil). Vision abnormally acute; double; dim and indistinct; blurred, hazy, misty.

Ears.—Sharp, shooting pains in the ears. Hissing, buzzing, ringing in the ears.

Nose.—Fluent coryza, sneezing; burning, smarting, itching and tingling of nostrils; nose stuffed and hot. Twitchings in nose and involuntary expansion of nostrils.

Face.—Face pale; flushings of the face (Ferr.). Neuralgic pain in right side of face. Sensation of contraction of left side of face.

Mouth.—Tongue sore on tip, and rough. Smarting of end of tongue; feels as if burnt (*Iris*). Tongue coated, more heavily at root. Numbness and tingling of tongue and lips, with constant desire to moisten them. Bad taste in mouth. Profuse salivation; thick, leathery saliva. Difficult speech (Caust., Coni., Gels., Hyos.). Power of speech retained long after inability to swallow.

Throat.—Sore throat, painful swallowing; tonsils and soft palate dark-red; burning, scraping, raw feeling; elongated uvula; small ulcers, with yellow centers in pharynx. Pain extending from throat to left ear when swallowing (Phyt.). Feeling as if a ball were coming up in throat (*Asaf., Lyc.*). Submaxillary gland tender and tumefied.

Stomach.—No appetite, disgust for food, tobacco and coffee, and *especially for cold drinks*. Tasteless eructations. Nausea and vomiting. In stomach: prickling, sharp pains; heaviness and weight, as from undigested food; griping; emptiness and weakness; sensation of nervousness and trembling. Soreness in region of stomach.

Abdomen.—Lancinating pains in hypochondria. Hard, sore pain in splenic region. Pain and soreness in umbilical region. Stitches in left side of abdomen. Much rumbling and distension in abdomen, with discharge of large quantities of flatus (*Aloe, Lyc.*). Colicky pains, with feeling as if diarrhœa would occur (Aloe). Sharp, cutting pains in lower part of abdomen. Dull pain in groins.

Stool and Anus.—Sphincter ani swollen and rigid; evacuation painful; rectum protruding, swollen and very sensitive; piles hard, protruding, painful and very sensitive. Tenesmus and burning, with diarrhœa; also tenesmus of bladder (*Merc. cor.*). Stools: copious; soft, thin; watery; yellowish; bilious; brown, black like tar; lumpy; dark and offensive. Constipation.

Urinary Organs.—Bruised, sore feeling in region of kidneys. Bladder feels distended. Frequent and copious urination (Phos. ac.). Urine yellow; high-colored; strong smell; clear; muddy.

Female Organs.—Leucorrhœa; metrorrhagia. Pain as if menses were coming on. Irregular. Menstruation, with palpitation; congestion of the eyes, with tonic spasms, rigidity, sighing respiration, consciousness retained.

Respiratory Organs.—Cough, from tickling in throat. *Labored, sighing respiration;* yawning. Stitches in the chest.

Heart and Pulse.—Dull pain, uneasiness and distress about the heart (Digit.). Violent palpitation of the heart (*Acon., Cact.*), °with feeling of pulsation through whole body. Heart's action irregular and tumultuous (*Digit.*), when lying on left side, better when lying on the back. Pulse variable; accelerated; small, frequent, slow, feeble, intermittent.

Neck and Back.—Stiffness in neck. Drawing on turning the head. Rheumatic pains in neck. Back very weak, unable to stand erect. Dull pain in the back. Creeping numbness from back of head down the spine. Cramp-like stitches up and down the spine. Pain under right shoulder blade (*Chel.*). Dull, heavy pain in lumbar region; also over left hip, extending to back. Pain in sacral region, worse on motion.

Limbs.—Limbs feel weary, as after great fatigue (Calc. c., Cinch.). Numbness and paralytic feeling in all the limbs (Acon.). Neuralgic pains in the limbs. Stiffness or bruised feeling in the joints. Staggering gait. Unsteadiness from knee downward when walking, especially with the eyes shut.

Generalities.—Great sense of fatigue and weariness; weakness (*Ars., Cinch.*). Convulsive twitchings (*Agar.*, Cic., Stram.). Violent trembling all over the body (Ant. tart.). Great prostration of the muscular system. Omits bath on account of horror for cold water. Sore and stiff all over, as from a cold. Severe, sharp pains in various parts of the body.

Sleep.—Irresistible desire to sleep; soporific sleep (*Op.*). Restless sleep, with dreams.

Fever.—Creeping, chilly sensation in back. Hands and feet cold (Sil., Verat. alb.). Cold, clammy skin. Heat in head and face: flushed and hot. Dry, burning heat in hands. Perspires very easily. Cold sweat in drops over whole body. Strong-smelling sweat around the genitals.

Aggravation.—Mostly in morning; from exercise; from mental activity.

Amelioration.—In open air and from walking; closing the eyes; from quiet; in warm room; from inhaling Camphor; from Arnica.

Compare.—Agar., Atrop., Gels., Jabor., Nux v., Op., Stram., Tabac.

THERAPEUTICS.

Physostigma has been used with some success in paralysis, traumatic tetanus, chorea, progressive locomotor ataxia, general paralysis of the insane; paralysis agitans and progressive muscular atrophy. Congestion of the spinal cord, with tetanic spasms. Numerous cases of tetanus in horses. Its chief homœopathic application has been in eye troubles, such as myopia, astigmatism, spasms of the ciliary muscles; torpor of the retina. Staphyloma; glaucoma; prolapsed iris; opacity of cornea; ulcers; keratitis, etc. On account of its extraordinary power to contract the pupil it has been used to tear up adhesions of the iris, especially when complicated with ulceration of the cornea at the margin.—*Allen.*

PHYTOLACCA.

Synonym.—Phytolacca Decandra. *Natural order.*—Phytolaccaceæ. *Common names.*—Poke Weed. Poke Root. Garget. *Habitat.*—An indigenous perennial plant. *Preparation.*—Tincture from the fresh root.

GENERAL ANALYSIS.

Acts especially upon the glandular system, particularly of the throat and mammæ, and the serous, fibrous and mucous tissues. It acts upon the kidneys, and produces symptoms of general lithæmia. It also acts prominently upon the periosteum and the skin, its effects resembling those of Mercury, the iodide of Potash, or of the syphilitic poison. The general condition produced by Phytolacca is one of inflammation, which, in the fibrous tissues, partakes of a rheumatic character, and, in mucous and glandular tissues, has a tendency to ulceration

PHYTOLACCA. 617

and suppuration. It also acts prominently upon the stomach and bowels, producing emesis and purging.

CHARACTERISTIC SYMPTOMS.

Mind.—Indifference to life. Loss of personal delicacy, complete shamelessness (Hyos.).

Head.—Vertigo, with dimness of vision. Sore pain over head, worse on right side. Sensation of soreness deep in the brain, as if bruised. Headache, with sick stomach (Iris, Nux v., Podo., Sang.); worse in forehead, or above eyebrows; comes every week (Sulph.). °Headache, worse from wet weather. Headache, commencing in frontal region and extending backward. Pain in the vertex, with dryness. Pressive pain in forehead or on top of head. Tinea capitis (*Graph., Hep. s., Merc., Nitr. ac., Sep.*).

Eyes.—Pupils contracted (*Merc. cor.,* Op., Phos., Physos.). Double vision (*Aur.,* Bell., Cic., Stram.). Feeling of sand in the eyes, with burning and smarting (Ars., *Caust.,* Ign., Natr. mur., *Sulph.*).

Nose.—Flow of mucus from one nostril while the other is stopped. Drawing sensation at root of nose (Acon.). Feeling in nose and eyes as if a cold would come on (Cepa, Euphr.). Acrid, excoriating discharge.

Face.—Paleness of the face. Pains in bones of face and head, at night. Chin drawn closely to sternum by convulsive action of muscles of face and neck; lips everted and firm; tetanus.

Mouth.—Tongue feels rough; white-coated blisters on both sides, and *very red tip* (*Ars., Rhus tox.*). *Great pain in root of tongue when swallowing.* Profuse saliva; tenacious, yellowish, ropy, with metallic taste (Cham.).

Throat.—*Throat sore; fauces congested, and of a dark-red color* (*Alianth., Arg. nit.,* Bapt., Naja); *dryness of the throat; tonsils swollen* (*Bell.*). Sore throat, swelling of soft palate in morning, with a thick, white and yellow mucus about the fauces. Feeling when swallowing as of a lump in the throat (*Bell., Lach.*), also when turning head to the left. Sensation of rawness and scraping in the throat and tonsils (Carb. v., Caust., Phos., Puls., Rumex). Dryness, soreness, smarting and roughness of the throat. Dryness in the throat provoking cough, with disposition to hawk and clear the throat. Difficult swallowing; *with every attempt excruciating shooting pains through both ears.*

Stomach.—Violent vomiting of clotted blood and slime, with retching, intense pain, and desire for death to relieve.

Abdomen.—Intense vomiting and purging, with griping pains and cramps in the abdomen.

Stool and Anus.—Neuralgic pains in anus and lower part of rectum, shooting along perineum to middle of penis; in middle of night. Diarrhœa of mucus and blood, or like scrapings from intestines. Bleeding hæmorrhoids (*Ham., Nitr. ac.*).

Female Organs.—°Menses too frequent and too copious (Amm. carb., Ars., *Bell.,* Borax, Calc. c., *Nux v.*). Metrorrhagia (Acon., Bell., Ferr., Ham., Ipec., Sabin.).

Urinary Organs.—Chalk-like sediment in the urine. Urine acid and albuminous (Osm., *Phos., Plumb.*). Slight suppression of urine, with pains in loins.

Respiratory Organs.—Hoarseness. Dryness of the larynx. Sharp pains through upper part of chest, preventing a long breath. Tenderness and lameness of the muscles of the chest, as if bruised. °Rheumatism of lower intercostal muscles from exposure to cold and dampness.

Neck and Back.—Hardness of glands in right side of neck. Stiff neck, worse on right side, and in bed; after midnight. Back very stiff every morning. Constant, dull, heavy pain in lumbar and sacral regions. Pains shooting from sacrum down both hips.

Limbs.—Rheumatic pains in arms and hands. Neuralgic pain in outer side of both thighs; sciatica. Rheumatic pains in lower extremities. Ulcers and nodes on legs. Nightly pains in periosteum of tibia (*Merc.*). Stitches in various parts, always from without inward and near surface. The pains are always in outer parts.

Skin.—°Syphilitic eruptions and ulcerations—secondary and tertiary (*Merc., Nitr. ac.*). °Squamous eruptions; tinea capitis; lupus; ulcers.

Aggravation.—Pain always worse at night and in wet weather.

PHYTOLACCA.

Amelioration.—Most symptoms better while lying down; pain better in the open air.

Generalities.—Great exhaustion and prostration. Convulsions. Feeling of soreness in all the muscles (Acon., Bry.). Bones and glands inflamed and swollen (Asaf., Hep. s., Merc., Nitr. ac.).

Compare.—Colch., Kali bi., Kali hyd., Lyc., Merc., Mez., Nitr. ac., Petrol., Rhus tox.

Antidotes.—Milk and Salt; Ign., Sulph. To large doses: Op., Coffee.

THERAPEUTICS.

Phytolacca has been found useful in syphilis, both primary and secondary. Syphilitic headache. Syphilitic periostitis. Spyhilitic sore throat. Chancres. Syphilitic eruptions and ulcerations. 'Syphilitic or gonorrhœal rheumatism, glands swollen, worse at night and in damp weather. Subacute rheumatism and gout; pains shift; joints swollen, red; periosteum affected, especially in mercurialization and in syphilis; pains in middle of long bones or attachment of muscles; worse in damp weather or at night. Intercostal rheumatism from exposure to cold and dampness. Rheumatism affecting dorsal muscles. Chronic endocarditis from rheumatism. Gouty heart. Fatty degeneration of the heart. Inflammation and swelling of bones and glands in general. By many considered our most valuable remedy both internally and locally for inflammation, swelling and suppuration of the breasts; pain whenever milk flows into the breast, especially when nursing; pains radiate from the nipple over the whole body, particularly up and down the backbone (a poultice of the fresh root is invaluable for dissipating recent inflammations and engorgements and lumps in the breast, and preventing suppuration). Abscesses or fistulous ulcers of the breasts (Sil.). Nipples sensitive, cracked and excoriated (Graph.). Mammary gland full of hard and painful nodosities. In the same line of glandular action comes the remarkable clinical value of Phytolacca in tonsilitis. The tonsils are swollen and bluish, usually worse on the right side, throat dry, swallowing difficult, with every attempt excruciating pains through both ears. Pharyngitis, and sore throat in general where the fauces are congested and have a dark-red color, with dryness, scraping, rawness and roughness in the throat, and stiffness of the muscles externally; sometimes ulceration; usually worse on right side. Much aching in the limbs. Often useful in diphtheria. Throat and fauces covered with a dirty, dark pseudo-membrane (Merc. iod., *Nitr. ac.*), like washed leather; mucus hawked with difficulty from posterior nares; hangs down in strings; cannot drink hot fluids. Severe pains in head, neck, back and limbs; great prostration; faint on rising. Urine often albuminous. Aphthous ulceration on cheeks and margin of tongue, thick, tenacious secretion in the mouth. Granular conjunctivitis. Blepharitis, with swelling of the meibomian glands, lids thickened, indurated, dark-red and tender; sometimes become ulcerated and covered with crusts. Hypopion. Suppurative choroiditis. Threatening suppuration of the cornea. Nasal catarrh, fluid, acrid discharge from one nostril, the other stopped; drawing pain at root of nose. Sometimes indicated during difficult dentition. Constipation. Bleeding hæmorrhoids. Diarrhœa. Ulcers and fissures in rectum, (Natr. m., Nitr. ac.). Metrorrhagia. Bright's disease; also for uræmic convulsions. Nephritis, with dull, heavy pain, heat and soreness in region of kidneys; most on right side; urine albuminous, dark-red, stains the vessel; chalk-like sediment. Catarrhal laryngitis, with hoarseness, burning in larynx and trachea, sensation of contraction of the glottis, labored breathing, spasm of the glottis. Sciatica. Squamous eruptions. Tinea capitis. Lupus. Chronic ulcers surrounded by small boils. Ringworms. Barber's itch (local application of tincture). Phytol. has been found useful in boils and carbuncles, with burning pains worse at night, usually swollen glands. Scarlatina, with characteristic sore throat; acrid coryza; urine dark-red; non-appearing eruption. Tetanus, alternate spasms and relaxation of muscles, especially of the face; general muscular rigidity.

PICRICUM ACIDUM.

Synonym.—Carbazotic Acid.   *Common name.*—Picric Acid. *Preparation.*—One part of pure Picric Acid is dissolved in ninety-nine parts of distilled water to make the 2x dilution. The 3x dilution is made with dilute alcohol, and subsequent dilutions with alcohol.

GENERAL ANALYSIS.

In poisonous doses Picric Acid acts profoundly upon the blood, causing disintegration of the blood corpuscles, and softening and degeneration of the cortex cerebri, cerebellum, medulla oblongata and spinal cord, and consequent paralysis. It also causes inflammation of the kidneys, the urine being loaded with phosphates, urates and uric acid. Albumen and sugar are also found in the urine. In smaller doses there is at first slight congestion followed by weariness, which may vary from a slight feeling of fatigue to actual paralysis. Associated with this is a mental inactivity, lack of will power, indifference to everything, and a desire to lie down and rest, thus simulating brain fag and neurasthenia, in which conditions is found its chief sphere of usefulness.

CHARACTERISTIC SYMPTOMS.

Mind.—*Great indifference; lack of will power to undertake anything* (Phos.). *Disinclination for mental or physical work. Aversion to talking or movement, with the headache. Mental prostration after reading a little; after writing a little. Inability to collect thoughts or to study.*

Head.—Vertigo and nausea. Vertigo on stooping (Acon., Bell., Puls., Sulph.); bending the head; lying down; rising from a seat (Bry., Sulph). Heat in head; in forehead. Burning along coronal suture. Headache worse on rising, better in the open air; worse on motion or on stooping; better from pressure, from bandaging the head (Arg. nit., Sil.). Heavy, blind, dizzy aching in vertex, worse from stooping. Pressure outward, as if the head would fly apart, worse from motion or study. Throbbing pain in left side of head, **worse in the eyeball and forehead, and extending back to occiput, better from quiet.** Aching over the eyes, worse from study and motion, better from sitting still. Heavy pain in supra-orbital region, extending to vertex, worse from motion or rolling the eyes. Sharp, shooting, cutting pains in the temples. Full heavy pain in vertex, worse on stooping and moving the eyes. *Pain in occiput and nape of neck. Heavy pain in occiput extending down neck and spine. Confusion in the base of the brain.*

Eyes.—Yellow sclerotica. *Conjunctivitis; worse right eye; better from washing with cold water and by cold air; worse in a warm room, with difficulty in keeping eyes open, and sticky sensation on reading.* Dryness and sensation of sand in the eyes (Ars., Caust., Hep. s., Ign., Merc., Puls., Rhus tox., Sep., Sil., Sulph.). Feeling of sticks in the eyes. Agglutination in the morning on waking. Heaviness of the lids on studying, cannot keep them open (Gels.). Vision dim and confused; as if looking through a veil (Caust., Croc., Natr. m., Puls., Sepia, Sulph.). Air looks smoky. Whirling of objects; sparks before the eyes.

Ears.—Ears burn and look puffy, with sensation as if worms were crawling in them. *Buzzing and hissing in the ears.*

Nose.—Sensation of a weight on bridge of nose (Kali bi.). Nose full of mucus; can only breath through the mouth, better in the open air.

Mouth.—White, frothy saliva hangs in strings to the floor. Taste sour; bitter; bad.

Throat.—Throat red, feels raw and scraped (Amm. c., Caust., Carb. v., Nux v., Phos., Puls., Sulph.); stiff and hot, as if burnt; with thick, white mucus on tonsils; great difficulty in swallowing, with sensation as if the throat would split open; soreness, worse on left side; worse after sleep (Apis, Lach., Sulph.); better after eating.

Stomach.—Appetite increased, then lost. Thirst unquenchable for cold water. Empty or sour eructations. Waterbrash. Nauseated, faint feeling in epigastrium, worse on rising and moving about. Sensation of weight at pit of stomach, with ineffectual desire to eructate.

Abdomen.—Rumbling. Emission of flatus. Sharp stitching

pains in hepatic region; in umbilical region; mostly on left side. Sensation of giving way in epigastrium.

Stool and Anus.—Stinging and itching in anus during and after stool. Stools yellow, copious, oily, frequent; light-colored, with straining; soft plugs, shooting away easy, then much flatus; quick, as if greased; sweetish smell, as of boiling soap.

Urinary Organs.—Dribbling micturition. Urine yellow; dark-yellow, with strong odor; *scanty;* copious and pale; urates abundant; *contained much indican, numerous granular cylinders and fatty degenerated epithelium.*

Male Sexual Organs.—*Terrible erections at night, with restless sleep. Great desire and violent erections all night, with emissions.* Desire, with almost constant priapism day and night.

Female Sexual Organs.—In left ovarian region, aching; twinges of pain. Yellowish-brown leucorrhœa in place of the menses, which are delayed. Voluptuous pruritus at night in bed, before menses.

Respiratory Organs.—Dry cough, as from dust in the throat. Tightness of chest, as if encircled by a band (Cact.).

Heart and Pulse.—Fluttering. Palpitation. Pulse slow, small, feeble and irregular.

Back.—Pain in back, worse from sitting. Heaviness and weakness in the back and limbs. Dragging pains in region of kidneys. Burning along spine, worse on trying to study, better on motion.

Limbs.—*Great heaviness of the limbs, especially the left; of arms and legs on exertion, especially legs; weakness and heaviness of the legs; and in region of hips; worse on left side.* Numbness of the lower limbs. Feet feel as if frostbitten (Agar.).

Generalities.—*Tired feeling on the least exertion; with lame sensation over the whole body. No desire to talk or to do anything; indifferent to everything.* Numbness, with pains, as when taking cold.

Skin.—Yellow. Pimples and boils, especially on face; painful.

Sleep.—Frequent yawning. Sleepiness; in evening; better from walking in the open air. Sleep sound, but unrefreshing. Sleepless all night. Restless sleep. Constant dreams.

Fever.—*Cold extremities; cold feet.* Chilliness predominates. Heat in lower dorsal and lumbar regions. Cold, clammy sweat.

Aggravation.—From study; after sleep (Lach.); from motion (except burning in spine).

Amelioration.—In open air; walking in open air; cold water; at rest.

Compare.—Arg. nit., Caust., Coccul., Gels., Lach., Petrol., Phos., Phos. ac., Puls., Sep., Sil., Sulph.

THERAPEUTICS.

Picric Acid has proved extremely valuable in brain fag (Phos.) and neurasthenia (Phos. ac.). The indications for its use are to be found in the pathogenesis. An important characteristic is the general prostration, both mental and physical, from any attempt at mental labor. A valuable remedy in occipital headache, worse from any mental effort. Has proved useful in hysteria; aching in left ovarian region; leucorrhœa in place of menses; great exhaustion during menses (Coccul.), etc. A case of hysteria is authentically reported as speedily alleviated by administering Picric Acid to the husband for "toothache"—in which is a thought worthy of consideration. A valuable remedy in sexual weakness, with seminal emissions and general exhaustion, even threatening paralysis. Dim vision from neurasthenia, especially sexual neurasthenia. Ophthalmia, better from cold water and in cold air. Chronic deafness following long-continued nervous headaches and prostration. Nephritis, chronic or subacute; dark, scanty urine; dragging pain in region of kidneys; great prostration. Probably an antipsoric remedy (see cases reported in *Medical Advance,* April, 1890). Pimples and boils on the face. Said to be especially useful when there is a disposition to boils on the back of the neck, or within the ears.

PLATINUM.

Synonym.—Platinum Metallicum. *Preparation.*—Triturations of precipitated Platinum.

GENERAL ANALYSIS.

Acts chiefly upon the nerve centers, depressing the sensorium, and producing in general a tendency to anæsthesia, torpor and paralysis, manifested mostly in women in deranged sexual health, hysterical conditions and melancholia.

CHARACTERISTIC SYMPTOMS.

Mind.—*Illusions; everything around her is very small, and everybody inferior to her in mind and body. Arrogant, proud, haughty* (Lach., *Stram.*); *looks down with pitiful contempt on others.* Low-spirited, sad, apprehensive, inclined to shed tears (Ign., *Natr. mur.*, Nux m., Puls.), worse evening in the house, better in the open air. Alternate cheerful or depressed mood (Croc., *Ign., Nux m.*, Stram.). Feels that she is all alone in the world, and that life is wearisome, but *dreads death, which she thinks is near at hand.* Deathly anxiety, with trembling of the limbs, oppression of breath and palpitation. Absent-minded and forgetful. Peevish, irritable, fretful mood; very sensitive to the least word or action, however innocent (Caps., Nux v., Staph.). Easily excited to anger. Physical and mental symptoms alternate.

Head.—Vertigo on sitting down or ascending stairs. *Sensation of numbness in the head, especially in forehead, as if constricted; intermittent, cramp-like. Tense, numb sensation in temples, zygomatic and mastoid processes, as if the head were screwed together, or too tightly bound* (Acon., Ant. tart., Chel., Gels., Merc.). °Periodical headache, increasing and decreasing gradually, worse from stooping, better from exercise in the open air. Numb pain on top of vertex, as if scalp would be contracted, and as if a heavy weight were lying on it. *Formication in one temple, extending to lower jaw, with sensation of coldness on that spot.*

Eyes.—Spasmodic twitching of the eyelids (Gels.). Intermittent, cramp-like pain near right outer margin of orbit. *Objects appear smaller than they really are.* Objects appear larger (*Hyos.*).

Ears.—Roaring, whizzing and ringing in the ears. Sticking jerking in right outer ear, with numbness and coldness extending through cheeks to lips.

Nose.—Numbness and crampy pain in nose and root of nose (Acon., Kali bi., Merc. iod.). Corrosive sensation on nose, as of something acrid.

Face.—Face pale and sunken. *Sensation of coldness, crawling and numbness in right side of face.* Sensation of burning and redness in face, without any visible change in color. *Cramp, pain, numbness and boring in malar bones, especially left.*

Mouth.—Toothache, with pulsating, digging pains. Numb pain in left lower teeth. Sensation as if the tongue were scalded (*Iris,* Puls.). Crawling sensation on the tongue.

Stomach.—Ravenous appetite, *and greedy, hasty eating,* with contemptuous mood. Empty eructations, after fasting, in morning; loud. Continuous nausea, with great weakness, anxiety, and trembling sensation through the whole body (*Ant. tart.*). *Fermentations in epigastric region.* Flatulent soreness towards hypogastrium.

Abdomen.—Sensation as if the abdomen were too tightly constricted. *Pressing and bearing down in abdomen, extending into pelvis* (*Bell.,* Cimic., Lil. tig., *Puls., Sep.*).

Stool and Anus.—Constipation; frequent urging, scanty stool, *with sensation of great weakness.* Crawling tenesmus in anus every evening before sleep. Stool indurated, as if burnt (*Bry.*); preceded and followed by pressure. Stool adheres to rectum and anus, like soft clay.

Urinary Organs.—Red urine.

Male Organs.—Excessive sexual desire, with violent erections, especially at night, with amorous dreams. Voluptuous crawling in genital organs and abdomen, with anxious oppression and palpitation, then painless pressure downwards in genitals, with sticking in sinciput and exhaustion.

PLATINUM. 627

Female Organs.—*Painful sensitiveness and constant pressure in mons veneris and genital organs*, with internal chill and external coldness, except face. Frequent sensation as if the menses would appear. *Menses too early and too profuse* (Calc. c., *Nux v.*); lasting too long; *flow dark and clotted* (Amm. carb., *Cycl., Croc., Ign.*); with much bearing down and drawing pains in abdomen. Stitches in right ovarian region. Leucorrhœa like the white of an egg (Amm. c., Borax, Bovis.).

Respiratory Organs.—Deep breathing, caused by a sensation as of a weight on the chest (*Ferr.*, Nux v., *Phos.*). Inclination to draw a long breath prevented by a sensation of weakness in the chest (*Stan.*). °Nervous, dry cough, with palpitation and dyspnœa. Cramp-like pain in left side of chest. Cramp-like constriction close to the shoulder.

Neck and Back.—Tensive, numb sensation in nape, close to occiput, as if tightly bound. Weakness in nape of neck; the head sinks forward (Aloe, Cimic., Kali c., Natr. mur.). Pain in back and small of back, as if bruised or broken (*Bell.*, Nux v.). *Numbness in sacrum and coccyx, while sitting*, as after a blow.

Limbs.—*Tension in the limbs, especially thighs, as if wrapped tightly.* Paralyzed sensation in left arm. Cramp-like pains; numbness in limbs and joints; trembling of right thumb, with numbness. Sensation of great weakness in and about the knee-joints. Pain as from a blow in left knee. Tremulous, restlessness and tired feeling in legs and feet, when sitting; *a numbness and rigidity*, worse evenings in bed.

Generalities.—Weakness and prostration. *Bruised pain on pressure in the parts affected by cramp-like pain.* Tremulous sensation at times, through whole body, with throbbing in veins, *Painful numbness here and there, as from a blow;* in spots, more on head. °Dull, pushing pains, as from a plug (Anac., Asaf., Ign.). °Pains generally increase and decrease gradually. Sudden heat; she thought she was very red, but color same as usual.

Sleep.—Great inclination to violent, almost spasmodic yawning. °Sleeplessness, with great nervous excitability. Awakes at night and has difficulty in collecting his senses.

Aggravation—In evening; before sleep; in room; °at rest.
Amelioration.—From motion in open air.
Conditions.—Especially suited to females.
Compare.—*Aur.*, Asaf., Bell., Croc., Hyos., *Ign.*, *Lyc.*, *Plumb.*, Puls., *Rhus tox.*, Sabad., Sep., Sulph., Verat. alb.
Antidotes.—Puls., sp. nitr. d.
Platinum Antidotes.—Bad effects of Lead.

THERAPEUTICS.

The chief use of Platinum is in the treatment of diseases of the female sexual system and certain forms of mental and nervous disturbances arising therefrom, the latter constituting the chief indication for its use. A peculiar haughtiness and pride, or a melancholia, or both combined, as described in the pathogenesis, are usually associated with the diseases referred to where Platina is indicated. It is very frequently called for in hysteria with the above symptoms; also hysterical spasms, from nervous excitement, with globus hystericus, and embarrassed respiration simulating asthma. Useful in mania, especially puerperal: nymphomania, especially in lying-in women (Verat. alb.), with voluptuous tingling extending from genitals into abdomen. Great sensitiveness of external organs, sometimes numbness. Melancholia, with fear of death, which she thinks near. Anxiety. Palpitation and weeping. Sexual melancholia in both sexes. Hysteria and other characteristic mental and nervous symptoms of a reflex character, such as a dry, nervous cough, palpitation, spasms, sleeplessness, etc., from suppression of the menses or other uterine or ovarian disorders. Pruritus vulva, with voluptuous tingling, anxiety and palpitation of the heart.

Useful in indurated and prolapsed uterus, with continued pressure in the groins and back, sensation of numbness, sensitiveness to touch. May be indicated in fibroid tumors and uterine cancer, with same symptoms, and also with metrorrhagia, flow dark and clotted. Ovaritis, especially right side, with burning pain, occurring in paroxysms, sensitiveness to touch, often sterility. Neuralgia, dysmenorrhœa, even spasms, with characteristic nervous symptoms, usually followed by a profuse flow of clotted blood. The Platina patient not only has the mental symptoms first mentioned, but also usually menorrhagia with dark, clotted blood, and an abnormal sexual appetite. In the male satyriasis. Bad effects of prepubic masturbation, melancholia, epileptiform spasms, etc. Otalgia. Nervous deafness. Facial neuralgia (see symptoms). Gastralgia, hysterical, flatulent pressure towards hypogastrium. Painter's colic; pain in umbilical region, extending through into back; patient screams and tries to relieve the pain by turning in all possible directions. Constipation, after lead poison or while traveling. Spasms caused by nervous excitement; during labor; from sexual erethism; spasmodic affections in general occurring in hysterical women or in children. (Asaf., Ign.). Neuralgia of various parts, characterized by tingling, and especially by numbness of the parts affected. Paralysis with numbness.

PLUMBUM.

Synonym.—Plumbum Metallicum. *Common name.*—Lead. *Preparation.*—Triturations of precipitated Lead.

GENERAL ANALYSIS.

Acts especially and with great power upon the spinal nerve centers, first producing irritation, giving rise primarily to increased sensibility, neuralgic spasms and convulsions. This condition of the nerve centers gradually gives way to softening or induration (also cerebral degeneration), and as a result of this process there are anæsthesia, paralysis, muscular atrophy, mental and physical decay, while at the same time there may occur, at longer or shorter intervals, neuralgia, epilepsy or kindred affections of the nervous system. Plumbum acts directly upon the kidneys, causing granular degeneration of these organs, and producing albuminuria; hence its use in Bright's disease and other renal affections. It may also cause degeneration of the heart, liver and other organs. According to Allen (*op. cit., p. 898*), "it produces general interstitial inflammation characterized by proliferation of connective tissue (nerve muscles, and parenchyma of organs)."

The chief feature of Plumbum is the well-known "lead colic," or "painter's colic," characterized by excruciating spasmodic pains in the abdomen, from contraction of the colon, with obstinate constipation.

CHARACTERISTIC SYMPTOMS.

Mind.—*Slow perception; apathetic* (Phos., Phos. ac.). *Loss of memory* (Anac., Natr. mur., Nux m., Merc., Phos. ac.); *unable to find proper word while talking* (Dulc.). Coma. Quiet and melancholy mood. Wild delirium with distorted countenance. Delirium; dread of assassination, poisoning; thinks every one about him a murderer.

Head.—Vertigo. *Aching.* Heaviness in the head, especially in cerebellum. Pain and heaviness in forehead. °Headache, as if a ball were rising from the throat into the brain.

Eyes.—Yellowness of the sclerotica (Cinch., Caust., *Chel.*); of conjunctiva. Hypopion. Diplopia. Loss of vision. Disc prominent, opaque, its outline hazy. Pain in eyeballs, as if too large (Carls., Phos. ac., *Spig.*). Paralysis of the upper lid (*Caust., Gels.*, Nitr. ac., Op.). Pupils dilated.

Face.—*Sallow, pale complexion, like a corpse* (Carb. v.). Expression of extreme anxiety and suffering (*Ars., Camph., Verat. alb.*). Lockjaw (Cic., Ign., Hyos., Laur.).

Mouth.—*Distinct blue line along margins of gums.* Tongue dry and white. Tongue paralyzed, cannot put it out (Caust., Dulc., *Gels.*, Hyos., Lach.). *Breath fœtid.* Imperfect articulation (Caust., *Gels., Hyos., Stram.*), sometimes only confused sounds. Margin of tongue red, brown fur down the center (Bapt., Phos.); slate-colored along border coated. Dryness of the mouth (*Apis, Ars., Bry., Nux m., Puls.*). Taste sweetish (Æsc., Bry., *Merc. cor., Sulph.*); bitter, metallic.

Throat.—*Constriction of the throat when trying to swallow* (*Bell., Hyos., Stram.*). Tonsils swollen, inflamed and indurated. Paralysis of the throat, with inability to swallow (*Bell.*, Op., Nux m.).

Stomach.—*Loss of appetite* (Alum., Ars., *Cinch.*, Phos.). Violent thirst (Acon., Ars., Bry., Merc., Phos. ac.). Eructations sweetish, sour (*Carb. v., Nux v.*, Phos., *Sulph.*); of offensive odor (Cham., Kreos., Phos., Sep., Verat. alb.). Hiccough. Nausea. *Incessant vomiting of food;* of fæcal matter; of brownish or blackish substances (Ars.,

Phos.); streaked with blood. Pressure and tightness about the stomach. Pains extending from the stomach to the loins and down the limbs. Feeling in epigastrium as if a ball ascended to throat, where it caused suffocation, preventing speaking and swallowing, with anxiety.

Abdomen.—*Violent colic; abdomen retracted to the spine, as if drawn in by a string* (Chel., Podo., Tabac.). Constriction of the intestines; navel violently retracted, recti muscles hard and knotty. *Excruciating pains in umbilical region, shoot to other portions of the abdomen and body; somewhat relieved by pressure.* Rumbling in the bowels. Sensitiveness to touch. Lacerating pains in the umbilicus and epigastrium.

Stool and Anus.—Anus drawn up; with constriction. Diarrhœa; alternating with constipation. *Constipation;* stools scanty, hard, in lumps or balls, like sheep's dung (*Alum.*, Kali c., *Op.*, Mag. mur.); *blackish* or green color; passed with difficulty.

Urinary Organs.—*Difficult micturition; urine passes only in drops* (Acon., *Bell.*, Canth.); ineffectual urging; strangury (*Merc. cor.*). *Urine dark-colored and scanty* (Osm.); *albuminous* (*Merc. cor.*, Osm., Phos., Phyt.); brownish-red, turbid, acid, flocculent sediment, consisting of red blood, corpuscles and cylinders; all the symptoms of acute diffuse nephritis; with amaurosis and cerebral symptoms.

Male Organs.—Loss of sexual desire (*Agn.*, Arg. nit., Camph.), or increased desire, and violent erections (Agar., Canth., Graph., Nitr. ac.).

Female Organs.—*Vaginismus* (Ham.). Milk scanty.

Respiratory Organs.—Cough short, dry, spasmodic, with purulent or bloody expectoration (Cinch., Dulc., Kali c., Lyc., Phos., Sep., *Sil.*). Suppuration of the lungs (Phos.). Pressure upon the chest (Psor.).

Heart.—Change in muscular structure without coincident disease of the valves, with or without atheromatous degeneration of vessels, usually hypertrophy and dilitation of left ventrical, sometimes with parenchymatous nephritis. Bruit de souffle. Palpitation, worse on ascending stairs or running. Pulse rapid, jerky, weak.

Limbs.—*Violent pains in the limbs, especially in muscular parts of thighs; worse evening and night. Sciatica.* Twitching and jerking in the limbs. Trembling. Coldness of the hands and feet. Paralytic weakness in limbs. Cramp in calves, worse at night. (Sulph.). *Wrist drop.* Trembling of the hands. Dilitation of veins on back of hands, arms and calves. *Sharp, lightning-like, neuralgic pains in lower limbs, mostly from hips to knees, occurring in paroxysms;* worse from movement. Pain in great toe at night.

Generalities.—*Extreme emaciation (Ars., Natr. mur., Phos.);* wasting of the muscles, especially paralyzed parts. *Anæmia. Anæsthesia. Hyperæsthesia. Convulsions, tonic* and *clonic.* Trembling. Restlessness. Epilepsy. *General prostration; lassitude faintness; restlessness.* Diminished sensibility of right side of body. *Arthralgic and neuralgic pains in trunk and limbs.* Wandering pains. Sensation of constriction, with pain and spasm in the internal organs. *Entire lack of perspiration.*

Skin.—*Dry, yellow* (Bry., Cinch.), *or bluish* (Lach.). Jaundice. Dry skin.

Sleep.—*Sleeplessness* at night; sleepy during the day. Restless sleep.

Aggravation.—At night; while lying in bed; from drinking.

Amelioration.—From friction and strong pressure.

Compare.—*Alum., Ars.,* Bell., Calc. c., Colch., Coni., *Cupr.,* Ferr., Led., *Lyc.,* Merc., Nux v., *Op., Phos., Plat., Rhus tox.,* Stram., *Sulph.,* Zinc.

Antidotes to Lead Poisoning.—Alumen, Alumina, Bell., Coccul., Hyos., Nux v., *Op.,* Plat., Stram., Zinc., Electricity. Alcohol as a preventive. Milk.

THERAPEUTICS.

Plumbum, from its profound action on the nerve centers, is one of our most important remedies in neuroses. In many forms of paralysis it is often valuable, as has already been indicated in the pathogenesis. Paralysis preceded by mental derangement, trembling, spasms, or by shooting, darting, intense tearing pains in track of larger nerves; the parts emaciate; wrist drop, caused by apoplexy, sclerosis of brain, or pro-

PLUMBUM. 633

gressive muscular atrophy; alternating with colic. Spinal paralysis of a rheumatic character. Often a valuable palliative, at least in multiple cerebro-spinal sclerosis, and locomotor ataxia, especially for the violent neuralgic pains. Paralysis of the face, eyes, throat, tongue, etc. Epilepsy, chronic forms; before the spell, legs heavy and numb; tongue swollen; afterward, long-lasting, stupid feeling in head; constipation. Convulsions, tonic and clonic, with other symptoms of the drug. Lockjaw. A valuable remedy in neuralgia, especially sciatica, accompanying cerebral and spinal disease, with marked consecutive muscular atrophy, or earlier when walking causes great exhaustion. General anæmia, mucous membranes very pale, great prostration and lassitude. Chlorosis inveterate, with constipation, tendency to neuralgia. Hypopion. Dim vision from paralysis of the optic nerve. Violent gastralgia, relieved by pressure and by eructations. Persistent or periodical vomiting from cerebral disease. Excruciating colic; abdomen retracted to the spine; recti muscles hard and knotty; tympanitic distension, obstruction of the bowels and frequent vomiting. Incarcerated hernia. Hepatitis, with characteristic pains. Jaundice, with constipation, vomiting, etc. Neuralgia of the rectum. Occasionally indicated in diarrhœa. Alternate diarrhœa and constipation. A valuable remedy in chronic constipation, with characteristic abdominal pains, retraction of the navel, marked spasm or contraction of the sphincter ani, stools dark, in lumps or balls, like sheep's dung. Paralysis of the bladder. Useful in the various forms of nephritis, acute and chronic, with symptoms given in pathogenesis. Chronic Bright's disease. According to Farrington there is very little dropsy or albuminuria, but a marked tendency to uræmic convulsions. Hæmaturia, with excruciating pains in course of the ureters. Dysmenorrhœa, with characteristic colic and retraction of navel. Vaginismus. Abortion from failure of the uterus to develop. Has been found useful in phthisis, stage of suppuration, short, dry cough, with purulent expectoration. Hæmoptysis.

PODOPHYLLUM.

Synonym.—Podophyllum Peltatum. *Natural order.*—Berberideæ. *Common names.*—May Apple. Mandrake. *Habitat.*—A perennial, herbaceous plant found abundantly in the Western and Middle states, and southward. *Preparation.*—Tincture from the fresh root.

GENERAL ANALYSIS.

Acts especially upon the liver and the digestive tract, its special affinity being for the mucous membranes, more especially of the duodenum and rectum, and for glandular structures, producing irritation, excessive secretions, inflammation and even ulceration or suppuration.

CHARACTERISTIC SYMPTOMS.

Head.—Morning headache, with heat in vertex (Nux v.). Giddiness and dizziness, with sensation of fullness over the eyes. °Headache preceded by blurring of vision, then gradually increasing pain, especially in the occiput, with nausea and vomiting (Iris). °Headache, rolling from side to side, with moaning (Hell.); during dentition, or *with bowel disorders*. Headache, alternating with diarrhœa.

Nose.—Soreness and little pustules in the nose.

Mouth.—°Grinding of the teeth (Ars., Cic., Hell., Hyos.), at night, especially during dentition. Offensive odor from the mouth (Arn., Aur., Hep. s., Iodi., Merc., Nux v.). Tongue coated white, with foul taste (*Nux v., Puls.*). Much viscid mucus in the mouth (Kali bi., Merc. cor.). Bitter, sour taste.

Throat.—Dryness of the throat (Apis, Ars., Bry., Nux m., Puls.). Soreness of the throat, extending to ears (Bell., Hep. s., Kali bi.).

Stomach.—Loss of appetite (Alum., Ars., Cinch., Phos.). Desire for something sour (Ant. tart., Hep. s., Phos.). Great thirst for large quantities of cold water (*Bry.*). Regurgitation of food, which is sour (*Phos.*), with acid eructations. Heartburn, with waterbrash, with heat in stomach (Ars.).

Nausea and vomiting, with fullness in head. Vomiting of food (Ipec., Nux v., Phos.); of thick, dark-green bile (Acon., Ars., Grat., Iris), mixed with dark, coagulated blood (Ham., Nux v., Op., Stram.); of hot, frothy mucus. *Hollow sensation in the epigastrium.*

Abdomen.—Fullness, with pain and soreness in right hypochondria. Pain and rumbling in transverse colon, at 3 A.M., followed by diarrhœa. Cramp-like pain in bowels, with retraction of abdominal muscles (Aloe, Chel., Plumb.), at 10 P.M. and 5 A. M. (Chel.). Heat in bowels, with inclination to stool.

Stool and Anus.—Hæmorrhoids (Ars., Nux v., Sulph.). Prolapsus ani (Ars.), with stool, or from least motion (*Ign.*). *Faintness, with sensation of emptiness in abdomen, after stool.* Protrusion of rectum after stool or any sudden motion, such as sneezing, and mental excitement, sometimes prolapsed for days owing to swelling and congestion. *Diarrhœa early in the morning* (Aloe, Nuph., *Rumex, Sulph.*); *stools green; sour* (Hep. s., *Rheum, Sulph.*), with much flatulence (Aloe, Coloc., Lyc.). Diarrhœa after much eating or drinking (*Coloc.*). Stools natural, but too frequent during the day, and exhausting. Alternate diarrhœa and constipation (*Ant. crud.*, Cimic., Natr. ars., Nux v.). Stool: *frequent, painless* (Nuph.), *watery* (Cinch.), *gushing, fœtid* (Ars.), *yellow, liquid; with mealy sediment; green, sour, watery; yellow, undigested fæces* (Arn., Cinch.); *mixed with mucus, offensive;* streaked with blood, and tenesmus; black only in morning; *preceded by griping and colic; with heat and pain in anus;* clay-colored, chalk-like (*Bell.*, Calc. c., Dol., *Hep. s.*, Myrica).

Urinary Organs.—°Enuresis; frequent nocturnal urinations (*Caust., Puls.*). °Suppression of urine (Acon., *Bell., Stram.*).

Female Organs.—*Pain in region of ovaries, especially right* (Bell.), *also with pain in uterus.* Sensation as if genitals would come out during stool. Prolapsus uteri, with aching and bearing down pains (Coni., Sep.). °Leucorrhœa of thick, transparent mucus (*Alum.*).

Generalities.—Pain under right shoulder blade (Abies). Pain between shoulders in morning.

Sleep.—*Sleepy, especially in forenoon.* Drowsy, half-closed eyes, moaning, whining, especially in children. Unrefreshed by sleep on waking in the morning. Restless sleep, especially forepart of night (*Phos.*).

Aggravation.—In morning, 2 to 4 A. M., of all symptoms except weakness in epigastric region.

Amelioration.—In the evening.

Conditions.—Bilious temperaments; especially after mercurialization.

Compare.—*Aloe,* Apis, Bry., *Chel.,* Colch., Hell., *Iris, Lept., Merc.,* Nitr. ac., Nux v., Puls., *Sulph.,* Sulph. ac., Verat. alb. After Ipec. Nux v. (vomiting).

Antidotes.—Lact. ac., Nux v. Salt increases its action.

Podophyllum Antidote.—Merc.

THERAPEUTICS.

The chief use of Podo. is in the treatment of hepatic disturbances—bilious conditions in general. Chronic congestion and torpidity of the liver. Chronic hepatitis. Tongue coated white or yellow, dull headache, liver swollen and sensitive, jaundice. Gall-stones, colic, with jaundice. Duodenitis, with jaundice. Ulceration of duodenum. Bilious headache. Bilious diarrhœa. Especially useful in morning diarrhœa, with sour, bilious stools. A valuable remedy in diarrhœa during hot weather, with a variety of stools such as have already been described in pathogenesis. A valuable remedy in prolapsus ani and protrusion of the rectum, especially when accompanying the characteristic diarrhœic conditions. Hæmorrhoids, with prolapsus ani; also when associated with prolapsus uteri. Constipation, stools clay-colored, prolapsus ani. May be found useful in dysentery characterized by prolapsus ani, hollow, sinking feeling in the abdomen, nausea, etc. Chronic dysentery, stools like washings of meat, with tenesmus and burning, nausea and vomiting. Catarrhal enteritis, with hot, watery stools. Often a valuable remedy in the diarrhœa of dentition, also reflex cerebral disturbances, grinding of the teeth, rolling head from side to side, with moaning. Will often prevent hydrocephaloid when the symptoms accompany profuse, exhausting stools. Gastric complications in liver disorders; also with uterine complaints. Acid dyspepsia. Enuresis. Prolapsus uteri, especially after confinement with aching and bearing down pains. Endometritis. Leucorrhœa of thick, transparent mucus. Suppression of menses, with hæmorrhoids, bearing down, etc. Ovaritis, especially on right side. Said to be indicated and useful also in ovarian tumors on right side. Often useful in bilious fever of a remittent type, with pronounced bilious symptoms. Bad effects from the use of Mercury.

PTELEA TRIFOLIATA.

Synonym.—Ptelea Viticifolia. *Natural order.*—Rutaceæ. *Common names.*—Wafer Ash. Hop Tree. Swamp Dogwood. *Habitat.*—An indigenous shrub growing west of the Alleghenies, in shady, moist hedges and in rocky places. *Preparation.*—Tincture from the fresh bark of the root.

GENERAL ANALYSIS.

Acts especially upon the mucous membranes of the digestive tract, producing symptoms of indigestion and bilious disturbance, and causing congestion of the liver, stomach and bowels; also, secondarily, of the lungs. Its action is not violent, but slow and pervading, giving rise to many chronic abnormal conditions.

CHARACTERISTIC SYMPTOMS.

Mind.—Disinclined to mental work, with languor rather than with inability. Great mental confusion, as in a bilious attack. Memory weak; forgetful, as if the intellect were slow to act; can remember by making a great effort.

Head.—Confusion; vertigo; worse when turning the head, or from sudden motion. Racking frontal headache, with red face and hurried manner. Constant dull headache; worse from walking. Headache in occipital region, passing to frontal, over the eyes. Pressive, bruised feeling at base of brain.

Ears.—Intolerance of loud talking or noise. Ringing in ears; slight giddiness. White blisters on a red sore on right ear, discharging watery fluid; later, desquamation or pus and scabs form; boils.

Face.—Sickly-pale expression, especially around the eyes. Face yellow; skin dry and hard.

Mouth.—Carious teeth sensitive; gums sore; teeth feel as if elongated (Merc., Nitr. ac.). Tongue coated with white fur; swollen; yellow; feels rough; papillæ red and prominent; brown-yellow, dry. Taste sour, mornings; bitter; food tasteless. Saliva profuse, drooling at night.

Stomach.—Voracious appetite; craves acid food (Ant. tart., Cinch., Phos. ac., Verat. alb.). Dislikes things formerly enjoyed. Repugnance to butter and fats (Hep. s., *Puls.*); also to animal food (Alum., Arn., Carb. v., Graph.. Puls.); and rich puddings. Hepatic and gastric symptoms worse after meals and in mornings (*Nux v.*). Eructations sour or bitter; tasting like rotten eggs (Arn., Ant. tart., *Psor.*, Sep.). Nausea, rising of a bitter fluid; confused head; dizzy; sweat on forehead; bilious. Sense of weight and fullness, even after a moderate meal. Burning distress in epigastrium; oppressing vomiting; chronic gastric catarrh. Pressure at pit of stomach, as from a stone (*Ars., Bry., Nux v., Puls.*); worse from a light meal.

Abdomen.—Liver swollen, sore on pressure, causing dull and aching pains. Weight and aching distress in hepatic region; dull pain, heaviness; better lying on the right side, turning to left causes a dragging sensation. Sharp, cutting pain in liver; worse from deep inspiration. Soreness and aching distress in abdomen. Pulsation in umbilical region, synchronous with the heart. Griping, colicky pains. with rumbling and discharge of wind from the bowels.

Stool.—Small hard stool, with much straining. Diarrhœa, bilious, thin, dark, offensive stools.

Urinary Organs.—Smarting in urethra during and after micturition; urine scanty, scalding (*Acon., Apis, Ars.*). Urine scanty, clear, or deep reddish-yellow; deposit of epithelia, phosphates and urates.

Respiratory Organs.—Pressure on lungs, with sense of suffocation; walls of chest feel as if they would sink in.

Back.—Severe aching distress in back.

Limbs.—Aching, bruised feeling in muscles and joints on awaking; drawing pains, especially with gastro-hepatic symptoms.

Generalities.—Restless, uneasy; malaise. Feeling of weakness; languid, irritable; sick, faint sensations, as in bilious patients. Smarting and prickling in mucous membranes.

Fever.—Chilliness, shivering; wants to be near the fire. Dry, general heat; worse in face and hands. Hot flushes and headache; feverish, hot head; dull, frontal aching. Sweat profuse on awaking; on forehead during stool.

Aggravation.—Lying on right side; from motion; walking in warm room; in mornings; on awaking; after meals.

Amelioration.—In open air.

Compare.—Berb., Hydras., Merc., Nux v., Podo.

THERAPEUTICS.

Ptelea has not been used clinically to any great extent, but has been found useful in bilious attacks; indigestion; gastralgia; congestion of liver; chronic hepatitis; diarrhœa; constipation, etc., the symptoms of the drug agreeing.

PULSATILLA.

Synonyms.—Pulsatilla Nigricans. Pulsatilla Pratensis. *Natural order.*—Ranunculaceæ. *Common names.*—Wind Flower. Meadow Anemone. Pasque Flower. *Habitat.*—A plant found on sunny, elevated places and pasture-grounds in sandy soil, and also in clear pine forests, in central and northern Europe. *Preparation.*—Tincture from the fresh plant.

GENERAL ANALYSIS.

Pulsatilla acts prominently upon all the mucous membranes of the body, and upon the synovial membranes, the veins, the eyes, the ears and the generative organs of both sexes, more especially the female. In the mucous membranes a catarrhal process is established, the secretions are modified, sometimes retarded, more often increased, the functions of the organs they supply are disturbed, the nervous system becomes irritated and depressed, and as a result we obtain the numerous symptoms of deranged digestion, respiratory troubles, genito-urinary disturbances, and catarrhal affections of the eye and ear, which so fully characterize the action of this drug. On the generative system Pulsatilla exerts a marked action outside of its catarrhal sphere, due probably to its influence over the cerebro spinal system. On the synovial membranes it produces arthritic or rheumatic inflammation, and in the veins varicose conditions.

CHARACTERISTIC SYMPTOMS.

Mind.—*Mild, gentle, timid, yielding disposition, with inclination to weep* (Apis, *Ign.*, Lil. tig., *Natr. mur.*, Nux m.). Tremulous anxiety, as if death were near (Acon., Ars.). Fears ghosts at night, or in the evening (Acon., Ars.). Anxiety about the heart in the evening, even to suicide. *Anxiety at night, as from heat.* Peevish and capricious, though not vexed. Irresolute. *Hypochondriac moroseness; out of sorts with everything* (*Nux v.*). Many wandering thoughts. Ill-humored, discontented, fretful (*Bry., Cham.*).

Head.—Confusion of head, with bruised pains or hollow feeling in head. *Vertigo; as if intoxicated* (Cinch., *Coccul., Nux v.*, Rhus tox.); on stooping (Bell.); better *while sitting; in morning on rising* (*Bry.*); *must lie down again; with nausea and inclination to vomit.* Heaviness on stooping, as if he could not raise it again. *Dullness of the head, and bruised sensation in forehead* (Cinch., Puls., Sang.). Headache on one side, as if the brain would burst (Bry., Caps., *Natr. mur.*), and the eyes fall out. Headache from stooping. *Headache from overloaded stomach* (Bry., Ipec., Iris, Nux v.), *or from fats.* Violent boring pain behind one side, as if a nail were driven in. *Headache, with aching pain in the eyes, in the evening. Throbbing, pressive headache, relieved by pressure* (Apis, Arg. nit.). *Pressive pain in forehead above the orbits, aggravated on raising the eyes.* Stitching, tearing pain in temples and through the whole head. Pulsation in the head in the evening (Nux m.). Biting itching of the scalp. Pressive and constrictive pain in temples. Constriction above eyes, worse on looking intently.

Eyes.—Dryness of the eyes and lids, with sensation as if darkened by mucus, which ought to be wiped away (Alum., Croc., Euph.). Pressure, as from sand in the eyes, when reading (Ars., *Caust.*, Ign., Natr. mur., *Sulph.*). *Conjunctivitis, with profuse, thick, yellow, bland discharge. Burning and itching in the eyes, provokes rubbing and scratching. Inflammation of eyes and margins of eyelids, with lachrymation and nightly agglutination* (Alum., Æth., Calc. c., Graph., *Lyc.*, Merc., *Sulph.*). *Subject to styes, especially on upper lids* (Graph., *Lyc.*). *Itching, biting and burning in the lids and canthi, in the evening. Profuse lachrymation, in the wind or open air* (*Sulph.*). *Dimness of vision, like a fog or veil before the eyes* (*Caust.*, Hyos., Laur., Merc., Phos., Petrol., Ranunc., *Sulph.*). *Dark before the eyes in the morning on rising* (Dulc.), *and on going into a warm room.*

Ears.—External ear and meatus red, swollen and hot (Acon., Apis, Bell.). Otalgia, with darting, tearing pains (*Bell.*, Sil.), and pulsating at night (Merc.). Itching deep in the ears. *Violent pain in the ear, as from something forcing outward. Hardness of hearing, as if the ears were stopped. Sensation as if the ear were stopped, with roaring in it like a loud, distant noise.* Humming, roaring, singing and ringing in the ears (Calc. c., Graph., Kali c.). Cracking in ears on moving head or body. Bland, nearly inoffensive discharge of mucus and pus from the ears.

Nose.—Coryza, fluent or dry; *frequent sneezing; loss of smell and taste* (Ant. tart.); *nostrils sore; wings raw* (Lyc.; later, *yellow-green discharge* (Graph., Merc.); *worse indoors* (Cepa, Nux v.); *chilliness; pale face; head confused; frontal headache* (Acon., Cepa, Sang.). Stoppage of nose in evening; and in warm room in morning; yellow, opaque, offensive mucous discharge (Nitr. ac.). Bad smell, as of old catarrh in the nose (Sulph.). Epistaxis with catarrh; with suppressed menses (Bry., Calc., Ferr., Sep.). Abscess at root of nose near inner canthus, as if lachrymal fistula would form. Ulceration of nostrils; wings of nose, and oozing of watery moisture.

sation at root of nose (Acon., Kali bi.). Nasal bones pain as if they would be forced asunder.

Face.—Paleness of the face. Boring in left malar bone. Lower lip swollen and cracked in the middle, with tensive pain.

Mouth.—Sharp, shooting pains in teeth, or *drawing, jerking, as if nerve were put on the stretch, and then let loose.* Toothache worse; *evening and night; in warmth of bed* (Cham.); *from taking anything warm in the mouth* (Cham.); when eating; from picking teeth. Pain in the gums as if sore. *Better in open air; from uncovering; when cold water taken into the mouth becomes warm.* Tongue dry; *covered with a tenacious mucus; as with a membrane;* coated thick, white or yellow (*Bry., Merc., Nux. v.,* Podo.). Sensation in middle, as if burned (Iris, Plat., Sang., Sulph. ac., Verat. vir.); insensible, even when moist; at night and in morning; painful blister on right side of tip. *Very offensive odor from the mouth* (Arn., Aur., Hep. s., *Merc.,* Nux v.) in morning; in evening after lying down; at night. *Mouth and pharynx dry and covered with tasteless, insipid, tenacious mucus in morning. Accumulation of sweet saliva in the mouth* (Cham., Phos.); watery saliva, like waterbrash. Taste: *of putrid meat, in morning, with inclination to vomit* (Arn., Merc.); *slimy; foul, clammy, insipid; bitter, especially after eating* (*Bry.,* Coloc., *Nux v.*); *or smoking, though food has a natural taste; bad taste in the mouth in the morning. Food, especially bread,* tastes bitter (*Bry.,* Cinch., Coloc., *Nux v., Sulph.*). or taste of food diminished. Great dryness of the mouth in the morning, without thirst (Apis, *Nux m.*).

Throat.—Rawness and scraping in the throat (Amm. carb., Carb. v., Caust., Phos.), with dryness of the mouth. Great dryness of the throat (Apis, *Nux m.*), in the morning. Throat internally covered with a tenacious mucus, in morning. Pressure and tension in throat on swallowing. Constriction. Sensation of a worm creeping up into the throat.

Stomach.—Desires food, but does not know what kind. Aversion to fat food (Hep. s., Ptel.), meat (Graph., Ptel.), bread (*Natr. mur.*), butter (Ptel.), milk; to smoking (Ign.).

Thirst for beer (Coccul., Petrol.), or alcoholic drinks. °*Thirstlessness, with all complaints (Ant. tart., Apis). Eructations after eating, tasting and smelling of food* (Ant. crud., Calc. c., Cinch., Graph., Phos.); *bitter, bilious, rancid, sour (Bry., Nux v., Phos.); tastes like putrid meat.* Hiccough when smoking. *Nausea; in epigastric region, worse from eating or drinking; waterbrash* (Led., Nux v.); *disagreeable risings, especially after eating and drinking (Ars.).* °Morning nausea, especially during menses, from suppressed menses, or during pregnancy (Graph., Kali c., Nux m., Sep.). Vomiting of bilious matter (Ars., Bry., Nux v., Podo.); *of food eaten long before,* or after each meal. Distension. Griping pains in pit of stomach and epigastrium. °*Stomach disordered from fat food* (Cycl., Tarax.), pasty (Ipec., Nux v.), fruit or ice-cream. *Pain in stomach an hour after eating (Nux v.).* Weight, as from a stone (Acon., Æsc., Ars., Bry., Nux v.), especially in morning on waking. Crampy pains in stomach, in morning, or after meals. *Gnawing distress in stomach, as from hunger* (Abies c.). Pressing, pinching, or choking pains in stomach after eating, impeding breathing. *Sensation as of having taken too much food, which rises into the mouth, as if one would vomit. Scraping sensation in stomach (Nux v.), and œsophagus, like a heartburn.* Tension in region of stomach in forenoon, better from moving about. Perceptible pulsation in pit of stomach (Ant. tart., Asaf.).

Abdomen.—*Flatulent colic; loud rumbling and gurgling* (Lyc.); *flatus moves about in abdomen (Aloe, Carb. v.), especially in evening; in bed.* Incarcerated flatus, pressing here and there; not relieved by passing flatus (Cinch.); after midnight. Colic and griping, especially in upper abdomen. Fullness and distension of abdomen and stomach; painful sensitiveness. Pain, in evening after drinking; after drinking; after stool; on touch. *Chilliness extending around from abdomen to lower part of back. Pressure in abdomen* (Berb.), *and small of back, as from a stone; limbs go to sleep while sitting;* ineffectual desire to stool. Drawing, tearing or forcing-down pains in abdomen, like labor-pains. Cutting low down in abdomen, pene-

trating into pelvis (Cham.). *Constriction as from a stone extending to the bladder.*

Stool and Anus.—*Painful, protruding, blind piles* (*Aloe*, Calc. c., Lach., Merc., Sil.), with stitches, smarting, soreness and *itching* (*Sulph.*). Pressure in rectum after stool. Frequent urging, as if diarrhœa would occur. Stools *watery at night, like bile, preceded by rumbling; green mucus* (Apis, Arg. nit., Ars., Bell., Ipec., Merc., Sulph.); *slimy; soft; mixed with mucus, or only mucus, with colic; frequent* (*Merc. cor.*); *bloody mucus, without colic;* not exhausting (*Phos. ac.*). Constipation; difficult evacuation, with painful pressure and pain in back; stools white; yellowish-white, mucus mixed with stool.

Urinary Organs.—Tenesmus of the bladder (Canth., Caps., Merc. cor.). Region of bladder painful to touch. Sharp pressure on bladder, without desire to urinate. Burning in orifice of urethra during and after micturition (*Can. sat., Canth.*). Frequent, almost ineffectual, urging to urinate, with acrid urine and cutting pains. *Involuntary micturition* (*Ars.,* Bell., Hyos.); *at night, in bed* (Arn., Cupr., Graph.), especially in little girls, while coughing or passing flatus (*Caust.*, Natr. mur.). Dribbling of urine while sitting or walking. *Frequent urinations, profuse flow* (Apis, Apoc., Arg., Cepa, Ber.). Urine watery, colorless; brown; bloody.

Male Organs.—*Drawing, tensive pains, from abdomen through spermatic cords, into testicles* (Berb., Ham., Merc.), *which hang low down. Swelling of the testicles, with soreness and tearing pains. Swelling of right side of scrotum* (Clem.). Desire in the morning on waking. Nocturnal emissions (Cinch., Phos.), without dreams. Itching biting on inner and upper part of prepuce. °Thick, yellow, or yellow-green discharge from urethra, in gonorrhœa (Agn., Hydras.).

Female Organs.—*During menses and with uterine troubles, heavy, pressive pain in abdomen and small of back, as from a stone* (Alum., Caul., Cimic.); *limbs tend to go to sleep; ineffectual urging to stool. Drawing, pressing pain extending toward uterus, with nausea in morning. Chilliness before the menses, with yawning and* **stretch-**

ing. *Constrictive pain in left side of uterus, like labor-pains, obliging her to bend double. Menses suppressed; after getting feet wet. Menses delayed, with coldness of body and chilliness and trembling of the feet. First menses delayed* (Graph.). *Menses too late, scanty, and of short duration* (Cimic., Sulph.): *suppressed,* or flow intermittent (Cimic.); flow thick and black (Ign.); more during day while walking about (at night, *Mag. carb.*). *Leucorrhœa thick, like cream or milk* (Calc. c., Coni., Sep., Sulph. ac.); *worse when lying down; with swollen vulva; painless; acrid, thin, burning* (Alum., Coni., Kreos., Merc., Phos.).

Respiratory Organs.—*Violent tickling and scraping in the larynx, bringing tears into the eyes and causing dry cough.* Constriction in larynx, especially at night when lying down. Hoarseness and roughness of throat; cannot speak a loud word (Caust., Hep. s., Phos.). *Dry cough at night or in evening, after lying down (Coni.,* Mez., Nux v., *Rumex, Sulph.); disappears on sitting up in bed, returns on lying down* (Hyos.); *causes dryness of throat; prevents sleep;* with nausea and vomiting; causes exhaustion. °Cough dry at night, loose during the day. *Expectoration difficult; yellow mucus* (Calc. c.), in morning after rising; bitter; scanty, of tenacious mucus; black clotted blood (*Nux v.*). Dyspnœa in lower part of chest, as if too full and tight, especially mornings (Bell., Phos.). Oppression of the chest. Cramp-like and constrictive tension in the chest. *Shortness of breath, anxiety and palpitation when lying on left side.* Scraping and soreness in chest, causing cough (Cham.). Pain in chest behind sternum, as if ulcerated (Psor.). Pressure and soreness in chest. Stitches in the chest and sides, when lying, at night, from inspiration or coughing (Acon., *Bry., Kali c.*).

Heart and Pulse.—Catching pain in cardiac region; better for a time from pressure of hand. Stitches in præcordial region, better while walking, with pressure and anxiety, impeding respiration. *Palpitation, with anxiety, after dinner; from lying on left side, with anxiety and want of breath;* °with menstrual irregularities, chlorosis, etc. The beat of the pulse is felt in the pit of the stomach.

Neck and Back.—Stiffness, and rheumatic, tensive, and drawing pains in nape of neck (Colch.). Sticking pains in nape of neck and back. Pain in nape at night, as if he had lain in an uncomfortable position. *Pain in small of back, as from long stooping* (Arn., Cinch.), *or from a sprain (Sulph.);* on motion; after sitting (Rhus tox.); in evening. Back painfully stiff. *Labor-like pains in small of back* (Caul., Cimic., Kreos.), as if constricted by a tight band. Pain as if suppurating. Drawing, tensive pain in loins. Pressive pains in sacrum, in evening, as from fatigue.

Limbs.—Redness and swelling of joints (Bry.), with stinging pains (Apis). Anxious tremulous sensation in limbs. Drawing, sticking, worse in joints, which are painful to touch. Weakness in limbs morning after rising, with relaxation without feeling weary. *Drawing, tearing pains in limbs* (Acon.), °*shifting rapidly from place to place;* worse at night, from warmth (*Merc.*); better from uncovering. *Pain in limbs in morning in bed, worse in joints, forcing him to stretch, with general heat.* On waking, the parts on which he has lain are asleep, with crawling and tingling (Acon.). Coldness of hands and feet; they seem dead.

Upper Limbs.—Sensation of numbness and heaviness in the arms, as if beaten. Drawing, tearing pains, in shoulder joints, and in arms, hands and fingers (Bry., Led., Rhus tox.). Swelling and wrenching pains in elbow joints.

Lower Limbs.—*Hip-joint painful, as if dislocated.* Acute, drawing, jerking pains from the hip to the knee. Bruised pains in the gluteal muscles, and in muscles and bones of thighs. *Drawing, tensive pains in thighs and legs at night, with great restlessness, sleeplessness and chilliness. Painless swelling of the knee. Knees swollen, with tearing, drawing pains.* Drawing, heaviness and weariness in legs and feet. Legs seem asleep on rising from a seat. Cramps in legs, in evening, after lying down (*Sulph.*). Feet inflamed, red-hot, swollen (*Bry.*), with tensive, burning pains; also soles. *Varices on the legs* (Ham., Zinc.); *on feet.* Weakness in feet. Pain in soles, as if beaten. *Boring pain in heels toward evening* (Zinc.). Chilblains, burning, sticking, itching (Agar., Nitr. ac.).

Generalities.—Violent trembling of the whole body; with cold

PULSATILLA.

sweat, anxiety and drawing pains. Excessive weariness and prostration (Ars., Phos., Ferr.). Everything about body seems too tight, wishes to throw off her clothes. Heaviness of the whole body. Inclination to stretch. Lies upon back with hands above head when sleeping; also with feet drawn up. *Longing for fresh air* (*Lyc*.). *Feeling of discomfort over the whole body, in morning, after rising, disappearing on moving about. Weaker the longer he lies in the morning.* °Wandering pains shift rapidly from part to part (Benz. ac., Kali bi., Led.). °Symptoms ever-changing. Pulsations through the whole body (*Glon*., Sep., Zinc.).

Skin.—*Burning, biting, itching here and there; worse from warmth of bed, in evenings and before midnight; from scratching; from becoming heated during a walk* (Clem., Merc., Mez., Sulph.). *Itching in the evening in bed.* °Measly-like eruption (Ant. crud., Bapt., Coff. c., Rhus tox.); nettle rash (Apis).

Sleep.—*Irresistible sleepiness in afternoon and early evening. Cannot go to sleep in evening; sleepless first part of night. Sleeps late in morning. Restless sleep, with sensation of heat;* wakes frequently, as in frights. Dreams; *confused;* vivid, frightful, disgusting, anxious (Arn., Aur., Rhus tox., *Sulph*.). Frequent yawning.

Fever.—*Constant chilliness, even in warm room; cold chills* all over, chilly, with the pains; *worse evenings* (Phos.). Shivering, creeping sensations. *Anxious heat, as if dashed with hot water. Intolerable, dry, burning heat, evening or night; with distended veins* (Cinch.), *and burning hands that seek out cool places, without thirst* (*Ign*., *Phos*.). Profuse sweat in morning (Calc. c., *Nitr*. ac., Rhus tox.), one-sided sweat.

Aggravation.—*In the evening and in succeeding hours till midnight;* every other evening; at night; from warmth of bed; °while lying down, especially on left side; °from lying on painless side; in warm room; after eating, °especially after fat food, pork, ice-cream, fruit, pastry.

Amelioration.—*In open air* (Ox. ac.); *in cool place; when lying upon the back;* °lying on painful side; °from cold drink; °from slow motion.

Conditions.—Sandy hair, blue eyes, pale face, inclined to silent grief and submissiveness; especially women and children. Slow, phlegmatic; peevish but not irascible.

Compare.—*Ant. crud.*, Ars., *Bell.*, Bry., Calc. c., *Caul.*, Cham., Cimic., Cinch., Coccul., Coloc., *Coni., Cycl.*, Euphr., Ferr., *Ham.*, Ign., Kali bi., *Lyc.*, Merc., Nux v., Nux m., Plat., *Phos., Rhus tox., Sep.*, Sil., *Sulph.*, Zinc.

Antidotes.—*Coff. c.*, Cham., Ign., Nux v. (Acetum).

Pulsatilla Antidotes.—Cinch.. Iron, Sulph., Sulph. ac. Vapor of Mercury or of Copper (Bell., Cham., Coff. c., Colch., Lyc., Plat., Stram.).

THERAPEUTICS.

The chief clinical use of Pulsatilla is in the treatment of catarrhal affections, characterized by thick, yellowish-green discharges, disorders of digestion and disturbances of the female sexual system. It is also useful in rheumatism, usually subacute, often arising from derangements of digestion, with drawing, tearing, shifting pains, better from cold, worse in the evening. Gonorrhœal rheumatism. Neuralgia, wandering pains, mostly tearing, with tendency to chilliness and the characteristic modalities. Chorea, epileptiform spasms or paralytic symptoms, arising from suppressed menses or other disturbances of the sexual sphere. Hysteria from similar causes; chlorosis and anæmia, patient always chilly. but wants to be in the open air; mental disorders; especially after the abuse of Iron and Quinine. Pulsatilla acts prominently on the venous system (*Ham.*), and is useful in varicose veins; in the hæmorrhages calling for the drug, the flow is passive and dark. In all the above conditions and those which are to follow, the temperament of the Puls. patient as mentioned under "Conditions," must be borne in mind, sadness and weeping, even to melancholia, being extremely characteristic. We will now consider the special clinical uses of Puls. in the customary anatomical order. Conjunctivitis thick, bland, yellow or yellowish-green discharge, after measles or from taking cold. Ophthalmia neonatorum. Pustular conjunctivitis. Styes. Blepharitis. Pustules or ulcers on cornea. Disease of the lachrymal duct with characteristic symptoms of drug. Episcleritis. Hyperæmia of the choroid. Retinitis. Occasionally useful in iritis.

PULSATILLA.

A valuable remedy in earache, with darting, tearing pains, relieved by cold. Otitis, external ear and meatus red, swollen and hot. Otorrhœa, discharge of mucus and bloody pus. Deafness from catarrh or after scarlet fever. A most valuable remedy in acute coryza from taking cold especially in the advanced stages, patient cold and chilly all the time (see symptoms). Chronic nasal catarrh, with characteristic discharge, etc., worse evenings, especially with loss of smell and taste. Neuralgic toothache; during pregnancy; with characteristic modalities. Occasionally useful in pharyngeal catarrh, parts dark-red, varicose dry, covered with mucus, bad taste. A frequently indicated and extremely useful remedy in various disorders of digestion. Gastric catarrh, dyspepsia and indigestion in general, characterized by putrid, slimy, greasy or bitter taste after eating or in the morning; tongue coated thick-white or yellow: loss of appetite; vertigo; bitter or rancid eructations; continual nausea and qualmishness; regurgitation of food; pain and weight in stomach; especially aggravated by fat foods (Cycl.). Dyspepsia from ice-cream, etc. (Ars.); ice-water; fruit; buckwheat cakes; fat food. Atonic dyspepsia. Gastralgia, with more or less of above symptoms. Morning sickness of pregnancy; also during menses or from suppressed menses; also colic from same causes. Flatulent colic, intestinal catarrh and diarrhœa from causes above named, and from taking cold, with gastric symptoms. Hæmorrhoids with characteristic gastric symptoms. Occasionally needed in dysentery, with bloody mucous stools, burning in anus, etc. Enuresis, especially in girls; while coughing (Caust.), or passing flatus. Catarrh of bladder from cold; during pregnancy or suppressed menses; with enlarged prostate; from suppressed gonorrhœa. Gonorrhœa with characteristic discharge and other symptoms. Orchitis. Enlarged prostate. Epididymitis. Neuralgia of testicles. Hydrocele, especially congenital. An extremely useful remedy in suppressed menstruation, especially from getting the feet wet; dysmenorrhœa from same causes. Amenorrhœa and dysmenorrhœa in general, with Puls. symptoms, and especially with characteristic temperament; gastric derangements. Vicarious menstruation. Leucorrhœa as noted in symptoms, especially with delayed or irregular menses and other Puls. symptoms. Prolapsus uteri. A valuable remedy for the disorders of pregnancy; also during the lying-in period. Is said to correct malpositions of the fœtus, by altering abnormal conditions of uterus. Inertia of uterus; during labor-pains slow, weak and ineffectual. Retained placenta. Tones up the uterus and prevents post-partum hæmorrhage. Phantom tumors; scanty or suppressed lochia; lochia becomes white, like milk. Phlegmasia alba dolens. Milk suppressed. Puls. is the remedy for lumps in the breasts of school girls, before puberty, or escape of thin, milky fluid. Puls. is not so often used in catarrh of the lower air passages. It may, however, be indicated in catarrhal laryngitis or bronchitis, or even in catarrhal pneumonia, the symptoms agreeing. Aphonia reflex, occasionally catarrhal. Asthma, in children, or in women with menstrual irregularities. Chlorosis. Occasionally indicated in whooping cough. Threatening phthisis, especially in girls near puberty, menses delayed or suppressed, chlorotic symptoms, soreness in apices of lungs, short breath; characteristic temperament. Hæmoptysis, blood black and clotted, soreness in chest. An excellent remedy for the ordinary "backache" of women, especially with menstrual derangements and other Puls. conditions; and during pregnancy; extending from small of back downwards into sacrum and hips; as if sprained; worse when lying on the back, better when lying on the side, or on changing position. Lumbago. Spinal irritation; neck and back stiff; small of back feels as if constricted by a tight band. Rheumatism of extremities as before mentioned. Gout. Varicose ulcers on limbs. A valuable remedy in measles, after Acon., etc., with dry cough, earache and other Puls. symptoms. Not often indicated in fevers, but may be useful in gastric, remittent or intermittent fevers with the characteristic gastric symptoms, and especially when chilliness is the predominating feature.

RANUNCULUS.

Synonym.—Ranunculus Bulbosus. *Natural order.*—Ranunculaceæ. *Common name.*—Bulbous Crowfoot. *Habitat.*—An indigenous plant, common in New England. *Preparation.*—Tincture from the entire fresh plant.

GENERAL ANALYSIS.

Acts upon the sensory nerves, the muscular tissues and upon the skin, its most characteristic effects being exerted upon the walls of the chest, where it produces a condition simulating pleurodynia, in which affection it is most prominently useful.

CHARACTERISTIC SYMPTOMS.

Mind.—Vanishing of thought on reflection. Obtuse intellect. Irritable and quarrelsome.

Head.—Vertigo; with danger of falling, when going from room to open air; making it difficult to think. Sensation as if the head were too large and distended (Mang. c.). Congestion of blood to the head (*Acon., Bell.*). Pain in head and eyes. Headache over the right eye, worse on lying down, better from walking or standing; in evening. Neuralgic headache in forehead and vertex, as if forced asunder, worse evenings, or on coming into warm room. Pressing pain in forehead, from within outward. Headache mostly caused or aggravated by passing from a hot to a cold place, and *vice-versa*.

Eyes.—Pressure in the eyeballs. Balls sore on moving them. Pupils insensible. Burning, soreness and smarting in lids. Smarting and sore feeling in right outer canthus. Smarting in eyes as from smoke. Mist before the eyes (*Caust.*, Hyos., Phos., Petrol.).

Ears.—Stitches in the ears, principally in the evening; in region of right tympanum.

Nose.—Redness and inflammatory swelling of the nose, with tension. Stoppage. Profuse, tenacious mucus. Blows blood from the nose. Internal tingling and upward pressure.

Mouth.—White saliva, with metallic taste.

Throat.—Much viscid phlegm in the throat. Inflammatory burning pains in the throat and on the palate.

Stomach.—Increased thirst afternoons. Frequent eructations. Spasmodic hiccough (Hyos., Ign.). Nausea in the afternoon, sometimes with headache. Pressure in the pit of the stomach (Ars., Bry., Puls.). Sensation of burning in pit of stomach, and in region of cardiac orifice.

Abdomen.—*Pain and soreness in hypochondria, as if bruised; evenings; with pain in back, lassitude and ill-humor. Stitches in the hepatic region, arresting the breathing with stitches and pressure on top of right shoulder* (Bry.). Stitches in left side of abdomen. Pinching, cutting colic. Abdomen sore on pressure, as if bruised and ulcerated. Pinching sometimes alternating with pain in chest.

Stool.—Frequent and easy. Hard stools every morning, with much urging; natural stool in afternoon.

Respiratory Organs.—*Short and oppressed breathing, with burning and fine stitching pains in the chest, and* inclination to draw a long breath, with much weeping. *Stitches in chest; increased by moving, stooping, inspiration* (Bry.), *or touch; with pressure and tightness across lower part of chest.* Rheumatic pains in the chest, as from subcutaneous ulceration. Burning pains. *Chest feels sore and bruised* (Arn.); *worse from contact and motion* (Senega).

Back.—Pain in back, lassitude and pain as if bruised, in region of short ribs. Pain in morning on rising. Stitches in right lumbar region when walking, with slight burning sensation.

Upper Limbs.—Spasmodic, rheumatic pains in the arms. Stitches in arms, hands and fingers. Crawling in single parts of fingers. Shining red, loose swelling of fingers, with inflammation, etc., changing to flat, spreading ulcers. Blister-like eruptions on palms of hands and fingers. Itching in hollow of hand.

Lower Limbs.—Drawing pains along the thighs. Great weakness in lower limbs when walking, forenoons. Pulsative stitches in left heel when standing.

Generalities.—Great heaviness and lassitude in the whole body. The whole body feels bruised (Arn., Ruta). Shooting, tearing, rheumatic and arthritic pains in limbs and muscles.

Skin.—Vesicular eruption, as from burns (Canth.). *Dark-blue vesicles, small, transparent,* in groups, with burning and itching, and forming hard, horny scurfs. Tettery eruptions over the whole body.

Sleep.—Falls asleep late and wakes frequently during the night. Restless, disturbed sleep.

RHEUM. 653

Aggravation.—From changes of temperature (Mang., Rhus tox.), *mornings;* evenings; touch; motion; °change of position; °from alcoholic drinks.
Compare.—Acon., *Bry.,* Cimic., Clem., *Puls., Rhus tox.,* Sabad.
Antidotes.—Bry., Camph., Puls., Rhus tox.
Inimicals.—Alcohol, Staph., Sulph., Vinegar, Wine.

THERAPEUTICS.

Ranunc. has been found most useful in neuralgic, arthritic and rheumatic conditions. Always worse from damp weather or from change of temperature. Rheumatic neuralgia. Intercostal rheumatism, chest feels sore and bruised, as from subcutaneous ulceration. Pleurodynia. Pleurisy. Diaphragmitis. Peritonitis. A very valuable remedy in herpes zoster; dark-blue, transparent vesicles, with characteristic neuralgic pains. Also herpes frontalis, with violent pains in and above the eyes. Vesicular eruptions, with burning and itching. Pemphigus. Malignant and rapidly spreading ulcers. Hay fever, with smarting, burning and tingling in eyes and nose, nostrils dry and obstructed, worse evenings. Has been found useful in delirium tremens and for the effects of intoxicating liquors in general.

RHEUM.

Synonyms.—Rheum Officinale. Rhubarbarum. *Natural order.*—Polygonaceæ. *Common name.*—Rheubarb. *Habitat.*—A plant native of China. *Preparation.*—Tincture from the dried root.

GENERAL ANALYSIS.

Acts especially upon the liver and intestinal canal, increasing the secretion of bile, stimulating the muscular activity of the bowels, and causing purging of fæcal matter, without symptoms of inflammatory action. Its chief characteristic is a diarrhœa, with an excessively sour-smelling stool.

CHARACTERISTIC SYMPTOMS.

Mind.—The child demands different things, with vehemence and crying.

Head.—Dull, stupefying headache. Heaviness of the head. Sweat on forehead and scalp after slight effort.

Face.—Cool sweat on face (Verat. alb.); most around nose and mouth.

Stomach.—*Desire for various things, but cannot eat them; they become repulsive* (*Bry., Cham., Cina*). Nausea, as from the stomach or abdomen, with colic. Fullness in stomach, as after eating too much (*Cinch., Lyc., Nux v., Puls.*).

Abdomen.—Violent, cutting colic, forcing one to bend double (Aloe, Caust., *Coloc.*, Iris). Tension. Griping in abdomen, with great urging to stool; better after stool; worse from plums.

Stool and Anus.—Frequent, ineffectual urging to stool (Ambr., Coni., Natr. carb., Nux v.); worse on motion and when walking. Colic before each stool (*Coloc., Merc.*). Desire for stool after a meal. *Thin, pasty, sour-smelling stools* (Arn., Hep. s., *Podo.*, Sulph.), *with straining before, and colicky, constrictive cutting in the abdomen after, and shivering during stool* (Merc.). Frequent, forcible, semi-liquid stools; brown, mixed with mucus; followed by tenesmus, and great burning in anus and rectum (*Ars., Sulph.*).

Back.—Violent cutting, as if in the lumbar vertebræ, increased from stool.

Limbs.—Pain in all the joints during motion. The limbs upon which he lies fall asleep. Weariness of the thighs, as after great exertion. Tensive, pressive pain in the hollow of the left knee, extending to the heel.

Sleep.—Restless sleep, with tossing about, and talking in sleep (Acon., *Rhus tox.*). Vivid, sad, anxious dreams. Snoring inspiration during sleep.

Generalities.—°Child smells sourish, even if washed or bathed every day. Heaviness of the whole body, as after awaking from a deep sleep.

Condition.—Often suitable for children, suckling or during dentition.

Compare.—Ars., *Bell.*, Cham., Coloc., Mag. c., Nux v., Podo., Puls., Rhus tox., *Sulph.* Complementary to Mag. carb., while Rheum, follows Ipec. well.
Antidotes.—*Cham.*, Camph., Coloc., Merc., *Nux v.*, Puls.
Rheum Antidotes.—Canth., Mag. carb.

CHARACTERISTIC SYMPTOMS.

The chief and almost only clinical use of Rheum is in the treatment of diarrhœa, especially in infants, teething children and lying-in women, characterized by excessively sour-smelling stools, and other symptoms as noted above. Not only are the stools sour, but the whole body smells sour, no matter how often bathed, thus showing an excessively acid state of the system.

RHODODENDRON.

Synonym.—Rhododendron Chrysanthemum. *Natural order.*—Ericaceæ. *Common names.*—Dwarf Rosebag. *Habitat.*—An evergreen shrub, native of Siberia, growing on mountain heights. *Preparation.*—Tincture from the dried leaves.

GENERAL ANALYSIS.

Acts upon the muscular and fibrous tissues, producing arthritic and rheumatic conditions, and upon the testes and epididymis, producing inflammation, swelling and induration. Its chief characteristic is the aggravation of all symptoms in cold, stormy weather, and before and during a thunder storm.

CHARACTERISTIC SYMPTOMS.

Mind.—Forgetfulness of what he is talking about.
Head.—Headache, almost depriving him of his senses, better on rising. Confusion. Pain in forehead and temples, when lying in bed, in the morning; worse from drinking wine (Nux v., Zinc.), and in wet weather, cold weather; better after rising and on moving about. Tearing, boring pains in left temporal region.

Eyes.—Sensation of dryness and burning in the eyes; worse in bright daylight, and from intent looking; on reading or writing.

Ears.—Violent pain in the right outer ear, commencing in morning, and continuing all day. Humming before ears, with ringing. Buzzing and sensation as if water running into the ears. Loud sounds re-echo long.

Nose.—Obstruction of left nostril, sometimes alternating with right; best in open air.

Mouth.—*Toothache, drawing, tearing pains; worse in stormy weather or before a storm* (Rhus tox.); *in cloudy or windy weather, with cutting.*

Throat.—Scraping and scratching sensation in the throat, as if lined with mucus.

Stomach.—Empty eructations. Contractive pressure in pit of stomach evenings when walking, with tight breath.

Stool.—Soft stool, evacuated slowly, and with much urging (Carb. v., Cinch.). Diarrhœa; in damp weather; from fruit; food passes undigested.

Urinary Organs.—Frequent urging to urinate, with drawing in region of bladder. Pain in urethra, as from subcutaneous ulceration. Urine somewhat increased, pale, of offensive acrid odor.

Male Organs.—Drawing pain from anus to testicles. *Testicles drawn up, swollen and painful* (Clem.). *Testicles, especially epididymis, intensely painful to touch. Contusive pain in testicle* (Arg. nit., Spong.), *with alternate drawing. Induration and swelling of testicles* (Acon., Arg., Caust.), *especially right, with violent drawing pains, extending to abdomen and thighs.* Sticking, stitching pains in right testicle. Itching, and increase of heat about the scrotum (Sil.).

Female Ogans.—°Pain in ovaries; worse in change of weather.

Respiratory Organs.—Dry, exhausting cough, morning and evening, with oppression of the chest, and rough throat; in paroxysms, from tickling in trachea. Transient, dull pain from chest to left hypochondrium when walking fast.

Neck and Back.—Rheumatic pain, with stiffness in nape of neck; early in morning, in bed or after rising. Bruised pain in small of back; *worse at rest,* and in rainy weather (Rhus

RHODODENDRON.

tox.). Sprained pain, or as if he had been sitting bent too long, or lying upon it too long. Pain in back when sitting, better from motion, worse from stooping.

Limbs.—Rheumatic, drawing, tearing pains in all the limbs (Acon., Coloc., Led., Puls.); worse at rest, and in rough weather (Rhus tox.). Sensation in the joints as if sprained; also tearing, drawing pains. Drawing and tearing in the periosteum, mostly in forearms and legs; in small spots; worse at night; at rest; *from change of weather* (Rhus tox.). Heat of the hands. Itching of right middle and ring fingers with erysipelatous redness.

Aggravation.—In morning; *while at rest* (Amm. carb., Rhus tox.); before a thunder storm; in cold, damp weather (Dulc.); *windy and cold weather; rough weather.*

Amelioration.—In bed the limbs drawn up.

Compare.—Aur., Bry., Calc. c., *Clem.*, Coni., Kalmia, Led., Lyc., Merc., Nux v., *Puls., Ranunc., Rhus tox.*, Sep., Sil., Sulph.

Antidotes.—Bry., Camph., Clem., Rhus tox.

THERAPEUTICS.

Especially useful in arthritic and rheumatic pains in various parts, aggravated before a storm, or in cold, damp, rough weather. Chronic rheumatism of small joints (Actea sp., Caul., Led.). Rheumatoid arthritis. According to Allen, Rhod. is useful in threatening glaucoma, always worse at the approach of a storm, better after the storm broke, patient strongly rheumatic. Muscular asthenopia, with darting pains through the eye, worse before a storm. Ciliary neuralgia Otalgia. Facial neuralgia and neuralgic toothache, with characteristic aggravation. Diarrhœa in damp, cold weather; from fruit. Catarrh of the bladder. Hydrocele. A valuable remedy in orchitis (see symptoms). Induration of testicles.

RHUS TOXICODENDRON.

Synonym.—Rhus Humile. *Natural order.*—Anacardiaceæ. *Common names.*—Poison Oak. Poison Ivy. *Habitat.*—A shrub growing in fields, woods and along fences all over North America. *Preparation.*—Tincture from the fresh leaves.

GENERAL ANALYSIS.

Acts prominently upon the organs of animal life, upon the mucous membranes, the lymphatic glands, the skin, the muscular tissues, and the tissue which compose the joints. The primary condition produced is one of irritation, and this may proceed to inflammation, or, if it stops short of that, produces serous discharges, in the form of evacuations or œdema. This condition of irritation affects most prominently the skin. "Even contact of the leaves of the plant, or proximity to them, produces an eruption, varying in intensity, from the slightest erythema to the gravest form of vesicular erysipelas."

The action of Rhus upon the mucous membranes resembles that which it has upon the external skin, simulating eczematous and vesicular eruptions; it acts most powerfully upon the conjunctiva, though affecting other mucous surfaces to a greater or less degree.

In the sero-fibrous tissues the characteristic primary irritation develops a rheumatoid inflammation of the joints and muscles, affecting particularly the fascia, tendons, sheaths of nerves, ligaments and fibrous tissues. The lymphatic glands throughout the body become enlarged and inflamed. The cellular tissues become infiltrated with a serous exudation, and the functions of nutrition are depressed and impaired.

On the organs of animal life Rhus acts secondarily, producing dullness of the senses, and a condition of the cerebral system closely resembling that present in low types of fever. The chief characteristic of Rhus is the prominent aggravation of its symptoms during repose, and amelioration by motion.

RHUS TOXICODENDRON.

CHARACTERISTIC SYMPTOMS.

Mind.—*Full of sad thoughts,* anxious, *apprehensive* especially in the evening and at *night* (Ars., Calc. c., Merc.), with desire for solitude (Carb. v., Ign.), and *inclination to weep* (Lyc., Natr. mur., Puls.); *worse in house; relieved by walking in open air. Anxiety, with great restlessness; cannot remain in bed* (Acon., Æth., Ars., Camph.). Discouragement and dissatisfaction; evening. Satiety of life, with desire to die, without sadness. Fretful; impatient, ill-humored, easily vexed (Bry.). Forgetful; difficult comprehension; cannot remember the most recent events (Phos. ac.). Low, mild, delirium, with stupefaction and insensibility (Phos., Phos. ac.).

Head.—Confusion, dullness of the head, and vertigo. *Giddy, as if intoxicated, with staggering* (Cinch., Coccul., Nux v., Puls.); *when rising from bed* (*Bry.*, Phos.). Fullness and heaviness of the head, with pressing downward, as from a weight in the forehead. Tearing in region of brows and in malar-bones, with drawing. Sensation as if the brain were loose, and hit against the skull (Cinch., Hyos, Nux m., Sulph. ac.), when stepping or shaking the head. Aching in occiput, which disappears on bending head backward. Sensitiveness of the scalp to touch (Cinch., *Merc., Mez.*). Moist, suppurative eruptions on the head, forming thick crusts, eating off the hair; offensive smell and itching; worse at night (*Graph.*, Lyc., *Merc.*, Staph., *Sulph.*).

Eyes.—*Inflammation of the eyes and lids, with redness, swelling and nightly agglutination* (*Ant. crud.*, Caust., *Graph.*, Lyc., *Merc.*, Puls., Phos., *Sulph.*, Zinc.). *Swelling of the whole eye and surrounding parts* (*Ars.*). Eyelids œdematous, or erysipelatous, with scattered watery vesicles; meibomian glands enlarged, cilia fall out. Burning and itching in the eyes and lids (Sulph.). Sharp pains running into the head. Lachrymation in evening, with burning pain. Aching in the eyes on exerting vision. Aching, pressive pains, as from sand in the eyes (Ars., *Caust.*, Hep. s., Puls., *Sep.*, *Sulph.*). *Heaviness and stiffness of lids, as if paralyzed* (*Kalm.*). Eyeball sore when turning the eye or pressing upon it (*Spig.*). Obscured vision, as if a veil were before the eyes (Caust., Petrol., Phos., *Puls.*, *Sulph.*)

Ears.—Lobule of left ear swollen. Inflammation, swelling and suppuration of parotid gland.

Nose.—Frequent, violent, spasmodic sneezing. Involuntary discharge of mucus in morning after rising, without coryza. Nosebleed in morning or at night; when stooping; °in typhus. Puffy swelling of nose (*Apis*). Tip of nose red (Bell.), and painful to touch; nose sore internally. Hot burning beneath left nostril.

Face.—Sickly expression, sunken face, blue rings around the eyes (Phos., Sulph.). *Erysipelatous inflammation and swelling of face* (Graph.), with much burning, smarting and tingling; also vesicular erysipelas of face (Cist.). Cramp-like pain in articulation of lower jaw, close to the ear. Pressive and digging pain in glands beneath angle of lower jaw. Lips dry, cracked and covered with a red crust. Corners of mouth ulcerated and sore (Ant. crud., *Graph.*, Lyc., Sil.). Moist eruptions and thick scabs on the face (Lyc., Merc., Staph.).

Mouth.—Toothache, tearing, jerking or crawling; better from external heat; at night. Teeth feel elongated and loose (Ars., *Merc.*, Sil.). Blisters on the tongue. *Tongue red, dry and cracked* (Bapt., Bell.); covered with a brown mucus; yellowish-white at root. *Sore sensation of tongue, with red tip* (Ars., Arg. met.). Mouth dry, with much thirst (Acon., *Ars.*, Bry.). ¡ Saliva runs from the mouth during sleep. Putrid breath (*Arn.*, Aur., Hep. s., Iodi., Kreos., *Merc.*, *Nitr.* ac., Nux v.). Taste putrid (Merc.); bitter (*Nux v.*); also of food (*Bry.*, Cinch., Coloc., *Puls.*, *Sulph.*); especially of bread (Natr. mur.).

Throat.—Sensation of *dryness* of throat (Apis, *Nux m.*). Sore throat; difficult deglutition, with stitching pains; throat swollen externally. Difficult swallowing of solids, as from constriction; of liquids, as from paralysis (*Bell.*, Hyos., Nux m., *Plumb.*). *Parotid and submaxillary glands hard and swollen* (Baryt. c., Calc. c., Iodi.); with sticking on swallowing.

Stomach.—*Great thirst for cold water* (*Acon.*, *Ars.*, Bry.), or cold milk, from dryness of mouth and throat. Hunger and emptiness in stomach, without appetite. Complete loss of appetite (Alum., Ars., Cinch., Hep. s., *Merc.*, Phos.,

RHUS TOXICODENDRON.

Sulph.). Eructations incomplete; nausea after eating and drinking. Fullness and heaviness in stomach, as from a stone, after eating (Ars., *Bry.*, Merc., *Nux v.*, Puls.). Pressure in stomach and pit of stomach after eating.

Abdomen.—Pressive drawing, from below upward, in left hypochondrium, with anxiety, with nausea in chest. Soreness, as if beaten, in hypochondria, and still more in abdomen; worse on side lain on, when turning and when beginning to move. Extensive distension of the abdomen especially after eating (Cinch., Lyc., Nux m., *Nux v.*). Cutting, griping and jerking pains in abdomen, especially after eating; better after stool (*Coloc.*). Colic pains and contraction in abdomen force him to walk bent (Aloe, Caust., *Coloc.*, Iris, Nux v., Rheum). Swelling. Pain in region of ascending colon. Swelling of the inguinal glands (*Calc. c.*, Clem., Iodi.).

Stool and Anus.—°Sense of constriction in rectum, as though one side had grown up. Stools thin, tinged with blood; loose, dark-brown (Ars.); mucus, mixed with blood; gelatinous (Colch., *Hell.*), and liquid, red and yellow.

Urinary Organs.—Frequent urging day and night, with profuse emission. Incontinence of urine, especially during repose (Arn., *Caust.*, *Puls.*). Urine hot, high-colored, scanty (Acon., Apis), irritating; dark, soon becoming turbid (Cina, Digit., Graph.).

Male Organs.—Swelling of the glans and prepuce; dark-red; erysipelatous. Scrotum and penis red; scrotum flaccid and hanging low. Scrotum becomes thick and hard, with intolerable itching. Paraphimosis. Œdema of scrotum. Humid eruptions on genitals, and between scrotum and thighs (*Hep. s., Graph.*).

Female Organs.—Menstrual flow light-colored and acrid, causing biting pain in the vulva. Soreness and pain in the vagina. Erysipelatous inflammation of the external genitals. Suppression of the milk, with general heat (Acon., Hyos., Puls.).

Respiratory Organs.—Hoarseness and scraping rawness in larynx, with roughness and soreness in chest (Osm.). Short, hurried respiration; oppressed and anxious. *Putting hand out of bed covers brings on a cough* (*Hep. s.*). *Short, dry* cough, from tickling in trachea and bronchi (Nux v., Rumex); worse evening and before midnight. Hacking cough in the evening after lying down. Cough in the morning, soon after waking. Spasmodic cough that shatters the head. Cough, with tearing pains, and stitches in the chest (Acon., *Bry., Kali c., Puls.*). Anxious oppression of the chest. Tension in chest in the evening, with short breath and weakness in the limbs. Stitches in chest and its sides; worse when at rest, and while sneezing and breathing. °Pneumonia, with typhoid symptoms, often after re-absorption of pus.

Heart and Pulse.—Violent palpitation when sitting still, so that the body moved with every pulse. Sensation of weakness and trembling in the heart (*Acon.,* Kalm.). Pulse rapid, small, compressible.

Neck and Back.—Rheumatic stiffness of neck (Bad., Chel.), with painful tension on moving (Acon., *Calc. phos.*). Pain in shoulders and back, as from a sprain (Acon.). Pain in cervical muscles, as if asleep, or as if head had beeen too long in an uncomfortable position, especially toward evening. Stitches in back, worse when walking or stooping; more when rising up after stooping. Rheumatic pain between scapulæ, better from warmth, worse from cold. Constriction of dorsal muscles when sitting, better bending back, worse bending forward. Cutting in sacrum when standing and bending backward. *Stiffness and aching* (Acon.); *bruised pains in small of back, when sitting still or when lying* (Berb.); *better from motion* °*or when lying on something hard* (Natr. mur.).

Limbs.—*Limbs swelling, stiffness and paralyzed sensations in joints, from sprains,* °*over-lifting or over-stretching. Lameness, stiffness and pain on first moving after rest, or on getting up in the morning; relieved by constant motion. Trembling or sensation of trembling, in the limbs. The limbs upon which he lies, especially arms, go to sleep. Rheumatic tension, drawing, tearing in limbs, during rest.*

Upper Limbs.—*Rheumatic tearing, stitching or sprained pains in shoulder joints, in arms, elbows, wrists, hands, and fingers* (Acon., Bry., Led.); *worse in cold, wet weather,* in bed and at rest (Rhod.). *Sprained pain in arm when carried far upward and backward. Weakness in upper part of forearm, and sprained pain in wrist on grasping anything.* Swelling of axillary glands (Baryt. c., Lyc., Sil.). Swelling of hands; of fingers. *Crawling, prickling sensation in palms, surfaces and tips of fingers.*

Lower Limbs.—*Great weakness and paralytic heaviness of the legs and feet; is scarcely able to walk. Great weariness in the legs while sitting, disappearing on walking* (*Ars.*). *Aching pains in legs; must change position every moment. Tingling pain in shafts of tibia at night when feet are covered, with constant necessity to move legs, preventing sleep. Tension and pain in hip and knee-joints, when sitting, when rising from a seat, or after over-exercise. Sprained pain in feet in morning on rising. Drawing like paralysis in feet when sitting.* Cramps in legs and feet; must walk about; especially at night. Swollen about the ankles after sitting too long; feet swell in evening.

Generalities.—*Great debility, paralytic weakness and soreness, especially when sitting and at rest* (Agar.). Great restlessness and uneasiness, must constantly change position (Natr. ars.) especially at night. Sensitiveness to cold open air (Aur., Petrol., Rumex, Sep.) Sufferings during cold weather and the prevalence of northeasterly winds.

Skin.—*Itching over the whole body* (Graph., *Sulph.*), especially on hairy parts. Red rash, like measles, all over the body (Ant. crud., Bapt., Coff. c., Puls.). *Vesicular* and *pustular eruptions, with burning and itching* (*Graph., Merc., Sulph.*). *Eczema: surface raw, excoriated; thick crusts, oozing and offensive* (*Graph., Hep. s., Lyc., Sulph.*). *Erysipelatous swelling and inflammation* (*Apis, Bell.*): *vesicular; phlegmonous.*

Sleep.—*Sleeplessness, with restless tossing about* (Acon.). Disturbed sleep, with anxious, frightful dreams (Arn., Aur., Puls.). *Anxious dreams about business as soon as he falls asleep.*

Fever.—Constant chilliness, especially evenings (*Phos.*). Chill in back and heat in anterior portion of body. Coldness of hands and feet. *Fever in evening, with shivering, over* the body; *stretching*, *headache and pains in the limbs.* Remittent type of fever; sometimes with brain symptoms. Profuse sweat in the morning (Calc. c., *Nitr. ac., Puls.*). Sweats from warm drinks.

Aggravation.—While at rest (Amm. carb., *Rhod.*); after midnight; before storms; on rising from a bed or seat; on beginning to move; from getting wet; in wet weather (Aran.); from northeasterly winds; cold air or taking cold; after drinking cold water.

Amelioration.—From continuous motion; from moving affected parts; in warm, dry weather.

Compare.—Anac., Ailan., Apis, Arn., Ars, *Bry.*, Caust., Clem., Con., *Crot. tig.*, Dulc., Euph., Ferr., Led., Lyc., Nux v., Phos., Phos. ac., *Puls., Ranunc., Rhod.*, Ruta, Sep., Sil., *Sulph.*, Viola tr.

These remedies precede Rhus tox. well: Arn., Bry., Calc. c., Calc. phos., Clem., Lach., Phos. ac., Sulph.; while these follow well: Ars., Bry., Calc. c., Coni., Nux v., Phos. ac., *Puls.*, *Sulph.* To Rhus Apis is inimical, while Bry. is complementary.

Antidotes.—Bell., *Bry.*, Camph., Coff. c., Crot. tig., Sulph.

Rhus Antidotes.—Ant. tart., Bry., Ranunc., Rhod.

THERAPEUTICS

Rhus is especially useful in rheumatism and rheumatoid affections in general with the characteristic modality of the drug—worse on beginning to move, better from continued motion. Rheumatism worse during cold, wet weather and from northeasterly winds; from getting wet, especially when overheated; from working in the water; from living in damp houses; from checked perspiration. Not ordinarily useful in acute inflammatory muscular rheumatism with high fever, etc., but more in chronic forms, or in acute attacks occurring in rheumatic subjects, from causes above named, but without much fever. A valuable remedy for sprains, and for soreness of muscles and tendons from over-lifting, or reaching high up with the arms. Rheumatic paralysis, and rheumatoid neuritis, with great stiffness and numbness of the parts involved, with characteristic modalities, and when brought on by causes above named. Rhus often becomes a valuable remedy in cellulitis after pus has formed, especially when the parts look dark-red, erysipelatous, and other Rhus symptoms. Boils. Carbuncles. Abscesses. One of our most valuable remedies in skin diseases, the vesicular character of the eruption always predominating, with much burning and itching. Acne rosacea. Urticaria. Erythema, with tendency to vesicular formations and œdema. Eczema (see symptoms). The chief remedy in vesicular erysipelas, especially of the scalp, face or genitals. Phlegmonous erysipelas. Suppuration of inflamed glands. Valuable in adynamic forms of scarlet fever, with characteristic restlessness, typhoid tendency, eruption irregular and dark-red, sometimes vesicular, swelling of cellular tissues and œdema, enlargement and threatening suppuration of the parotid or cervical glands. Purpura hæmorrhagica. Variola, pustules turn black, diarrhœa, dark, bloody stools, restlessness, typhoid symptoms. Œdema is a prominent feature in the action of Rhus, reminding us of Apis, from which it is readily differentiated. An invaluable and very frequently used remedy in typhoid fever, and in low, typhoid states in general occurring in the course of other diseases, such as diphtheria, peritonitis, typhlitis, enteritis, pneumonia, dysentery, puerperal diseases, etc. Mild delirium, stupefaction, restlessness; red, dry and cracked tongue; sordes; epistaxis; diarrhœa, yellowish-brown, offensive stools, etc. Useful in many affections of the eyes, especially when characterized by œdematous swelling of the lids and surrounding parts, and when aggravated by cold air or in wet weather. Only second to Apis in orbital cellulitis. Purulent ophthalmia, worse at night, intense photophobia. Conjunctivitis. Iritis, especially rheumatic. Glaucoma. Paralysis of the upper lids from exposure to cold, especially cold, damp winds. Inflammation of middle or external ear. Otalgia, with pulsation of the ear at night. Parotitis, especially after suppuration. Nasal catarrh in rheumatic subjects, worse from cold, wet weather. Facial neuralgia, from cold or wet, numbness and stiffness, cramp-like pains. Sometimes indicated in sore throat. Hæmorrhoids. Fissures in anus. Diarrhœa or dysentery from getting wet, stools of darkbrown or bloody mucus, tearing pains down thighs during stool, etc. Rheumatic cystitis. Paralysis of the bladder. Oxaluria. Useful in various affections of the genital organs, some of which have already been outlined in pathogenesis. Uterine displacements. Ovarian cysts. Membranous dysmenorrhœa, worse in wet weather and from getting wet. Abortion impending from straining or over-exertion. Lochia vitiated and offensive; lasting too long or often returning. Milk leg; also metritis, with typhoid symptoms. Laryngitis, with hoarseness, scraping and rawness, worse in wet weather. Bronchitis. Typhoid pneumonia. Hæmoptysis. Hypertrophy of the heart from over-exertion, such as wood-chopping, etc., also from rheumatism. Rheumatism of the heart. Organic diseases of the heart, with painful lameness and numbness of the left arm (Acon., Kalmia). Lumbago, with characteristic modalities. Sciatica. Locomotor ataxia. Sometimes useful in intermittent and other forms of malarial fever with characteristic Rhus symptoms.

ROBINA.

Synonym.—Robina Acacia. *Natural order.*—Leguminosæ. *Common name.*—Yellow Locust. *Habitat.*—An indigenous tree, common in the Middle and Southern States. *Preparation.*—Tincture from the fresh bark of the young twigs.

GENERAL ANALYSIS.

Through the pneumogastric nerve Robina acts especially upon the stomach, arresting digestion, and causing excessive acidity, resulting in emesis, the vomited matter being so intensely sour that the teeth are set on edge.—*Burt.*

CHARACTERISTIC SYMPTOMS.

Mind.—Very low-spirited; irritable.
Head.—Constant, dull, heavy, or throbbing frontal headache, aggravated by motion and reading.
Stomach.—Constant eructations of a very sour fluid. Nausea, followed by profuse *vomiting of an intensely sour fluid,* setting the teeth on edge. Violent vomiting. Sour stomach. Sharp pain in stomach and epigastrium. Burning in stomach and region of gall-bladder. Dull, heavy, aching distress in the stomach. Great distension of stomach and bowels, with flatulence; severe colic and acid diarrhœa.

RUMEX. 667

Stool.—Desire for stool, but only flatulence passes off; finally constipated stool. Diarrhœa, stools yellow, green, burning. °Sour stools of infants (Calc. c., Pod., *Rheum*).
Generalities.—°The whole child smells sour (*Rheum*).
Compare.—Calc. c., Iris, Mag. carb., Puls., *Rheum*.

THERAPEUTICS.

Especially useful in gastric disturbances, indigestion and *sick headache,* characterized by excessively sour eructations and vomiting. Acid dyspepsia. Heartburn. Cholera infantum.

RUMEX.

Synonym.—Rumex Crispus. *Natural order.*—Polygonaceæ. *Common name.*—Yellow Dock. *Habitat.*—A plant native of Europe, but introduced into this country where it is found in pastures, dry fields, waste grounds, etc. *Preparation.*—Tincture from the fresh root.

GENERAL ANALYSIS.

Rumex affects the mucous membranes, lymphatics and skin, but its prominent action is upon the mucous membrane of the larynx and trachea, diminishing its secretions, and exalting, in a very marked degree, its sensibility, indicating an excessive morbid irritability, yet not passing into an inflammatory condition.

CHARACTERISTIC SYMPTOMS.

Head.—Dull headache, and slight bruised feeling in the forehead.
Nose.—Epistaxis; violent sneezing and painful irritation of nostrils. Fluent coryza, watery discharge, with violent sneezing (*Acon., Cepa,* Sang.); worse evenings and night; with headache; desire to pick the nose.
Mouth.—Tongue coated yellow (*Chel.,* Cinch., Iodi.).

Throat.—Excoriated scraping feeling in the throat (Amm. carb., Carb. v., Caust., Phos., Puls.), with secretion of mucus in upper part of throat.

Stomach.—Heaviness in epigastrium soon after a meal (*Bry., Nux v., Puls.*). Feeling of repletion. Sensation of fullness on pressure, in pit of stomach, extending up into throat; every empty swallowing carrying it downward, but it immediately returns. Shooting from pit of stomach to chest.

Stool.—*Morning diarrhœa* (*Aloe, Podo., Sulph.*); *brown and watery* (*Ars., Kali bi.*); preceded by urging, with pain in abdomen. Constipation (*Alum., Bry., Nux v., Op.,* Phos., Sulph.).

Respiratory Organs.—Tenacious mucus in larynx (Kali bi., Nux v.), with constant desire to hawk, but without relief; worse at night. Irritation in larynx when eating, causing cough. Pain in larynx (Phos.); hoarseness (Carb. v., Caust.). Frequent feeling as though she could not get another breath; as if the air did not penetrate the chest. *Dry, incessant, fatiguing cough* (*Nux v.*), *caused by tickling in throat-pit* (Hep. s., *Phos., Sang., Sep.*); *aggravated by pressure, talking, and especially by inspiring cool air, and in evening, after lying down* (Coni., Dros., *Hyos., Mez.,* Nux v., *Puls.*). Dry, spasmodic cough, like the early stage of whooping cough, preceded by tickling in the throat. *Sensation of soreness and rawness in larynx, and behind the sternum* (*Ambr.,* Aral., *Phos.,* Rhus tox.). *Stitches in substance of left lung.* Aching over anterior portion of both lungs. Acute stitching or burning, stinging pains in left side of chest, near heart; worse from deep breathing, and on lying down in bed at night; °rheumatism (Bry.).

Limbs.—Legs densely covered with a rash; small, red pimples.

Generalities.—Great languor and weakness. Restless in the evening. *Very sensitive to the open air* (Amm. carb., Aur., Coccul., Sep., Sil., Rhus tox.).

Sleep.—Restless, disturbed, with short naps, and unpleasant fancies, even when awake.

Skin.—Itching in various parts (Graph., Rhus tox., Sulph.); worse on lower limbs, while undressing and on rising in morning, better from warmth of bed. Stinging itching, or

RUTA. 669

pricking itching of the skin. Vesicular eruption; itching when uncovered and exposed to cool air.
Aggravation.—In evening on lying down; from cool air; in raw, cold weather.
Compare.—*Apis, Bell., Caust.,* Hep. s., *Lach., Phos., Podo., Spong., Sulph.*

THERAPEUTICS.

Rumex is a valuable remedy in acute catarrh of the larynx or bronchi, and coughs from laryngeo-tracheal irritation, with the peculiarities mentioned in pathogenesis; always produced by tickling in throat pit and associated with sensation of soreness and rawness behind the sternum. Asthma. Sympathetic gastric cough. Catarrhal aphonia. Gastralgia, pains extend to chest or back. Dyspepsia. Affections from excessive tea-drinking. Diarrhœa, early in the morning, driving out of bed, stools brown and watery, especially when associated with characteristic cough.

RUTA.

Synonym.—Ruta Graveolens. *Natural order.*—Rutaceæ. *Common names.*—Rue. Bitter Wort. *Habitat.*—A plant widely cultivated in gardens; indigenous to Southern Europe. *Preparation.*—Tincture from the fresh plant.

GENERAL ANALYSIS.

Ruta acts especially upon the periosteum, bones, joints and cartilages, producing symptoms of a rheumatic character. It also has a special action upon the eyes, producing a somewhat similar condition. It also acts profoundly upon the uterus, causing both active determination of blood to that organ, and contraction of its muscular walls, hence its use as an emmenagogue and aborti-facient.

CHARACTERISTIC SYMPTOMS

Mind.—Fretful. Inclined to anger and vexation.
Head.—Pulsative, pressive pain in the head. Stitching, draw-

ing pain in frontal bone; extending to temporal bones. Bruised pain in periosteum, extending from temporal bones to the occiput.

Eyes.—Itching at the inner canthus, and on lower lid, smarting after rubbing; eye becomes full of water. Bruised pain in orbicular cartilages. Pressure deep in the orbits. Cramp in lower lid, followed by profuse lachrymation. *Eyes burn, ache, feel strained; sight blurred; from fine sewing or reading too much, or otherwise overtaxing them; worse on using eyes in evening* (Myrica, Natr. ars., Natr. mur., Phos., Sep.). Coldness beneath left eye.

Ears.—Scraping pressure, as with a blunt piece of wood.

Face.—Pain as from a blow behind mastoid process.

Stomach.—Frequent eructations; odorless. Burning or gnawing in the stomach. Nausea in pit of stomach. Tension in stomach *worse from drinking milk*. Epigastric region sensitive.

Abdomen.—Pressing, gnawing pain in the hepatic region.

Rectum and Anus.—Tearing stitches in rectum when sitting. Frequent, unsuccessful urging, with prolapsus ani and emission of flatus. Rectum protrudes immediately on attempting a passage.

Urinary Organs.—Pressure on bladder as if continually full, with constant urging, as if urine could not be retained, yet little is voided; feeling as if bladder moved up and down. °Incontinence at night.

Female Organs.—Metrorrhagia as a forerunner of miscarriage. Bearing-down pains. Miscarriage; at seven months;

Respiratory Organs.—Hacking cough, awakens about midnight. Pressure in the sternum. Gnawing pain in the chest; in right side with biting and burning.

Neck and Back.—Pain as if sprained or bruised in nape and shoulder. *Pain as if beaten, and lame in the spine; and like lumbago.* Bruised pain in back in coccyx, extending to sacrum. Digging as if bruised just above sacrum, when sitting after a long walk, better from continued walking, returning when standing still and sitting. Coldness down the spine.

Limbs.—Pains in the limbs, joints and bones, as if beaten, or as after a blow or fall (Arn.). Falling from side to side when walking, legs will not support him, no power or steadiness in thighs. Legs give out on ascending or descending stairs. Ankles pain as after a sprain or dislocation; as if ulcerated. Pains in bones of feet, cannot step heavily thereon.

Generalities.—Great weakness after a walk; *limbs feel bruised* (Arn.). Small of back and loins painful. *All parts of the body on which he lies are painful, as if bruised* (Arn., Bapt.). Bruised pain on touch, worse in hips and bones of legs.

Sleep.—Sleepiness during the day, with stretching. Frequent waking at night. Confused dreams; vivid.

Skin.—Itching all over the body (Graph., Rhus tox.); relieved by scratching (*Sulph.*).

Aggravation.—Pains usually worse in cold, wet weather.

Amelioration.—From motion.

Compare.—Amm. carb., *Arn.*, Bry., Calc. c., *Euphr.*, Lyc., Merc., *Mez.*, Phos. ac., *Phyt.*, *Puls.*, *Rhus tox.*, Sep., Sil., *Sulph.*

Antidote.—Camph.

Ruta Antidote.—Merc.

THERAPEUTICS.

Ruta has been found especially useful in bruises and other mechanical injuries of bones and periosteum; periostitis; rheumatism, etc; always characterized by a general feeling of soreness, as from a bruise. Usually worse in cold, wet weather; better from motion. Lameness after sprains, especially of wrists and ankles. Synovitis from strains. Ganglia, especially on wrist. A very valuable remedy in bad effects from overstraining the eyes; asthenopia. Weakness of accommodation. Has been used in dyspepsia resulting from a strain of the abdominal muscles; also when meat always disagrees, causing great distress and an eruption like nettle-rash.

SABADILLA.

Synonyms.—Veratrum Sabadilla. Asagræa Officinalis. *Natural order.*—Melanthaceæ. *Common names.*—Indian Caustic. Barley. Cevadilla. *Habitat.*—A bulbous plant indigenous to Mexico, and countries south of it. *Preparation.*—Tincture from the seeds.

GENERAL ANALYSIS.

Through the cerebro-spinal nervous system Sabadilla affects especially the vegetative sphere, the mucous surfaces being more particularly involved by its action.

CHARACTERISTIC SYMPTOMS.

Head.—Vertigo on rising from a seat, on waking at night. Pressive stupefying headache in forehead and temples, causing a reeling sensation. Head feels dull and heavy. Headache, especially after every walk; °after eating. Headache from much thinking, or too close attention. Corrosive burning point on top of the head.

Eyes.—Lachrymation, as soon as the least pain is felt in some other part. Lachrymation during exercise in the open air. Margins of the eyelids red.

Ears.—Tickling in the ears.

Nose.—Itching and tingling in the nose. Sensitive dryness of upper part of nose. Epistaxis. Violent spasmodic sneezing, shaking the abdomen, then lachrymation. Fluent coryza; influenza; °hay fever. One or other nostril stuffed up; inspiration through nose labored; snoring.

Face.—Heat of the face, with fiery burning redness (Ferr.). Beating and jerking in the muscles of the left upper jaw, with itching. Face feels hot, as after wine; red face and eyes; °hay fever.

Mouth.—Shooting pains in the molar teeth. Tongue coated mostly whitish-yellowish, more in the middle and back part. Feels sore and full of blisters. Mouth and tip of tongue burning and sore as if scalded. Bitter taste in the mouth (*Bry., Nux v., Puls.*).

Throat.—Dryness of the throat; when swallowing. Sensation in the throat as if a lump were lodged, obliging him to swallow. Roughness and scraping in the throat with inclination to swallow. Constriction in fauces as from an astringent drink.

Stomach.—Aversion to meat (Sepia). Nausea; with constant spitting of insipid water. Pain as if a sore spot were pressed below pit of stomach, on pressure and inspiration. Corrosive, burning pain in the stomach and œsophagus; when walking.

Abdomen.—Cutting in the bowels, as with knives. Burning in the abdomen (Ars.). Rumbling in the abdomen, as if empty (Lyc.).

Stool and Anus.—Crawling in rectum and anus, as from ascarides. Diarrhœa; stools brown, as if fermented.

Urinary Organs.—Urging to urinate, especially in the evening. Urine dark, muddy, thick, turbid; like muddy water. Burning in the urethra when urinating.

Respiratory Organs.—Oppressed breathing, with anxiety. Dry cough at night (Hyos.). Short, dry cough, produced by scraping in the throat. Stitches in sides of chest, especially when inspiring or coughing (*Bry.*).

Limbs.—Weariness and heaviness in all the limbs, worse towards evening, obliging her to lie down. Stinging sensation in the thighs. Tension in the calves. Coldness of the limbs. Heaviness of the feet.

Generalities.—Lassitude and weakness. Intense but transient bruised pain in various parts of the body. Intense pains in all the bones, especially in joints, as if the anterior of bones were cut and scraped with a sharp knife. °Great sensitiveness to cold air, which aggravates. Symptoms appear first on right, then on left side. °General aggravation at the same hour each day. Most symptoms better when lying down; in the open air.

Sleep.—Great inclination to sleep during the day. Disturbed and unrefreshing sleep at night, with anxious, confused dreams.

Skin.—Red spots and stripes, more marked when in the cold air.

Fever.—*Fever without thirst* (Apis, Puls.); shivering, with isolated attacks of heat, mostly in head and face. Chill afternoon or evening, returning at the same hour; often without subsequent heat. Feverish; feels sick, anxious, starts easily, trembles, breath short and hot. Chill predominates, particularly on extremities, with heat of face.
Compare.—Acon., Bry., Cinch., Natr. mur., Puls., Sep., Verat. alb.
Antidote.—Pulsatilla.

THERAPEUTICS.

Sabadilla has been found useful in intermittent fever with above symptoms, paroxysms recurring at the same hour each day (Ced.). An excellent remedy for worms; ascarides; lumbrici; tænia; fever from worms. Nymphomania and pruritus caused by ascarides. Ovaritis, with cutting pain. Influenza and hay fever with symptoms already mentioned in pathogenesis. Tonsilitis, commencing on left side and extending to right side. Measles, with violent sneezing, etc. Gastric disturbances, with longing for sweet things, honey or pastry; aversion to meat, symptoms better after eating. Has been found useful in a mental condition where the patient imagines himself sick, or has imaginary diseases.

SABINA.

Synonym.—Juniperus Sabina. *Natural order.*—Coniferæ.
Common names.—Savin. *Habitat.*—A woody evergreen shrub found mostly in the southern Alps in Austria and Switzerland.
Preparation.—Tincture from the fresh tips of the younger branches.

GENERAL ANALYSIS.

Acts chiefly upon the generative organs of women, but also affects prominently the urinary organs and the gastro-intestinal canal. The general condition produced is one of intense irritation, resulting in congestion and inflammation, which in the uterus gives rise to hæmorrhages and abortion, in the urinary organs to strangury, and in the bowels to purging and bloody stools.

CHARACTERISTIC SYMPTOMS.

Mind.—Hypochondriacal mood (*Nux v.*). Great anxiety and apprehension (Acon., Ars.). Music is intolerable (Digit.).

Head.—Vertigo when standing, as if she would fall; with obstruction of vision; with orgasm and heat in head. Pressive headache, especially in temporal eminences, suddenly appearing, and slowly disappearing. Circumscribed pain in temples. Painful stricture in temples. Dull, pressive frontal headache.

Nose.—Dry coryza.

Face.—Drawing pain in right angle of jaw, in masseter muscles, worse on touch.

Mouth.—Dryness in mouth (Apis, *Nux m.*). Throbbing toothache in evening and at night. Tearing in roots of molars.

Throat.—Dryness, with drawing pain. Sensation as if he had to swallow over a foreign body. Stools hard and painful, followed by discharge of blood from anus.

Stomach.—Desire for acid things (Ant. tart., *Cinch.*, Hep. s., Phos., Podo., Verat. alb.), especially lemonade. Poor appetite. Heartburn and eructations (Nux v., Lyc.).

Abdomen.—Griping, twisting, labor-like pains in the abdomen to the groins; with sensation as if vomiting would come on without nausea.

Stool.—Blood and mucus, or diarrhœic stools. Stools hard and painful, followed by discharge of blood from anus.

Urinary Organs.—Frequent, violent urging to urinate, with copious emission (Apis, Apoc., Arg. met.). Retention of urine; discharge by drops, with burning (*Bell.*, Canth.; Can. sat.). Burning pain in vesical region.

Male Organs.—Burning sore pain in glans, and in figwarts.

Female Organs.—*Menses too profuse, too early, and last too long* (*Bell.*, Calc. c., *Kali c.*, *Nux v.*). Passes clots of blood after rising. Almost insatiable desire for coition with corresponding gratification. Contractive pain in region of uterus. *Hæmorrhage from the uterus in paroxysms; worse from motion; blood dark* (*Kali nit.*) *and* clotted (*Croc.*); *red, profuse; from loss of tone in uterus* (*Caul.*); *after abortion or parturition; with pain from back to pubis.* Miscarriage, especially at third month (Sec.). Leucorrhœa, °thick, yellow, fœtid; after suppressed menses (Puls.).

Respiratory Organs.—Crawling and tickling in larynx, excited cough and a slimy expectoration. Dry, hacking cough and tickling in the trachea. Hæmoptysis (Acon., Cinch., Ferr., Ham.). Tensive, pressive pain in sternum, not affected by respiration. Stitches in left nipple. Intermittent stitches in clavicle.

Neck and Back.—*Drawing pains and dragging in small of back, extending into the pubic region.* Pain in back obliging him to bend inward. Paralytic pain in back.

Limbs.—Drawing, tearing pains, especially at night; most in wrist-joints and toes; with red, shiny swelling; worse from motion and touch. *Middle of anterior surface of thighs feel bruised and painful.* Stitches in elbows; in heels, extending outward.

Generalities.—Great weakness and weariness in all the limbs; with despondency. Heaviness and indolence of the body, obliging him to lie down. Throbbing in all the blood vessels. Symptoms cease in open air, return on entering the house.

Sleep.—Restless, disturbed sleep.

Compare.—Arn., *Bell.*, Calc. c., *Croc.*, Coccul., Ipec., Millif., *Puls.*, Rhus tox., Ruta, Sulph., *Tril.*

Antidotes.—Camph, Puls.

THERAPEUTICS.

The chief use of Sabina is in uterine hæmorrhages and menorrhagia, with the symptoms above described. Said to be especially useful in women of gouty diathesis. Dysmenorrhœa, with characteristic pain from back to pubis. Threatening miscarriage, with hæmorrhage and pain from back to pubic region. Leucorrhœa after menorrhagia or suppressed menses; during pregnancy; acrid, much biting and itching, thick, yellow, fœtid. Chlorosis, with tendency to hæmorrhages; also hysteria. Useful in arthritic affections, better in open air, worse from warmth. Arthritic nodes. Facial neuralgia, better in open air.

SAMBUCUS.

Synonym.—Sambucus Nigra. *Natural order.*—Caprifoliaceæ. *Common names.*—Black Elder. European Elder. *Habitat.*—An indigenous shrub, common in thickets and waste grounds. *Preparation.*—Tincture from the fresh leaves and flowers.

GENERAL ANALYSIS.

Affects especially the mucous membranes and the respiratory organs and the skin, causing in the former obstructive catarrh, and in the latter profuse debilitating perspiration.

CHARACTERISTIC SYMPTOMS.

Mind.—Constant fretfulness; very easily startled; trembling, anxiety and restlessness (Acon.).
Face.—Bloated or dark-blue.
Abdomen.—Griping colic, as after taking cold, with emission of flatus.
Urinary Organs.—Frequent desire to urinate, with copious discharge. °Deposits a heavy sediment.
Respiratory Organs.—*Hoarseness, with much tenacious, glutinous mucus in the larynx* (Kali bi., *Rumex*). Oppression of the chest with pressure in the stomach, nausea and weakness. Oppression and stitches in left side of chest, below the nipple (Kali c.). °Suffocative attacks after midnight (Acon., Ant. tart., Ars., Cinch.); wakens suddenly, sits up in bed, turns blue, gasps for breath (Ipec.). °Quick, wheezing respiration, suffocative cough, with crying in children.
Generalities.—Hands and feet bloated and blue. Dropsical swelling of the body.
Sleep.—Sleepiness, without sleep (*Bell.*, Cham., Lach.).
Fever.—During heat, dread of uncovering (reverse, Led.). Sensation of burning heat in the face, with moderate warmth of body, and icy-coldness of feet, without thirst. *Very pro-*

*fuse, debilitating perspiration, while awake **without thirst**;* skin dry and burning, without sweat during sleep. Profuse night sweats (*Cinch., Phos.,* Phos. ac., *Sulph.*).

Aggravation.—While at rest.

Amelioration.—From motion; on sitting up in bed.

Compare.—*Acon.,* Ars., Bell., Cinch., *Ipec.,* Rhus tox., Sep., Sulph.

Sambucus follows well after Opium.

Antidotes.—Ars., Camph.

Sambucus Antidote.—Abuse of Arsenic.

THERAPEUTICS.

Sambucus is of use chiefly in respiratory affections characterized by suffocative attacks as above described. Laryngismus stridulus; acute laryngitis; suffocative catarrh; croup; whooping cough; asthma of Millar. Cough, etc., always worse after midnight and lying with the head low. Useful in dropsy, especially from acute nephritis, with characteristic urine and sweat.

SANGUINARIA.

Synonym.—Sanguinaria Canadensis. *Natural order.*—Papaveraceæ. *Common name.*—Blood Root. *Habitat.*—An indigenous perennial plant. *Preparation.*—Tincture from the fresh root.

GENERAL ANALYSIS.

Affects chiefly the respiratory mucous membrane, producing irritation and catarrhal irritation. It has a decided influence upon the pneumogastric nerve, and through it creates derangement of the liver and digestive tract.

CHARACTERISTIC SYMPTOMS.

Head.—*Vertigo* in morning on rising from a sitting or stooping position (Bry.); on quickly turning the head (*Calc. c.*) or looking upward (Calc. c., Cupr.). ***Determination of***

SANGUINARIA.

blood to the head, with whizzing in the ears, and flushes of heat (Acon.). Headache in morning; worse from stooping and moving about. Dull, pressive frontal headache (Euph., Merc. cor.). *Headache occurring in paroxysms* (Cinch.). °Headache begins in occiput (Verat. vir.), *spreads upward, and settles over right eye.* Headache, as if it would burst (Bry., *Caps.*, Cinch., Puls., *Natr. mur.*), in forehead and temples; mostly right; better in open air (Puls., Sep.). Pain over eyes in morning lasting all day; on rising from a seat, with vertigo. Pain in occiput and nape in afternoon. *Headache with nausea and chilliness, followed by flushes of heat, extending from head to stomach.* Throbbing headache, worse from motion or stooping; with bitter vomiting.

Eyes.—Pupils dilated (*Ailanth.*, *Bell.*, Cic., *Hyos.*). Burning dryness in the eyes, followed by copious lachrymation (*Ars.*, Euphr.). Pain in eyeballs on moving them. Balls sore, with darting through them and dim vision.

Ears.—Burning of the ears; cheeks red. °Earache, with headache, with stinging in the ears and vertigo. °Humming and roaring in the ears, with painful sensitiveness to sudden sounds, in the women at the climacteric.

Nose.—Fluent coryza, with frequent sneezing (*Acon.*, Ars., *Cepa*, Gels., Iris, Rumex); watery, acrid; with tingling; with heavy pain at root of nose and stinging in nose. Dry coryza, as from a sudden cold. Alternately fluent and dry coryza. Loss of smell.

Face.—°Circumscribed redness of one or both cheeks (Kreos.). Paleness of the face, with disposition to vomit. Sensation of dryness of the lips. Pain in cheek-bones. °Neuralgia in upper jaw, extending to nose, eye, ear, neck and side of head; shooting, burning pains; must kneel down and hold head tightly to the floor.

Mouth.—Loss of taste, with burnt feeling on the tongue (Puls.). Sores on gums and roof of mouth.

Throat.—Feels swollen, as if to suffocation, when swallowing, worse on right side. Pain on swallowing. Feeling of dryness in the throat; not relieved by drinking. Throat sore, as if raw and denuded (Arg. nit., Arum.).

Stomach.—Craving for he knows not what; for spiced things

(Phos.). Deathly nausea, in paroxysms (*Ant. tart.*), with much salivation; with headache, chill and heat. Nausea; not relieved by vomiting. Vomiting of bitter water; of sour, acrid fluids; of ingesta (Ipec., Phos., Verat. alb.); °of worms (Acon., Sabad.). Sensation of emptiness in the stomach, with faint, feverish feeling. Soreness and pressure in epigastrium; worse after eating. Burning in the stomach (Ars., Canth., Iris, Verat. alb.).

Stool.—Diarrhœic stool, mixed with much flatus (Aloe). °Diarrhœa following coryza; pains in chest, and cough.

Urinary Organs.—Copious and frequent nocturnal urination, clear as water (Natr. mur., Phos. ac.).

Female Organs.—°Climacteric disorders, especially flushes of heat, and leucorrhœa (Lach.). Abdominal pains, as if menses would appear (Aloe, *Caul.*, Cimic., *Puls.*). Stitches in nipples, especially right.

Respiratory Organs.—*Dry, hacking cough, caused by tickling in throat* (Hep. s., *Phos., Rumex, Sep.*), *with dryness of throat; crawling sensation, extending down behind the sternum; evenings after lying down.* Dry cough, awaking from sleep; not ceasing until after he sits up in bed and passes flatus, upward and downward. °Cough, with circumscribed redness of the cheeks; pain in the chest and coryza. Severe dyspnœa and constriction of chest, with inclination to take deep inspirations. Constant pressure and heaviness in upper part of chest, with difficult breathing. Sharp, pinching, myalgic pain midway between sternum and right nipple. Intense pain and burning under sternum, and in right side of chest. Burning below right arm and clavicle, streaming down to hepatic region at 4 P.M. Acute stitches in right side of chest, near nipple (*Bry.*). °Expectoration tough, difficult; rust-colored; extreme dyspnœa; pneumonia; hepatization. Pain in right chest to the shoulder; can only with difficulty place hand on top of head. Burning pain between breasts in afternoon. worse on right side. °Exceedingly offensive breath (Caps., Croc.) and expectoration.

Heart and Pulse.—Irregularity of the heart's action, and of the pulse, with coldness, insensibility, etc. Pulse slow, irregular, feeble.

Neck and Back.—Rheumatic pains in nape of neck, shoulders and arms.
Generalities.—Great weakness and prostration, especially in morning on waking. General torpor and languor. Sensation as if hot water were poured from breast into abdomen. An uncomfortable prickling sensation of warmth spreading over whole body. Ulcers about the nails.
Fever.—Burning heat, rapidly alternating with chill and shivering. Heat flying from head to stomach. Flushes of heat; glow of warmth over body (Calc. c.).
Aggravation.—Morning and evening; from light, noise and motion.
Amelioration.—When lying quiet; in the dark room; after vomiting.
Compare.—Ant. tart., Bell., *Bry.*, *Chel.*, Hep. s., *Iris*, Lyc., Merc., Natr. mur., *Phos.*, Rumex, *Squilla*, Sang., Spong.; follows Bell. well in scarlet fever.
Sanguinaria Antidotes.—Op., Rhus tox.

THERAPEUTICS.

The chief use of Sanguinaria is in the treatment of certain respiratory diseases and various forms of headache. Nasal catarrh, with dull frontal headache, pain over root of nose, sore throat, etc. Acute coryza, frequent sneezing with pain over and in eyeballs, at root of nose, etc. Aphonia. Laryngitis. Croup. Whooping cough. Œdema of glottis. Asthma. Especially valuable in pneumonia, rather subacute in character. After exudation, dry cough, tough, rust-colored expectoration, extreme dyspnœa, circumscribed redness of cheeks, better when lying on the back. Hypostatic pneumonia. Typhoid pneumonia. A valuable remedy when phthisis follows pneumonia. Often of great service in tuberculosis, hectic fever, circumscribed redness of one or both cheeks, hœmoptysis. Hydrothorax. May be indicated in a variety of headaches, catarrhal, gastric and climacteric. The most characteristic is a sick headache, beginning in the occiput, spreading upwards and settling over the right eye. Other forms of headache are detailed in pathogenesis. Catarrhal conjunctivitis, especially of right eye, with other characteristic symptoms. Blepharadenitis. Polypus of the ear. Nasal polypus. Neuralgia of face (see clinical symptoms under "Face"). Pharyngitis, feeling of dryness and burning as if scalded, feels raw and denuded, worse on right side. Ulcerated sore throat. Diphtheria, pearly coating on palate and fauces. Gastric derangements. with nausea, not relieved by vomiting, headache, etc. Nausea during pregnancy. Ulcer in stomach with Sang. symptoms, flushes of heat rising into the head, better from vomiting. Sometimes useful in jaundice; hepatic derangements. Catarrhal diarrhœa or dysentery following or accompanying characteristic coryza. Often a useful remedy for the flushes of heat, headache, leucorrhœa, etc., occurring at the climacteric period. Polypus of uterus. Profuse, irregular or suppressed menstruation. with other Sang. symptoms. Ulceration of os uteri; fœtid discharge. Sore, painful nipples. Sometimes indicated in rheumatism of nape, shoulders and arms, worse at night in bed.

SARSAPARILLA.

Synonyms.—Smilax Medica. Smilax Officinalis. *Natural order.*—Smilaceæ. *Common name.*—Wild Liquorice. *Habitat.*—A plant indigenous to Mexico and as far south as the Northern part of South America. *Preparation.*—Tincture of the dried root (Honduras variety). Triturations of the dried root-bark.

GENERAL ANALYSIS.

Acts powerfully upon the blood, giving rise to herpes and other skin eruptions. It also acts prominently upon the urinary system, producing symptoms similar to those of gravel, in which affection it is an excellent remedy.

CHARACTERISTIC SYMPTOMS.

Mind.—Anxiety with the pains, also after seminal emissions. Cheerful.
Head.—Heaviness in the head. Pressing and stitching pains in left side of head. °Shooting pains from left ear to root of nose; base of nose and eyes swollen. °Neuralgic head-

ache, right side, throbbing, stitching, starting from occiput. Throbbing pains in the head.

Eyes.—Shooting pain in eyes. Red stripe from cornea to outer canthus. Cloudiness before the eyes, as from a fog (*Caust., Phos., Ranunc., Sulph.*).

Face.—Eruptions on the face; like milk crust (Viola tric.). Stiffness and tension in the muscles and articulations of the jaw.

Mouth.—Bitter taste in the mouth, in the morning (*Bry., Nux v., Puls.*).

Stomach.—Bitter eructations after eating.

Abdomen.—Rumbling, with sensation of emptiness in the abdomen. Stitches in sides (left) of abdomen.

Stool.—Painful, difficult evacuations. Stools hard. Obstinate constipation.

Urinary Organs.—Frequent desire to urinate, with scanty discharge, accompanied by burning (Acon., Canth.). Frequent and profuse discharge of pale urine, day and night (Apis, Apoc., Verbas.). °Urine contains gravel or small calculi. Urine scanty and turbid, like clay-water as soon as passed. Severe pain at the conclusion of urination, the last urine containing blood.

Respiratory Organs.—Spasmodic oppression of the chest.

Back.—Pains from small of back down spermatic cords; worse at night and from motion; after emissions.

Upper Limbs.—Stitches in the joints of the arms, hands and fingers. Deep rhagades on fingers, with burning pains. Finger tips feel as if ulcerated, or as from salt in a wound.

Lower Limbs.—Weariness in the thighs. Stitches in the thighs, knees and legs.

Skin.—Herpes on almost all parts of the body: especially on prepuce. Deep, burning, painful rhagades (Graph.). Itching sometimes over the whole body, especially in evening in bed and in morning when rising. °Moist eruptions, with excoriating discharges. Dry, red pimples, only itching when exposed to the heat. Shriveled skin.

Fever.—Frequent rigors, running from below upward. Heat in the evening in bed; with feeling of strength. Sweat on forehead; during the evening heat.

Conditions.—Frequently useful after the abuse of Mercury.

Compare.—Amm. carb., Bell., Cham., Merc., Sep., Sulph.
Antidotes.—Bell., Merc.

THERAPEUTICS.

Sarsaparilla is used chiefly in cystitis with bloody urine, and other symptoms above mentioned. Gravel, especially in children. Discharge of gas in urine, showing fermentation in bladder. Herpes preputialis. Swelling of spermatic cords, pain from small of back down cords, after sexual excitement or nocturnal emissions. Secondary syphilis. Herpes and other eruptions. Eruptions during hot weather, becoming ulcers. Rhagades. Bone pains, especially after Mercury, worse from dampness. Marasmus, with characteristic urine, emaciation, shriveled skin. Useful in syphilitic and Mercurial headaches, extending from occiput to eyes.

SECALE CORNUTUM.

Synonyms.—Acinula Clavus. Ergota. *Natural order.*—Fungi. *Common names.*—Spurred Rye. Ergot. *Preparation.*—Tincture from the fresh fungus.

GENERAL ANALYSIS.

Acts powerfully upon the cerebro-spinal system, giving rise to two distinct and characteristic conditions known as convulsions and gangrenous ergotism; the former resulting directly from nerve poisoning, while the latter is due to secondary blood disorganization, or, as is well maintained, to the power Ergot possesses over the unstriped muscular fiber, producing persistent contraction of the arterial coats, diminishing their caliber, and so reducing their current of blood. This, too, might produce cerebral and spinal anæmia, and thus also cause the convulsive form of Ergot poisoning. A full description of these conditions may not be presented here, but sufficient may be gathered from the annexed list of symptoms.

To the powerful action of Ergot on the unstripped muscular fiber also is due the important effects it displays upon the gravid uterus, exciting contractions thereof, and expelling its contents. To avert such a disaster Secale is often the true homœopathic remedy, but to give it in parturition, in order to hasten delivery is an inexcusable practice.

CHARACTERISTIC SYMPTOMS.

Mind.—Stupid, half-sleepy condition (Bell., Op.). Dullness of all the senses. Moaning. Mild or raving delirium (Bell., Hyos., Stram.). *Great anxiety and fear of death* (*Acon., Ars.*).

Head.—Stupefaction. Vertigo. Aching. Dullness. Heaviness of the head and tingling in the legs.

Eyes.—*Eyes sunken, and surrounded by blue margins* (Phos., Cinch., Kali iod., Sulph.). *Eyes look fixed, wild, staring* (*Canth., Bell., Hyos.*). Obscuration of sight. Pupils generally dilated (*Bell., Hyos., Stram.*). Cataracts, hard and soft, with headache, vertigo and roaring in the ears.

Ears.—Roaring in the ears, with great difficulty in hearing. (Calc. c., Merc., Phos. ac., Sulph.). °Hard hearing after cholera.

Nose.—*Bleeding of the nose* (Acon., Bell., Bry.. Ham.).

Face.—*Pale, sunken, Hippocratic, anxious expression* (*Ars., Camph., Verat. alb.*). Lips bluish or deathly pale. Risus sardonicus.

Mouth.—Tongue clean or coated white (*Ant. crud., Bry., Nux v., Puls.*). Painful crawling in tongue; burning and tingling. Very offensive breath (*Ars., Hep. s.,* Iodi., *Merc., Nitr. ac.,* Nux v.). Increased secretion of saliva (*Hep. s., Merc., Kali iod.*). Feeble stuttering, indistinct speech. as if the tongue were paralyzed (*Caust., Gels., Hyos., Stram.*).

Throat.—Dryness of the throat (Apis, Ars., *Nux m.*).

Stomach.—*Ravenous hunger* (Bry., Cina, Ferr., *Lyc.*). Violent, unquenchable thirst (*Acon., Ars., Bry., Rhus tox.. Sulph.*). Hiccough. Nausea and inclination to vomit (*Ant. tart., Ipec.*). Vomiting of matter (Bry., Iris, v., Nux Podo.); of mucus; of d⸺ n., coffee-grounds fluid (Coni.); of all food and drink⸺ hæmorrhage from the stomach (Ham., Phos.). Great ⸺ and oppression in stomach, with great sensitivene⸺ touch. Violent pressure in the stomach, as fro⸺ weight (Acon.,

Ars., *Bry.*, *Nux v.*, Puls.). Burning in the stomach (Ars., Canth., Iris, Sang.), with pain in abdomen.

Abdomen.—Abdomen distended and tympanitic (Arn., *Cinch.*, Phos.). In liver: enlargement; inflammation; gangrene. Painful colic, with convulsions. Continual bearing down in lower abdomen. Cold feeling in abdomen and back. Pains in hypogastric region.

Stool and Anus.—Paralysis of rectum and anus. Anus wide open. *Diarrhœa;* frequent brown, slimy discharges; dark-colored (Ars.); very offensive (*Ars., Asaf.*); *thin, olive-green;* involuntary (*Arn., Ars., Hyos.*); very exhausting (Cinch., Phos.); pernicious. Hæmorrhage from the bowels (Ham., Op.). Constipation (Alum., *Bry., Nux v., Op., Phos., Sulph.*).

Urinary Organs.—Paralysis of the bladder (Bell., Caust., Coni., Hyos.). Retention of urine (*Bell., Op., Stram.*). Suppression of urine. Urine pale and watery (Natr. mur., Phos. ac., Staph.).

Female Organs.—Menses too profuse and of too long duration (Amm. carb., Ars., Calc. c., Kali c., *Nux v.*). *Uterine hæmorrhages; worse from the slightest motion* (Erig., Sab.); discharge black, fluid, and very fœtid. *Pains as of an expulsive character in the uterus* (*Caul.*). Irregular, stormy contractions. Uterus and right ovary congested and sensitive to touch. Pain in uterus and ovaries. Threatened abortion, especially at third month (Sab.). After abortion uterus does not contract (*Caul.*); thin, black, foul-smelling discharge. Gangrene of vaginal mucous membrane, with a dark, slate-color. *Suppressed lochia, followed by fever and inflammation of the uterus* (*Acon., Bell.*). Suppression of milk.

Respiratory Organs.—Voice feeble, inaudible, stammering. Spitting of blood, with or without cough. *Anxious, labored inspiration. Expectoration of blood during violent efforts to breathe. Constant sighing* (Calc. phos., Ign.); hiccough (Cic., Nux v., Hyos., Stram.).

Heart and Pulse.—Palpitation of the heart. *Pulse small, very rapid, contracted; frequently intermittent* (*Coni., Digit.*, Kali c., Natr. mur.); fluttering, slow, depressed.

Back.—Pain in back and small of back (*Bell.*, Cimic., Nux v.,

Puls.). Tingling in the back, which is numb, extending to fingers and toes (*Acon.*).

Limbs.—Convulsive movements of the limbs (Cic., Bell., Hyos., Stram.). Contraction of hands, feet, fingers and toes. Heaviness and trembling of the limbs. *Limbs become cold, pale, and wrinkled, as after being a long time in hot water. Numbness, insensibility, and coldness of the limbs, especially tips of fingers and toes.* Disagreeable sensation of sleep and formication in the limbs. Cramps in legs, calves, arms, hands and toes. Crawling and tingling in the limbs (Acon.). Drawing pains in the limbs. Burning of the hands and feet (Ars., Sulph.). *Fuzzy feeling in the limbs.* Cold gangrene of the limbs (Ars.); the dead part separates at joints and drops off.

Generalities.—*Extreme debility, prostration and restlessness* (*Ars.*). Unsteadiness of the whole body; trembling. Rapid sinking of strength (*Ars.*, Camph., Carb. v.). Convulsions; tonic; of all extensors; epileptiform spasms. Epilepsy. Cramps in legs, arms and chest.

Skin.—Cold and dry. Formication over the whole body. *Sensation of something creeping under the skin.* Petechia Arn., Ars., Phos.); ecchymosis (Arn., Phos.); gangrenous blisters (Ars.). Swelling and pain without inflammation; coldness, blue-color, gangrene. Anthrax becoming gangrenous.

Fever.—Coldness of the surface of the body, especially the extremities and face; dryness. Heat in internal organs; hands and feet. Profuse cold, clammy sweat over the whole body (*Ars.*, Camph., *Merc.*, Phos.).

Aggravation.—During menses; from warmth; *heat applied to any part.*

Amelioration.—In the cold air, and from getting cold; from sweat.

Conditions.—Particularly useful in tall, scrawny women, of lax muscular fiber; feeble, cachetic; in very old decrepit persons.

Compare.—Ars., *Bell.,* Cham., Carb. v., *Caul.,* Colch., Lyc., Phos., Plumb., Puls., Rhus tox., Sabin., Sulph., Tabac., Ustil., Verat. alb. After Sec. follows Cinch. Resembles Colch. in cholera morbus.

Antidotes.—Camph., Op.

SECALE CORNUTUM.

THERAPEUTICS.

Especially useful in uterine hæmorrhages, from atony of the uterus; after parturition or abortion; during climacteric; flow black and offensive; worse from slightest motion; skin cold; threatening collapse. Often used after labor to cause contraction and prevent post-partum hæmorrhage. Allen says (*Handbook of Materia Medica, p. 993*): "During labor or uterine hæmorrhage it should be used with great discretion; it is extremely dangerous when there is albuminuria, for it is liable to bring on convulsions; if used too freely during labor it is extremely apt to cause puerperal metritis." The drug should never be given during parturition in large doses to hasten delivery. Sometimes if the pains are prolonged and ineffectual, irregular, spasmodic, weak or entirely wanting, a dose of the potentized drug may be of benefit. Hour-glass contractions causing retained placenta. Suppressed lochia, with metritis, or offensive, purulent discharge. Often valuable in puerperal fever, with putrid discharges, tympanitis, coldness, threatening collapse. Has cured fibroid and other uterine tumors. Milk suppressed, threatened abortion. A valuable remedy in spasms; epilepsy; puerperal convulsions; extensor muscles especially involved. Paralysis of flexor muscles (Plumb.). Paralysis with flexor muscles (Plumb). Paralysis, with numbness and formication; spinal anæmia. A valuable remedy in gangrene, especially senile (see symptoms). Ulcers. Anthrax. Petechia. Ecchymosis. Lymphatic tumors. Collapse with choleroid and other diseases (Carb. v.), skin cold, but external warmth intolerable. Asiatic cholera, with collapse, icy-coldness, but cannot bear covering or warmth, face sunken and distorted, particularly about the mouth. Dysentery, threatening collapse. Cholera infantum, watery, offensive, causing great prostration.

SELENIUM.

An element. *Preparation.*—Triturations.

GENERAL ANALYSIS.

Acts chiefly upon the larynx, and upon the male sexual organs, producing inflammation of the former, and weakness tending to complete impotence; in the latter, the general tendency of the drug being to produce exhaustion and debility.

CHARACTERISTIC SYMPTOMS.

Mind.—Great dullness, with complete insensibility and indifference to his surroundings (Carb. v., Cinch., Phos.). Forgetful, especially in business; but when lying half asleep, everything recurs to him. Difficult comprehension, mental labor fatigues; unfit for any kind of work.

Head.—Vertigo, as if intoxicated (Agar., *Nux v.,* Stram.). Hair falls off when combing; also of eyebrows, whiskers and genitals.

Nose.—Itching in nose and on borders of wings. Inclination to bore fingers into nose (*Cina*). Yellow, thick, jelly-like mucus in nose.

Face.—Greasy, shining skin of face. Comedones (Sulph.). Great emaciation (Natr. mur.) of face and hands.

Mouth.—Teeth covered with mucus. Stammering speech; articulates with great difficulty (Can. ind., Caust., Stram.).

Throat.—Hawking of lumps of transparent mucus every morning (Argent.).

Abdomen.—Pains in right side, around under last ribs, especially on inspiration, extending to region of kidneys, which were sensitive to external pressure.

Stool.—Threads, like hairs, in stools. Constipation, hard stools, with blood at end.

Urinary Organs.—Urine dark, scanty; red in evening. Involuntary urination when walking; dribbles after stool or urination when walking. Biting in the top of urethra.

SELENIUM.

Male Sexual Organs.—Erections slow, insufficient; semen emitted too rapidly, and with long-continued thrill; weak and ill-humored after an embrace; weakness in loins. Semen thin, without normal odor. Lewd thoughts, but physical impotence. Prostatic juice oozes while sitting, during sleep, when walking, and at stool (Agn., Sil.).

Respiratory Organs.—Voice hoarse when beginning to sing, or from long talking (Arg. met., Arum., Phos.); has to clear the throat, hawks transparent lumps of mucus every morning, sometimes bloody. Cough in morning, straining the chest, with expectoration of lumps of mucus and blood.

Neck and Back.—Neck stiff on turning the head. Pain, as from lameness, in small of back, in morning.

Limbs.—Tearing in hands at night, with cracking in wrists. Emaciation of hands and legs. Itching of palms, also of ankles, in evening. Ulceration on legs; blisters on toes. Cramps in calves and soles (*Calc., c., Sulph.*). Legs feel weak, with fear of paralysis, after typhus.

Generalities.—Irresistible desire to lie down and sleep; strength suddenly leaves him. Throbbing in vessels of whole body (Glon., Sep.), especially felt in abdomen. Every draft of air, even warm, causes pain in limbs, head, etc. Great emaciation, especially of face, thighs and hands.

Fever.—Chill, alternating with heat. External heat, burning in skin, and only in single spots. Profuse sweat on chest, armpits and genitals, from least exertion; as soon as he sleeps; stains yellow or white, and stiffens the linen.

Aggravation.—Pains and most other symptoms worse after sleep; from draft of air; on hot days.

Compare.—Arg. met., Caust., *Phos.,* Stan.

Antidotes.—Ign., Puls. Incompatible: Cinch., Wine.

THERAPEUTICS.

Selenium is an excellent remedy in general debility, especially of old people, or after typhoid fever or other exhaustive diseases; early exhausted both mentally and physically; after coition or seminal emissions; bad effects from sexual excesses. Impotence. Nervous headache over left eye, worse from heat of the sun, strong odors, tea or acids (lemonade); periodical every afternoon; hysterical with profuse flow of urine, and melancholy. Headache of drunkards, enlargement of liver, stitching pains, sensitiveness, worse on motion and pressure, rash over hepatic region. Constipation from atony of the bowels. Follicular laryngitis. Paralysis of vocal cords. Hoarseness, especially of singers and public speakers, must hawk and clear the throat of mucus. Incipient tubercular laryngitis.

SENECIO AUREUS.

Natural order.—Compositæ. *Common names.*—Golden Ragwort. Squaw Weed. *Habitat.*—An indigenous perennial plant, growing on banks of creeks and on low marshy grounds throughout the North and Northwest. *Preparation.*—Tincture from the entire fresh plant.

GENERAL ANALYSIS.

Acts powerfully upon the mucous surfaces, causing irritation and increased mucous discharge. It has especial affinity for the generative and urinary organs, and to a less degree, the bronchial and intestinal tracts. It also produces a condition of nervous irritability and prostration similar to that present from reflex causes in hysteria and other affections of the female generative organs.

CHARACTERISTIC SYMPTOMS.

Mind.—Inability to fix the mind on any one subject for any length of time.
Head.—Dull, stupefying headache. °Catarrhal headache from suppressed secretions.
Eyes.—Sharp, lancinating pains in left eye and left temple. °Catarrhal inflammation from suppressed secretions.
Nose.—Sneezing and sense of burning and fullness in the nostrils. Coryza.
Mouth.—Dryness of the mouth, throat and fauces.
Stomach.—Nausea on rising in the morning (Graph., Nux m., Puls., Sep.).
Abdomen.—Griping, colic-like pains, relieved by bending forward (Coloc.).

Stool.—Stool: thin, watery; dark-colored; containing hard lumps.

Urinary Organs.—Tenesmus of the bladder, with heat and urging; pain in region of kidneys and frequent urination. Urging to urinate followed the chilliness; urine tinged with blood. Urine scanty and high-colored. Frequent copious flow of urine. Slight pains in region of kidneys.

Male Organs.—Full, heavy pain in left spermatic cord, moving along the cord to the testicle. Prostate gland enlarged, and feels hard and swollen to the touch.

Female Organs.—°Suppressed menses from cold (Cimic.). °Dysmenorrhœa, with urinary sufferings. °Premature and profuse menstruation, with backache. °Retarded and scanty menstruation (Sep.). °Irregular menses, at times too soon, at times retarded. °Leucorrhœa instead of the menses, or with urinary troubles.

Respiratory Organs.—°Loose, catarrhal cough; especially when attended with irregular or suppressed menses. Increased secretion from bronchial mucous membrane; the bronchi and lungs seem full, but it cannot be coughed up.

Back.—Pain in back and loins at night. Dull pain in the lumbar region in morning. Lancinations in lumbar region.

Generalities.—Nervousness, sleeplessness and hysterical moods. Great sleeplessness, with vivid, unpleasant dreams.

Aggravation.—Symptoms generally worse in the afternoon.

Compare.—Calc. c., Helon., Phos., Puls., Sang., Sep.

THERAPEUTICS.

Senecio has been found of most value in disorders of menstruation (see clinical symptoms above mentioned). Bronchial catarrh and pulmonary diseases, especially associated with suppressed menses, chronic cystitis with heat, strangury and bloody urine. Nephritis, pain in back, tenesmus and urging. Scanty and bloody urine. Ascites with scanty, high-colored urine. Insomnia from uterine irritation.

SENEGA.

Synonym.—Polygala Senega. *Natural order.*—Polygalaceæ. *Common name.*—Seneca Snake Root. *Habitat.*—An indigenous perennial plant, most common in the Western States. *Preparation.*—Tincture from the dried root.

GENERAL ANALYSIS.

Chief action is upon the mucous lining of the respiratory tract, where it produces catarrhal inflammation. It produces a similar effect upon the conjunctiva, and also acts upon the eye itself. It causes irritation of the gastric and intestinal lining, resulting in vomiting, colic, and diarrhœa, and has a marked action upon the pleura and joints, as shown by the chronic exudations from these parts. It also produces paralytic symptoms, which are most pronounced in the eye and larynx.

CHARACTERISTIC SYMPTOMS.

Head.—Confused feeling in head. Slight vertigo before the eyes; reeling sensation in head. *Dullness of the head, with pressure and weakness of the eyes.* The head feels heavy. Sort of aching in forehead, sinciput and occiput; comes every day, is felt when sitting in a warm room, and is accompanied by pressure in eyes, that does not bear touch, though headache is not worse from pressure, better from exercise in open air. Pressing pain in forehead and orbits after dinner, especially in left side of head; relieved in open air.

Eyes.—Aching over the orbits; eyes tremble and water when he looks at any object intently or steadily; eyes weak and watery when reading. Burning in eyes when reading or writing. Drawing and pressure in eyeballs, with diminution of visual power. Dryness, with sensation as if balls were too large for orbits. Weakness of sight and flickering before the eyes when reading; must wipe them often. When walking toward the setting sun, seemed to see another smaller sun beneath the first, assuming a somewhat oval shape on looking down *disappearing on bending the head backward and on closing the eyes. Double vision relieved* *by bending head backward.* Cilia hang full of hard mucus; smarting of the conjunctivæ, as if soap were in the eyes; mornings; blepharitis; sometimes lids stick so after sleep they must be soaked before they can be separated.

Nose.—Troublesome dryness of Schneiderian membrane. Sneezes so often and so violently head grows dizzy and heavy; followed by thin coryza.

Face.—Paralytic feeling in left half of face.

Mouth.—Tongue coated white, yellowish-white, or slimy, in morning, with slimy, unpleasant taste.

Throat.—Mouth and throat dry; tenacious mucus difficult to hawk up; scraping and roughness; constriction in fauces; hawking; rawness; burning. Irritation and roughness in œsophagus; burning sensation as if abraded.

Stomach.—Eructations which relieve the mucus and hawking. Pressure below pit of stomach; sense of gnawing hunger; burning; deranged digestion.

Stool.—Watery stools spurting from the anus (Crot. tig., Grat., Thuja).

Urinary Organs.—Diminished secretion of urine; dark-colored and frothy; acrid. After cooling, urine becomes turbid and cloudy, or deposits a thick sediment, yellowish-red, with upper stratum yellow and flocculent.

Respiratory Organs.—Tenacious mucus, causing hawking or coughing. Sudden hoarseness when reading aloud. Tearing and stinging in larynx and trachea. *Hacking cough from irritation in the larynx.* Short breathing and oppression of chest on going up stairs. Dry cough, with oppression of chest and roughness in throat; short, hacking cough from mucus, or from irritation or tickling in larynx, worse in open air, *and from walking fast.* Cough ends in a sneeze, as in a common cold. Soreness of chest, dry cough, throat dry, hoarseness; later much mucus in bronchi and trachea. °Cough worse evenings, at night, during rest, sitting, lying on (left) side, and in warm room. Orgasms of blood; oppression, with flushes of heat; oppression especially during rest. Tightness and oppression of the chest (Merc. cor.), worse during rest. Violent aching pain in chest, especially at night and while at rest. Walls of chest sensitive or painful when touched, or on sneezing; better from deep inspira-

tions; °often remaining after colds on chest (Ranunc.). Certain movements cause pain, as if chest were too tight; disposed to expand the chest; this leaves soreness. Burning, sore pain under sternum, especially during motion and on deep inspiration. Shooting stitches in chest, worse during inspiration, and during rest. Accumulation of much mucus in larynx, trachea, and chest (Ant. tart., Ipec., Stan.).
Heart.—Violent boring pain in region of heart (Stil.).
Generalities.—Great debility, with stretching of the limbs, and confusion in head. Lassitude and slight trembling of upper limbs. Faintness when walking in open air.
Fever.—Chilliness; shuddering over back; heat in face; weak; burning eyes; beating headache; difficult breathing; body feels bruised; hot skin; accelerated, hard pulse.
Aggravation.—During rest; walking; in open air.
Amelioration.—From sweat.
Conditions.—Best suited for the phlegmatic, also for fat children predisposed to catarrh; or to the sluggish, who react from colds imperfectly.—*Hering.*
Compare.—Baryt. c., Bry., Calc. c., *Caust.,* Hep. s., Phos., Spong., Squilla.

THERAPEUTICS.

The chief use of Senega is in the treatment of catarrhal affections of the respiratory tract, with symptoms above outlined, especially laryngeal and bronchial catarrh. Catarrhs that tend to leave sore and tender places in walls of chest, as though there had been left circumscribed spots of inflammation. Bronchial catarrh in the aged, especially during cold weather, much tough mucus, which cannot be raised, difficult breathing. Anxiety. Whooping cough, with characteristic expectoration. Congestion of lungs. Pneumonia, especially right side. Œdema of the lungs. Hydrothorax after pleuro-pneumonia. Exudations in pleura, after Bry. with tightness and great oppression. Useful in various affections of the eye. Promotes the absorption of lens fragments after operations for cataracts. Iritis. Catarrhal conjunctivitis. Hypopion in scrofulous subjects. Double vision, relieved only by bending the head backward. Muscular asthenopia. Catarrhal pharyngitis. Catarrhal cystitis.

SEPIA.

Synonyms.—Sepia Octopus. Sepia Succus. *Natural order.*—Dibranchiata. *Common names.*—Cuttlefish. Squid. *Preparation.*—Triturations from the inky juice of the cuttle fish.

GENERAL ANALYSIS.

Affects especially the portal, hepatic, and the female sexual systems, and diminishes in general the reproductive energies of the vegetative sphere. Its action is sluggish, and its pains and isolated symptoms feebly pronounced, the general condition being one of torpidity and depression.

The functions of the liver are not greatly disturbed, but the secretions are altered, becoming sour and foul, and their consistence changed, as is indicated by a special analysis of the symptoms produced. Sepia exerts its chief local action upon the female sexual organs, producing weakness and irritation, and upon the skin producing herpetic eruptions.

CHARACTERISTIC SYMPTOMS.

Mind.—Excessively nervous; sensitive to the least noise (Coccul., Sil.). Great sadness and dejection, with much weeping (Lyc., *Natr. mur.*, Plat., *Puls.*): in evening; when walking in the open air. Gloominess, and dark forebodings of the future; about her health. Depression on awaking in the morning. Anxiety, with flushes of heat in the evening (Acon.). *Very irritable, fretful, and easily offended* (Bry., Cham.). *Great apathy; indifference to everything* (Berb., *Phos. ac.*); *even to one's own family*. *Indolent mood;* indisposed to any exertion, mental or physical (Nux v., Phos., Sulph.). Absent-minded. Dullness of comprehension. Stupid. Heavy flow of ideas; language coming slowly (Nux m., Phos.); unable to collect thoughts; weak memory (*Anac.*, Kreos., Lach., Merc., Natr. mur., *Nux m.*).

Head.—Painful confusion of the head, particularly in the forehead. Rush of blood to the head. Vertigo when walking in the open air (Agar., Calc.); with nausea and anxiety.

SEPIA. 697

Violent pressive headache, as if the head would burst (Natr. mur., Puls., Sang.); worse from stooping, motion, coughing or shaking the head (Bell., *Bry.*). Headache, with mental depression in the morning. Headache, with nausea, beginning in the morning (Natr. mur., *Nux v.*), and lasting till noon or evening; better in the open air (Puls., Sang.). Heavy, pressing pain in the left orbit and left side of head, *with darting pains from left eye over side of head toward occiput; better after meals.* Headache worse from mental labor. Pain over eyes; over left eye; worse on motion in the house; better on walking in the open air, and on lying down; with nausea. Intense frontal headache, dull pressure, or stitching, tearing pains. Jerking pains in forehead. Tearing pains from left temple to upper part of left side of head. Fullness in forehead and temples, with throbbing in carotids. *Great falling out of the hair* (*Ambr., Graph., Hep. s., Lach., Lyc., Merc., Natr. mur., Nitr. ac., Petrol., Phos.*). Moist eruptions on vertex and back part of the head (*Graph.,* Hep. s., Lyc., Rhus tox., *Sulph.*). Scalp and roots of the hair very sensitive to touch (Cinch., Ferr., Hep. s., Staph., Sulph., Verat. alb.). Much itching of the scalp (Caust., Graph., *Sulph.*).

Eyes.—Inflammation of the eyes, with swelling, redness, and burning, smarting, pressive pains; lachrymation, which relieves. *Lachrymation morning and evening.* Eyes feel heavy, and *lids inclined to close, as from paralysis* (*Caust.,* Coni., *Gels.,* Plumb.). *Soreness, roughness and burning in the eyes, from walking in cold wind;* aggravated by gas-light, and from reading. *Pressure as from sand in the eyes; aggravated by rubbing and pressing lids together* (Ars., Caust., Hep. s., Puls., Rhus tox., *Sulph.*). Whites of eyes become yellow. Eyes become easily fatigued from reading and writing, especially by candle-light (Myrica, Phos., *Ruta.*) Nightly agglutination of the eyes (Calc. c., *Graph., Lyc., Merc., Rhus tox., Sulph.*). *Red, herpetic spot on upper lid, scaly and peeling off.* Pustules on conjunctiva. Heat and dryness of the margins of the lids, with much itching (*Staph., Sulph.*). Vision obscured, as from a veil (Caust., Croc., Natr. mur., Petrol., Phos., *Sulph.*). Sight vanishes during the menses, better on lying

down. Intolerance of reflected light from bright objects.
Fiery sparks (Bell., *Cycl.*, Natr. mur., *Phos.*, *Sulph.*) and
zigzags before the eyes. Many black spots before the eyes
(*Agar.*, *Merc.*, *Phos.*).

Ears.—Very sensitive to noise (Acon., *Bell.*, Lyc., Sil.). Loud
sounds and humming in the ears. Itching.

Nose.—Nose inflamed and swollen; nostrils sore and ulcerated
(Alum., Ant. crud., Graph., Merc.). Painful eruption on tip
of nose. Severe dry coryza, especially of left nostril. Fluent coryza, with frequent sneezing (Acon., Cepa). Violent
bleeding of the nose, especially during menses.

Face.—Face *pale; yellow* (Hep. s., Natr. mur.); red; flushed;
swollen. *Yellow saddle across the nose and upper part of
cheeks; also yellow spots on the face* (Ferr.). Yellowness
around the mouth. *Herpetic eruption on the lips.* Red
roughness on face; on forehead. Skin swollen on forehead.
Itching pimples on the skin.

Mouth.—Early decay of the teeth. Toothache, drawing, tearing, stitching, extending to the ear, especially after eating,
drinking, or taking anything hot or cold into the mouth.
Toothache during the menses. Gums painful, swollen darkred, ulcerated, and easily bleeding (*Merc., Nitr. ac., Phos.*).
Vesicles on the tongue (Borax, Nux v., *Nitr. ac.*). Tongue
coated white (Ant. crud., *Bry., Nux v., Puls.*). Tongue
feels as if scalded (*Iris,* Merc., Plat.). Bad smell from the
mouth (*Arn.*, Hep. s., Iodi., *Merc., Nitr. ac.*, Nux v.).
Dryness of lips, mouth and tongue (Apis, *Nux m.*). Taste
bitter (*Bry., Cinch., Nux v., Puls., Sulph.*), sour (Calc. c.,
Cinch., Mag. carb., Nitr. ac., *Nux v.*), slimy, foul, mostly in
morning.

Throat.—Dryness and soreness in throat, with tension and
scraping. Much mucus in throat. Pressure in throat in
region of tonsils, as if neck-cloth were too tight. Roughness
and burning in fauces; aggravated by hawking. Soreness
of throat, with swelling of cervical glands.

Stomach.—Excessive appetite, never satisfied, or no appetite
at all. Aversion to meat (Sabad.). Desire for vinegar
(*Hep. s.*). Frequent eructations, sour, bitter (*Nux v.,*
Phos., *Puls.*), or like rotten eggs (Agar., *Arn., Borax*), especially after eating and drinking. Hiccough after a meal.

Nausea, mornings, passed off after eating something; after a meal; from smell of food; with weakness, vertigo, and darkness before the eyes. Vomiting of bile and food (Nux v., Podo.) during pregnancy (Kali c., Nux m., Puls.); straining so hard that blood comes up. Sensitiveness of pit of stomach to touch (Hyos., Natr. carb., Sil.). *Painful sensation of emptiness in stomach and abdomen* (Cimic., Hydras., *Ign.*, Petrol., *Puls., Sulph.*). Pressure in stomach as from a stone, after eating (*Bry., Nux v., Puls.*). Pulsation in pit of stomach (Ant. tart., Asaf., Puls.). Stitches or burning in pit of stomach.

Abdomen.—In region of liver, stitches (Ars., Bry., Cinch., Kali c.); fullness; pressure; soreness (Apis, *Bell.*, Bry.). Severe stitches in left side of abdomen. Attacks of contractive pain in right hypochondrium. *Pressure and heaviness in the abdomen.* Abdomen distended and sensitive (Bry., Cinch., *Graph.*). Abdomen puffed up; °pot-belliedness of mothers. Loud rumbling in abdomen (Agar., Aloe, Lyc.), especially after eating. Pain across hypogastrium at night on lying down, better from micturition. Brown spots on the abdomen.

Stool and Anus.—Burning and itching in the rectum and anus (*Sulph.*). Prolapsus of rectum. Weak feeling in rectum in evening in bed. *Painful protruding hæmorrhoids; during stool; when walking;* bleeding when walking. Soreness, aching, or stitches in the anus. Inactivity of the bowels (*Alum.*, Camph., *Op.*). °Rectum feels full all the time, even after a soft stool. Ineffectual urging to stool, with discharge of mucus or flatulence only; with sensation of a plug. Stool insufficient, retarded; like sheep's dung (Alum., Kali c., *Op.*, Plumb.); difficult, mixed with mucus. Bloody. Diarrhœa, °after boiled milk. Whitish or brownish color of the stools. Expulsion of ascarides (Ferr., Merc., Spig.).

Urinary Organs.—*Urging to urinate from pressure on the bladder and tension in hypogastrium. Frequent micturition, even at night* (Ambr., Borax, Coni., Phos. ac.). Feeling as if the bladder were greatly distended. Burning in the urethra, when *urinating* (Acon., Ars., Canth., Coni., Natr. carb.); stitches; smarting. Urine; *turbid, clay-col-*

ored, *with reddish sediment;* thick, slimy, very offensive (Calc. c., Kreos.), *depositing a yellowish, pasty sediment;* becomes turbid and offensive, with white sediment (Calc. c., Colch., Graph.); *staining bottom of vessel.*

Female Organs.—*Pain in the uterus, and sensation of bearing down in all the pelvic organs, with strong pressure, as though the contents would issue through the vulva* (Bell., Lil. tig., Natr. mur., Plat.); *must cross her limbs to prevent protrusion of the parts, with oppressed breathing.* Dull, heavy pain in the ovaries; especially left. *Great dryness of vulva and vagina, especially after menses; painful to touch. Prolapsus uteri* (Arg. nit., Coni.), *with congestion, with yellow leucorrhœa.* Prolapsus, with inclination of fundus to left (Puls., Nux v., right side), causing numbness in left lower half of body, with pain, better when lying, especially on right side, tenderness of os uteri. Menses too early; and scanty, appearing only in the morning. Too late and scanty; regular but scanty; flow dark (Nux v.). Soreness and redness of the labia; in the perineum, and between the thighs (Kreos.). *Leucorrhœa yellow; like milk* (Calc. c., Coni., Lyc., Sulph. ac., Puls.); *excoriating* (Alum., Ars., Kreos.); like pus; of bad-smelling fluids; *before the menses; with soreness of pudenda.* Abortion after the fifth month. Itching of nipples which bleed and seem about to ulcerate (Graph.).

Respiratory Organs.—*Dry, hacking cough, especially in the evening, on lying down and at night* (Coni., Hyos., Puls., Sil.). Spasmodic; from tickling in larynx (Hep. s., Phos., Rumex, Sil., Sang.); much rattling of mucus in the chest (Ant. tart., Ipec., Phos.). *Short, dry cough, as if proceeding from the stomach* (Bry.); with pain in stomach; with nausea and bitter vomiting. Expectoration profuse, purulent, offensive, tasting salty (Ambr., Carb. v., Lyc., Phos.). Expectoration of blood while lying down. Oppression of the chest and shortness of breath when walking or from slightest exertion (Acon., Ars.). *Oppression of the chest morning and evening.* Stitches in chest when coughing (Bry., Kali c.); especially in left side (Phos.). Brown spots on the chest (yellow, Phos.).

Heart and Pulse.—Palpitation; in evening, in bed with beating in all arteries; during digestion; with stitches in left side of chest.

Neck and Back.—*Pain in the back, and small of back particularly with stiffness; improved by walking* (*Rhus tox.*). Aching pain between the shoulders, and under left scapula. Tearing in back during the menses, with chills, heat, thirst and contraction of chest. Aching and dull pain in lumbar and sacral regions, extending to thighs and legs. Heaviness in back in morning on waking, almost as if asleep. *Weakness and tired pain in small of back* (Hydras.), *when walking*. Sprained pain over hips, in evening in bed, and in afternoon.

Limbs.—Heaviness of the limbs. Drawing, paralytic pains, and weakness in limbs, especially in joints. Arthritic pains in the joints. Limbs go to sleep easily (Sil., Sulph.). Coldness of the hands and *feet;* but moist.

Upper Limbs.—*Itching eruption in bends of elbows.* Tension in meta-carpal joints.

Lower Limbs.—Lancinating stitches over right thigh; must get out of bed for relief; sore as if ulcerated. Bruised feeling in lower limbs, desires to sit down, and when sitting feels that she must stand up. Pains in hips and thighs, extending to knees. Soreness and burning pain between the thighs. Swelling and heaviness of the feet. Sticking pain in heel; and corns. Offensive foot-sweat (Baryt. c., *Nitr. ac.*), causing soreness between the toes (*Sil.*).

Generalities.—Frequent trembling of the whole body. *Excessive prostration, exhaustion and faintness in morning during menses;* in morning on waking; in morning on rising. *Indolence;* after a meal. Easily fatigued from the least exercise. °Excessive sensitiveness to pain (Aur., Cham., Cinch., Coff., Ign.). Sensitive to cold or damp air (Aur., Nux v., Petrol., Rhus tox., *Rumex*, Sil.). Violent ebullition of blood, also during the night. Feels pulse beating through the whole body (*Glon.*, *Puls*, Sil., Zinc.), especially in whole of left chest.

Skin.—Itching on various parts of the whole body (Rhus tox., Sulph.), face, arms, hands, back, hips, feet, abdomen and genitals. Red, herpetic eruptions; with itching and burning. Brown or reddish liver spots on the skin. Indolent ulcers, with itching, stinging and burning.

Sleep.—Great sleepiness in the day-time, especially in forenoon. Difficult waking in the morning, with much weariness. Restless, unrefreshing sleep; wakes up tired and aching. Wakes at night in a fright, and screaming. Talking in sleep.

Fever.—Want of natural body warmth (*Led., Sil.*). Chilliness in the evening, in the open air, and from every motion. Chilly in the warm room, during the day. Flushes of heat, as if hot water *were poured over him,* or from least motion. Anxious heat afternoons and evenings. Heat ascends to the head and face. Profuse perspiration; at night (Calc. c., *Cinch., Merc., Phos.,* Sil., Stan., Sulph. ac.), in morning after awaking (Calc. c., *Nitr. ac.,* Nux v., Puls., Sulph.); while walking; from slightest motion (Ambr., Calc. c., *Hep. s.,* Lyc., Phos., Sil.). Cold sweat at night on breast, back and thighs.

Aggravation.—Morning and evening; from 12 till 1 P.M., and from 4 till 6 P.M.; after eating; while sitting; after sexual excesses.

Amelioration.—In the open air; during violent exercise.

Conditions.—Especially suited to persons with dark hair; for women, and particularly during pregnancy, child-bed, and while nursing.

Compare.—Acon., Ars., Bell., Berb., Bry., *Calc. c.,* Carb. v., Cinch., Graph., *Lil. tig., Lyc.,* Merc., *Natr. mur.,* Nux v., Podo., *Puls., Rhus tox.,* Sil., *Sulph.* After Puls., Sil., Sulph., then Sep. follows well. Inimical to Sep. is Lach.

Antidotes.—Vegetable acids, Nitr. sp. d., Acon., Ant. crud., Ant. tart., Rhus tox.

Sepia Antidotes.—Calc. c., Cinch., Merc., Phos., Sars., Sulph.

THERAPEUTICS.

The chief clinical use of Sepia is in the treatment of diseases of the female organs. In general it stands at the head of all remedies in the treatment of uterine displacements, especially prolapsus, with engorgement and the characteristic bearing-down sensation as if the organs would protrude, has to cross her limbs to prevent it. Has cured many cases of prolapsus without this symptom, but where other indications for Sepia were present, especially a sensation of "goneness" in the stomach. In general it is the chief remedy in chronic endometritis, and uterine leucorrhœa, with pain in back, yellow or milky excoriating discharge, etc. Congestion and induration of the cervix, with soreness and burning. Useful in all disorders of menstruation. Especially valuable in chronic amenorrhœa; scanty irregular menstruation. Dysmenorrhœa. Metrorrhagia. Chronic vaginitis, parts dry and painful, especially during coition. Morning sickness. Threatening miscarriage; disposition to miscarry; sore nipples. Pot-belliedness of mothers. Flushes during climacteric period. Ovarian irritation. Indurations; of mammary glands and ovaries. Chlorosis. Often useful in melancholia and hysteria, associated with uterine troubles. Hemicrania. Anæmia. Jaundice. Epithelioma of lip, stomach or vagina, with burning pain. Herpetic eruptions, especially on face and in bends of joints. Acne. Eczema. Indolent ulcers, and ulcers around joints, especially of fingers. "Liver spots," especially on abdomen and chest. Often used in eye affections. Asthenopia associated with uterine disease, worse evenings; also from loss of semen in the male. Sudden vanishing of sight during the menses. Scrofulous conjunctivitis, subacute mucopurulent discharge in the morning, eyes dry in the evening. Supra-orbital neuralgia from uterine disease. Granulated lids. Paralysis of upper lid from uterine disease or disordered menstruation. Phlyctenular conjunctivitis. Blepharitis ciliaris. Pustular keratitis. Tarsal tumors. Cataract. Dry catarrh. Nasal polypi. Epistaxis during menses. Facial neuralgia during pregnancy, with chronic amenorrhœa; intermittent worse at night. Toothache from same causes. Frequently useful in dyspepsia during pregnancy, or with uterine disease or amenorrhœa, with hypochondriacal mood, also from severe mental labor or sexual excesses; desire for acids, "gone" feeling in stomach, etc. Acid dyspepsia, enlargement and congestion of the liver, with heaviness and soreness. Useful when the liver is sluggish and torpid, with headache, bad taste mornings, sallow complexion, especially "yellow saddle," across bridge of nose, constipation, etc. Constipation from inactivity of the rectum. Bleeding, painful, protruding hæmorrhoids, especially with uterine or hepatic disease. Diarrhœa from boiled milk, especially in teething children. Chronic cystitis, with characteristic urine and sediment, constant urging and pressure, etc. Atony of the bladder. Nocturnal enuresis. Chronic urethritis. Gonorrhœa. Bladder troubles, with uterine displacements. Chronic bronchitis, cough worse evenings, with gastric, hepatic and other Sepia symptoms. Whooping cough, worse before midnight, cough seems to come from the stomach. Reflex coughs from uterine or gastric troubles. Often indicated and useful in the course of phthisis pulmonalis, particularly in women, with characteristic Sepia symptoms. Functional heart troubles with uterine disease, menstrual disorders or at climacteric, especially palpitation, fainting, flushes, etc. Arthritic affections. Sometimes indicated in intermittent fever.

SILICIA.

Synonyms.—Acidum Silicum. Silex. *Common names.*—Flint. Silica. *Preparation.*—Triturations of pure Silica.

GENERAL ANALYSIS.

Acts powerfully upon the vegetative sphere, affecting more especially the organic substances of the body and involving prominently mucous surfaces, glandular structures, bones and joints. The general condition of system produced, representing a perverted nutrition, resembles the two great dyscrasias—scrofula and rachitis—while the action of the drug, like that of the disease, is also slow, deep and long-lasting. The chief property of Silicia is its power to produce a suppurative process, either in soft tissues, in the periosteum, or in the bone itself.

As a secondary result of the morbid processes set up by Silicia, the nervous system becomes involved, giving a condition of erethism conjoined with exhaustion, and resulting in various nervous disorders, spinal irritation, exalted activity of the senses, followed by depression and paralysis.

CHARACTERISTIC SYMPTOMS.

Mind.—Difficulty in fixing the attention; mind confused (Gels., Nux v.). Restless and fidgety; *startled and anxious from*

SILICIA. 705

the least noise, to which he is very sensitive (Coccul.). Desponding, melancholy, tired of life; lachrymose. Irritable, *peevish,* low-spirited (*Nux v.*). Excitement, with easy orgasm of blood. Compunctions of conscience about trifles (Ign.).

Head.—Vertigo ascending from dorsal region, through nape of neck into head, constantly inclined to fall forward; all day, while stooping at work. Congestion to the head, with redness and burning in the face. Difficulty in holding the head up. *Heat of head.* Pressing, bursting headache, as if the eyes and brain were forced outward (Acon., Bry., Kali iod.). *Headache, rising from the nape of the neck to the vertex.* Violent headache, with loss of reason and unconsciousness. Headache at night, with confusion of mind. Roaring and shattering sensation in the brain, when stepping hard, or knocking the foot against anything. Violent pressive headache in the morning, with chilliness and nausea. *Violent tearing in the head, frequently one-sided, starting from occipital protuberances; extending upward and forward. Headache, consisting of a bruised pain above the eyes, so that he could scarcely open them.* Jerking headache extending deep into the brain. *Tearing to vertex as if it would burst, extending through the head, with throbbing and chilliness, necessity to lie down and toss about in bed, better from binding the head tightly.* Stitches in the forehead and temples. Weight over the eyes. Jerking pain in middle of forehead, renewed by suddenly turning around, stooping or talking. *Pressive headache in occiput.* Headache worse from mental exertion; *noise;* motion; *jarring;* light; stooping; cold air; better from *binding head tightly* (*Arg. nit.*); *wrapping head warmly* (Mag. mur.); hot compresses; in warm room. *Head is wet from profuse sweating at night* (Cinch.); *likes wrapping up. Scalp very sensitive to touch, even of the hat* (*Carb. v., Cinch., Merc.*). Eruption on back of head, moist, dry, or offensive; scabby, burning, itching; discharging pus (Hep. s., *Graph.,* Lyc., Rhus tox., *Sulph.*). *Itching on scalp* (Camph., Sep., Sulph.); *painful and sore after scratching* (Merc.). Itching pustules on scalp and neck; better from wrapping up warm.

Eyes.—Inflammation of the eyes: red, with smarting, burning and profuse lachrymation (*Alum.*, *Calc. c.*, *Lyc.*, *Merc.*, *Puls.*, *Sulph.*). Agglutination of the lids at night (*Calc. c.*, *Graph.*, *Lyc.*, *Phos.*, *Rhus tox.*, *Sulph.*). Painful dryness of the eyes, as if full of sand, in the morning (*Ars.*, *Caust.*, *Hep. s.*, *Puls.*, *Rhus tox.*, *Sep.*). Tearing shooting pains in the eyes, on pressing them together. Weakness. Heat. twitching. *Swelling of the right lachrymal gland and sac; skin inflamed.* Dimness of vision; mist or flickering before the eyes (*Phos.*, *Sil.*). Blackness before eyes after headache. Letters run together (*Natr. mur.*); appear pale. Black spots before the eyes (*Agar.*, *Cycl.*, *Merc.*, *Phos.*, *Sep.*, *Sulph.*). Ulcers, spots and opacities of the cornea (*Euphr.*, *Nitr. ac.*, *Sulph.*).

Ears.—Swelling of the external ear, with thin discharge from the inner ear, accompanied by a hissing noise. Otalgia, with drawing, stitching pains (*Puls.*). Itching in the ears (*Baryt. c.*, *Hep. s.*, *Sulph.*), especially when swallowing. Stoppage of the ears (*Coccus.*, *Mang.*), which open at times with a loud report. Difficult hearing, especially of the human voice (*Phos.*). Roaring and singing in the ears (*Cinch.*, *Merc.*, *Sulph.*). *Over-sensitiveness to loud sounds* (*Acon.*, *Bell.*, *Lyc.*, *Sep.*).

Nose.—Frequent, violent sneezing, or inefficient efforts to sneeze. Acrid, corroding discharge from the nose (*Ars.*, *Amm. carb.*, *Arum.*, *Merc. cor.*). Discharge of much mucus without coryza. Dry coryza; complete stoppage of the nostrils (*Nux. v.*). Alternate fluent and dry coryza (*Alum.*, *Nux v.*, *Phos.*). *Sore, painful spots below septum of nose, with sticking on touch.* Nose inwardly dry, painful, excoriated, covered with crusts. Drawing in root of nose and in right malar bone. Bleeding of the nose (*Acon.*, *Bell.*, *Bry.*, *Phos. ac.*). Itching in the nose (*Sulph.*). Voluptuous itching about the nose, in evening. Soreness as if beaten, in nasal bones.

Face.—Pale, suffering expression. Pimples and ulcers in vermillion border of lower lip. Blisters on margins of upper lip, sticking or smarting on touch. Painful ulcers in corners of mouth (*Ant. crud.*, *Graph.*, *Lyc.*, *Rhus tox.*), with itching. Burning about the mouth. Herpes on the chin

(Hep. s., *Graph.*). Painful swelling of the submaxillary glands (Hep. s.); pain on touch.

Mouth.—Teeth become loose and feel elongated (Ars., *Merc.*, Rhus tox.), with swelling and painful soreness of the gums; inflamed gums; gum boils. *Gums painfully sensitive on taking cold water into the mouth.* Soreness of the tongue. *Sensation of a hair lying on forepart of tongue* (back part, Kali bi., Natr. mur.). Offensive odor from the mouth (Arn., Hep. s., Iodi., *Merc.*, *Nitr. ac.*) in the morning. Taste sour after eating. Dryness of the mouth (Apis, Ars., *Nux m.*, *Puls.*, Sep.).

Throat.—Sore throat, as if swallowing over a lump or an excoriated surface; especially on left side. Swelling of uvula. Sticking on swallowing, with pain on touch. Pressive pain or prickling in throat when swallowing. Paralysis of the velum palati; food is ejected through the nose.

Stomach.—Ravenous hunger, or loss of appetite. *Excessive thirst* (*Acon.*, *Ars.*, *Bry.*, *Rhus tox.*, *Sec.*). Bitter taste in the morning (*Bry.*, *Cinch.*, *Puls.*, *Sulph.*). Sour, acid eructations (Carb. v., Nux v., Phos., Puls.); after a meal, with burning in throat. °Water tastes bad; vomits after drinking. Nausea, with good appetite and natural taste of food. Heaviness and pressure in stomach after eating (Ars., *Bry. Nux v.*, Sep.). Burning in pit of stomach (*Ars.*, Canth Phos., Sang.). Sensitiveness of pit of stomach to pressur (Hyos., Natr. carb., Puls., Sep.). Squeezing and clawing i pit of stomach, especially after meals.

Abdomen.—Swelling; uneasy and pressive pain in region (liver. *Abdomen distended, hard and tense* (*Ars.*, Bary c., Calc. c., *Merc.*). Flatulence, with much rumbling (Agar Aloe, Hep. s.). *Emission of very offensive flatus* (*Alo Bry.*, *Graph.*). Cutting and pinching pains in abdome with constipation. Inflamed inguinal glands, large as pea painful to touch.

Stool and Anus.—*Cutting and stinging in the rectur* Burning or stinging in rectum during stool. *Moisture the anus* (Carb. an., Carb. v., Merc. cor.). *Burning in t anus* (*Ars.*, *Canth.*, *Sulph.*), *especially after a dry, ha stool. Constriction in anus during stool.* Constant b ineffectual desire for stool (Nux v.). *Stool remains lo* *in rectum.* Diarrhœa; *stools horribly offensive (Ars., Asaf.,* Lept.). Pasty, liquid mucus. *Constipation; stools scanty or composed of hard lumps, light-colored; expulsion difficult, as from inactivity of the rectum (Alum.); when partly expelled, it slips back again.* Painful hæmorrhoids; protrude during stool (Aloe, Calc. c., Lach., Mur. ac., *Puls.*).

Urinary Organs.—Frequent micturition, with distress, from irritable sphincter. Urging at night.

Male Organs.—Sexual desire increased or very weak. Violent erections at night (Graph.). Nocturnal emissions (Cinch., Digit., Phos. ac.). Lascivious thoughts. Discharge of prostatic fluid while straining at stool (Agn., Selen.). Itching and moist spots on scrotum (Petrol., Sulph.). Hydrocele. Sweat on scrotum (Rhod.).

Female Organs.—Increased menses, with repeated paroxysms of icy coldness over the whole body. Suppressed menstruation (Caul., Cimic., *Puls.*). Menses too early and too feeble. Profuse, acrid, corrosive leucorrhœa (Ars., Kreos.); °purulent; milky; in paroxysms. Pressing-down feeling in vagina. Itching, burning and soreness in pudenda (Sulph.); during menses. Mammæ swollen hard, and painful (Coni.), as if "gathering" (Merc., Phyt.), near the nipple. *Darting, burning pains in left nipple.* Nipple ulcerates; is very tender.

Respiratory Organs.—Hoarseness; roughness of the larynx (Carb. v., Hep. s., *Kali bi.*, Rhus tox.). Dry, hacking cough with hoarseness; with soreness in the chest, caused by tickling and irritation in the throat (*Phos., Rumex, Sang.,* Sep.). Cough, especially in the evening on lying down, during the night (Coni., Puls., Sep.), and after waking in the morning. *Expectoration thick, yellow, lumpy; purulent* (Carb. v., Lyc., Staph.); tenacious mucus (*Kali bi., Phos.*); profuse; greenish (Stan.). Obstructed respiration; shortness of breath; oppression. Bruised pain in chest when coughing (Apis., Arn.). Sticking pain in the chest and sides (Bry., *Kali c., Phos.*, Sep.). Pressive pain in the sternum.

Heart.—Palpitation and throbbing over the whole body while sitting. Violent palpitation on every movement.

Neck and Back.—Cervical glands and parotids swollen; indurated (Baryt. c., Calc. c., Iodi.). *Stiffness of the nape of neck; with headache* (*Chel.,* Ign.). Weakness in back, and paralyzed feeling in limbs; could scarcely walk. Burning in back when walking in the open air and becoming warm. Aching, shooting, burning and throbbing in lumbosacral region. Stitches between the hips. Tearing between and beneath the scapulæ. Stiffness and pain in small of back on rising from a seat, or on getting out of bed in the morning. *Pain as if beaten,* in the small of back and hips. *Coccyx painful, as after a long carriage ride. Stinging in os coccygis on rising; painful to pressure.* Scabby elevation on coccyx, above fissure of nates.

Limbs.—Nails dirty-yellow, crippled and brittle. *Ulcers about nails. Weakness of the limbs; can scarcely walk.* Limbs go to sleep easily (Sep., *Sulph.*). *Icy-cold legs and feet* (*Verat. alb.*). Soreness and lameness in the limbs.

Upper Limbs.—Heaviness and paralytic weakness of the arms. Trembling in all the limbs, especially in the hands. Great swelling of the axillary glands (Baryt. c., Lyc.). Tearing pain in wrists and ball of hand. Arms go to sleep when resting on them. Skin cracked in arms and hands. Cramp-like pain and lameness of the hand after slight exertion. Profuse sweat of the hands. *Falling asleep of the hands at night. Finger nails rough and yellow.* Dryness in tips of fingers. Contraction of flexor tendons; very painful when moving fingers. *Tearing, drawing, sticking pain and numbness in fingers, as if suppurating, or as if a panaritium would form.*

Lower Limbs.—Heaviness and weariness of the lower limbs. *Tearing, stitching pains in the hips and thighs. Ulcer on leg, with sticking, burning pains.* Suppurating pains in hip-joint. Drawing pains extending from the hips to the feet. *Knee is painful, as if too tightly bound.* Tearing in knee when sitting, better from motion. Cramp-like tension in the calves, and contraction. Swelling and redness of the feet. *Intolerable carrion-like odor of the feet, without sweat, every evening. Offensive foot sweat* (Baryt. c., *Nitr. ac., Graph.*), *with rawness between the toes* (Sep.). Burning of feet. Cramp in soles of feet (Carb. v., *Sulph.*). *Corro-*

sive ulcer on heel, with itching. Soreness of the soles; also burning (Calc. c., *Sulph.*). Itching, suppurating scabs on toes. Constant, violent boring or tearing in the great toes. °Ingrowing toe nails (Mar. ver.); offensive discharge. Stitching pains in corns (*Sulph.*); also under toe nails.

Generalities.—*Weakness and sense of great debility; wants to lie down;* in morning after waking; on rising; evening; after walking; at night, even to faintness. *Emaciation;* with pale, suffering expression. Trembling when writing. Coldness of left side of body. Epileptiform spasms; starting, distortion of eyes, twitching of lips, lolling of tongue, stretching and distortion of head and limbs. *Restlessness, with excitement.* Want of vital warmth (Led., Sep.), even when taking exercise. *Sensitive to cold air* (Aur., Coccul., Kreos., Sep.); *takes cold easily* (Calc. c.). *Painful, bruised feeling over the whole body* (Arn., Bapt.); *after coition; at night, as if he had lain in an uncomfortable position. Whole side of body on which he lies is painful, as if ulcerating, with chilliness on uncovering;* thirst, and flushes of heat to the head (Calc. phos.). Itching and sticking in various parts of the body. Feeling as if knives were running into her.

Skin.—*Small wounds heal with difficulty, and suppurate profusely* (Borax, Graph., Hep. s., Sulph.). *Painful pustular eruptions* (Cic., Crot. tig., Sulph.); *at last forming suppurating ulcers; on forehead, occiput, sternum and spine.* Eczematous or herpetic eruptions (*Graph., Hep. s., Lyc., Sulph.*). *Disposition to boils; boils in various parts; with stinging on touch.* Ulcers, *with stinging, sticking, burning pains;* offensive, with ichor and proud flesh (Ars., Carb. v., Graph.). Itching on various parts, worse at night, with sticking. Painless swelling of glands; also with suppuration (Graph., Hep. s.). Fistulous openings; discharge offensive; parts around hard, swollen, bluish-red.

Sleep.—Great sleepiness after eating (Kali c., Nux m.), *and in the evening.* Yawning. Sleepiness all day. *Restless, uneasy sleep;* starting from sleep in fright, with trembling of whole body. Talking in sleep. Sleepiness after 2 A.M., with rush of thoughts. Dreams confused; *frightful, of his* *youth;* of past events; anxious; lascivious, with emissions (*Phos. ac.*).

Fever.—Constant chilliness, even when exercising or in a warm room (*Puls.*). Shivering creeping over the whole body.. Fever, with violent heat in the head (*Bell.*); *afternoons; at night, with thirst and catching inspiration.* Frequent flushes of heat, especially face and head. *Fever worse at night* Profuse perspiration at night (Cinch., Stan. ac., Sulph.); *sour or offensive* (Arn., Ars., Carb. an.). *Perspiration on slight exercise* (Ambr., Calc. c., Hep. s., Lyc., Phos., Sep.,

Aggravation.—*During new moon* (Caust.); *from motion;* at night; in morning; from uncovering the head; open air; cold and wet; lying on painful side; wine.

Amelioration.—From wrapping head; from warmth; in the room.

Conditions.—Scrofulous children; large bellies, weak ankles, and much sweat about the head. Over-sensitive; imperfectly nourished, not from want of food, but from imperfect assimilation.

Compare.—Arn., Bell., *Calc. c.*, Carb. v., *Fluor. ac.*, Graph., *Hep. s.*, Hyper., Kali c., Lach., *Lyc., Merc.*, Mur. ac., Nitr. ac., Nux., *Phos., Phos. ac.,* Picr. ac., Puls., Rhus tox., Ruta, Sep., *Sulph.*, Thuja. After Bell., Bry., Calc c., Cina, Graph., Hep. s., Ign., Nitr., ac., or Phos., then Sil. follows well. After Sil. come Fluor. ac., or Hep. s., Lach., Lyc., Sep.

Antidotes.—Camph., Hep. s., Fluor. ac.

Silicia Antidotes.—Merc., Sulph.

THERAPEUTICS.

The chief clinical value of Silicia is in the treatment of slow suppurative processes in general—long-lasting suppurations; glands, abscesses ulcers, felons, boils, carbuncles, cancers, caries, etc. Bad effects of splinters, needles, etc., penetrating the flesh. Indurations following suppurative inflammations, to cause absorption. Valuable in scrofulous and rachitic conditions in general. Defective nutrition in scrofulous children, not from want of food, but from imperfect assimilation; open fontanelles; head large; body emaciated: large abdomen; sweat on the head, earthy complexion. Child slow in learning to walk. Diseases of bones (Fluor. ac.); of glands. **Caries of bones,** especially long bones, with stabbing pains. **Caries of vertebræ.** Spinal curvature. Necrosis. Enchondroma. **Exostoses.** Hip-joint disease. Felons sometimes aborted; they are generally better from warmth. Abscesses, especially about joints, with fistulous openings, offensive discharge, surrounding parts hard, swollen, bluish-red. Mild and malignant suppurations, cellular tissues. Disposition to boils. Pustular, eczematous and herpetic eruptions. Herpes zoster. Ulcers, with stinging, burning pains, offensive, proud flesh. Ailments from impure vaccination. Finger nails become yellow and brittle. Ulcers about the nails. Ingrowing toe-nails. Offensive feet. Offensive foot sweat. Useful in a variety of chronic diseases of the nervous system. Epilepsy, with well-marked aura starting from the solar plexus. Paralysis, more often a paralytic weakness arising from defective nutrition. Spinal irritation. Locomotor-ataxia. Often useful in nervous affections following injuries of the spine. Chronic effects of fright or shock. In all nervous diseases the patient is extremely sensitive to all external impressions. The surface of the body is tender to the touch, and the spine cannot bear the least jar or pressure, also mental irritability and restlessness. Often valuable in nervous headaches, with symptoms noted in pathogenesis, especially when better from bandaging the head tightly or wrapping it up warmly. Useful in various diseases of the eye. A valuable remedy in inflammation of the lachrymal sac and in lachrymal fistula (Fluor. ac.). Caries of the orbital bones. Scrofulous conjunctivitis. Blepharitis. Tarsal tumors. Ulcers and opacities of cornea; corneal fistulæ. Senile cataract. Keratitis. Hypopion. Sclero-choroiditis. Irido-choroiditis. Big styes; also to prevent their recurrence. Inflammation of external, middle or inner ear; especially chronic suppurative inflammation of middle ear; hissing noises most characteristic; ichorous discharge. Caries of mastoid processes. Chronic nasal catarrh, offensive purulent discharge, or thin, bloody, excoriating; ulcerated membrane; Eustachian tube involved, with itching and tingling. Hay-fever, with symptoms given in pathogenesis. Necrosis of the jaw (Phos.). An extremely valuable remedy in abscesses at the root of the teeth and dental fistulæ. Tonsilitis, when the tonsils have suppurated and the process does not cease. Hepatic abscess. Hæmorrhoids. Fissures of the anus, with irritability and moisture. Diarrhœa, stools painless, offensive, lienteric, with constitutional symptoms of the drug. Constipation, from inactivity, stool when partly expelled slips back again. Diabetes, with general Silicia symptoms. Nocturnal seminal emissions. Sexual weakness. Hydrocele. Chlorosis. Suppuration of mammary tumors. May be useful in bronchial troubles of Silicia children; also in old people, especially phthisis mucosa. Suppurative stage of tuberculosis, with offensive, purulent expectoration. Sometimes useful in asthma following a suppressed fistulous discharge of long standing. Hectic fevers, with night sweats. Sometimes useful in chronic rheumatism.

SPIGELIA.

Synonym.—Spigelia Anthelmia. *Natural order.*—Loganaceæ. *Common name.*—Pink Root. *Habitat.*—An annual plant found in the West Indies and South America. *Preparation.*—Tincture from the freshly dried herb.

GENERAL ANALYSIS.

Acts especially on the nerves of animal life and of special sense, and upon the fibrous and muscular tissues of the eye and the heart. It produces irritation of the nerves, resulting, in the motor sphere, in spasmodic movements of the facial muscles, subsultus tendium, and even convulsions; in the sentient nerves, to neuralgic pains, especially of the fifth pair and of the heart, which, together with the rheumatic condition of the eye and heart which it produces, is the most important action of the drug.

CHARACTERISTIC SYMPTOMS.

Mind.—Weak memory. Mental exertion difficult.
Head.—Vertigo on looking down, as if he would fall; better when lying down. Dullness of the whole head, *with pressive pain from within outward, in the forehead.* Sensation of a tight band around the head (Ant. tart., Gels., Kali

iod.), especially when stooping. Burrowing pain in forehead, occiput and left side of vertex, worse from motion, loud noise, better from lying down. *Tearing pains in temples and forehead, extending toward the eyes; worse on motion, especially on making a false step. Brain feels loose on turning the head.* Pressive headache, mostly in right temple, and involving the eye; worse from motion, noise, jarring or straining at stool. Shooting through frontal sinuses; behind and above right eminence. Neuralgic pains flying from one part to another. Feeling as if the head would burst asunder (Bry., *Caps.*). Periodical headache. Shaking in the brain; worse when moving the head or stepping hard (*Bell.*, Nux m., Rhus tox.); swashing sensation. Scalp sore and sensitive to the touch (Acon., Cinch., Merc., Natr. mur., Sil., Sulph.); worse on moving the scalp.

Eyes.—*Eyes hurt on motion, as if too large for their orbits* (Carls., Paris, Phos. ac., Plumb.). Sharp, shooting, cutting pains radiate from the eye in every direction. Itching in right eye-ball, returning after rubbing. *Intense, pressive pain in eyeballs, especially on turning them* (*Bry.*, Physos.). Pain in the eyes, deep in the sockets (Aloe, Cimic.). Vision dim.

Ears.—Sensation of distant ringing in the ears, with sensation as if the ear were loosely stopped, or a thick mist were in front of it. Itching in right vesicle. Otalgia, with pressive pain, as from a plug.

Nose.—Copious mucus flows through the posterior nares, causing choking at night; mucus at one time white, at another yellow. Tickling on back of nose, as if lightly touched by hairs, or as if a gentle wind were blowing across it.

Face.—*Prosopalgia, mostly left-sided* (Acon.), *with tearing, shooting, burning pains, especially in cheek-bones, lower jaw extending to ears, above the eyebrows, and in the eyeball; periodical; from morning until sunset; worse at noon; worse from motion or noise* (Cinch., Chin. sulph.). Burning in right side of upper lip.

Mouth.—Toothache, pressing outward; throbbing, tearing, and jerking, especially in hollow teeth (Merc.); aggravated by cold water (Ant. crud., Graph., Staph., Sulph.); cold air (*Acon.*); after eating (Ant. crud., Lach.); better when lying down. *Toothache in the evening after smoking.* Tongue cracked (Bapt., Bell., *Rhus tox.*). Stitches in right side of tongue. Salivation, white, frothy.

Throat.—Discharge of mucus from fauces all day, most from posterior nares

Stomach.—Pressing in pit of stomach, as from a hard lump. Dull stitches in pit of stomach (Bry., Kali c., Merc., Nux v., Sep.), worse from inspiration, with oppression of the chest.

Abdomen.—Griping in abdomen, as if constricted, with anxiety and difficult breathing. Sharp stitches in the abdomen. Pain in abdomen as if it would burst, worse evening before a soft stool, then slight relief.

Anus.—Itching and tickling in anus and rectum; °ascarides (Ferr., Merc., Sep.). Boring stitches in perineum.

Urinary Organs.—Discharge of prostatic fluid from the urethra.

Sexual Organs.—Erections, with voluptuous fancies, but without sexual desire. Itching stitch in right testicle and penis, from behind forward.

Respiratory Organs.—Constriction in chest, with anxiety and difficult breathing. Tearing constriction in pectoral muscles when standing. Stitches in the chest; worse from the least movement, or when breathing (*Bry., Kali c.*). *Cutting, tearing beneath the left nipple, extending to region of scapulæ and upper arm, worse during inspiration and deep breathing.* Dyspnœa and suffocating attacks when moved in bed, or raising the arms; must lie on right side, or with head high.

Heart and Pulse.—*Palpitation* (*Cact.*, Calc. c.), *violent, visible and audible* (Glon., Kali nit., Thuja, Verat. alb.); *when bending forward, on sitting down, or after rising from bed in the morning;* from deep inspiration, or holding the breath; *with anxious oppression of the chest* (Acon., Sulph., Verat. alb.); *Trembling of the heart.* Heavy aching in region of apex, with feeling as if a dull-pointed knife were slowly driven through it. Stitches in the heart (Arn., Ascl., Bry., Cact., *Kali c.*); sometimes synchronous with the pulse. Pulse weak, irregular, trembling.

Back.—Bruised feeling in spine, even during rest.

SPIGELIA.

Limbs.—Trembling of the upper limbs. Fatigue. **Drawing, tearing, twitching pains in limbs and joints (Bry., Led.).** The limbs are affected mostly when walking.

Generalities.—Body painfully sensitive to touch or jarring; causes pain, or tingling, or crawling. Great weakness, especially mornings.

Sleep.—Restless sleep, with frequent waking. Late falling asleep. Confused dreams, which cause him to awaken wearied, and which he cannot remember.

Fever.—Chilliness from the slightest motion. Chilliness every morning on rising, without thirst. Clammy sweat on the hands, from motion of arms; lying on back.

Aggravation.—From motion; noise; inspiration; touch; turning the eyes; from 10 A.M. till 12 M. Better about 3 or 4 P.M.

Compare.—*Acon.*, Arn., *Bell.*, *Bry.*, Cactus., Calc. c., Cimic., Cinch., *Cina*, Digit., Kali c., Kalmia, Laur., Lyc., Merc., Nux v., Phos., *Puls.*, Rhus tox., Sep., *Sulph.*, Zinc. After Acon. (endocarditis), then Spig. follows well. After Spig. comes Ars., Digit., Kali carb. (heart symptoms), Cimic., Zinc.

Antidotes.—Aur., Coccul., Camph., *Puls.*

Spigelia Antidote.—Merc.

THERAPEUTICS.

Spigelia is chiefly useful in neuralgia, especially of the fifth pair of nerves, and in rheumatic and neuralgic affections of the heart. A general characteristic in neuralgia is that the pain begins at one point and radiates in different directions, generally worse in stormy weather. Neuralgic headaches, with symptoms already described. The chief remedy in ciliary neuralgia. Rheumatic ophthalmia. Inflammation of the eyes, with red injected sclerotica, violent ciliary pains. Rheumatic iritis. Ptosis, with sharp pains and profuse lachrymation. Asthenopia. Post-nasal catarrh, supra-orbital pains. An extremely valuable remedy in facial neuralgia, especially supra-orbital, also involving the eyeball, worse on left side, begins in the morning, grows worse towards noon and diminishes towards evening. Neuralgic toothache. Enteralgia. Inter-costal neuralgia. A valuable remedy in organic disease of the heart, with symptoms noted in pathogenesis. Rheumatic pericarditis, or endocarditis; purring feeling over the heart; wave-like motion not synchronous with the pulse. Systolic blowing at apex. Always great dyspnœa and extremely violent palpitation. Nervous palpitation of the heart, irregular tremulous action, intermittent pulse. Neuralgia about the heart. Angina pectoris. Hydrothorax. May be useful for the pains and general reflex symptoms resulting from worms.

SPONGIA.

Synonyms.—Spongia Officinalis. Spongia Tosta. *Natural order.*—Ceratospongiæ. *Common name.*—Sponge. *Preparation.*—Tincture or triturations from the turkey-sponge, roasted brown, but not burnt.

GENERAL ANALYSIS.

Affects chiefly the larynx, trachea, thyroid gland, heart, and testicles, producing irritation, inflammation, swelling and sometimes fibrous exudations. Its action upon glandular structures—enlargement and induration, as well as its inflammatory effects upon the larynx and trachea—resembles closely the action of Iodine.

CHARACTERISTIC SYMPTOMS.

Mind.—Irresistible desire to sing, with excessive mirth, then distraction of mind and disinclination to work.
Head.—Dull headache in right side of brain, on coming into warm room from the open air. Sharp stitches in left temple extending to forehead. Congestion of blood to the head. (Acon., Bell.).
Eyes.—Yellow, crusty eruption, painful to touch, on left eyebrow.
Nose.—Fluent coryza, with much sneezing (Acon., Cepa). Dry coryza; nose stopped up (Alum., Nux v., Sep., Sil.).
Face.—Bloated, red, or bluish, with anxious expression. Heat of face. Swollen gland beneath left lower jaw, painful to touch. Stitches transversely through left upper jaw.

Cramp-like pain from left jaw-joint to cheek, in evening when eating.

Mouth.—Swelling of the submaxillary glands.

Throat.—*Thyroid gland swollen and hard* (Iodi.), *with suffocative attacks at night;* stitching pains and pressure.

Stomach.—Increased appetite. Hiccough. Bitter taste (Ars., Bry., *Nux v.*, Puls.), especially in throat.

Urinary Organs.—Frequent urging to urinate.

Male Organs.—*Pressive, painful swelling of the testicles* (*Clem.*, Rhod.). *Pinching, bruised, squeezing pain in the testicles* (Acon., *Arg. nit.*, *Rhod.*). Stitches from testicles into spermatic cord (Clem.). *Spermatic cord swollen and painful.*

Respiratory Organs.—*Hoarseness;* voice cracked. Great dryness, of the larynx, worse from hawking. Pain in the larynx on touching it (Acon., *Lach.*), and on turning the head; when singing. Scraping in larynx, with burning and constriction. Sensation in region of thyroid and cervical glands on breathing, as if forced in and out. *Sensation of obstruction in the larynx, as from a plug* (Lach.), *with impeded respiration. Incessant cough from low down in chest, where there is a sore pain. Cough dry, barking* (Bell.), *hollow, croupy, or wheezing and asthmatic. Dry cough day and night, with burning in the chest.* Cough worse from lying with head low; °from too warm room; °dry, cold winds (Acon., Hep. s.); *better after eating or drinking.* °Wheezing, whistling, sawing, anxious breathing; worse during inspiration, and when lying down. °Expectoration yellow, tenacious, hard or slimy; tasting salty. *Dyspnœa and great weakness in chest, so that she could hardly talk after slight exercise* (Hep. s., Stan.). *Short, panting respiration, surging from heart into chest, as if it would force out upward.* °Awakens from sleep with suffocative sensation. *Burning sore pain in chest and bronchi, with rawness in throat, when coughing.* Sensation as if he had to breathe through a dry sponge. °Chronic cough, violent attacks, brought up small, hard tubercle.

Heart and Pulse.—*Violent palpitation of the heart* (Acon., *Ars., Bell.*, Lycopus, *Spig., Sulph.*), with pain and gasping respiration; awakens after midnight with suffocation, great alarm, and anxiety. Pulse full, hard and frequent (*Acon.*, *Bell.*, *Verat. vir.*).

Back and Neck.—Painful stiffness of muscles of neck and throat; on left side when turning head to the right. Coldness in back, not relieved by warmth of stove.

Limbs.—Twitching of the muscles about the left shoulder joint. Cramp-like pain in the ball of the right thumb; on moving hand, extends to thumb.

Generalities.—*Extreme exhaustion and heaviness of the body after slight exertion, with orgasm of blood in chest, heat of face, vessels hard and distended, great anxiety, and difficult breathing.* Heaviness when walking in open air, must sit down.

Sleep.—Sleepy, yawning, no activity, afternoons. Sleep interrupted by dreams.

Fever.—Feverish heat, with hot, dry skin (Acon., Ars.); anxious heat; red face; weeping; inconsolable; wants to die.

Aggravation.—At night; lying with head low; in the room; when ascending.

Amelioration.—When descending; after eating and drinking, especially the cough; when resting in horizontal position.

Conditions.—Children and women, especially with light complexion and lax skin and muscles.

Compare.—Acon., Bell., *Brom.*, *Bry.*, Calc. c., Carb. v., Coni., Dros., *Hep. s.*, Ign., *Iodi.*, Kali bi., Lyc., Merc., Nux v., *Phos.*, Puls., Rhus tox., Sep., Spig., Stan., Sulph. Acon. or Hep. s. precede Spong. well. After it, Brom., Hep. s.

Antidote.—Camph.

THERAPEUTICS.

The most common use of Spongia is in croup, in which it is a most valuable remedy, though it is often prescribed when a careful selection of Iodine or Bromine would answer better. The virtues of Spongia largely depend upon the small amount of Iodine and Bromine which the drug contains, especially the former. Spongia is not indicated in croup with high fever and dry hot skin, but in cases when this condition is not present, or after it has been subdued by Acon., a dry, barking croupy cough, and anxious, wheezing, whistling, sawing respiration, with suffocative attacks, still remaining. If Spongia fails to relieve, consult Iod. or Brom. If the symptoms are similar to Spong. but more moisture, there being a slight mucous rattling in the respiration, give Hep. sulph. Acon., Hep. sulph. and Spongia are all indicated in croup arising from dry cold winds. Suffocative attacks are more common in Spong. than any other drug except Bromine. Generally of little value after membranes have formed. Acute laryngitis, with similar symptoms to those first mentioned, larynx very sensitive to touch and sore when turning the head. Laryngismus stridulus. Laryngeal phthisis, with great hoarseness; voice gives out when reading or talking (Phos.). Bronchial catarrh. Whooping cough, worse about midnight and from cold air. Pneumonia, stage of resolution, patient cannot lie down, profuse mucus expectoration. Phthisis, especially following pneumonia: beginning in apex of (left) lung; hoarseness; suffocative attacks, worse from exposure to dry cold air. Often useful in organic diseases of the heart, when the patient cannot lie flat with the head low without bringing on suffocative attacks. Rheumatic endocarditis; loud blowing with each beat of the heart. Angina pectoris; contracting pain in chest; heat, suffocation, faintess, anxious sweats. Aneurism of aorta: dry, paroxysmal cough; worse lying down. A valuable remedy in goitre (consult pathogenesis). Sometimes useful in enlarged and indurated testicles, after maltreated orchitis, or following checked gonorrhœa; spermatic cords swollen and painful, etc.

SQUILLA.

Synonym.—Scilla Maritima. *Natural order.*—Liliaceæ. *Common names.*—Squill. Sea Onion. *Habitat.*—A perennial plant found generally in countries bordering on the Mediterranean. *Preparation.*—Tincture from the fresh bulb.

GENERAL ANALYSIS.

Squilla acts upon the mucous membranes of the respiratory and digestive tracts, producing irritation, even to inflammation. It also acts upon the kidneys, causing excessive secretion; sometimes bloody urine and even suppression.

SQUILLA.

CHARACTERISTIC SYMPTOMS.

Head.—Cloudy dizziness in the head. Stitching pain in right side of forehead. Contractive pain in both temples. Sudden transient drawing pain in occiput from left to right.

Eyes.—Contraction of the pupils.

Ears.—Tearing pain behind the left ear.

Nose.—Acrid, corrosive, fluent coryza in the morning; sneezing and watering of the eyes (*Ars., Cepa, Euphr.*). Sensation of soreness of the margins of the nostrils.

Throat.—Burning in palate and throat. Irritation and tickling in throat, inducing cough.

Stomach.—Sweet or bitter taste of food. Insatiable appetite. Excessive nausea in back of throat, with accumulation of saliva in mouth. Pressure in the stomach, as from a stone (*Ars., Bry.,* Nux v., *Puls.*).

Abdomen.—Painful sensitiveness of the abdomen and region of bladder.

Urinary Organs.—Continuous painful pressure on the bladder. Great desire to urinate, with profuse emission of watery urine (Apis, Apoc.). Red, deep-colored urine (Acon., Ars., Canth.). Scanty urine. Greatly increased secretion of urine (Apis, Apoc.).

Respiratory Organs.—*Cough violent, with stitches in the side;* caused by tickling beneath thyroid cartilage; *with expectoration of mucus;* short and dry on inspiration. *Cough in morning, with profuse, slimy expectoration.* Cough causes retching. Violent, dry cough, causing shattering in abdomen and dryness in throat. Difficult respiration; frequently obliged to take a deep breath, which excites cough. Oppression and tightness in chest. *Dyspnœa, with stitches in chest; worse during inspiration. Stitches in chest, especially when inhaling or coughing;* pleurisy (*Bry.*).

Neck and Back.—Stiffness of the neck. Painful jerking above left scapula. Painless drawing on left scapula.

Limbs.—Convulsive twitching of the arms and legs.

Generalities.—Stretching and yawning, without sleepiness. *Great weakness and weariness of the whole body.* Excoriation in bends of limbs (Graph., Mang.).

Sleep.—Restless sleep, with much tossing about (Acon.).

Fever.—Icy-cold hands and feet, with warmth of the rest of t
body. Dry, burning heat, with shivering and pain when
the least uncovered.

Compare.—Ant. tart., Bry., Caust., Cepa, Kali c., **Nux v.**, Rh
tox., Sulph.

THERAPEUTICS.

Squilla has been used almost exclusively in catarrhal affe
tions of the respiratory tract. Influenza; bronchitis; pne
monia, later stages; pleurisy; pleuro-pneumonia. Said to
especially useful in pleurisy and pneumonia after blood-lettin
Cough during measles. Whooping cough. In all coughs the
is considerable rattling of mucus; spasmodic cough; causi
urine to spurt; stitches in chest; dyspnœa, etc. Has been us
in nephritis; cystitis; diabetes; abdominal dropsy, with scan
urine; atony of the bladder, urine spurts when coughing, snee
ing or blowing the nose (Caust.).

STANNUM.

Synonym.—Stannum Metallicum. *Common names.*—Ti
Preparation.—Triturations.

GENERAL ANALYSIS.

Acts primarily upon the cerebro-spinal system, giving ris
in the motor sphere to profound prostration (neurasthenia), a
well as paralysis and convulsions, and in the nervous sphere t
neuralgic pains. It also acts prominently upon the respirator
mucous membrane, producing catarrhal inflammation, an
profuse muco-purulent expectoration, with dilitation of th
bronchi, together with excessive prostration of the respirator
nerves. Tin has formerly ranked as an important vermicide
acting, according to Hahnemann, as a narcotic to the para
sites, so that they may readily be dislodged by appropriate pu
gatives It has also proved of service for the removal of thos
symptoms of the digestive sphere, which usually accompan
vermicular affections, whether the parasites be actually presen
or not.

STANNUM.

CHARACTERISTIC SYMPTOMS.

Mind.—Great anxiety and restlessness, melancholy and disposition to weep (Ign., *Natr. mur.*, *Puls.*, Rhus tox.). Quiet fretfulness; answers unwillingly and abruptly. *Sad.* Discontented, discouraged. Aversion to and dread of people. Restless and distracted, not persistent in work. Fruitlessly busy.

Head.—Vertigo. Heaviness in the evening. *Neuralgic headache; begins lightly and increases gradually to its highest point, and then gradually declines.* Dull pressure from within outward in the forehead. Constriction as from a band, and pressure in whole upper part of head, and in forehead, *slowly increasing and decreasing.* Intermittent tearing pain in right half of forehead, worse on stooping. Crashing pain in forehead. Sharp jerking in right anterior lobe of brain, above orbit. Pressive, tearing frontal headache. Painful jerks through left temple, forehead and cerebellum, *leaving a dull pressure* worse during rest; better from motion. Throbbing headache in the temples.

Eyes.—Pustular swelling of left inner canthus, like a lachrymal fistula. Pressive pain in left inner canthus, as from a stye. Agglutination of the lids at night (Calc. c., *Lyc.*, Merc., Rhus tox., Sil., *Sulph.*).

Face.—Pale face and sunken; sickly expression; features elongated.

Mouth.—Tongue coated with a yellowish mucus. Fœtid smell from the mouth (*Arn.*, Hep. s., Iodi., Kreos., *Nitr. ac.*).

Throat.—Accumulation of thick, viscid, grayish, bloody mucus in throat; efforts to expel excite vomiting. Extreme dryness and rawness of throat; worse when swallowing (Alum., Arg. nit., *Hep. s.*). Cutting in pharynx on swallowing. Scraping and roughness in throat in the morning. Ulcerated sensation in right side of throat.

Stomach.—Excessive hunger; cannot eat enough (Bry., Cina, Ferr., *Lyc.*). Bitter eructations, after eating (Bry., Cinch., *Nux v.*). Nausea, especially after a meal, followed by vomiting of bile (*Nux v.*). Vomiting of blood (Ham., Nux v., Op., Podo.). Heavy pressure in stomach, with soreness to touch. Cramps in the stomach.

Abdomen.—Sensation of emptiness in the abdomen (*Phos.*,

Sep.). Digging; soreness. Abdomen sore, and sensitive to touch (Apis, *Bell.*, Bry.).

Stool.—Ineffectual desire for stool.

Male Organs.—Emission without dreams.

Female Organs.—Prolapsus of the vagina, with hard stool.

Respiratory Organs.—*Hoarseness and roughness in the larynx, with great weakness and emptiness in the chest; at times hoarseness better from an expulsive cough* (Carb. v., Phos.). *Great accumulation of mucus in the trachea* (*Ant. tart., Ipec., Osm., Phos.*), *easily detached by a slight cough. Inclination to cough before midnight, with scanty expectoration. Scraping cough, with profuse greenish expectoration* (Sil.) *of an offensive, sweetish taste* (Calc. c.); *worse in evening before lying down; producing soreness in trachea and chest* (Caust., Nux v.). *Dry cough in the evening, in bed, till midnight, with scanty expectoration. Short cough from weakness of chest, having a hoarse, weak sound. Shattering, deep cough. Fatiguing, paroxysmal cough, so that epigastric region was painful, as if beaten.* Constant hacking cough, caused by tickling in the chest, as from mucus. Expectoration yellow, foul-tasting (Calc. c.), globular, *grayish lump of thick mucus* (*Lyc.*); thick mucus and blood; *greenish, profuse* (Sil.); taste putrid, sweet (Calc. c.) or salty (Ambr., Calc. c., Carb. v., Phos., Sep.). Dyspnœa and want of breath on ascending (Acon., Amm. carb., Ars., Cact., Calc. c.), or from the slightest motion. *Short, difficult inspiration, from weakness of chest, with emptiness of stomach.* Dyspnœa in the evening; must loosen the clothing. *Sensation of great weakness and emptiness in chest.* Oppression of chest as from constriction, with disposition to take a deep breath, and anxiety. Sensation of mucus, with rattling when breathing. *Sensation of great soreness in the chest.* Sharp, cutting stitches in left side of chest (Kali c., Phos., Sep.); worse from stooping.

Limbs.—Great heaviness and paralytic weakness in arms and legs. Swelling of the hands and feet in the evening.

Generalities.—Extreme weakness and prostration; must sit or lie down continually (Sil.). Emaciation. Faintness in going down stairs; can go up without difficulty. Reading aloud or talking produces great exhaustion (Cocc.). Pains commence lightly, increase gradually to a very high degree, and decrease again as slowly. Chilliness over the whole body. Profuse, debilitating sweat, night and morning (*Cinch.*, *Phos.*, Sulph. ac.); hot, even on slight movement; °with moldy, putrid smell (Nux v., Staph.).

Aggravation.—From motion; from talking; when descending.

Amelioration.—From walking (except weakness); when lying on the back.

Compare.—*Arg. nit.*, Ars., Bell., Bry., Calc. c., *Caust.*, Cina, Cinch., *Cupr.*, Hell., Lyc., *Phos.*, *Puls.*, Rhus tox., *Sep.*, Spig., Sulph., Zinc. After Caust. then Stan. follows well.

Antidote.—Puls.

THERAPEUTICS.

The chief use of Stannum is in the treatment of respiratory diseases characterized by profuse mucous or muco-purulent expectoration, and great weakness in the chest. The expectoration of balls of sweetish mucus is also characteristic. Valuable in acute and chronic bronchial catarrh. Catarrh of the larynx. Especially useful in laryngeal phthisis with characteristic symptoms. Phthisis pulmonalis. Pleurisy. Intercostal neuralgia. Chronic catarrh of the pharynx, hawking up balls of mucus. °Leucorrhœa, transparent and yellow; at times watery, with bearing down. Prolapsus of vagina; of uterus; worse during stool, with great weakness and emptiness in chest (in stomach, Hyd., Ign., Sepia, etc.). Vermicular affections. Often useful in the neuroses, especially neuralgia of different parts, the pains gradually increasing and decreasing. Neuralgic headaches. Chronic gastralgia. Epilepsy, reflex from abdominal irritation, especially worms. Hysteria, with characteristic weakness. Functional paralysis, from fatigue or mental emotions. Neurasthenia, general nervous exhaustion. Anæmia.

STAPHISAGRIA.

Synonym.—Delphinium Staphisagria. *Natural order.*-Ranunculaceæ. *Common names.*—Staves Acre. Lark Spur *Habitat.*—A plant found growing in poor soil in Southern Europe. *Preparation.*—Tincture from the ripe seeds.

GENERAL ANALYSIS.

Staphisagria acts chiefly on the genito-urinary organs affecting especially the prostatic portion of the urethral mucous membrane, causing irritation and chronic inflammation sometimes extending into the ejaculatory canals and seminal ducts, often presenting in its symptoms a picture of spermatorrhœa, in which disease it has proved of great value. Staphisagria affects also the cerebrum, the digestive tract, and the skin as shown by its pathogenesis, resembling in its action somewhat the syphilitic and scrofulous miasms.

CHARACTERISTIC SYMPTOMS.

Mind.—*Very peevish; throws or pushes things away indignantly (Cham., Cina); in the morning.* Disinclined to mental work. Apathetic; gloomy. Very sensitive to the least impression; the least word that seems wrong hurts her (Nux v., Plat.). Weakness of memory (*Anac.,* Kreos., Lach., Merc., Nux m.); °especially after sexual excesses or onanism (*Cinch.,* Phos. ac.).

Head.—Heaviness of the head relieved by resting it upon the hand. Vertigo. Sensation of a round ball in forehead, sitting firmly there, even when shaking the head. Pressive, stupefying headache, especially in forehead. Headache, as if the brain were compressed; worse in forehead. Dullness in small spot in middle of forehead. Violent pressing, boring stitches in left half of forehead, from within outward, in the morning. Burning in left temple; internally and externally, as if the bones would be pressed out, worse from touch. Fine, burning, needle-like stitches, externally on the vertex. Hard, pressive pain in vertex. Feeling as if the occiput were compressed, internally and externally. Moist, itching, fœtid, scurfy eruption on occiput, sides of head and behind the ears (*Graph.*, Lyc., Sil., *Sulph.*); worse from scratching.

Eyes.—Eyes sunken with blue-raised rings around them. Dryness and pressure in the eye-balls and lids. Pain in upper lid, worse on closing the eye. Pain as if a hard substance were beneath the left upper lid. Biting, smarting in inner canthi. *Itching of the margins of the lids* (Sep., Sulph.). Inflammations of margins of lids, with nightly agglutination (Calc. c., *Graph.*, Sep., *Sulph.*); blepharitis. Pupils dilated.

Ears.—Tensive stitches in left ear.

Nose.—Coryza, with ulcerated nostrils. Coryza; at first discharge of only thick mucus, after of thin water. Sneezing without coryza.

Face.—Inflammation of the bones of the face. Sharp, burning stitches in left cheek, which provoke scratching. Sensitive induration beneath chin, pain on swallowing and on touch.

Mouth.—Painfulness of the submaxillary glands, with or without swelling. Teeth turn black, crumble and decay (*Merc.*); have black streaks across them. Tearing pains in decayed teeth; worse after eating (Lach.) and chewing (Ant. crud.); after drinking anything cold (Ant. crud., *Calc. c.*, Coccus, Sulph.), and in the open air; teeth sensitive to touch, especially at night and in the morning. °Hard pressure frequently relieves the toothache. Constant accumulation of mucus in the mouth. Gums swollen, ulcerating, spongy; bleed when touched (Carb. v., *Merc.*, *Nitr. ac.*, Phos.). Tearing in gums of lower incisors, and their roots when eating. Excrescences and painful nodosities on the gums.

Throat.—Dry and rough, with soreness, when talking and swallowing. Submaxillary glands painful, as if swollen and bruised.

Stomach.—Thirstlessness. Frequent hiccough.

Abdomen.—A feeling of weakness in the abdomen, as if it would drop. Passage of hot flatus. Painful swelling of the inguinal glands (Calc. c., Iod., Nitr. ac., Rhus tox.). Griping pain, twisting about, here and there, in the whole abdomen; incarcerated flatus. Hard pressure in right side beneath umbilicus. Pinching stitch in left viscera. Swollen abdomen, in children, with much colic.

Stool and Anus.—Smarting, sore pain in rectum after stool. Itching in the anus, while sitting. Constipation; stool scanty and hard. Loose stools, with much flatulence (Aloe).

Urinary Organs.—Frequent urging to urinate, with scanty discharge in a thin stream, or discharge of dark urine, in drops (Acon., *Bell.*, Canth.). Burning in the urethra during micturition (Ant. tart., *Canth.*, *Can. sat.*, Coni.). After micturition, urging as if the bladder were not emptied, with dribbling of urine (Acon., Caust., Stram.). Profuse discharge of watery, pale urine (Natr. mur., Phos. ac., Sec.).

Male Organs.—Sexual desire increased. °Effects of onanism; face sunken, abashed look; melancholy; nocturnal emissions; backache; legs weak; organs relaxed. Seminal emissions, followed by great prostration (Agar., Cinch., Kali c., Phos. ac.). Pressing pain in left testicle when walking; and after rubbing; worse from touch. Drawing, tearing in right testicle, as if compressed. Drawing, burning, extending from right inguinal ring, as if in spermatic cord, into right testicle. °Soft, moist excrescences on and behind the glans (Nitr. ac., Thuja). Dyspnœa toward the end of coition.

Female Organs.—Painful sensitiveness of the sexual organs, especially when sitting. °Granular vegetations of vagina.

Respiratory Organs.—Cough, with purulent, yellow expectoration, especially at night (Lyc., Sil.). Itching stitches in the costal cartilages. Itching in sternum beneath pit of throat.

Heart.—Palpitation of the heart from the least motion (Merc.).

Neck and Back.—Painful swelling of the glands of the throat, neck and axillæ (Calc. c., Iodi., Merc.). Pain in small of back, as if broken or sprained; worse at rest; on rising from a seat; turning the body; principally at night and in the morning (*Rhod.*, *Rhus tox.*). Itching stitches in region of kidneys.

Limbs.—Drawing, tearing, stitching pains in extremities. Limbs feel beaten and painful, as after a long walk, below shoulders and below hip-joint.

STAPHISAGRIA.

Upper Limbs.—Stitches in shoulder joints, worse on touch and motion. Paralytic pain in arms, worse on motion and touch; jerking and tearing in muscles of fingers and thumbs, worse in tips. Burning itching in left thumb. Paralytic drawing in meta-carpal joints, worse on motion. Numbness in tips of fingers. Arthritic nodosities on the fingers. Ostitis of phalanges of fingers.

Lower Limbs.—Itching on inner side of thigh. Pain in thigh when walking. Stitches in knee-joint, worse on motion. Boring stitches in right tibia during rest. Tearing in muscles of leg when sitting and standing. Stitches in right calf. Nates ache while sitting.

Generalities.—Weakness of whole body; especially of knees; when walking; with bruised pain. Itching in various parts. Pain in all bones. In the morning in bed, weary, without sleepiness; *limbs pain as if bruised, and as if there were no strength in them* (*Arn., Cinch.*). Weariness and sleepiness after eating; needs to lie down. °Pain, swelling and suppuration of the bones and periosteum (Asaf., Hep. s., Phos. ac.). °Mechanical injuries from sharp cutting instruments. Drawing pain here and there in all the muscles of the body, while sitting (Puls.). General bruised sensation when walking; weary pains as if beaten; can scarcely drag the feet. Sweat, smelling like rotten eggs.

Skin.—Herpes. Itching in the evening; *burn after scratching* (Ars., Rhus tox.). Chronic miliary eruption. Painful swelling of glands (Calc c., Iodi.).

Sleep.—Sleepy all day, with frequent yawning; awake all night; body aches all over. Amorous dreams with emissions.

Aggravation.—At night and in morning; from loss of fluids; sexual excesses; onanism; from touch; from motion.

Compare.—Acon., Ambr., Calc. c., *Caust.*, Cimic., Cinch., Clem., Cocc., Coff. c., Coloc., Kreos., Lyc., Merc., Phos. ac., *Thuja*, *Sulph.* Staph. precedes or follows Coloc. well.

Antidote.—Camph.

Staphisagria Antidotes.—Merc., Thuja.

THERAPEUTICS.

Useful in many affections resulting from scrofula, especially of glands and bones. Pain, swelling and suppuration of the bones and periosteum. Scorbutic affections; ulcers; spongy excrescences on gums; bleeding gums, etc. Antidotes the chronic effects of Mercury; of Thuja. Bad effects of sexual excess or onanism. Incised wounds after surgical operations; neuralgia; colic after intra-abdominal operations. The individual affections in which the drug is useful will be briefly considered in the usual anatomical order. Hysteria or hypochondriasis, from sexual excesses or onanism; anger, chagrin or wounded pride; with peevishness, violent temper, great sensitiveness, etc. Neuralgic headache. Moist eczema on and about occiput. Often a valuable remedy in affections of the eyelids. Especially valuable for styes, tumors, nodosities, steatoma, polypi; chalazæ, one after the other, sometimes ulcerating. Anchylops, leaving a small, hard tumor. Scrofulous or arthritic ophthalmia; eyes burn on least exertion as if very dry, yet lachrymation is constant. Deafness after the abuse of Mercury. A valuable remedy in caries of the teeth; they turn black and crumble, especially in scrofulous or syphilitic children, or in women during pregnancy. Valuable in toothache (see symptoms). Scorbutic gums. Dental fistula. Aphthous sore mouth. Sometimes useful in the diarrhœa of scrofulous children, who have eruptions on the skin, crumbling teeth, etc.; stools hot and offensive. Enlarged prostate. Staphisagria stands next to Thuja for figwarts and condylomata, and is preferable to that remedy when the general constitutional symptoms of Staph. are present. The excrescences are soft, moist and offensive and are chiefly located on or behind the glans penis; granular vegetations in the vagina. Secondary syphilis, orchitis, especially as metastasis of mumps (Puls.). Bad effects of onanism. Prolapsus uteri, with relaxed, hanging-down feeling in abdomen, generally from disappointed love, or allowing the mind to dwell on sexual subjects, even onanism. Also ovarian troubles and irregular menstruation from the same causes. Often valuable in moist itching eruptions; eczema; herpes; burn after scratching; after scratching the itching appears in another place. Herpes zoster, with shooting pains extending down the thighs. Gout; arthritic nodes.

STICTA PULMONARIA.

Synonym.—Lichen Pulmonarius. *Natural order.*—Lichenes. *Common names.*—Lungwort. Lung Moss. *Habitat.*—Found growing on the trunks of large trees in the mountainous counties of England; also in New England and as far south as Carolina. *Preparation.*—Tincture from the fresh lichen, grown on the sugar maple.

GENERAL ANALYSIS.

Acts upon the mucous lining of the respiratory tract, producing symptoms of a catarrhal character.

CHARACTERISTIC SYMPTOMS.

Mind.—General confusion of ideas; inability to concentrate them.

Head.—Dull sensation in the head, with sharp, darting pains through the vertex, side of face and lower jaw. *Dull, heavy pressure in forehead and root of nose* (Acon., Kali bi., Phyt.); *increasing during the day.* °Catarrhal headache before the discharge sets in.

Eyes.—Burning in eyelids, with soreness of the ball in closing the lids or turning the eyes, increasing in intensity all day. °Catarrhal conjunctivitis, with profuse, mild discharge.

Nose.—*Feeling of fullness and heavy pressure at root of nose* (Acon., Kali bi.); °tingling in right side of nose; loss of smell; dry coryza. °Acute catarrh of nasal passages; influenza (Acon.). °Constant need to blow nose, but no discharge results. °Excessive and painful dryness of mucous membrane; secretions dry rapidly, forming scabs, difficult to dislodge.

Stool.—°Diarrhœa, with much mucus, associated with cough.

Respiratory Organs.—°Dry cough; worse evening and night; can neither sleep nor lie down. °Severe, dry, racking cough, caused by tickling in larynx and bronchia. °Incessant, wearing, racking cough in consumptives. °Spasmodic stage of whooping cough. Oppression of the lungs.

Limbs.—Darting pains in arms, fingers, joints, thighs and toes.
Generalities.—°General feeling of dullness and malaise. as when a catarrh is coming on (Gels., Hydras.). °Legs feel as if floating in the air; she feels light and airy, without any sensation of resting on the bed (Asar.); hysterical chorea.
Compare.—Acon., Dulc., Hydras., Kali bi., Merc., Rumex. Sang.

THERAPEUTICS.

Sticta pulmon. is especially useful in catarrhal affections as indicated in the above symptoms. Influenza. Conjunctivitis. Nasal catarrh. Hay fever. Bronchitis. Whooping cough. Phthisis. Cough during measles. Occasionally useful in hysteria. Inflammatory rheumatism of the small joints. Rheumatism of the wrists; of the knee. Housemaid's knee.

STILLINGIA SYLVATICA.

Synonym.—Sapium Sylvaticum. *Natural order.*—Euphorbiaceæ. *Common names.*—Queen's Root. Yard Root. *Habitat.*—An indigenous perennial plant found growing in pine barrens and sandy soils from Virginia to Florida and Louisiana. *Preparation.*—Tincture from the fresh root.

GENERAL ANALYSIS.

Acts prominently upon the periosteum and fibrous tissues, causing painful nodes, bone pains, and rheumatic symptoms, resembling those associated with secondary syphilis and chronic rheumatism, in both of which affections it has been successfully used. It also acts upon the cartilages of the larynx. and upon the mucous lining of the respiratory tract, giving symptoms of laryngeal and bronchial irritation and inflammation. The lymphatic glands are enlarged, and their secretions increased in quantity and perverted in character. The skin becomes eczematous, and the seat of ulcerations characterized by excessive discharges.

STILLINGIA SYLVATICA.

CHARACTERISTIC SYMPTOMS.

Mind.—Depression of spirits, *and gloomy forebodings.*
Head.—Throbbing and giddiness of the head. °Bony swellings on head and forehead. °Mercurial periostitis of the skull. °Moist, brown, excoriating eruption on the scalp.
Eyes.—Inflamed and watery, with severe headache and general muscular soreness, as though he had taken cold.
Nose.—Catarrhal discharge from the nose, at first watery, then muco-purulent; nostrils sore on inner surface. °Inflammation and necrosis of bones of nose (*Aur.*).
Throat.—Dryness, rawness, stinging and smarting of fauces.
Stomach.—Pyrosis every afternoon, lasting until bed-time. Burning in stomach and bowels (*Ars., Iris,* Canth.). Distress and griping pains in epigastrium, with rumbling in bowels, followed by diarrhœic stool (*Aloe*).
Stool.—Diarrhœa; stools irregular, frothy, acrid, bilious; white, resembling curds. Constipation.
Urinary Organs.—Severe dull pain in region of kidneys. Urine high-colored, frothy, thick and milky (Phos. ac.); abundant white sediment, soon deposited; white, flocculent, or brick dust sediment (Lyc.); brownish-red sediment, like sausage meat. Violent, sharp, smarting, burning pains throughout entire course of urethra; aggravated by micturition, with difficulty in passing urine, and dull pain in region of kidneys; pains in urethra so severe as to cause perspiration to start.
Female Organs.—°Copious, muco-purulent leucorrhœa, with rheumatic pains.
Respiratory Organs.—Excessively dry cough toward evening, caused by tickling in trachea. Sensation of lameness, seemingly in cartilages of trachea. Constriction in region of larynx, with stinging and burning in fauces. Cough short, hacking, deep, loose, spasmodic.
Heart and Pulse.—Boring pains in region of heart (Senega). Pulse very irregular.
Limbs.—In the evening, pains in right elbow and right leg of an aching and pulsating character, with soreness. Sharp, shooting pains in arms extending to fingers. Shooting in upper side and inner third of forearm. Aching pains in hips, legs and feet; more on right side. Burning and itching of

legs below knees. Eruptions, ulcers and periosteal enlargements on limbs.

Generalities.—Malaise; drowsiness; general feeling of distress. °Tubercular eruptions, which tend to ulcerate. °Enlarged cervical glands.

Fever.—Feverish heat, especially in face, as from catarrh.

Aggravation.—Afternoons; from damp air; motion.

Compare.—Arg., Aur., Hep. s., Kali iod., Merc., Mez., Phyt., Rhus tox., Sulph.

THERAPEUTICS.

Stillingia sylvat. has been successfully used in the following conditions, the symptoms agreeing: Secondary syphilis; syphilitic periosteal rheumatism; nodes; chronic rheumatism; sciatica in syphilitic patients; laryngitis, especially if of a syphilitic character; mercurial periostitis; urethritis; gonorrhœa; gleet; leucorrhœa; venereal or scrofulous ulcers and eruptions.

STRAMONIUM.

Synonym.—Datura Stramonium. *Natural order.*—Solanaceæ. *Common names.*—Thorn Apple. Jamestown Weed. Stink Weed. *Habitat.*—Supposed to be a native of Asia, but growing in many parts of the world. Found on road-sides, near dung-heaps, pig-styes or rubbish. *Preparation.*—Tincture from the ripe seeds.

GENERAL ANALYSIS.

Acts chiefly upon the sensorium, increasing its activity, perverting its function, and giving rise to nausea, delirium and to hallucinations; simulating in kind the action of Belladonna and Hyoscyamus, yet differing in degree. The delirium is more furious, the mania more acute; while the congestion, though greater than in Hyoscyamus, is much less than in Belladonna, never approaching a true inflammatory condition.

Stramonium also produces great dryness of the throat and skin, on the latter causing a fiery red rash, resembling that of scarlatina. On other portions of the body Stramonium only acts through sympathetic irritation from the brain. In this manner it produces dilated pupils, diminished general sensibility, perversion of the special senses, convulsive motions, intense sexual excitement, suppressed urine, etc.

CHARACTERISTIC SYMPTOMS.

Mind.—*Delirium; furious* (Bell., Canth., Œnan.); *full of fear* (Bell., Verat. alb.); *tries to escape; struggles to get out of bed* (Bell.); *incessant and incoherent talk; laughing* (Hyos.); *carphologia* (Bell., Hyos.); *sexual excitement. Mania; desire for light and company* (Kreos.; aversion, Hyos.); *attacks of rage, with beating or striking; proud, haughty* (Lach., Plat.); *screaming, biting, scratching; terrified; merry; exaltation; singing and dancing* (Croc.). *Hallucinations* (Anac., Hyos., Can. ind.), *which terrify the patient* (Absinth.); *horrible images; sees strangers, or imagines horrible animals are jumping sideways out of the ground, or running at him. Hydrophobia* (Bell., Hyos.); *excessive aversion to liquids; water, a mirror, or anything bright, excites convulsions; spasmodic constriction of throat, etc.* Symptoms resembling delirium tremens. Dullness of all the senses. Alternate exaltation and melancholy. Stupid indifference to everybody and everything (Berb., Phos., Phos. ac.). °*The child on waking is frightened at everything that first meets its eyes* (Bell.); *wants to run away from them.* °Strange, absurd ideas; thinks herself tall, double or lying crosswise; one half of body cut off, etc. (Bapt., Petrol.). Unconscious snoring; jaws hang down; hands and feet twitch; pupils dilated (Op.). Weak memory (Anac., Kreos., Lach., Nux, Natr. mur.); looses thoughts before she can utter them; calls things by wrong names.

Head.—*Vertigo;* cannot walk in the dark; falling to the or backward (Bell.); reeling as if drunk (Agar.). *Violent congestion in the head* (Bell.). Aching. Heat in head; throbbing about vertex and in forehead; fainting; dim sight and hearing; face bloated and turgid. Convulsive movements of the head, mostly to the right side; inability to raising the head up.

Eyes.—*Eyes wide open, staring, prominent*

STRAMONIUM.

Hyos., Naja, Op.); *brilliant, contorted.* **Pupils dilated** (*Bell., Hyos., Op.*); *sometimes immovable, and insensible to light* (Cic., Digit.). *Conjunctiva injected, as if the vessel were filled with dirty liquid. Total blindness, transient.* Light dazzles; shuns the light; *bright light or brilliant objects cause convulsions.* Double vision (*Aur.,* Bell., Cic., Phyt.): sees obliquely.

Ears.—Hardness of hearing.

Face.—*Face hot, red and bloated* (Acon., Bell., Op.); *eyes wild; expression of terror.* Twitching in muscles of face (Agar., Ant. tart., Cic., Ign.); frowns on forehead. Lips dry and sticky.

Mouth.—Tongue swollen, stiff, dry, moved with difficulty. *Stammering* (Can. ind., Caust., Selen.), *speech difficult and unintelligible, or entirely speechless* (Hyos.). Great dryness of mouth and fauces. *Dribbling of glairy saliva from the mouth.*

Throat.—*Difficult deglutition, from spasmodic constriction of the throat* (*Bell., Hyos.,* Laur., *Plumb.,* Verat. alb.). *with paralysis.* Great dryness of the throat (Apis, *Nux m.,* Rhus tox.).

Stomach.—*Violent thirst;* especially for acid drinks (Ant. tart., Cinch., Phos., Verat. alb.). Hiccough. Nausea. Vomiting.

Abdomen.—Abdomen distended, not hard.

Stool and Urine.—*Suppression of both stool and urine.* Discharge of coagulated blood from rectum. Constipation. Urine dribbles away slowly and feebly (Acon., Caust.). Involuntary urination (*Ars., Bell.,* Cic., *Hyos., Op.*). Onanism, causing epilepsy.

Sexual Organs.—Exalted sexual desire in both sexes; in females, nymphomania (Canth., Cinch., *Plat.*). Metrorrhagia, with characteristic mental symptoms.

Respiratory Organs.—*Voice hoarse and croaking; high, fine, squeaking; indistinct.* Difficult, hurried respiration. Great sense of suffocation, from constriction of the chest (Asaf., Ign.). Oppression, with desire for open air.

Neck and Back.—Spine sensitive; the slightest pressure causes outcries and ravings. Drawing pains in the middle of spine; in sacrum.

STRAMONIUM. 737

Heart and Pulse.—Palpitation (Acon., *Bell., Spig.*). Pulse rapid, full, strong; soft, feeble, frequent.

Limbs.—Convulsive motions of hands and arms; carphologia (Hyos.). *Twitching of the hands and feet* (Bell., Hyos.). *Twitching of the tendons* (Hyos., Kali iod.). *Trembling of the limbs* (Coccul., Coni., Gels., Merc.). The limbs fall asleep.

Generalities.—*Suppression of all secretions and excretions. Trembling of the whole body as if from fright* (Gels.). Frequent twitchings (Agar., Cic.); sudden jerks through the body. Subsultus tendinum. *Convulsions: from the sight of bright, dazzling objects; from water, touch (Nux v.), or being spoken to (Cic.).* Choreic convulsions (Agar., Cic., Cimic., Hyos., Ign., Laur.); °especially from fright. *Constant, restless movements of the limbs and whole body. Great restlessness.*

Skin.—*Intense, bright, scarlet-red rash over the whole body* (Apis, Arum., Bell., Rhus tox.).

Sleep.—Snoring; deep sleep (Laur., *Op.*). Restless sleep, with tossing about, twitching and screaming.

Fever.—Coldness of the whole body, *especially the limbs*. During chill head is hot; doesn't want to be covered. Hot, red face, with cold feet. Violent fever; skin dry and *burning hot, especially head and face (Bell.)*. Cold sweat over the whole body (Ant. tart., Ars., Cupr., Digit., Verat. alb.).

Aggravation.—In forenoon; when alone; in the dark; from being touched; from looking at glistening objects; when attempting to swallow, especially liquids.

Amelioration.—In the house; from light and company; from cold water.

Conditions.—Especially in children, and in young plethoric persons.

Compare.—*Agar.*, Ars., *Bell.*, Bry., Can. ind., Cham., Cic., Hyos., *Ign.*, Lyc., Merc., Nux v., Op., Plumb., Puls., Secal. c., Sulph., Verat. alb.

Antidotes.—Bell., Hyos., *Nux v.* To large doses: Lemon juice, vinegar, tobacco injections.

Stramonium Antidotes.—Merc., Plumb.

THERAPEUTICS.

The chief use of Stramonium is in the treatment of acute mania, of the character already described, the chief element being one of terror, attempts to escape, terrifying halluciantions, especially of horrible animals, etc.; rage, screaming, biting and scratching. Also useful for similar symptoms in delirium tremens, and in the delirium of typhus and other fevers. In fevers delirium characterized by an allusion, as to the proportions of the body (see symptoms). Stram is acknowledged by all schools of practice to be the best remedy for hydrophobia; its action is strictly homœopathic. Mania, chorea, epilepsy, convulsions, etc., caused by fright. Chorea, affecting especially the muscles of the face. Hysteria, with mental characteristic and distorted features. Spasmodic conditions from non-appearance of eruptions in children. Strasbismus. Stammering. Early stages of locomotor ataxia. Catalepsy. Paralysis after apoplexy. Erysipelas, with violent cerebral symptoms, characteristic delirium, etc. One-sided erysipelas, with meningitis; spasmodic symptoms alternate with paralytic. Occasionally useful in abscesses, especially in left hip-joint, or in panaritum, with pain so intense as to almost cause convulsions. As a rule, there is an absence of pain under this drug, but in the conditions named, and in some others, it relieves the pain of suppuration. Often indicated in scarlet fever, especially of the malignant type; from suppression of the eruption. Anasarca after scarlet fever.

Measles. Hydrocephalus. Cerebro-spinal meningitis. Prosopalgia nervosa; pains maddening; spasmodic starts and shocks through body; throws arms upward; skin of forehead wrinkled. Diaphragmitis; delirium, burning along diaphragm: spasms; aversion to water, etc. Cholera infantum; foul smelling stools; strabismus; awakes in fright; twitching. Satyriasis. Nymphomania. Dysmenorrhœa, with characteristic mental and spasmodic symptoms. A valuable remedy in puerperal mania. Puerperal convulsions. Spasmodic asthma, desire to be in the open air, suffocative cough. Whooping cough. Cough of drunkards. Sometimes indicated in pneumonia by the characteristic delirium. Typhoid fever, with characteristic delirium, black, putrid stools, suppression of urine, sometimes red rash on chest. Remittent and other fevers in children; cry out in sleep; start as from fright; jerk, twitch; eyes half-open; pupils large; suppressed urine. Ailments from the vapor of Mercury.

SULPHUR.

Synonym.—Flores Sulphuris. *Common names.*—Brimstone. Flowers of Sulphur. *Preparation.*—Triturations of pure Sublimed Sulphur. Sulphuris tincture is a saturated solution with Alcohol, and is equivalent to the 2x dilution.

GENERAL ANALYSIS.

Acts especially on the ganglionic nervous system, affecting primarily the venous capillary system, and through it affecting profoundly the entire vegetative sphere, penetrating deeply every recess of the human body. Precisely how this mighty agent operates, and exactly the channels through which it produces its wonderful changes in organic and functional life, may not be definitely known; the effects of these operations are ever before us, and offer conclusive evidence as to the character of the remedy in its general constitutional action, tainting the system, as it does, with a chronic miasm, peculiar to itself, yet simulating a vast array of pathological states which have, for their peculiar expression, some character of cutaneous eruption. Thus, as we have indicated, the chief local action of Sulphur is found to be upon the skin, producing various forms of eruption, papular, vesicular, pustular and herpetic, its most noted action being an itching, vesicular formation, holding a marked resemblance to scabies or itch, and other kindred affections of the skin.

Sulphur also affects particularly the lymphatic glandular system, the mucous membranes, especially of the eyes, bronchi, urethra and rectum, and the portal system, especially the hæmorrhoidal vessels. However, as Allen remarks (*Hand-book of Materia Medica, p. 1056*): "Since Sulphur is an integral part of every form of protoplasm, it follows that all tissues become affected by its abnormal exhibition, and no particular limit or character can be assigned to it."

CHARACTERISTIC SYMPTOMS

Mind.—*Melancholy, sad, despondent, inclined to weep* (Aur., Ign., Natr. mur., Plat., Puls., Rhus tox.). Discouraged and weary of life. *Peevish, irritable; fretful; ill-humored; quarrelsome* (*Bry., Cham., Nux v.*). Indolence of mind and body; indisposed to anything—work, talk, pleasure, or motion (*Nux v.*, Phos. ac.). *Great anxiety and apprehension in the evening* (Calc. c., Merc., Rhus tox.). °Great tendency to religious and philosophical speculations (Verat. alb.). Uneasiness and involuntary haste in everything (Sulph. ac.). Weak memory (*Anac.*, Kreos., Lach., *Nux m.*), particularly for names. Mental distraction; cannot think, or fix his mind on any subject (Calc. c., Gels., Natr. mur., Phos. ac., Sep.). Awkwardness at his work.

Head.—*Great confusion of the head, with dizziness; with aching, as if a band were tied tight around the forehead* (Coccul., Gels., Merc., Puls., Spig.). *Vertigo; while walking in the open air* (Arg. nit., Calc. c., Glon., Sep.), *when stooping* (Acon., Bell., Puls.), *on looking down;* when rising from a seat (Bell., *Bry., Sulph.*); when crossing a stream (Ferr.); with nosebleed mornings (*Bell., Bry.*). *Heaviness, fullness, and pressure in the forehead. Rush of blood to the head;* with pulsation, heat, and pressure in the brain (*Acon., Bell.*). *Pressive headache, especially in temples, in the morning, after rising.* Pain as if the brain were beating against the skull, especially when nodding, or moving the head (Ars., Glon., Hyos., Nux m.). Every step is felt painfully in the head. Stitches in the head and out of the eyes. *Tearing, tensive, jerking, or hammering pains in the head. Heavy, pressive, frontal headache, especially in the morning* (*Nux v.*), *with restlessness.* Headache, as from a board in front of the head (Acon., Bell., Gels., Merc., Nitr. ac.). *Pressive headache in vertex, as from a weight on top of the brain* (Aloe). *Scalp, especially the vertex, painfully sensitive to touch* (Cinch., Merc., Natr. mur., Nitr. ac.). *Profuse falling out of the hair* (*Graph.*, Hep. s., Lyc., Merc, *Nitr. ac.*, Phos., *Sep.*). Roots of hair painful, especially to touch (Cinch., Ferr.). *Violent itching of the scalp* (Caust., Carb. ac., Graph., Sep., Sil.). *Painful elevations on sinciput and vertex. Painful, inflamed, itching pimples on scalp and forehead* (Hep. s., Sep., Sil.). °Fontanelles close too late. *Humid, offensive eruption, with thick pus, yellow crusts,*

SULPHUR. 741

itching, bleeding and burning (Ars., Graph., Hep. s., Merc., Sil.).

Eyes.—*Inflammation of the eyes or lids, with swelling, redness of conjunctivæ, and much itching, burning and smarting (Ant. crud., Arg. nit., Calc. c., Graph.). Dryness of the eyes in the room; lachrymation in the open air (Puls.). Lachrymation in the morning, with burning.* °Retinitis, caused by over-use of eyes; congestion of optic nerve. *Burning, dryness, smarting and itching of the margins of the lids. Pain in lid, as if rubbed against spiculæ of glass. Burning and rubbing, dry sensation between the lids, as if sand were in them* (Ars., Caust., Hep. s., Thuja). *Agglutination of the lids at night* (Calc. c., Lyc., Merc., Puls., Rhus tox., Sil.). *Dryness in balls, and sensation as if they rubbed against the lids.* Shooting pains in the eyes, *and cutting stitches as from a knife, especially in right eye. Aching in the eyeballs in evening, with weight and loss of vision.* Pustules and ulcers on and around the cornea (Hep. s., Nitr. ac., Sil.), with redness of the eye, photophobia and lachrymation. Ulceration of the margins of the lids (*Graph.*). *Great sensitiveness of the eyes to the light of the sun* (Acon., Bell., Graph., Ign., Merc.). *Burning in the eyes, and easy fatigue when reading. Dimness of vision, as of a veil before the eyes* (Croc., Natr. mur., Petrol., Phos., Sep., Thuja). *Dark points and spots floating before the eyes* (Agar., Chel., Kali c., Merc., Phos., Sep., Sil.). *Flickering before the eyes* (Carls.). Dazzled by looking long at an object.

Ears.—Pressure and pain in the ear when swallowing and sneezing, as if ulcerated. Sharp, shooting or drawing pains in the ear, sometimes extend to throat and head. *Stitches in the left ear* (Ars., Coni., Graph., Kali bi., Kali c.). Itching in the ears (Baryt. c., Hep. s., Merc. bin.). *Ringing and roaring in the ears* (Cinch., Merc., Sil.); *in evening in bed with rush of blood to the head.* Hardness of hearing, preceded by over-sensitiveness of hearing. Something seems to come before the ears. Swashing in the ears. Purulent, offensive otorrhœa, worse left ear. °Ears very red with children.

Nose.—Nose swollen, red and inflamed (Bell., Phos.); internal ulceration. *Violent, fluent coryza, with frequent sneezing* (Acon., Cepa, Sang.); *in evening and morning.* Burning coryza in open air; stopped up when in the room. Bloody mucous discharge, when blowing the nose. Profuse secretion of thick, yellow, purulent mucus (Calc. c., Hydras., Puls.). *Offensive odor of nasal mucus, as of a old catarrh* (Puls.). *Comedones on the nose.* Dryness of the nose. Tip of nose red and shiny. *Itching and burning in the nostrils, as if sore.*

Face.—*Paleness of face, and expression of great suffering as after long illness.* Eyes sunken, and blue rings around them (Cinch., Kali iod., Phos.). *Heat and burning in the face,* with dark-red face, or circumscribed red cheeks (Bapt.). Pressure and tearing pains in malar bone. Black comedones on face (Selen.), especially on *forehead, nose, upper lip and chin.* Swelling of the lips, especially the upper lip (Bell., Calc. c.). *Swelling of lower lip, with eruption on it. Upper lip and margins of nose dry, scaly, rough and burning. Burning and sticking in upper lip in morning on rising, as if raw.* Dryness of the lips. Painful eruptions around the chin. Herpes at the corners of mouth (Ant. crud., Ars.). *Painful glandular swelling of the lower jaw; drawing, jerking pains.*

Mouth.—*Drawing, throbbing, or boring toothache;* in the open air, or in slightest draft of air (Cinch.); from cold water (Ant. crud., Calc. c., Coccus, Staph.); in the evening and night, with pain in submaxillary glands. Swelling of the gums, with throbbing pain. Bleeding gums. Taste bitter (Bry., Cinch., Coloc., Nux v., Puls.); *pasty; offensive; sweetish* (Ars., Bry., Merc., Plumb.); *metallic* (Esc., Coccul., Merc., Naja); *sour; in the morning.* Tongue coated white, with red tip and borders (°mostly in acute diseases). Blisters on the tongue and in the mouth (Borax, Nitr. ac., Nux v.). Burning pain in tongue. *Great dryness of the mouth, tongue and palate, with much thirst* (Ars.). *Mouth dry, insipid, and sticky in the morning.* Fœtid or sour smell from the mouth, especially in morning and after eating. *Accumulation of saliva in mouth* (Merc.); bloody (Nitr. ac.), or salty (Ant. crud., Merc. cor., Phos.); *after eating.*

SULPHUR.

Throat.—Roughness, rawness, and dryness of the throat. *Scraping in the throat; hawking and clearing throat* (Amm. carb., *Carb. v., Phos.*). Sore throat, with great burning and dryness; soreness begins on right side and goes to left; redness of tonsils. *Stitches in throat when swallowing* (Alum., Arg. nit.). A hard ball seems to rise in throat and to close the pharynx, and take away the breath (*Asaf.*, Lyc.). Painful contraction of the throat when swallowing (Bell., Plumb.). Burning up into the throat, with sour eructations. Stitches and swelling in parotid and submaxillary glands.

Stomach.—*Excessive, ravenous hunger; must eat frequently; if he does not eat, headache and lassitude. Complete loss of appetite* (Alum., Ars., Cinch., Plumb.); *feels full and aversion to food when beginning to eat* (*Lyc.*). Constant thirst; thirst for beer (Acon., Coccul., Phos. ac., Sulph.). Milk disagrees, and causes much distress (Carb. v.), waterbrash (Natr. carb.), mornings or after meals (Ars., Nux v.). Heartburn. *Sour or empty eructations, especially after meals and in morning* (Ambr., Bry., Carb. v., *Nux v.*, Phos.); tasting of bad eggs. Burning in the stomach (Ars., Canth., Iris, Lob., Mez.). *Nausea and qualmishness; mornings* (Calc. c., *Nux v.*, Puls.); before meals; during stool. Vomiting of food or acid substances, mornings, evenings, or after meals. *Feeling of fullness in stomach after eating but little* (Cinch., Led., *Lyc.*). Anxious pain in pit of stomach; at night with palpitation. Pain in region of stomach; after eating; at night, better from eructations. °Empty, gone, faint feeling (Cimic. Hydras., Ign., Petrol., Puls., Sep.), about 11 o'clock a. m. *Pressure and heaviness in the stomach, also after eating* (Ars., Bry., *Nux v.*, Puls.). Stitches in stomach and pit of stomach.

Abdomen.—Stitches, or dull, pressing pain in region of liver (Acon., Ars., Bry., Calc. c., Chel., Cinch., Kali c., Nux v., Sep.). *Bile increased.* Swelling and induration of the liver (Cinch., Phos.). Soreness in both hypochondria, which are sensitive to the touch, mornings. Stitches in region of spleen (Natr. carb., Natr. mur.); in left side of abdomen, on deep breathing. *Griping pains about the* *vel, relieved by emission of flatus* (Carb. v., *Coloc.*). Tension and pressure in the umbilical region. *Distension of the abdomen (Carb. v.,* Cinch., *Graph.).* Rumbling and gurgling in the abdomen (Agar., *Aloe, Lyc.,* Zinc.). *Stitches. Fullness and tension in abdomen, as from incarcerated flatulence (Carb. v., Cinch., Lyc.,* Kali c., Phos.). *Bruised pain in muscles of abdomen on touch. Emission of much flatus, smelling of rotten eggs (Arn.); worse evening and night.* Colic and griping in abdomen, relieved by bending double (Aloe, *Coloc.,* Iris, Nux v., Rheum); *before stool. Cutting in hypogastrium, with thin stool. Pressure downward in abdomen, toward anus. Painful sensitiveness of the abdomen to touch* (Acon., *Bell., Cupr., Merc.*).

Stool and Anus.—*Burning and pressure in rectum during stool; burning in anus after stool* (Natr. ars.). *Violent stitches and crawling in rectum, especially in evening. Violent itching in rectum and anus* (Caust., Nux v., Sil.). *Sticking and sore pain in anus.* Anus red, inflamed, swollen, covered with red veins. Much moisture about anus, with soreness and itching. *Bearing-down* in anus, in forenoon when sitting, with tenesmus. *Sensation in rectum after stool as if something remained (Nux v.).* Itching in perineum, with soft stool. *Frequent ineffectual urging to stool* (Ambr., Coni., Natr. carb., Nux v., *Sil.*). *Moist,* blind, or bleeding hæmorrhoids. *Diarrhœa some hours after midnight, or driving out of bed early in the morning* (Agar., *Aloe,* Dros., Natr. ars., *Rumex, Podo.*). *Dysenteric stools, with colic; straining and violent tenesmus (Merc.,* Nux v.), *especially at night.* Involuntary stool when sneezing or laughing, with emission of flatus. Stools watery; frothy, *green,* or bloody mucus; *pappy, greenish-yellow;* fœtid; *slimy; tough; gluey; bloody; excoriating (Ars., Merc.); semi-fluid;* involuntary (Ars.). Passing of thread-worms during stool. *Constipation; stools hard, as if burnt* (Bry.); *scanty, difficult and insufficient.*

Urinary Organs.—Retention of urine (Acon., *Bell.). Frequent and sudden desire to urinate, especially at night, with copious discharge.* Constant desire, with scanty urine. Dragging in bladder in the morning after urinating. Pressure soon after urinating, as from a full bladder. Nocturnal enuresis (Arn., *Caust.*, Cupr., Graph., *Puls.*). *Burning in the urethra, also while urinating* (Ars., Canth., Can. sat., Coni.). *Stitches and shooting pains in urethra; in fore part. Itching in the urethra.* Stream intermits, or is thinner than usual. Urine *turbid* (Ant. tart., Bell.); reddish; offensive (Calc., Kreos.); excoriating (Merc.); fatty pelicle.

Male Organs.—Involuntary emissions (Cinch., Phos. ac.). Coldness of penis; *sexual powers much weakened* (*Agn.*, Berb., Caps.). *Increased sexual powers* (*Phos.*) Inflammation and swelling, with redness and burning of the prepuce, with phimosis. Stitches in penis. *Itching in glans penis* (Mez.). Pressure and tension in testicles and spermatic cords. Testicles relaxed (Camph.); hanging down (Clem.). Offensive sweat around the genitals. Itching of scrotum; in morning on waking. Soreness and moisture of scrotum (Petrol.).

Female Organs.—Menses too early, *too profuse, but of too short duration; too late;* suppressed (Cimic., *Puls.*). Menstrual blood thick, dark, and excoriating (Amm. carb.). *During menses, headache, rush of blood to the head, nosebleed* (Bry., Ham.); *pressure in pit of stomach;* before menses, headache; fullness in chest. °Profuse, yellowish, corrosive leucorrhœa (Ars., Sep.). Burning in the vagina; is scarcely able to keep still. Troublesome itching of the genitals, with papular eruption around them (Merc.). Erysipelatous inflammation of mammæ (Rhus tox.); they are red, hot, hard, with red rays extending from nipple, and stitching pains.

Respiratory Organs.—*Voice rough and hoarse, especially mornings; aphonia* (*Carb. v.*, *Caust.*, *Phos.*). Roughness and scraping in throat, with much mucus in the chest; causes cough (Cham., *Nux v.*). Shortness of breath from talking (Dros.), or when walking in open air. *Dyspnœa; oppression and anxiety* (*Acon.*, *Ars.*, *Puls.*); at night when lying on the back. Attacks of suffocation, especially at night in bed; wants doors and windows open (*Ars.*, Bapt., Carb. v.). *Dry cough in the evening in bed, or waking from*

sleep, at night (*Coni., Hyos.,* Mez., Nux v., *Puls., Rume*.
Dry cough, with hoarseness, dryness in the throat, a
watery coryza. Short, dry, violent cough, with pain in
sternum, or with stitches in the chest. *Cough caused
rawness in the larynx* (*Phos., Rumex*). Congestion
blood to the chest. Heaviness. *Weakness of the ch
when talking* (*Carb. v., Stan.*); also in evening when
ing down. Bruised pain in upper part of chest. Pain in
chest as if sprained. Sensation of constriction in che
Pain in the sternum on moving arm, with oppressed brea
ing. Tightness in chest, as if something had grown fa
*Pressure in the chest, so she could hardly breathe. Stitch
in chest, extending to back, or to left scapula* (Kali
Merc.); *worse from breathing* (Bry.), and from mot
(Bry.), and when lying on the back. Burning in the che
rising to the face. °Exudation after pneumonia.

Heart and Pulse.—*Palpitation of the heart, with anxi*
(Acon., *Ars., Spig.,* Verat. alb.); *at night; in bed;* wh
ascending. Pulse hard, full, and *accelerated* (Acon., *Bell*
Stitches in præcordial region.

Neck and Back.—Stiffness in neck and back. Inflammati
of cervical glands. Cracking in the cervical vertebræ, esp
cially on bending head backward. Drawing, tension a
stitches in nape of neck. Paralytic sprained pain in ne
Tensive pain between the scapulæ, on motion and when
ing down. Pain in back, as if sprained (*Puls.,* Rhus tox
or bruised. *Violent bruised pain in small of ba*
(*Cupr.*), and in the coccyx, especially when stooping
rising from a seat (Rhus tox.). Drawing pain in back, wi
weakness. Stitches in the shoulder blades, back and *sma
of back.* Curvature of spine; vertebræ softened.

Limbs.—Weakness and trembling of the limbs, especial
hands and feet. Unsteadiness of joints. Limbs "go
sleep" (Sep., Sil.), especially when lying down. Bruise
feeling, and *drawing, tearing pains in the limbs* (Bry
Coloc., Led., Lyc., Merc.). Cramp-like pain in muscles
limbs, on motion.

Upper Limbs.—*Rheumatic, drawing, tearing pains
shoulders* (*left*), *arms and fingers.* Stitches between t
right shoulder, on motion, extending into the chest. Se

SULPHUR. 747

sation of weakness and weariness in upper arms. Sprained pain and stiffness in wrist, worse in morning. *Very disgusting, offensive sweat in the axillæ. Great burning in the palms of the hands* (Lach.). *Skin of the hands hard, dry and cracked* (Natr. mur.). *Hang-nails* (Natr. mur., Thuja). *Itching vesicles on back of hand.* Thick, red chilblains on fingers. Numbness of the fingers. *Ulcers about the nails.*

Lower Limbs.—Weakness and heaviness of the limbs when walking; violent, shooting pains in hip-joint; worse from touch or motion; from turning over in bed; cannot rise from bed. Cramp-like, tensive pain in muscles of thigh. Itching and soreness between thighs when walking. *Stiffness of the knee and ankle-joints. Tension in hollow of knees, as if contracted on stepping. Sticking in the knee and tibia.* Weary pain in calves at night in bed. Sprained pain in left ankle, when standing and walking. *Stiffness of maleoli. Cramps in the calves of the legs and soles of the feet* (Carb. v., Selen.), *principally at night* (Calc. c., Camph., Cham., Ferr., Nitr. ac., Nux v., Sil.); *even when walking the calves are painful, as if too short. Burning in the soles* (Calc. c., Lach., Sil.); *wants them uncovered* (Cham.). Sticking, cutting pain in toes; about the nails. *Corns, with aching and sticking pains.* Coldness of the feet, especially the soles. Cold sweat on feet.

Generalities.—*Extreme emaciation* (Ars., Ferr., Phos.). *Great debility and trembling* (Alum., Cinch.); *weariness and prostration.* °Sensitive to the open air; inclined to take cold (Calc. c., Kali c., Phos., Sil.). Unsteady gait; tremor of hands. Cannot walk erect; stoop-shouldered. Standing in the most disagreeable position. °Child dislikes to be washed and bathed (Ant. crud.). °Child jumps, starts and screams. °Epilepsy, with stiffness; sensation as from a mouse running up arms to back, before the fit. Dry, flabby skin. Glandular swellings, indurated or suppurating. °Body offensive, despite washing.

Skin.—*Voluptuous itching and tingling, with burning and soreness after scratching* (Carb. ac.). *Vesicular and herpetic eruptions, with much itching and burning* (Crot. tig., Merc., Rhus tox.). *Itching; worse from the warmth* *of the bed* (Alum., Merc., Mez., *Puls.*). *Formication over the whole body. Slight cuts and injuries inflame and suppurate* (Borax, Cham., Graph., *Hep. s., Sil.*). Soreness in the folds of the skin (Graph., Hydras., Ign., Lyc., Merc.). °Ulcers, with raised, swollen edges, bleeding easily (Asaf., Merc., Mez.); surrounded with pimples, and discharging fœtid pus.

Sleep.—*Irresistible sleepiness during the day* (*Ant. tart., Apis, Nux m.*); *wakefulness the whole night. Yawning. Restless sleep, with frequent waking. Late falling asleep. Violent starting on falling asleep* (Ars., Bell., Hyos.). *Vivid, frightful, vexatious, anxious dreams* (Arn., Aur., Puls.).

Fever.—Chilliness every evening in bed, followed by heat and profuse perspiration; in morning. *Frequent internal chilliness, without thirst* (*Puls.*). *Chill creeping up the back.* °Chill and fever; no reaction; constantly sinking. Heat in afternoon and evening, with dry skin and excessive thirst. *Frequent flushes of heat;* sometimes ending with a little moisture and faintness. Morning sweat setting in after waking (Sep.). Sweat smelling of sulphur. *Profuse night sweat* (*Cinch., Phos.,* Sil., Sulph. ac.). Perspiration from the least exertion (Ambr., Calc. c., Hep. s., Phos., Sil.).

Aggravation.—In evening, or after midnight; from warmth of bed; *during rest;* when standing; from touch; from washing or bathing; in the open air.

Amelioration.—*During motion; on walking.*

Compare.—Aloe, Ars., Bell., Calc. c., Cinch., Colch., Hep. s., Iodi., Lyc., Merc., Natr. m., Nitr. ac., Nux v., Phos., Psor., Puls., Rhus tox., Sep., Sil.

Antidotes.—Acon., Camph., Cham., Cinch., Merc., Puls., Rhus tox., Sep.

Sulphur Antidotes.—Cinch., Iod., Merc., Nitr. ac., Rhus tox., Sep.

THERAPEUTICS.

As has been already suggested, Sulphur may be indicated in any disease, regardless of its character or of the tissue involved. It will, therefore, be impossible to give a complete résumé of its clinical range. Its chief use is in chronic diseases.

Oftentimes it may be prescribed as an intercurrent remedy, even when its individual symptoms are absent, in both chronic and acute diseases, for the purpose of arousing the reactive energies of the system, when carefully selected remedies have failed to produce a favorable effect. This power of Sulphur depends upon its relation to Hahnemann's psora; and while we must admit that the latter theory was based upon false premises so far as the single disease, itch, was concerned, science having at that time failed to discover the parasitic nature of this disease, yet it is evident that Hahnemann only used the term scabies or itch to indicate some form of cutaneous eruption, and the term psora to indicate a constitutional taint dependent upon, or having for its external manifestation, some form of cutaneous eruption, not necessarily always identical with itch. This might be hereditary, or due to the suppression of an eruption; and while some skin diseases of a parasitic nature may be cured solely by external means, without immediate bad results, yet remote consequences are possible, and in many instances at least a constitutional dyscrasia is thus established which afterwards more or less modifies and controls the course of any disease with which the individual may suffer. Sulphur is the chief remedy with which to combat this constitutional condition, often restoring the suppressed disease, and, if not, so controlling the dyscrasia that the action of other indicated remedies may not be interfered with. It is especially useful in people who are subject to eruptions upon the skin, and those in whom the skin is rough and harsh and the hair coarse; light-complexioned; lean, stoop-shouldered; offensive odor from the body; general dislike to and aggravation from washing or bathing. Said to be indicated for people who have very red lips, and redness of the other orifices of the body, often accompanied by soreness and burning. Diseases which alternate with some form of eruption on the skin. All forms of scrofulous disease. Rachitic complaints. Sufferings from the abuse of Mercury or Cinchona, and metals generally. In briefly considering some of the individual pathological states in which Sulphur is especially useful, the remarks just made on the general action of the drug, especially as regards the retrocession of eruptions, must be borne in mind in order to save repetition. It is useful in some forms of nervous disease; hysteria; epilepsy; chorea;

paraplegia; neuralgia of various sorts, sometimes periodic. Sulphur does not produce any spinal or cerebral changes, but its nervous manifestations are due to spinal weakness and general constitutional conditions. Marasmus; tuberculosis; tubercular meningitis; hydrocephalus; open fontanelles in sickly, scrofulous children—may be readily differentiated from Calc. by the characteristics of the patient. Characteristic eruptions on the scalp (see symptoms). Alopecia. A valuable remedy in many diseases of the eyes and lids, especially of a scrofulous nature. Conjunctivitis. Blepharitis. Styes. Tarsal tumors. Ulceration of lids. Painful inflammation from foreign bodies in the eye (after Acon.). Pustular inflammation of conjunctiva; of cornea; ulcers on and about cornea; abscesses; always great pain, photophobia and lachrymation; usually worse at night; sharp, burning, sticking and itching; nightly agglutination, etc. Keratitis. Kerato-iritis. Iritis. Retinitis. Asthenopia. Opacities of the vitreous. Cataract. Inflammation of the external and middle ear. Chronic nasal catarrh. Comedones. Tonsilitis. Pharyngitis. Dyspepsia and gastric troubles in general, with weak, faint feeling at stomach about 11 A. M. Dyspepsia from milk. Swelling and induration of liver. Engorged liver, with piles and other resulting conditions. Various abdominal troubles, with symptoms agreeing; usually follows Nux well. Ascites. An invaluable remedy in constipation, hæmorrhoids and various conditions of the rectum, according to symptoms. Diarrhœa, especially in morning; great variety of stools (see symptom). Dysentery. A valuable remedy in chronic nephritis. Catarrh of the bladder. Chronic gonorrhœa. Gleet. Hæmaturia. Sexual weakness and neurasthenia. Phimosis. Hydrocele. Pruritus in both male and female. Amenorrhœa. Dysmenorrhœa. Menorrhagia. Vicarious menstruation. Leucorrhœa. Chlorosis. Uterine displacements, and various forms of uterine and pelvic inflammation, with Sulphur symptoms. Often useful in chronic respiratory diseases. Aphonia. Laryngeal and bronchial catarrh. Whooping cough (vapors of Sulphur said to be extremely beneficial). Often useful in chronic asthma, especially after suppressed eruptions or discharges, even many years after. An extremely valuable remedy in chronic pneumonia, and in the later stages of acute pneumonia, when resolution does not take place, hepatization remaining, with dry cough, etc.; also in first stage of phthisis following pneumonia. Phthisis, with general Sulphur indications. Hydrothorax. Cardiac dropsy. Spinal irritation. Chronic rheumatism. Rheumatic gout. Synovitis. Lumbago. A most important remedy in skin diseases as already mentioned; vesicular, herpetic and pustular eruptions in general, with much itching and burning; worse at night from warmth of bed; also complaints from their suppression by external applications. The chief remedy in "itch" or scabies. Eczema. Acne. Intertrigo. Ulcers. Abscesses. Erysipelas. Eruptive fevers. Bilious fevers. Typhoid fever. Hectic fever. In fevers Sulph. may be indicated by the symptoms of the case, or may be useful as an intercurrent remedy, as already mentioned.

SULPHURICUM ACIDUM.

Synonym.—Hydrogen Sulphate. *Common name.*—Sulphuric Acid. *Preparation.*—The 1x and 2x dilutions are made with water; the 3x with dilute Alcohol; subsequent dilutions with Alcohol.

GENERAL ANALYSIS.

Acts especially upon mucous tissues, particularly of the alimentary canal and the respiratory tract, and upon the skin, though, owing to its chemical action, its dynamic physiological effects are comparatively little understood.

CHARACTERISTIC SYMPTOMS.

Mind.—Fretful, ill-humored, peevish (*Bry.*, Cham.). Despondent. Impatient; must do everything in a hurry (Sulph.).
Head.—Sensation in the forehead as if the brain were loose, and falling from side to side (Nux m., Hyos., Rhus tox.); worse when walking in the open air; better when sitting quiet in the room. Painful shocks in the forehead and temples; worse in the forenoon and evening. Gradually increasing, and suddenly ceasing headache. External pain over the whole head, as if suppurating, painful to touch.

Eyes.—Sensation of a foreign body in right outer canthus, in the morning when walking. Lachrymation.

Ears.—Hardness of hearing (Calc. c., Sulph.).

Nose.—Dry coryza, with loss of smell and taste (Ant. tart., Puls.). Coryza: thin, lemon-colored discharge.

Face.—Face deadly pale. Face feels as if the white of an egg had been dried on it (Alum.).

Mouth.—Breath very offensive (*Arn.*, Hep. s., *Nitr. ac.*, Nux v.). Pain from submaxillary glands into tongue; tongue feels burnt (*Iris,* Plat., Puls., Sang.). Teeth on edge. Aphthæ in the mouth (*Borax,* Hell., Hydras., Iodi.). Mucous membrane of palate and pharynx swollen, injected and ulcerated.

Throat.—Swollen, as if a lump were in it; sensitive; impeded deglutition (*Bell.*). Swelling of uvula and root of palate. Soreness in evening on swallowing; worse on left side. Rawness in the throat (*Arg., Arum.*, Nux v., Sang.). Constriction. Swelling and inflammation of the submaxillary glands. °Stringy, lemon-yellow mucus hangs from posterior nares, in diphtheria.

Stomach.—Sour eructations (Alum., Carb. v., Phos.). Violent hiccough (Bry., Cic., Hyos., Ign., Verat. alb.). Vomiting; °of drunkards (Nux v.). Every drink chills the stomach, unless some spirit is mixed with it. Pain in epigastric region after eating; worse from hard food, with sensitiveness of stomach.

Abdomen.—*Weak feeling,* as if the menses would appear. Violent protrusions of an inguinal hernia.

Stool and Anus.—Hæmorrhoids; itching, burning, sticking; with moisture. Pressing in anus during and after pasty stool. Chronic soft stool. Diarrhœa, with great debility. *Soft stool, followed by a sensation of emptiness in abdomen. Stool as if chopped* (Acon.), *saffron-yellow, stringy, and slimy, in children.* Stool; soft, pasty; yellowish-white; partly solid, partly liquid, with much thin mucus and streaks of blood; very ofiensive.

Urinary Organs.—Pain in bladder, as if the call to urinate is postponed.

Female Organs.—Menses too early and too profuse (.*Ars.,* Calc. c., *Nux v.*). Leucorrhœa, acrid and burning, or like milk (Calc., Coni., Puls., Sep.).

SULPHURICUM ACIDUM.

Respiratory Organs.—Hoarseness, with roughness in throat and larynx. Shortness of breath. Cough from irritation in the chest, with expectoration in the morning, of dark blood, or of a thin, yellow, blood-streaked mucus, of a sourish taste. Belching after the cough. Pressure in left side of chest. Cough, with hæmoptysis (Acon., Ham., Ferr., Sabad.). Profuse hæmorrhage from the lungs.

Generalities.—*Extreme weakness and exhaustion*, with sensation of tremor all over the body, without trembling. Pain in lumbar region. Pains appear gradually, and cease suddenly. Hæmorrhages of black blood from all the outlets of the body (Ham., Phos.).

Skin.—Blue spots like ecchymoses (Arn., Phos., Sec.). Gangrenous tendency after a bruise (Ars.).

Sleep.—Falls asleep late, and wakes early. Sleepiness.

Fever.—Chilliness, worse in-doors; better out-doors; when exercising. Profuse perspiration with great debility; also at night (*Cinch., Phos.*, Phos. ac.).

Aggravation.—In open air; after dinner; in cold, wet weather.

Amelioration.—From pressure over epigastrium.

Conditions.—In old people, particularly women; light-haired people. In climacteric years, flushes of heat.

Compare.—Mineral acids, *Arn.*, Digit., Puls.; *Sulph.*

Antidote.—Puls.

Sulphuric Acid Antidotes.—Bad effects of lead water.

THERAPEUTICS.

Sulphuricum Acidum has been successfully used for general debilitated states of the system, especially with tendency to hæmorrhages from the outlets of the body. Catarrhal ophthalmia. Hectic fever. Hæmoptysis. Tuberculosis. Apthous sore mouth, especially during protracted diseases; particularly in children with marasmus, sour vomiting, characteristic diarrhœa, etc. A valuable remedy in certain forms of dyspepsia, especially where the stomach feels cold and weak, and the patient craves stimulants. Acid dyspepsia; dyspepsia of drunkards, especially with enlarged liver, piles, diarrhœa and other digestive troubles; digestion feeble; vomiting; patient shriveled and cold. Sulph. acid is said to remove the craving for liquor (crude acid in water). Vomiting of pregnancy. Hiccough. Stomach cough; belching after cough. Tonsilitis. Diphtheria, bad cases; abundant membrane; drowsiness; liq uids escape through the nose; stringy, lemon-yellow mucus hangs from the posterior nares. Enlarged spleen. Inguinal hernia. Sometimes useful in typhoid fever, great prostration, hæmorrhages, drowsiness, vomiting, sour discharges. Purpura hæmorrhagica. Bad effects from mechanical injuries, bruises, chafing, etc.; long-lasting blue spots.

TABACUM.

Synonym.—Nicotiana Tabacum. *Natural order.*—Solanaceæ. *Common name.*—Tobacco. *Habitat.*—Probably native of Central America, but widely cultivated. *Preparation.*—Tincture from the dried leaves of the genuine Havana tobacco.

GENERAL ANALYSIS.

Acts especially upon the pneumogastric nerve and the medulla oblongata, producing complete relaxation and paralysis of the involuntary muscular system, causing nausea, vomiting, feeble heart and pulse, low temperature, vertigo, delirium and collapse. Its long-continued use may result in degeneration of nerve tissue, causing atrophy and general muscular paralysis. Through the vagi also the digestive system is powerfully affected, even to causing violent gastro-enteritis. According to Bartholow, "the emetic effect of tobacco is doubtless the product of three factors: its cerebral action, its local irritation of the gastric mucous membrane, and its specific emetic property. The secretions of the intestinal mucous membrane are increased, and the muscular layer is thrown into tetanic contraction, whence the catharsis which follows its administration." Its chief characteristic is a deathly nausea, accompanied by pallor, vertigo, cold sweat and intermittent pulse.

CHARACTERISTIC SYMPTOMS.

Mind.—Anxiety; better after weeping. Difficult concentration of the mind.

Head.—Vertigo, with qualmishness of the stomach; worse indoors; better in the open air. °Neuralgic headache, sensation as of sudden blows struck by a hammer. °Headache from one temple to the other, involving the orbits, or with shooting in left eye, better from cold. Heaviness of the head.

Face.—*Death-like paleness of the face, with sick stomach* (Ant. tart., *Ars.*, Ipec.). *Face pale, collapsed; covered with cold sweat* (Ox. ac.). Violent tearing in facial bones and teeth, in evening.

Mouth.—Frothing from the mouth (Cic., Coccul., Laur.). *Profuse salivation* (*Hep. s., Merc., Nitr. ac.*). *Accumulation of white, tenacious mucus in mouth and throat, which must be frequently expectorated.*

Stomach.—Great thirst; worse at night. *Qualmishness, nausea and vomiting; worse on motion. Deathly nausea, with vertigo, in paroxysms; body covered with cold sweat* (Verat.); °*seasickness* (Coccul.). Violent vomiting; easy, of sour liquid; watery, insipid, sometimes bitter, in morning. Feeling of coldness in stomach (Camph., Colch.), with nausea. *Sinking at the pit of stomach;* sensation of relaxation (Ipec.).

Abdomen.—Painful retraction of the navel; contraction of the abdominal muscles (*Chel., Plumb., Podo.*). °Incarcerated hernia.

Stool.—Violent pain in small of back during soft stool, with tenesmus and burning. Diarrhœa, yellowish-green, or greenish, slimy stools. Cholera-like stools; watery, urgent, painless (Ars., *Camph., Cupr., Verat. alb.*).

Respiratory Organs.—Difficult respiration. Violent constriction of the chest. °Hiccough after every paroxysm of whooping cough.

Heart and Pulse.—Violent palpitation (Acon.. *Ars.*, Aur., *Spig.*). Action weak. Paroxysms of præcordial oppression, at night, with palpitation, and pain between the shoulders. Pulse very feeble, soft and slow; imperceptible, small, intermittent.

Neck.—Neuralgia, with tightness of the throat.

Generalities.—*Great weakness and debility* (*Ars., Cinch.*). Restlessness, wants to change place continually. Gait slow and shuffling, difficulty in ascending stairs. Stupefying sleep at night. Itching over the whole body.

Fever.—Icy-coldness from knees to toes. Body warm; ha[nds] and legs icy-cold (Menyanth.). Cold sweat on hands, f[ace] head and face (Verat. alb.). *Cold, clammy sweat* (A[rs.] Camph., *Merc.*, Phos., Tereb.).

Aggravation.—On left side; from great heat or great c[old] and especially in stormy weather; from walking, riding [in] a carriage, and jar of a railway train.

Amelioration.—In open air; from vomiting.

Compare.—*Ant. tart.*, Arsen., Bell., Coccul., *Digit.*, Ipec., L[ach.] Nux v., Op., Phos., Stram., Verat. alb.

Antidotes.—Ars., Cham., Ign., Ipec., Nux v., Puls.

Tabacum Antidotes.—Cic., Stram.

THERAPEUTICS.

Tobacco has been found useful in diseases originating [in] cerebral irritation, followed by marked gastric sympto[ms] characteristic of the drug. Effects of sunstroke. Nervous [dis]eases and heart affections, accompanied by deathly nau[sea,] feeble, irregular pulse, clammy sweat, etc. Angina pecto[ris,] pains radiate from center of sternum, especially towards [left] side, extending down left arm with nausea, faintness, [etc.] Gastralgia, with same symptoms. Asthma. Asphyxia. Re[nal] colic. Strangulated hernia. Cholera infantum, with nau[sea,] faintness, etc. Seasickness. Characteristic nausea and vo[mit]ing wherever found. Vomiting of pregnancy.

TARAXACUM.

Synonyms.—Taraxacum. Dens leonis. Taraxacum off[ici]nale. *Natural order.*—Compositæ. *Common names.*—Dan[de]lion. Puff Ball. *Habitat.*—A perennial herb found growing [in] the greater portion of the Northern Hemisphere. *Prepa[ra]tion.*—Tincture from the entire fresh plant.

GENERAL ANALYSIS.

Acts especially upon the mucous membranes of the dig[es]tive tract, and upon the liver.

TARAXACUM.

CHARACTERISTIC SYMPTOMS.

Head.—Drawing pain in left temple while sitting, ceasing when walking and standing. Needle-like stitches in left temple when sitting, ceasing when standing. Tearing pain in occiput. Pressure and heaviness in lower part of occiput, after lying down.

Eyes.—Burning in left eyeball.

Ears.—Drawing pain in external ear.

Face.—Hot and red. Pustule in right corner of lips.

Mouth.—Teeth set on edge as from acids. *Tongue covered with a white coating, which peels off in patches, leaving dark, red, tender, very sensitive spots.* Accumulation of saliva in the mouth, with sensation as if the larynx were pressed shut. Bitter taste in the mouth after eating (*Bry., Nux v.*).

Stomach.—Bitter eructations; hiccough. Nausea, as if from too fat food, with inclination to vomit (*Puls.*).

Abdomen.—Stitching pains in sides (left) of abdomen; in hypogastrium. Motions in the abdomen, as if bubbles were forming and bursting.

Stool.—Difficult, but not hard stool.

Urinary Organs.—Pressure to urinate without pain; frequent desire to urinate, and copious urine.

Respiratory Organs.—Stitches in the chest (Bry.). Twitching in right intercostal muscles.

Neck and Back.—Twitching and dull sticking pain in left side of nape of neck; when standing; better when sitting. Tensive stitches towards right side of back; outward in right scapula. Vibration in right scapula, with quivering.

Upper Limbs.—Twitching in muscles of left forearm. Finger tips icy-cold. Pressive pain in three last fingers of right hand.

Lower Limbs.—Stitching pain in left thigh. Pressive pain in left calf. Jerking pain in right calf, ceasing quickly when touched. Drawing pain in dorsum of right foot, when standing; stitches when sitting. Severe or fine stitching pains in right sole. Burning in the toes.

Sleep.—Yawning and sleepiness during the day. Vivid, unremembered dreams.

Fever.—Chilliness after eating or drinking (*Caps.*).

Aggravation.—Almost all symptoms appear when sitting, or disappear when walking.

Compare.—Bry., Caps., Chel., Hydras., Nux v., Puls., Spig.

THERAPEUTICS.

Taraxacum has been found useful in headaches; gastric affections; bilious attacks; enlargement and induration of the liver; jaundice, etc., usually with chilliness, soreness over the liver, bitter taste and "mapped" tongue. Bilious fever. Rheumatism. Neuralgia.

TARENTULA HISPANICA.

Synonym.—Lycosa Tarantula. *Natural order.*—Araneideæ. *Common name.*—Tarantula. *Preparation.*—Triturations of the live spider.

GENERAL ANALYSIS AND THERAPEUTICS.

The action of this poison differs only from other spider poisons in that it is more persistent, the cerebro-spinal system being the seat of its primary effects, through which it causes, together with restlessness and great mental and physical depression, choreic phenomena of a marked character, being more severe and terrible in their manifestations than are those produced by great sexual excitement. The chief characteristic is that the paroxysms are quieted, sometimes entirely removed through the influence of music, a cure sometimes resulting therefrom. It is said that the patients will cause their bodies to move to the measure of the music, and are often led to execute a kind of a dance. Its chief clinical use, accordingly, is in chorea, which it is said to have cured in the most aggravated forms. It is also useful in hysteria, and some other nervous affections of a like character, such as hystero-epilepsy, etc. According to Allen, "its curative powers in these and other forms of mental disturbance rest upon a very slender basis, for it is probable that most of the mental symptoms attributed to the bite of this spider are purely imaginary." It has also been used in nymphomania, and in dysmenorrhœa, menstrual irregularities, and various forms of diseases of the female sexual organs, with the characteristic nervous phenomena of the drug. Spinal irritation. Multiple sclerosis. Intermittent fever, with choreic convulsions.

Compare.—Agar., Cimic., Myg., Stram.

TELLURIUM.

An element. *Preparation.*—Triturations.

GENERAL ANALYSIS.

Acts chiefly upon the skin, producing vesicular and herpetic eruptions, sometimes resembling herpes circinatus. It also causes sensitiveness of the spine, and pain down the sacrum and thigh, resembling sciatica.

CHARACTERISTIC SYMPTOMS.

Mind.—Very forgetful and negligent.

Eyes.—°Deposit of a chalky-looking white mass on anterior surface of lens. °Purulent discharge; eczema impetignoides on lids. °Herpes conjunctiva bulbi; veins enlarged, running horizontally toward the cornea, ending in little blisters near edge of cornea; worse from crying.

Ears.—Dull throbbing pain day and night; thin, watery, excoriating discharge. °Vesicular eruption on membrane; suppuration and perforation; membrane permanently injured, and hearing greatly impaired. *Itching and swelling, with painful throbbing in external meatus; in three or four days, discharge of a watery fluid, smelling like fish pickle, which causes vesicles wherever it touches; ear is blistered, as if œdematous; hearing impaired.*

Nose.—*Fluent coryza, lachrymation, and hoarseness when walking in open air;* also short cough and pressure under sternum.

Mouth.—Breath has a garlic-like odor.

Abdomen.—Burning in hepatic region.

Male Organs.—Increased sexual desire. Herpes on scrotum and perineum.

Back.—*Painful, sensitiveness of spine, from last cervical to fifth dorsal vertebræ; sensitive to pressure and touch; dreads even to have it approached.* Pain in sacrum, passing into right thigh down sciatic nerve; worse when pressing at stool, coughing, laughing, also when lying on affected side.

Generalities.—Restless. Weakness.

Skin.—*Vesicular and herpetic eruptions, resembling ringworms, covering whole body; more distinct on lower limbs; on single parts; more on left side; itching worse at night after going to bed.* Sticking and pricking in various parts; worse during rest.

Compare.—Ars., Rhus tox., Xanthox.

THERAPEUTICS.

Ringworms; vesicular and herpetic eruptions; eczema of the external ear (see symptom). Otorrhæa. Deafness. Scrofulous ophthalmia. Eczema and herpes of lids (see symptoms). Spinal irritation. A valuable remedy in sciatica, usually on right side, worse on lying down at night, etc. (see symptom).

TEREBINTHINA.

Synonym.—Oleum Terebinthinæ. *Common name.*—Oil of Turpentine. *Preparation.*—One drop to ninety-nine of alcohol makes the 2x dilution.

GENERAL ANALYSIS.

The chief action of turpentine is upon the kidneys, where it produces irritation, congestion and inflammation, together with hæmaturia and albuminuria. It also affects to some extent all mucous surfaces, producing a tendency to congestion and catarrhal inflammation; it affects the bronchial and intestinal mucous membranes, causing cough and loose, bloody stools, with marked tympanitis; but more especially does it act upon the mucous lining of the bladder and urethra, giving rise to inflammation and strangury.

CHARACTERISTIC SYMPTOMS.

Mind.—Stupefaction; inability to fix attention; comatose condition (uræmia). (Bell.).
Head.—Vertigo; headache; intense pressure and fullness of the head.
Nose.—Violent nosebleed (Acon., Bell., Bry., Ham.).
Face.—Pale, earthy color of the face (Ars.).
Mouth.—Tongue red, smooth, and glossy, as if deprived of papillæ.
Stomach.—Loss of appetite. Vomiting of mucus. Burning in the stomach.
Abdomen.—*Excessive distension of the abdomen* (Cinch., Graph., Hep. s.): *meteorism* (*Acon., Phos. ac.*). Colic.
Stool.—Stools of mucus and water; worse in the morning. Intestinal catarrh and diarrhœa, with nephritis.
Urinary Organs.—Heaviness and pressure in region of kidneys. Inflammation of the bladder. Burning in bladder and urethra; when urinating. Frequent desire to urinate. Urine suppressed. *Violent burning, drawing pains in region of kidneys. Distressing strangury, followed by soreness* (Canth.). *Urethritis, with painful erections. Urine scanty and bloody* (*Ars.*, Canth., Colch., Ham.). Urine having the odor of violets.
Respiratory Organs.—Difficult respiration, as if from congestion of the lungs. Breath short, hurried and anxious. Great dryness of the mucous membranes of the air passages. Expectoration streaked with blood.
Pulse.—Quick, small, thready, almost imperceptible.
Generalities.—*Great prostration* (*Ars., Cinch., Phos.*). Occasional subsultus (Hyos., Stram.). Cold, clammy perspiration all over the body (Camph., *Tabac.*, Verat. alb.).
Compare.—*Canth.*, Carb. v., Copab., Erig. Phos., Secal. c.

THERAPEUTICS.

The chief use of Tereb. is in the treatment of urinary diseases, especially albuminuria; Bright's disease; nephritis particularly when following acute diseases; always burning, drawing pains in region of kidneys, with heaviness and pressure. Strangury, and scanty, bloody urine. Especially useful in the congestive stage of renal disease, before disorganization has taken place or soon after. Cystitis. Violent urethritis. Dropsies of renal origin. Pelvic peritonitis and cellulitis with bladder complications and tympanitis. Metritis, peritonitis, scarlet fever or typhoid fever, with characteristic urinary symptoms and marked tympanitis. Particularly valuable in intestinal hæmorrhage. Bronchitis, with burning in chest. Capillary bronchitis, child drowsy, lungs seem filled up, urine scanty and dark. Hæmoptysis. Purpura hæmorrhagica. Bed sores. Diarrhœa. Red, glossy tongue. Tympanitis. Recommended for various eye diseases, especially when dependent upon kidney disease. Ciliary neuralgia, over right eye. Epi-scleritis. Rheumatic iritis. Adhesions of the iris. Amblyopia from alcohol. Urticaria, after eating shell fish (Urtica.). Exanthema, with renal symptoms.

TEUCRIUM MARUM VERUM.

Synonym.—Marum Verum. *Natural order.*—Labiatæ. *Common name.*—Cat Thyme. *Habitat.*—A plant growing in Southern Europe and Africa, cultivated in Northern countries. *Preparation.*—Tincture from the fresh plant.

GENERAL ANALYSIS.

Acts especially upon the mucous membrane of the lower bowel, where it produces much irritation, leading to its successful use in the treatment of ascarides. It also acts prominently upon the Schneiderian membrane, producing violent sneezing, congestion and inflammation.

CHARACTERISTIC SYMPTOMS.

Mind.—Irresistible desire to sing.
Head.—Dullness and dizziness. Pressure in forehead above the eyes (Hydras., Kali bi., Puls., Sang.). Very painful pres-

sure in right temple, frequently alternating with same sensation in right frontal eminence, and in left temple.

Eyes.—Red and inflamed; look watery as if from weeping; biting sensations; upper lids red and puffy.

Ears.—Otalgia, with lancinating pains (*Bell.*, Cham., *Puls.*, *Merc.*).

Nose.—Frequent sneezing, with crawling in nose, without coryza. Violent crawling in right nostril, with lachrymation of right eye. *Sensation as if nostrils were stopped; blowing nose or sneezing does not remove the obstruction; nasal polypus* (Calc. c., Phos.).

Mouth.—Violent tearing in roots and gum of right lower incisors. Smarting, as from pepper, at root of tongue.

Throat.—Biting and scraping sensation posteriorly in fauces; worse left side.

Stomach.—Unusual hunger; prevents falling asleep. Frequent very violent hiccough.

Abdomen.—Dull pressing, as from incarcerated flatulence. Frequent noiseless emission of warm flatus.

Rectum.—Crawling in rectum after stool. Crawling and violent sticking in anus, in evening in bed. °Ascarides, with creeping and itching (Ferr., Sep., Spig., Sulph.), and nightly restlessness; worse from warmth of bed (*Merc.*).

Urinary Organs.—Increased discharge of pale, watery urine (Phos. ac.).

Limbs.—Rheumatic pains, mostly in bones and joints; worse evenings, better on motion (Rhus tox.). Inflammation in right toe, with pain as if the nail had grown into the flesh. °*Ingrowing toe nails with ulceration* (Sil.).

Generalities.—Very indolent; inclined neither to physical nor mental exertion.

Sleep.—Restless sleep; excited; vivid dreams.

Fever.—Frequent feeling of flushing heat in face, without external redness.

Conditions.—Especially useful in old people and children.

Compare.—Calc. c., Caust., Cina, Lyc., Sil., Staph., Sulph.

THERAPEUTICS.

Teucr. mar. ver. has often been successfully used in nasal polypi; polypus of the vagina; fibrous polypi of all kinds. Useful in ascarides; also in rheumatism, etc., the symptoms corresponding. Has been highly recommended for ingrowing toe nails.

THERIDION.

Synonyms.—Theridion Curassavicum. Aranya. *Class.*—Arachnida. *Order.*—Araneideæ. *Common names.*—Orange Spider. Black Spider of Curacoa. *Preparation.*—Tincture from the live spider.

GENERAL ANALYSIS.

Acts upon the cerebro-spinal system, giving rise to headache, vertigo, and neuralgia, which may be accompanied by gastric disturbances due to reflex action.

CHARACTERISTIC SYMPTOMS.

Mind.—Time passes too quickly. Easily startled (Coccul., Sep., Sil.). Aversion to work.

Head.—Vertigo, with nausea, even to vomiting; worse from stooping; from least movement; on closing eyes; on board a vessel; with cold sweat. Head feels thick; thinks it belongs to another; that she cannot lift it off. Headache on beginning to move. Violent frontal headache, with throbbing extending to occiput. Headache, which she cannot describe, nor even make clear to herself. Throbbing over left eye and across forehead; worse on rising after lying down; worse from persons walking over the floor; from least noise. Headache behind the eyes; hard, heavy, dull pressure.

Eyes.—Flickering before eyes in frequent paroxysms, even when closing the eyes, like a veil before the eyes; she must lie down.

Ears.—Rushing in both ears like a waterfall.

Nose.—°Chronic catarrh; discharge offensive, thick, yellow or yellowish-green.

Face.—Face feels immovable mornings when waking.

Mouth.—Teeth sensitive to cold water (Ant. crud., Calc. c., Staph.). Every sound penetrates the teeth. Salty taste; mouth feels numb and slimy.

THERIDION. 765

Stomach.—Much thirst; desire for acid drinks; for wine, brandy or tobacco; for food or drink, but knows not what. Nausea on rising in morning; from sounds; with vertigo; on closing eyes; like sea-sickness (Coccul., Petrol.); from sparkling before eyes; on motion; from talking; from fast riding in a carriage.

Abdomen.—Violent burning pain in hepatic region; worse from touch; retching, bilious vomiting. °Abscess of liver; relieves vertigo and nausea. Pain in groins after coitus; on motion.

Stool.—Small, soft stool daily, with much straining.

Male Organs.—Desire lessened; emission during siesta.

Female Organs.—°Hysteria during puberty; at climacteric.

Respiratory Organs.—Inclination to take deep breaths; to sigh (*Ign.*). Violent stitches up high in chest, beneath left shoulder, through into throat. °Violent cough, with spasmodic jerking of the head forward, and the knees upward.

Generalities.—Weak; limbs tremble; sweating. Faints after every exertion. Sounds and reverberations penetrate through her whole body, particularly the teeth, and increase the vertigo, which then causes nausea. During sleep bites point of tongue.

Fever.—Shaking chill, with foam at mouth; during headache, with vomiting. Bones pain as if they would fall asunder; coldness, cannot get warm. Sweats easily after walking.

Compare.—Acon., Aranea., Bell., Calc. c., Graph., Ign., Lyc., Spig., Sep.

Antidotes.—Acon., Graph., Mosch.

THERAPEUTICS.

Theridion is useful in headache, especially sick headache; nasal catarrh, offensive, thick, greenish-yellow discharge. Seasickness; in nervous women, deathly nausea on closing the eyes. Sunstroke, with violent headache, nausea and vomiting. Neuralgia. Hysteria. Dysmenorrhœa. Spinal irritation. Abscess of liver. Phthisis florida, in beginning. Violent stitches high up in left chest, through to the back. Climacteric troubles. Scrofula, when other remedies fail; rachitis; caries; necrosis, "to reach the root of the evil and destroy the cause."

ing pains in temples, forehead and over eyes. Intermittent drawing pain in left side of forehead. *Pain in left frontal eminence, and right side of head, as if a nail were driven in* (Agar., Arn., Anac., Coff. c.); *worse on touch.* °Hair becomes hard, dry and lusterless, and falls out. Scalp very sensitive to the touch (Acon., Bell., Cinch., Merc., Natr. mur., Nitr. ac.).

Eyes.—Sclerotica inflamed and red (Bell.), like blood. Pressure and dryness in the eyes, as if sand were in them (Ars., Caust., Hep. s., *Sulph.*), with weakness. Pupils dilated. Violent burning and stinging in the eyes and lids (Ars.). Inflammatory swelling of the eyelids, with hardness. Sensation as if a foreign body were in the eyes. Tearing in left eyebrow, better from touch. Nocturnal agglutination of the eyelids (Calc. c., *Graph., Lyc., Sulph.*). Dimness of the vision, as if a mist or veil were before the eyes (Croc., *Caust.,* Natr. mur., Phos., Petrol., Sep.); in open air with confusion of head; with pressure in eyes, as if they would be pressed out of the head, or as if they were swollen. Flickering before the eyes; flames of light, like fire-flies (Agar., Cycl., Merc). Short sighted.

Ears.—Roaring in left ear, with cracking when swallowing saliva.

Nose.—*Painful ulceration and scabs in the nostrils* (Alum., Ant. crud., Kali bi., Puls.). Swelling in wings of nose, with hardness and tension. Red, itching eruption on wings of nose, at times humid. Discharge of offensive, purulent mucus from the nose (Graph., Hep. s., Nitr. ac.). Dry coryza; nose very dry and stopped; worse evenings. Painful pressure at the root of the nose (Acon., Kali bi., Merc. iod.).

Face.—Boring and digging pains in face and cheek bones; relieved by touch. Stitches between left ear and zygomatic arch. Jerking sensation in upper lip, near corner of mouth. Red, itching, elevation on upper lip. Sensitiveness of upper lip. Flushes of heat in the face.

Mouth—°The teeth become dirty-yellow, and sore (Iod.). Painful ulcers and burning vesicles on the tongue (*Nitr. ac.*). Tongue swollen and sore; *tip of tongue painfully sore to the touch.* Apthæ: ulcers; mouth feels as if burnt (*Iris*, Puls., Sang., Sulph. ac.).

Throat.—Much tenacious mucus in throat; hawked up with difficulty (Alum., Amm. carb., Kali bi.). Throat dry and rough.

Stomach.—Loss of appetite. Eructations. Increased thirst, especially at night.

Abdomen.—Stitches in the hypochondria. Abdomen enlarged and puffed; *protrudes here and there as from the arm of a fœtus; movements and sensation as if something were alive, without pain (Croc.).* Abdomen much enlarged after eating (Cinch., *Nux v.*). Abdomen distended by flatulence; much rumbling and croaking, as if an animal were crying in the abdomen (Coloc.). Pressure in hypogastrium. Painful swelling of inguinal glands (Calc. c., Clem., Nitr. ac., Rhus tox.).

Stool and Anus.—Condylomata about the anus, sore to touch; stitches when walking. Moisture. Painful contraction of anus during an evacuation. Anus sore and very sensitive (*Sulph.*). Hæmorrhoids, painful to the slightest touch; pressure and burning. Painful stitches in the anus. Stitches in rectum towards small of back. Pressing, itching and burning in the hæmorrhoidal vessels, with dragging. Swelling of hæmorrhoidal veins. Itching in the anus (Nux v., Sep., Sil., Sulph.). Burning pain in perineum. Tubercle on perineum, becoming moist and smarting when walking. Diarrhœa daily, °*in the morning* (*Aloe, Rumex, Sulph.*); *after breakfast; at times painless; at times with colic.* °*Stool bright-yellow* (*Chel.*), *watery; expelled forcibly* (Crot. tig., Grat.), *with much noisy flatus* (*Aloe*); *gurgling, as water from a bung-hole.* Constipation (*Alum., Bry., Nux v., Op., Phos., Sulph.*).

Urinary Organs.—Frequent urging to urinate, with profuse emission; at night. Boring in region of bladder, with painful drawing up of testes. After urination, sensation as if a few drops were running down the urethra. Dribbling after urination. Urine stops several times before the bladder is emptied (Coni.). Burning in the urethra during emission of urine (Ars., Coni., Natr. carb.); with gleety discharge, stream small and split; next day yellow discharge; like gonorrhœa. Jerking, voluptuous formication in fossa navicularis. Urine scanty; burning; dark-colored; profuse, watery, after standing becomes cloudy. Yellowish or wine-colored. Orifice of urethra agglutinated by mucus.

Male Organs.—*Sycotic, moist excrescences on the prepuce and glans (Nitr. ac.,* Staph.*).* Swelling of the prepuce. Painful jerking in penis. Sensitiveness of glans. Itching in the glans and prepuce (Sulph.); alternating with stitches. Feeling as if the testicles moved. Nightly painful erections; emissions. Profuse sweat about the genitals, especially on scrotum and perineum (Sil., Sulph.). °Checked gonorrhœa, causing articular rheumatism; prostatitis; sycosis; impotence.

Female Organs.—Sycotic excrescences.; moist, bleeding and offensive (Nitr. ac.). Biting and itching in the genitals; after urination. Burning and biting in vagina. Mucous leucorrhœa; yellowish-green. °Vagina extremely sensitive during coition (Arg. nit., Kreos., Sulph.).

Respiratory Organs.—Shortness of breath; convulsive asthma (Ars.); at night. Cough immediately after eating. Hacking, dry cough.

Heart.—Visible palpitation (Glon., *Spig.*), without anxiety. Stitches in region of heart.

Neck and Back.—Painful drawing in sacrum, coccyx and thighs, while sitting; after long sitting prevents standing erect. Drawing pain in nape of neck. Tension and stiffness of nape and left side of neck.

Limbs.—Nails crippled (Ant. crud.); brittle or soft. Hangnails (Natr. mur., Sulph.). Stitches in shoulder. Drawing pain in arms. Trembling of hands and feet. Crawling in tips of fingers as if asleep.

Lower Limbs.—Painful laxity in both hip-joints, as if the capsules were weak and relaxed. Weakness of legs when sitting, changing into cutting in muscles of calf when walking. Perspiration on the feet (*Nitr. ac.,* Sep.,; *Sil.,* Sulph.). °Toe-nails crumble, brittle. Feet go to sleep.

Generalities.—Jerks of the upper part of the body. Cramp-like jerking in circumscribed spots. Emaciation and anæsthesia of affected parts. Weakness. Œdema about the joints; affects prominently epithelia, first causing hardening, hypertrophy; then softening. Stitches in various parts, changing to burning.

Skin.—*Wort-shaped excrescences* here and there, especially on hands and genitals (Nitr. ac., Phos. ac., Staph.). Violent itching on different parts, as from flea-bites.

Sleep.—*Persistent sleeplessness* (Cimic., Coff.). *Sleepiness.* Restless sleep. Troublesome, anxious dreams, when sleeping on the left side.

Fever.—Shaking chill, with yawning. The warm air seems cold, and the sun has no power to warm him. Shivering from slightest uncovering in warm air. Cold hands and internal heat of face. Heat, with activity of mind, and thirst. Flushing, without thirst. Profuse night sweat, staining the clothes yellow, *as if saturated with oil.*

Aggravation.—In morning and forenoon; after 3 A.M. and 3 P.M.; during rest; from heat of the bed; from spirituous liquors; from tobacco.

Amelioration.—In the open air; from warmth; from movement.

Conditions.—Especially useful in persons of a lymphatic temperament; people with dark complexion, black hair, dry fiber and not very fat.

Compare.—Aur., *Can. sat., Canth., Copab.,* Ign., *Merc., Nitr. ac., Puls.,* Staph., Sulph.

Antidotes.—Camph., Cham., Merc., Puls., Sulph.

Thuja Antidotes.—Abuse of tea, Merc. iod., Nux v., Sulph.

THERAPEUTICS.

Probably the most important use of Thuja is in the treatment of sycotic diseases, not only for the condylomata, or wart-like excrescences, occurring on various parts, but also for various diseases which may have their origin in the condition of system which Hahnemann designated as sycosis—a constitutional taint following gonorrhœa, or more apt to occur in those who have what Grauvogle termed a hydrogenoid constitution. Vaccination is more apt to cause bad results in sycotic constitutions, so we find Thuja a remedy for the bad effects of vaccination (Sil.); especially when the pustules are very large, and the patient has diarrhœa. The mental symptoms of the drug are very peculiar, and indicate it in some forms of insanity, particularly melancholia. Neuralgia of the head and face, especially as if a nail were driven in; violent stabbing pains; neuralgia of tea-drinkers. Ciliary neuralgia. Kerato-iritis. Opacity of the cornea. Iritis, especially syphilitic, with gummata on the iris; sharp sticking in the eye, with much heat above and around the eye. Episcleritis. Granular lids, when granules are large, wart-like. Chronic conjunctivitis, worse whenever his night's rest is disturbed. Dry, bran-like tinea ciliaris; lashes imperfect and irregular. Excellent for tarsal tumors.

Polypi of the ear. Watery, purulent otorrhœa, smelling like putrid meat. Nasal catarrh. Syphilitic ozœna, thick, green discharge. Toothache, teeth decayed, especially about margins of gums, which become retracted. Aphthous sore mouth, feels as if burnt. Ranula bluish; surrounded by varicose veins. Indurations in the stomach. Flatulent colic (see peculiar symptoms). Warts and condylomata about anus. Hæmorrhoids. Diarrhœa (see symptoms). Gonorrhœa; also bad effects after checking gonorrhœal discharge, especially articular rheumatism and inflamed prostate. Secondary syphilis; syphilitic herpes; obstinate chancroidal ulcers, with sticking pains, as from a splinter. Balanorrhœa. Condylomata and warts about the genitals of both sexes. Fungous growths about cervix; cauliflower excrescences, with burning and yellowish-green leucorrhœa. Uterine polypi. Chronic ovaritis; after gonorrhœa. Left ovary inflamed, worse at each menstrual nisus; distressing pain; burning when walking or riding; must lie down. Prolapsus uteri. Polypi of the vocal cords. Asthma. Sciatica. Offensive foot-sweat (Sil.). Fungoid excrescences on various parts, bleeding on slightest touch. Warts. Lupus. Varicose ulcers. Pemphigus. Eczema. Variola; as soon as the vesicles become filled; said to cause rapid dessication and prevent scars.

TRILLIUM.

Synonym.—Trillium Pendulum. *Natural order.*—Trilliaceæ. *Common name.*—White Beth Root. *Habitat.*—An indigenous plant common in Middle and Western States, growing in rich soils, in damp, rocky and shady woods. *Preparation.*—Tincture from the fresh root.

TRILLIUM.

GENERAL ANALYSIS.

Through the cerebro-spinal system, Trillium acts upon the mucous membranes and the capillary blood-vessels, more especially of the uterus, producing both active and passive hæmorrhages.

CHARACTERISTIC SYMPTOMS.

Nose.—°Profuse nose-bleed (Acon., Bell., Bry., Ham.).

Mouth.—°Bleeding from gums, or after extraction of tooth (Ham.).

Stomach.—°Sinking in stomach with heat. °Hæmatemesis (Ham., Ipec.).

Stool and Anus.—°Dysentery, when passages are almost pure blood. Diarrhœa thin, watery, tinged with blood; painless.

Urinary Organs.—Hæmaturia.

Female Organs.—°*Hæmorrhage from uterus; with sensation as though the hips and back were falling to pieces, better from a tight bandage.* °*Metrorrhagia at the climateric;* pale; faint; flow returns every two weeks. °Displaced uterus, with consequent menorrhagia. °Gushing of bright-red blood from the uterus at least movement; later, blood pale from anæmia. °Hæmorrhages from fibroid tumors. °Threatened abortion; profuse hæmorrhages. °Pain in back and cold limbs, with hæmorrhages. °Too profuse menstrual flow after exhaustion by exercise. °Profuse, exhausting leucorrhœa. °Profuse, long-lasting lochial discharges (Caul.).

Respiratory Organs.—°Cough, with purulent or bloody sputum. °Hæmoptysis (Ipec.).

Generalities.—°*Hæmorrhages usually bright-red, profuse; also when sacro-iliac synchondroses feel as if falling apart; wants to be bound tightly.* °Feels as if bones were broken, with hæmorrhages. °Crowding sensation in the veins, like a tightening up of the parts; worse in legs and ankles.

Compare.—Ham., Ipec., Sabina, Secal. c.

THERAPEUTICS.

Trillium is especially useful in hæmorrhages, both active and passive, as described above, the symptoms being mostly of clinical origin. Particularly useful in uterine hæmorrhages.

URANIUM NITRICUM.

Synonyms.—Uranii Nitras. Uranic Nitrate. *Common name.*—Nitrate of Uranium. *Preparation.*—Triturations.

GENERAL ANALYSIS AND THERAPEUTICS.

The chief action of Uranium nitr. is upon the kidneys, where it causes a degeneration, with albuminuria or glycosuria. It increases the total quantity and specific gravity of the urine, and produces acridity, with mucus discharges and incontinence. Its chief therapeutic application has been in the treatment of diabetes (both mellitus and insipidus) and in Bright's disease. Dr. Hughes considers it best suited to cases of diabetes originating in dyspepsia or assimilative derangement, while Phosphoric Acid is better adapted to those of nervous origin. In this I can, from my own experience, fully concur. Its most marked clinical symptom is "great emaciation, debility, and tendency to ascites or general dropsy."
Compare.—Ars., Arg. nit., Merc. cor., Phos., Phos. ac.

URTICA URENS.

Synonym.—Urtica Minora. *Natural order.*—Urticaceæ. *Common names.*—Dwarf Stinging Nettle. Common Nettle. *Habitat.*—Found in North America, Europe and Asia. *Preparation.*—Tincture from the entire fresh plant.

GENERAL ANALYSIS.

Acts especially upon the skin, producing an inflammation very similar to nettlerash, in the treatment of which affection we find its chief use.

CHARACTERISTIC SYMPTOMS.

Head.—Dull headache, mostly on right side. Urticaria of scalp, determining internally.

Eyes.—Pressing pain in eyeballs, as from a blow (Arn., Cin[ ]Ruta.).
Throat.—Burning in the throat (Ars., Canth., Caps.).
Stool and Anus.—Dysenteric stools, with burning and it[ ]ing in anus.
Skin.—The skin of the face, arms and shoulders and chest w[ ]affected with extremely distressing burning heat, with f[ ]mication, numbness, and violent itching (Apis). Excessi[ ]swelling of the breasts; discharging at first serum, aft[ ]ward perfect milk; a very copious secretion of milk lasti[ ]for eight days. Itching swellings all over the hands. Ur[ ]caria; hives; the skin becomes elevated, with a white ce[ ]tral spot and a red areola, attended by stinging, burni[ ]pains; relieved by rubbing the parts.
Generalities.—Symptoms return at the same time every yea[ ]
Compare.—Apis, Canth., Led., Rhus tox.

THERAPEUTICS.

Urtica urens is used chiefly in nettlerash and hives, above described. Urticaria after eating shell fish (Tereb.). Su[ ]pression or deficiency of milk. Pruritus of the genitals in bo[ ]sexes.

USTILAGO.

Synonym.—Ustilago Maidis.   *Natural order.*—Fun[ ]*Common names.*—Corn Smut. Maize Smut. *Preparation.[ ]*Tincture from the fresh ripe fungus.

GENERAL ANALYSIS.

Through the cerebro-spinal system, Ustilago affects prim[ ]rily the circulation, producing long-lasting contraction of t[ ]arterial capillaries, and dilatation of the venous capillaries, [ ]resting arterial circulation, and producing passive venous co[ ]gestion. The especial local action is upon the female generati[ ]system, producing uterine contractions, abortion, hæm[ ]rhage, and a general atonic condition.

USTILAGO.

CHARACTERISTIC SYMPTOMS.

Mind.—Irritable, and depressed in spirits (Bry., Nux v.).
Head.—Feeling of fullness of the head. Dull, pressive frontal headache. Nervous headache. Scald head; scalp a mass of filthy inflammation; hair falls out; watery serum constantly oozing from the scalp (Mez.).
Eyes.—Aching distress in eyeballs (Cimic., Ruta, Spig.).
Nose.—Dryness of nostrils, as from taking cold.
Mouth.—Toothache. Saliva very abundant, of slimy, bitter taste. Slimy, coppery taste in the mouth (Merc.).
Throat.—Tonsils painful, sore and dry. Feeling as of a lump in throat, with dry, burning sensation all along the œsophagus to the stomach (Caps.).
Stomach.—Hungry and thirsty. Constant distress in region of the stomach. Acid eructations. Burning pain in stomach (Ars., Bell., Colch., Phos.).
Abdomen.—Fine, cutting, colicky pains in abdomen.
Male Organs.—Depression of sexual system profound (Agar., Agn., Coni.). Severe neuralgic pain in one or both testicles (Staph.). Irresistible tendency to masturbation. °Seminal weakness, melancholy, etc. (Cinch., Phos. ac.).
Female Organs.—Constant aching distress in the mouth of the uterus. °Tendency to miscarriage (Sep.). Yellow, offensive leucorrhœa. Tenderness of left ovary, with pain and swelling. Menses copious, bright-red, not coagulating easily. °Os uteri dilated and relaxed; pains feeble (Caul.). °Menorrhagia from atony of the uterus (Caul., Cinch.). °Blood dark and clotted (*Croc., Cycl.*, Ign., *Sabina*). °Post-partum hæmorrhage from a flabby, atonic condition of the uterus (Caul.). °Pain in left mammary region.
Aggravation.—From motion; better during rest.
Compare.—Caul., Cinch., Croc., Cycl., Ham., Ign., Sabina.

THERAPEUTICS.

Ustilago is used chiefly in uterine hæmorrhages, especially from atony of the uterus; discharge sometimes bright-red, sometimes dark and clotted. Post-partum hæmorrhage. Hæmorrhage from fibroid tumors; seems to cure the tumors, as they sometimes disappear under its use. Ovarian neuralgia, left side, menses profuse; yellow, offensive leucorrhœa. Ovarian congestion. Amenorrhœa. Membranous dysmenorrhœa. Said to be especially useful during the climacteric period, and in tall, slender women (Phos.), with clear, white skin.

VALERIANA.

Synonym.—Valerina. Officinalis. *Natural order*—Valerianaceæ. *Common names.*—Valerian. All heal. *Habitat.*—An herbaceous perennial plant found growing in Europe and Asia, and cultivated in other countries. *Preparation.*—Tincture from the dried root.

GENERAL ANALYSIS.

Through the cerebro-spinal system Valeriana affects directly the nervous centers, producing a high degree of irritation, which results in excessive nervous excitability, pain and spasms, all partaking of a hysterical character, which latter is the most important feature of the action of the drug.

CHARACTERISTIC SYMPTOMS.

Mind.—Unusually joyous mood. Intellect clouded. Mild delirium, with trembling excitement.

Head.—Headache, the aching especially violent over the orbit. Violent pressure in the forehead, followed in a few minutes by sticking in the forehead, and especially over the orbits. *The pressure over the orbits alternates between a pressure and a sticking; the sticking is like a darting, tearing, as if it would pierce the eyes from within outward.*

Eyes.—Pressure in the eyes in the morning after rising; the margins of the lids seem swollen and sore. Smarting in the eyes, as if occasioned by smoke (Croc.). Sparks and flashes before the eyes (*Bell., Cycl., Glon., Sulph.*): objects seem on fire.

Face.—Neuralgic pains in the face (Bell., Cinch., Merc.). Crampy jerkings in different parts of the face (Ign.).

Mouth.—Toothache. Previous to dinner he has a taste and

smell as of fœtid tallow. *Flat, slimy taste in the mouth, early in the morning after waking.*

Stomach.—Frequent empty eructations. Gulping up of rancid fluid not rising into the mouth. *Nausea, as if a thread were hanging in the throat,* arising from the umbilicus and gradually rising to the fauces, exciting accumulation of saliva. Disposition to vomit; vomiting. Pressure in the epigastric region.

Abdomen.—Abdomen distended, hard. Twisting colic; hysterical.

Stool.—Diarrhœa. Stools frequent and pasty.

Urinary Organs.—Frequent emission of urine. Urine contains a white, red, or turbid sediment.

Respiratory Organs.—When walking feels pressed across the lower half of chest, with oppression of breathing. Sudden stitching in chest and in region of the liver, *from within outward.* Violent stitches and pressing *from within outward* in the region of the last true ribs, when standing. Dull stitches, resembling a pressing from within outward, in the left side of the chest during an inspiration.

Neck and Back.—Intense pain in the left lumbar region above the hip, as if he had strained the part much; *worse when standing, and especially when sitting than when walking.*

Limbs.—A very painful drawing, mixed with stitches, from left shoulder down to fingers; change of position did not relieve, but it *disappeared when walking.* Violent stitch in knee. Painful drawing in upper and lower extremities *when sitting quietly, relieved by walking.*

Upper Limbs.—Crampy, darting, tearing, like an electric shock, repeatedly through the humerus; intensely painful. Crampy drawing in region of biceps, in right arm from above downward while writing.

Lower Limbs.—Crampy tearing in outer side of thigh, extending into hip. Twinging pain in outer side of calf *when sitting.* Pulsative, tearing in right calf *when sitting, in the afternoon.* Transient pain, as if sprained in right ankle, most felt while standing, but seems to disappear when walking. Lower limbs contracted. Sudden pain, as if

bruised in outer malleolus of right foot, *worse when standing, less when walking.* Drawing in tarsal joint *when sitting.* Stinging pain in heels *when sitting.*
Generalities.—*Drawing in many places, now here, now there, like transient jerks.*
Sleep.—Wide awake in evening, restless at night, could fall asleep only towards morning, when he had vivid dreams.
Fever.—Chilliness. Sensation of icy-coldness. Constant heat in whole body, and uneasiness. Dry heat in face and whole body *in the evening when sitting.* Flushes of heat over cheeks for two hours, several times *in the evening.* Frequent sweat. Much perspiration during night.
Aggravation.—In morning; in evening; *while sitting or standing, Better from walking.*
Compare.—Ambr., Asaf., Ign., Mosch., Puls.
Antidotes.—Camph., Coff.

THERAPEUTICS.

The chief use of Valerian is in the treatment of hysteria, and other nervous affections where the hysterical element predominates. Usually great restlessness, excitability, and sleeplessness; globus hystericus, with sensation of something warm rising from the stomach to the throat; afraid of the dark or of being left alone. Nervous headache. Supra-orbital neuralgia. Trismus from a decayed tooth, with sensation as if a thread were hanging in the throat. Gastralgia, eructations of a rancid fluid, tympanitis. Sciatica. A valuable remedy to promote sleep, where the sleeplessness is caused by nervous excitement. The aggravation of pains and other symptoms when sitting, and amelioration when walking, is very characteristic.

VERATRUM ALBUM.

Synonym.—Helleborus Albus. *Natural order.*—Melanthaceæ. (Liliaceæ). *Common names.*—White Hellebore. European Hellebore. *Habitat.*—A perennial herbaceous plant growing in the mountainous portions of Middle Europe, and as

VERATRUM ALBUM.

far east as Asiatic Russia. *Preparation.*—Tincture from the dried root.

GENERAL ANALYSIS.

Through the cerebro-spinal nervous system Veratrum acts especially upon the system of nutrition, affecting profoundly the entire vegetative sphere. The blood becomes disorganized, and separated into its constituent elements, the circulation is embarrassed, and, as a result, general torpor of the vegetative system occurs, giving rise to a true choleraic condition, general coldness, prostration, collapse, copious watery vomiting and purging, spasmodic colic, cramps, spasms, rigid contraction of the muscles, and profuse, cold, clammy perspiration. It also affects, but to a less degree, the sensorium, causing excitation of the cerebral nerves, resulting in delirium and mania. It also produces exhaustion of nerve power, even to complete extinction. The chief feature of Veratrum is the choleraic condition above described.

CHARACTERISTIC SYMPTOMS.

Mind.—*Mania; persistent* raging, with desire to cut and tear, especially clothes (Bell., Stram.); *with inconsolable weeping, howling* (Cic.), *and screaming over some fancied misfortune.* Delirium; talks about religious things (Ars., Aur.); praying, cursing, and howling all night; loquacious. °Disposed to talk about the faults of others, or silent; but if irritated, scolding, calling names. °Despair about his position in society; feels very unlucky. Depression of spirits; despondency and discouragement. *Anxiety* and apprehension, as after committing a great crime (Coccul., Ign.).

Head.—Vertigo, with cold perspiration on the forehead (*Op.,* Tabac.). Congestion to the head when stooping. Heat of head. Paroxysms of headache, as if the brain were bruised or torn, with pressure (Coff. c., Mur. ac.). Headache, with vomiting of green mucus. Dull pressure on vertex; on movement becomes throbbing. *Coldness on the vertex* as if ice were lying there (Agar., Calc. c.). Painful sensitiveness of the hair (Cinch., Ferr., Sulph.). Crawling, bristling sensation, as if the hair were electrified.

Eyes.—Eyes distorted, protruding (*Bell., Stram.*); fixed, sunken (Ars.), lusterless; surrounded by blue or black rings (Cinch., Kali iod., Phos., Sec., Sulph.). Lachrymation, with redness of the eyes. *Excessive dryness of the lids;* feel sore; are stiff and agglutinated; as in coryza. Sensation as if salt were under upper lid. Pupils contracted (Merc. cor., *Op.*, Phos., Physos., Phyt.); dilated. Double vision.

Nose.—Grows more pointed; seems to be longer; face cold and sunken (Ars., Camph.). Dryness as from dust. Epistaxis (Acon., Bell., Bry., Ham., Ipec.).

Face.—*Face pale, cold, sunken. Hippocratic; nose pointed (Ars., Camph.);* face bluish. °Face is red while lying in bed, but becomes pale on rising (Acon.). Heat and burning of the cheeks. Cold perspiration on the face, *especially of forehead* (Cina). Stiffness of the masseter muscles. Lockjaw (Cic., Hyos., Ign., Laur., *Nux v.*). Risus sardonicus.

Mouth.—Tongue *cold* (Camph., Naja); dry, blackish (Op., Phos.); cracked; red and swollen (*Bell., Rhus tox.*). Inability to talk. *Dryness of the mouth and palate, with thirst. Much flow of saliva from the mouth, like waterbrash.* Biting taste, as from peppermint in the mouth.

Throat.—Throat dry and burning. Roughness, dryness and scraping in the throat (*Arg. nit.*, Rumex).

Stomach.—*Violent hunger; craves fruit, juicy, acid things* (Ant. tart., Cinch., Phos. ac., Ptel.), or cold or salt food. *Excessive thirst, especially for cold water (Acon., Ars., Bry.,* Phos.). Aversion to warm things. Violent empty eructations (Ipec., Merc., Phos.). Hiccough (Cic., Hyos., Ign., Sulph. ac.). *Violent vomiting,* with continued nausea; with great exhaustion, and desire to lie down. Nausea, with profuse salivation and violent thirst (Merc.). *Vomiting violent, forcible, excessive; of food* (Ipec., Kreos., Phos.); *of green mucus; of slimy, acid liquid;* whenever he moves or drinks; *with cold sweat.* Painful distension of pit of stomach. Violent pressure in pit of stomach, which extends into the sternum, the hypochondria, and the hypogastrium. Acute pains in the stomach and epigastrium (Æsc., *Ars.,* Canth., Iris, Phos.).

Abdomen.—Great sensitiveness of the abdomen to the touch

(*Acon., Bell., Coloc*). Distension of the abdomen (Aloe, Cham., Cinch., Colch.). Colic; *cutting*, griping and twisting, especially about navel, better after stool (Aloe, *Coloc.*); *as if intestines were twisted in a knot; flatulent; cold sweat;* worse after eating.

Stool and Anus.—*Diarrhœa, violent, painful, copious, with profuse perspiration.* Stools watery, greenish, mixed with flakes; rice water; sudden, involuntary. *Copious, frequent, with shivering.* Constipation; stools hard and too large size (Bry.).

Urinary Organs.—Urine suppressed (Acon., *Bell., Stram.*); involuntary (Ars., Bell., Cic., Hyos.); greenish. Dysuria. Diuresis.

Female Organs.—Menses too early and too profuse (Calc. c., *Nux v.*).

Respiratory Organs.—Paroxysms of constriction of larynx; suffocative fits, with protruded eyes. *Difficult respiration, with tightness and constriction of the chest (Phos.).* Tickling low down in air tubes, provoking cough, with slight expectoration. Pressure in chest, in region of sternum. Shortness of breath on slightest motion (Acon., Ars.). *Deep, hollow cough, occurring in shocks.* Cough, with much expectoration, blueness of the face, and involuntary micturition (Alum., *Caust.*, Colch.). °Cough on entering warm room from cold air (*Bry.*).

Heart and Pulse.—*Palpitation, with anxiety (Acon., Ars., Spig., Sulph.), and rapid, audible respiration.* Pulse rapid; slow; feeble; irregular; intermittent (Coni., *Digit., Natr. mur.*); imperceptible.

Neck and Back.—Neck so weak child can scarcely keep it erect (*Coni.*), °especially in whooping cough. Rheumatic pain in neck, extending to sacrum. Pains in loins and back, as if beaten (Arn., Ars., Bry.).

Limbs.—*Painful paralytic weakness in all the limbs.* Falling asleep of the limbs (Sep., Sil., Sulph.). Pain as from fatigue. *Nails blue from coldness.* °Pains in limbs resembling a bruise; worse during wet, cold weather; worse in warmth of bed; better walking up and down. Pain in middle of left forearm, as if bones were pressed together. *Icy-coldness of the limbs; of hands and feet (Sil.).*

Lower Limbs.—Difficult walking; first right, then left hip-joint feels paralytic. Cramps in the calves (Calc. c., Camph., Cham., Nitr. ac., Nux v., Sil., Sulph.). Pain in bone below knee, as if broken, when stepping. Stinging in toes when standing.

Generalities.—Trembling of the whole body (Colch.). *Sudden sinking of strength* (*Ars.*, Camph., Sec.). *Extreme weakness and prostration* (*Ars.*, Ferr., *Phos.*); in the morning with shivering. Excessive chronic weakness. Spasms, with convulsive motion of the limbs. °Attacks of pain, with delirium, or driving to madness. Pressure and bruised sensation in muscular parts of body.

Skin.—Wrinkled skin; remains in folds after pressure. Skin blue, purple, cold. Dry eruption, resembling itch.

Sleep.—Unusual sleepiness (*Ant. tart., Apis, Nux m.*). Yawning.

Fever.—*Coldness and chilliness over the whole body* (Bry.); with thirst; creeping, running from head to toes. External coldness, with internal heat. *Cold perspiration* (Euphorb.) *over the whole body, especially on forehead* (*Camph.*).

Aggravation.—After drinking; before and during stool; on rising.

Amelioration.—While sitting and lying (except weakness).

Conditions.—Especially useful in children.

Compare.—*Acon., Ant. tart.,* Arn., *Ars.,* Cinch., *Colch.,* Coff. c., *Cupr., Digit.,* Dros., Ferr., Ipec., Iris v., Op., Phos. ac., Rhus tox., Sec. cor., Zinc.

Antidotes.—Acon., Camph., Cinch., Coff. c.

Veratrum Antidotes.—Ars., Cinch., Ferr., Op., Tabac.

THERAPEUTICS.

The chief use of Verat. alb. is in the treatment of cholera and choleraic conditions characterized by terrible colic, even cramps, cramps in the calves, cold sweat on forehead, very profuse, watery, flaky stools, violent retching and vomiting, great prostration, burning in the stomach, sensitiveness to touch. The violent retching and vomiting with cold sweat on the forehead and violent pain are the most characteristic, and differentiate the drug from other cholera remedies. With this class of symptoms the drug may not only be indicated in true

VERATRUM ALBUM.

cholera, but also in cholera morbus, worse at night, after fruits; colic from taking cold, or from fruits and vegetables; peritonitis; diarrhœa, coming on suddenly at night, in summer; intussusception of the bowels. The drug is also valuable in constipation when the stools are large and hard (Bry.). Dyspepsia, with craving for fruit and juicy things, characteristic vomiting, etc. Verat. alb. is often a valuable remedy in nervous diseases. Mania; melancholia, especially religious; delirium, especially after severe illness, etc., as indicated in symptoms. Neuralgic headaches, with coldness on vertex. Neuralgia in the head, convulsive shocks on raising up the head, vomiting, pains so severe they cause delirium, better from pressure on vertex. Facial neuralgia, with cold sweat on forehead, vomiting, pinched features, violent neuralgic toothache, with other Verat. symptoms. Violent tonic spasms, palms and soles drawn inward. Trismus. Tetanus. Chorea. Paralysis, especially after cholera or from debilitating causes. Rheumatism, pains like electric jerks, worse during wet weather (Rhus tox.); getting worse in warmth of bed (Merc.); better on walking about. Hemeralopia, before the menses, with cramps, vomiting, etc., suppression of urine. Suppressed menses, with despair of salvation, vomiting, purging, etc. Dysmenorrhœa, with vomiting and purging, or exhausting diarrhœa and cold sweat. Nymphomania of lying-in women (Cinch., *Plat.*); preceding menses. Puerperal mania. Chronic metritis, with great sensitiveness of uterus to touch, and Verat. characteristics. Endometritis, with violent pain, vomiting, purging, cold sweat, etc. Bronchitis in old people or children, with profuse expectoration, or great accumulation or inability to expectorate, blueness of face, cold sweat, involuntary micturition. Spasmodic cough, with suffocative fits, from constriction of larynx. Whooping cough, attacks followed by great exhaustion; cough worse on entering warm room from cold air. Cardiac debility following acute diseases; tendency to faint on moving; on sitting up suddenly the red face turns deadly pale; very weak, thready pulse, cold sweat. Congestive chills, with characteristic Verat. symptoms. Typhoid forms of fever, especially in cholera seasons; also when vital forces suddenly sink. Chronic affections from abuse of cinchona; from copper, especially colic. Bad effects of fright, fear or vexation.

VERATRUM VIRIDE.

Synonym.—Helonias Viridis. *Natural order.*—Melanthaceæ. Liliaceæ. *Common names.*—American White Hellebore. Indian Poke. Swamp Hellebore. *Habitat.*—A coarse plant found growing in wet meadows and swamps from Canada to Georgia. *Preparation.*—Tincture from the fresh root.

GENERAL ANALYSIS.

Acts upon the cerebro-spinal system, especially upon the pneumogastric nerve, producing profound paralysis of the cerebro-spinal nerve-centers, the reflex motor nerve-centers, and of the whole circulatory apparatus, which results in intense congestion and inflammation of the brain and other organs, especially those under the control of the pneumogastric nerve, notably the lungs and stomach. Thus the action of Veratrum will be seen to differ from that of Belladonna and other remedies which produce congestion, by excitation of the nerve-centers, rather than by paralysis.

On the motor nerves it first produces prostration, but has the power of causing both tonic and clonic spasms, especially the latter, giving rise to a condition similar to chorea. The most essential feature of Veratrum is its influence upon the heart and circulation, being indicated by a loud, strong beating of the heart, quick pulse, and a very slow respiration.

CHARACTERISTIC SYMPTOMS.

Mind.—Quarrelsome and delirious. °Furious delirium, with screaming, howling and striking. °Delirium, with incessant muttering, dilated pupils, etc.

Head.—Vertigo: in morning on rising: better on closing the eyes and resting the head; on rising from a seat or bed, with nausea and vomiting. Headache, with vertigo. Headache proceeding from the nape of the neck (*Sang.*); head feels full and heavy: mornings. Active congestion of the head (*Acon., Bell.*). Neuralgic pain in right temple close to the eye. Severe frontal headache, with vomiting (*Iris*).

VERATRUM VIRIDE.

Eyes.—Dilated pupils (Ailanth., Bell., Cic., Op., Stram.). Dimness of vision, especially on rising or attempting to walk, with partial syncope. Unsteady vision.

Ears.—Humming, with sensitiveness to noise.

Face.—Face *flushed* (Bapt., Bell.); pale, cold, bluish; covered with cold perspiration (Verat. alb.). Convulsive stitches of the facial muscles (Agar., Cic., Ign., Nux v.).

Mouth.—Mouth and lips dry; thick mucus in mouth. Tongue feels as if it had been scalded (Coloc., *Iris,* Plat., Sang., Sulph. ac.). Tongue yellow, *with red streak in the middle.*

Throat.—Burning in the fauces and œsophagus, with constant inclination to swallow. Spasms of the œsophagus, with or without rising of frothy, bloody mucus.

Stomach.—Thirst in the morning after rising, with nausea. Painful, almost constant hiccough (Cic., Hyos., Ign., Sulph. ac.), with spasms of upper part of œsophagus. Violent nausea and vomiting; in morning on rising; with cold sweat (Verat. alb., *Tabac.*). Smallest quantity of food and drink is immediately rejected. Excruciating pain in lower part of the stomach. Intense, twisting, tearing pains in the stomach.

Abdomen.—Pain at right of umbilicus, passing down to groin. Pain in abdomen with flatulence. Pain and soreness across the abdomen, *just above the pelvis.*

Stool.—°Bloody, black, in typhoid; copious, light, mornings.

Urinary Organs.—Urine very clear.

Respiratory Organs.—Difficult, slow, labored breathing. (°Falls from 49 to 16 in pneumonia). Convulsive breathing, almost to suffocation. Oppression of the chest. Active congestion of the chest (*Acon.*).

Heart and Pulse.—Constant, dull, burning pain in region of heart. °Heart beats loud, strong, with great arterial excitement (Acon., *Bell.*).

Neck and Back.—Aching in the back of neck and shoulders.

Limbs.—Cramps of the legs, fingers and toes. Violent, galvanic-like shocks in the limbs.

Generalities.—Convulsive twitchings and contortions of muscles of face, neck, fingers and toes. Chorea (*Agar.*, Cic., Ign., Nux v.). Trembling, as if child were frightened and on verge of a spasm. Paralysis; tingling in the limbs;

VERATRUM VIRIDE.

cerebral hyperæmia. °Congestions, especially of bas
brain, chest, spine, stomach. °Dropsy, with fever;
scarlet fever.

Fever.—Chilliness, with nausea; in morning after rising.
ness of the whole body; cold sweat on face, hands,
(*Ars., Camph., Tabac., Verat. alb.*). °Fever, with
hard, frequent pulse (*Acon., Bell.*). Profuse sweat;
and sense of utter prostration (*Phos.*).

Aggravation.—On rising; on waking; in the evening;
motion.

Amelioration.—From hot, strong coffee.

Conditions.—In full-blooded, plethoric persons (Bell.).

Compare.—*Acon., Ant. tart., Bell.,* Coccul., *Digit.,*
Gels., Hell., Hyos., Phos., Tabac., Verat. alb.

THERAPEUTICS.

The chief value of Verat. vir. is in the treatment of inf
matory and eruptive fevers, characterized by intense
rial excitement, full, strong, incompressible pulse.
cially valuable in the congestive stage of pneumonia, b
exudation has occurred. Occasionally in pleurisy. Bronch
In pulmonary congestions and inflammations there is alv
extreme dyspnœa, and the face is usually livid. A valuable
edy in active cerebral congestions, especially at the base of
brain. Effects of sunstroke. Cerebro-spinal meningitis;
ingitis with high fever; intense congestion; later, rollin
head; vomiting; or, face haggard, cold; pulse slow, breat
labored. Cerebral apoplexy. Intense congestive heada
throbbing, double vision, etc. Insanity from cerebral con
tion; furious delirium, with screaming and howling. Ir
tive fever in children, with cerebral congestion, causing con
sions. Acute inflammation of middle ear (Ferr. phos.),
cerebral symptoms. Œsophagitis, with burning and cons
tion. Gastritis. Enteritis with high fever, great vasc
excitement; vomiting, dark, bloody stools. Menstrual di
ders, with intense cerebral congestion (*Bell.*); someti
opisthotonos. Puerperal mania (Bell., Hyos., Plat., Stra
convulsions. Puerperal fever. Congestive dysmenorrhea,
convulsions. Pelvic congestions and inflammations.
os during labor, with cerebral congestion and character

pulse. Carditis. Pericarditis. Endocarditis. Hypertrophy of the heart. Valvular insufficiency. Chorea, from congestion of the nerve-centres. Violent opisthotonic convulsions, either with congestions, or in anœmic subjects, from exhausting diarrhœa. Epilepsy. Hysteria. Hystero-epilepsy. Tetanus, threatening from the violent congestion. Paralysis; from cerebral hyperæmia. Inflammatory rheumatism. Eruptions and eruptive fevers—measles, scarlatina, small-pox, with intense fever, great arterial excitement; sometimes convulsions precede eruptions. Dropsy after scarlet fever. Has been found useful in opium poisoning.

VERBASCUM.

Synonym.—Verbascum Thapsus. *Natural order.*—Scrophulariaceæ. *Common names.*—Mullein. Flannel Plant. *Habitat.*—A plant native of Europe, but naturalized in North America, where it is found in fields and on roadsides. *Preparation.*—Tincture from the fresh plant.

GENERAL ANALYSIS.

Acts upon the cerebro-spinal nerves, giving rise especially to headache and prospalgia. Clinically it is indicated for a hoarse, dry, cough, in which condition its therapeutic range is almost entirely limited.

CHARACTERISTIC SYMPTOMS.

Head.—Attacks of vertigo on pressing the left cheek. Pressing, stupefying headache, principally in the forehead. Stitches deep in right temple when eating; worse from pressure; extending into upper teeth of right side. *Sensation as if the temples were pinched and crushed together by pincers.* Pressing, slow stitch from behind forward, through the left hemisphere of the brain.

Ears.—Numbness in left ear. Tearing, drawing pains in left ear; sensation as if ear would be drawn inward. Sensation as if the ears were obstructed, first the left, then the right.

VERBASCUM.

Face.—Violent, stupefying, pressive or tensive pains in left malar and cheek bones, aggravated on pressure and in the open air, or in a draught of air; °from changes of temperature; °from motion of muscles of face. Violent tension in the integuments of the chin, masseter muscles and throat. Stitches in left zygomatic arch.

Mouth.—Root of tongue brown, without bad taste, in morning and during forenoon.

Stomach.—Empty or bitter eructations. Frequent hiccough.

Abdomen.—Violent, painful pressure as from a stone upon the umbilicus (*Puls.*), aggravated by stooping.

Urinary Organs.—Frequent, profuse urination (Apis, Apoc., Cepa, Puls.); afterward scanty.

Respiratory Organs.—Hoarseness, when reading aloud. (Phos.). °Catarrh, with hoarseness and oppression of the chest. Stitches in the chest (Bry., Kali c.). °Deep, hoarse, dry or hollow cough, especially in the evening and at night (Spong.).

Upper Limbs.—Stitches like a sprain (or paralysis), where carpal bone of thumb articulates with radius.

Lower Limbs.—Cramp-like pain in muscles of right thigh, while walking in the open air. Sudden pain through right knee. Cramp-like pressure in sole of right foot, while standing, disappears when walking.

Generalities.—Tearing, stitching pains in different parts (Bry., Kali c.). Much stretching and yawning. Great sleepiness after a meal. Coldness of the whole body.

Compare.—Nux v., Plat., Stan.

Antidote.—Camph.

THERAPEUTICS.

Useful in headache and prosopalgia; the symptoms agreeing. Infra-orbital and supra-orbital neuralgia. Particularly valuable for chronic catarrhal coughs, especially in children. (See symptoms.) Asthma. Constant dribbling of urine. Nocturnal enuresis. An ancient and popular remedy for deafness, now used mostly locally in the form of an oil (Mullein oil).

VIBURNUM OPULUS.

Synonym.—Viburnum Edule. *Natural order.*—Caprifoliaceæ. *Common names.*—Cranberry Tree. High Cranberry. Sheep's Berry. Snowball. *Habitat.*—A shrub growing in low grounds along streams. Common in the Alleghenies as far south as the borders of Maryland. *Preparation.*—Tincture from the fresh bark of the root.

GENERAL ANALYSIS.

Through the cerebro-spinal system Viburnum exerts its most marked action upon the female generative organs, its chief clinical use being in the treatment of congestive or neuralgic dysmenorrhœa, where it has proved of remarkable value. Its action is undoubtedly due to the Valerianic acid which it contains.

CHARACTERISTIC SYMPTOMS.

Mind.—Depressed; irritable. Unable to perform mental labor.
Head.—Vertigo. Dull, frontal headache; and throbbing, extending to eyeballs, worse on mental exertion; better moving about. Dull, heavy headache, mostly over eyes, worse on left side, at times extending to vertex and occiput, principally when delayed menses should appear (Cimic.); worse on sudden jar, bending over, false step or movement; from every cough.
Eyes.—Heaviness over eyes and in balls; must, at times, look twice to be sure of seeing an object. Sore feeling in eyeballs (Bry., Physos., Spig.).
Face.—Flushed and hot.
Mouth.—Tongue dry, broad and white; center brown; leaves impress of teeth (*Merc.*). Taste coppery; disagreeable. Lips and mouth dry (*Ars., Bry., Nux m., Puls.*).
Stomach.—Constant nausea; with faintness; relieved by eating; followed by vomiting; deathly nausea every night. Faint, nauseated feeling in stomach; must lie down; fol-

lowing menses after flow ceases. Empty, gone feeling in stomach (Cimic., Ign., Sep.); food lies heavy.

Abdomen.—Deep-seated, darting pain in region of spleen. Sensation of hot fluid running through splenic vessels. Intense pain in splenic region, faintness better by sweat. Severe throbbing pain under left floating ribs; better from hard pressure and walking; cannot lie on left side. Abdomen tender and sensitive, worse about umbilicus. Cramping colic pains in lower abdomen, almost insupportable, coming suddenly and with terrible severity.

Stool.—Inactivity of rectum (*Alum.*); stools of large, hard, dry balls, voided with difficulty, requiring mechanical aid; tenesmus. Dark blood after stool. Diarrhœa profuse, watery, with chills, and at same time cold sweat that rolls off the forehead.

Urine.—Profuse, frequent, clear, watery.

Female Organs.—Before menses: severe bearing-down, drawing in anterior muscles of thighs; heavy aching in sacral region and over pubis; occasional sharp, shooting pains in ovaries; pains make her so nervous she cannot sit still; excruciating, cramping, colicky pains in lower abdomen and through womb; pains begin in back and go around, ending in cramps in uterus; pains worse in the early part of the evening, and in a close room; better in the open air and when moving about.

During menses: nausea. Cramping pain and great nervous restlessness; feeling as if the breath would leave the body and the heart cease to beat; pain as if the back would break; flow ceases for several hours, then returns in clots. Flow scanty, thin, light-colored, with sensation of lightness of head; faint when trying to sit up Congested feeling in pelvic organs, as if menses would appear. Leucorrhœa thin, yellow-white, or colorless, except with the stool, when it is thick, white, blood-streaked.

Neck and Back.—Neck stiff, with pain in occiput. Tired, bruised pain in muscles of back.

Generalities.—Inability to lie on the affected side.

Limbs.—Buzzing feeling in hands, as if they would burst. Swelling and numbness of the fingers, worse from washing in cold water.

Sleep.—Restless, unrefreshing.
Aggravation.—Evening and night; in warm room; left side most affected.
Amelioration.—In open air; from moving about; from pressure.
Compare.—Caul., Cimic., Gels., Sec., Sep., Xanthox.

THERAPEUTICS.

Viburnum has proved to be an invaluable remedy in dysmenorrhœa, especially of the *congestive* or *neuralgic* type, and often temporarily relieves in the membranous and obstructive varieties. It appears that its action becomes exhausted in about three months, and another remedy is required, though some cases of congestive and neuralgic dysmenorrhœa have been permanently cured. The symptoms indicating the drug have already been detailed. It is a valuable remedy for after-pains. Threatened abortion; intense cramp in uterus, and bearing-down; or pain around from back, ending in excruciating pain in lower abdomen. Leucorrhœa. Has been used in hysteria, with painful menstruation. Spasmodic dysuria.

VIOLA TRICOLOR.

Synonym.—Jacea. *Natural order.*—Violaceæ. *Common names.*—Pansy. Heartsease. *Habitat.*—The pansy is indigenous to Europe and Northern Asia, but is cultivated in all civilized countries. *Preparation.*—Tincture from the whole plant when in flower.

GENERAL ANALYSIS.

Acts chiefly upon the skin, giving rise to impetignous and eczematous eruptions, which are the chief indications for its use.

CHARACTERISTIC SYMPTOMS.

Mind.—Ill-humored, morose, with disinclination to talk.
Head.—Pressive headache, chiefly in forehead and temples, ex-

tending outward. Tearing stitch externally in left temple. Scurfs on head, unbearable burning, most at night. Impetigo of the hairy scalp and face. °Crusta lactea in children (Graph., Mez., Nitr. ac.) recently weaned. Thick incrustations, pouring out a large quantity of thick, yellow fluid, which mats the hair (Graph.).

Eyes.—Contraction and closing of the lids.

Face.—Tension in the integuments of the face and forehead. Milk crust (Sars.), burning, itching, especially at night, with discharge of viscid, yellow pus; also behind ears. Impetigo on the forehead.

Abdomen.—Cutting pains in the abdomen.

Urinary Organs.—Frequent and profuse emission of urine (Apis, Apoc., Cepa, Valer., Verb.). Urine very offensive (*Benz. ac.*); like cat's urine.

Male Organs.—Involuntary seminal emissions (Phos. ac., Cinch.), with lascivious dreams.

Respiratory Organs.—Stitches in the left side of chest; worse during inspiration and expiration.

Back.—Tension between the shoulder blades, with cutting and crawling in the skin.

Skin.—Eruption over face (except eyelids) and behind ears, with burning, itching, worse at night, a thick, hard scab formed, cracked here and there, from which a tenacious yellow pus exuded, and hardened into a substance like gum.

Sleep.—Sleepless; frequent waking. Vivid, amorous dreams.

Aggravation.—°In winter and in cold weather.

Compare.—Clem., Graph., Hep. s., Petrol.

Antidotes.—Camph., Merc. sol., Puls.

THERAPEUTICS.

Viola tric. has been used almost exclusively for impetignous and eczematous diseases, especially crusta lactea; plica polonica; scrofulous ophthalmia, with crusta lactea. Incontinence of urine at night in children, urine smelling like cat's urine, especially with crusta lactea.

XANTHOXYLUM.

Synonym.—Xanthoxylum Fraxineum. *Natural order.*—Rutaceæ. *Common names.*—Prickly Ash. Yellow Wood. *Habitat.*—An indigenous shrub found growing in most portions of the United States. *Preparation.*—Tincture from the fresh bark.

GENERAL ANALYSIS.

Acts upon the nervous system, producing irritation and stimulation of the nerves of sensation, and to a less extent of the nerves of motion. Secondarily, paralysis or torpor of both sets of nerves is established, and as a result a marked depression of the vital forces is produced, affecting both the sensorial and bodily functions. The mucous membranes and the muscular and glandular tissues are especially influenced by its irritant action. The most important practical feature is its action upon the female generative organs, where it gives rise to early and profuse menstruation, accompanied by severe neuralgic pains, constituting neuralgic dysmenorrhœa.

CHARACTERISTIC SYMPTOMS.

Mind.—Nervous, frightened feeling. Mental depression and weakness.
Head.—Head feels full and heavy. Bewildered feeling; pain in back of head. Throbbing headache over right eye, with nausea. Pain over eyes, with throbbing above root of nose. Aching and flashes of throb-like pain, as if top of head would come off. Tightness of the scalp.
Nose.—Right nostril seems filled up. Discharge of mucus; of dry and bloody scales.
Face.—Pain in lower jaw, left side.
Mouth.—Peppery taste in mouth, fauces and throat.
Throat.—Soreness, with expectoration of tough mucus. Feeling of a bunch in left side of throat when swallowing, shifting to right.

Stomach.—Loss of appetite; eructations; nausea. Sense of oppression, with frequent chills. Feeling of fullness or pressure; fluttering.

Urine.—Profuse, light-colored urine, °in nervous women.

Female Organs.—Ovarian pains, extending down the genito-crural nerves. Dreadful distress and pain; headache; menses too early and too profuse; pains down the anterior of thighs; very nervous, easily startled and hysterical; neuralgic dysmenorrhœa. °After-pains when of the above character, with profuse lochia.

Respiratory Organs.—Hoarse, husky feeling in throat. Desire to take a long breath; tight feeling about the chest; inclined to gape.

Limbs.—Severe neuralgic pains in course of genito-crural nerves. Excessive weakness of lower limbs. Pains in limbs, neuralgic, shooting; numbness and weakness.

Generalities.—Pricking sensations; gentle shocks, as from electricity. Mucous membranes smart, as from pepper; catarrh.

Fever.—Chills; pain in limbs; flushes of heat; sense of heat in veins.

Compare.—Bell., Cimic., Gels.

THERAPEUTICS.

Especially useful in neuralgic dysmenorrhœa, particularly in women of a spare habit, and of a delicate nervous temperament; with profuse menses, and with symptoms above described. Amenorrhœa, from getting the feet wet; hysterical depression and weakness, nausea, etc. After-pains. Neuralgia, especially sciatica; worse in hot weather; neuralgia of anterior crural nerves. Ovarian neuralgia, worse on left side, extending down the thighs. Facial neuralgia. Paralysis. Chlorosis.

ZINCUM.

Synonym.—Zincum Metallicum.   *Common names.*—Zinc. Spelter.   *Preparation.*—Triturations.

GENERAL ANALYSIS.

Acts profoundly upon the cerebro-spinal system, producing a condition of erethism in the brain, medulla oblongata and spinal cord, characterized by delirium, spasms, neuralgia, tremors, extreme hyperæsthesia, followed by cerebral depression, and an exhaustion of the nerve-centers (paralysis) which latter is its most important homœopathic application. In the blood it produces marked anæmia (deficiency of red corpuscles).

CHARACTERISTIC SYMPTOMS.

Mind.—Weak memory (*Anac.*, Kreos., Lach., Merc., *Nux m.*); forgets what has been accomplished during the day. Fretful, despondent, sullen mood, especially in the evening. Easily offended; sobbing from vexation. Anxiety. Mental operations difficult (Gels., Nux v., Phos. ac., Thuja); loss of thought, and a *soporous condition of the mind* (Nux m., Op.). Aversion to work (Cinch., Nux v., Phos. ac.).

Head.—Vertigo in the occiput, with falling to the left when walking. Frequent attacks of vertigo, preceded by sharp pressure at root of nose, and a sensation of drawing together of the eyes, as if by a cord, followed immediately by excessive nausea, faintness and trembling of the hands. Pressure on root of nose, as if it would be pressed into the head (Kali bi.). Sharp pressure on a small spot in forehead, evenings. Hemicrania; worse after dinner; tearing and stinging. Pain in sinciput, with dullness, extending into the eyes. Headache from drinking even small quantities of wine (*Nux v.*, Rhod.). Drawing, pressing, tearing on top of head. Tearing stitches in right temple. Sensitiveness of vertex to touch, as if ulcerated; worse evenings. *Heaviness and dullness in occiput.* Hair falls out on vertex, causing complete baldness (Baryt. c.), with sensation of soreness.

Eyes.—*Inflammation and redness of conjunctiva;* wor[se] inner canthus; pains worse evening and night, as [of] sand, with frequent lachrymation (*Ars., Caust., P*[uls.]) also during menses. Much burning in the eyes and [lids] in the morning and evening, with feeling of dryness [and] pressure in them (Alum., Ars., *Sulph.*). Itching, b[urning] and tickling, especially in right eye; as from dust; ph[oto]phobia and lachrymation; worse evenings. *Itching* [and] *stitching pain in inner angles of eyes, with cloudine*[ss of] *sight.* Pressure on margin of lower lid, near inner cant[hus]. Burning of lids as if too dry. Upper lids heavy as if [par]alyzed (*Caust., Gels.*). *Agglutination of lids at n*[ight] (Caust., *Graph., Lyc., Merc., Rhus tox., Puls., Sul*[ph.]) with pressing, sore feeling. Dim vision. Photoph[obia] (Acon., *Bell.*, Merc., Sil., *Sulph.*)

Ears.—Frequent, acute stitches in right ear, near tympan[um].

Nose.—Nose feels sore internally. Cutting, crawling in e[ar,] ing, then sneezing. Severe pressure on root of nose. S[top]page of nose (Nux v., Sil.).

Face.—Pale; °alternating with redness (Acon.). Tearing [and] sore pain in the facial bones. Sudden stitches from ri[ght] zygoma, to upper margin of orbit, deep in bone, in eveni[ng,] then soreness. Lips dry and cracked (Ars., Bry.).

Mouth.—Drawing, tearing, jerking pains in teeth. Gums bl[eed] on slightest touch (Carb. v., *Merc., Nitr. ac., Phos.*). B[lis]ters on tongue. Copious secretion of saliva, with crawl[ing] on inner surface of cheeks. Sticking, biting on palate cl[ose] to and in the roots of incisors.

Throat.—Dryness of the throat, with accumulation of muc[us,] especially from posterior nares; with inclination to ha[wk.] Sore throat. Tearing, drawing pains, more on poster[ior] sides of pharynx; worse between acts of swallowing th[an] on empty swallowing.

Stomach.—Salty taste in the mouth (Merc., Natr. mur.). [Vo]racious appetite and insatiable hunger (Bry., Ferr., I[od.,] *Lyc.*). Aversion to sugar; to wine and brandy. Loss [of] appetite (Alum., Ars.). Thirst, with heat in the palms; [in] afternoon. Sour, empty eructations (Carb. v., *Nux,* Phos.). Heartburn after eating sweet things. Hiccou[gh.] *Nausea* and vomiting (Ant. tart., Ipec., Lob.). Retchi[ng] of bloody mucus. Tearing stitches in and beneath pit of stomach; from both sides towards each other. Burning in the stomach and epigastric region (Ars., Canth., Iris). Pain and pressure in pit of stomach.

Abdomen.—Cramp-like pains in the hypochondria, with dyspnœa and oppression of the chest after eating. Sticking in right hypochondrium (Ars., Bry., Cinch., Merc., Sulph.); in spleen. Enlarged liver. Pain after a light meal, with tympanitis. Pain as from an internal induration in a spot beneath navel. Great fullness and distension of the abdomen. Pressure and tension of the abdomen, after eating (Carb. v., Cinch., *Nux v.*). Flatulent colic, especially in the evening; loud rumbling, gurgling and rolling (Aloe, *Lyc.*, Sulph.); frequent emission of hot, fœtid flatus (Aloe, Bry.). Severe stabbing pains in the abdomen. *Griping after breakfast or cutting after dinner.*

Stool and Anus.—Itching in the anus (*Sulph.*). Crawling in the anus as from worms (Sep., Spig.). Burning in anus during stool. Obstinate constipation; stools small, hard, dry and crumbling (Amm. mur., Natr. mur.); insufficient; difficult; expelled with much pressure (*Sulph.*). Diarrhœa.

Urinary Organs.—Pressure in region of left kidney. Violent pressure of urine in the bladder. Acute drawing in forepart of urethra and in penis. Urine turbid, loam-colored in the morning. °Can only pass water while sitting bent backward. Involuntary urination while walking, coughing and sneezing (*Caust.*, Natr. mur., *Puls.*).

Male Organs.—Long-lasting and violent erections. Drawing in the testicles, extending up to the spermatic cord (Reverse, Berb., Ham., Merc., Puls.). One or the other testicle drawn up. Easily excited; the emission during an embrace is too rapid, or difficult and almost impossible. Emissions at night, without lascivious dreams. Copious discharge of prostatic juice without any cause.

Female Organs.—Irresistible sexual desire at night; desire for onanism. Menses too early. °Suppressed or painful menstruation. Discharge of large clots during the menses; when walking. Leucorrhœa of thick mucus; bloody mucus (Alum.); excoriating after the menses (*Puls.*).

Respiratory Organs.—Hoarseness. Burning and sore pain

in the chest. Dull stitches in the right side of chest. Stitches in a spot in left side of chest, with feeling as if corroded and bruised. Burning inside of chest. Tightness and oppression of the chest. Tightness in evening, with sticking and pressure in middle of sternum; small, rapid pulse. Roughness and rawness in chest. Dry, spasmodic cough (*Hyos., Sep.*, Sil., *Sulph.*); with bloody expectoration; *before and during the menses;* morning and evening.

Heart.—Tension and stitches in the præcordial region. Stitches at apex. Palpitation without special anxiety. Rapid pulse.

Neck and Back.—Stiffness and pain in cervical and upper dorsal muscles. Tearing in right side of neck. *Nape of the neck feels weary, from writing, or any exertion.* Bruised pain and weakness in small of back, when walking. Pain in region of kidneys; stitches; cutting; pressure. Pain in lumbar region when walking, often forcing him to sand still, better on continuing to walk. Pressive tension beneath the right scapula. Sticking pain in back and small of back, when sitting and walking. Burning pressure upon spine above small of back.

Limbs.—Stiffness of the joints, with sharp, lancinating pains above the joints, *always transverse, not lengthwise of the limb.* Drawing in middle of almost all bones, so that they had no steadiness. Weakness, weariness and bruised feelings in the limbs. Coldness of the extremities. Drawing, tearing pains in all the limbs (Bry., Coloc., *Puls., Sulph.*). Violent itching in all the joints.

Upper Limbs.—Burning in left forearm at night. Weakness and trembling of the hands when writing (Natr. mur.); also during menses. Tearing near left shoulder. Tearing in first joints and phalanges of the fingers.

Lower Limbs.—*Varices in the legs* (*Ham., Puls.*). Rheumatic, drawing pains in right lower limb. Legs œdematous (Apis, Ars., Rhus tox.). Itching of thighs and *hollow of knees.* Heaviness of the lower limbs. *Uneasiness in lower limbs at night. Burning pain in the tibiæ.* Stitches in tibiæ to back of foot. Tearing in calves. Drawing in right tendo-Achillis. Weakness of the legs; worse when walking. Erysipelatous inflammation of the tendo-Achillis. Nervous, fidgety moving of the feet (Natr. mur.); after retiring and during sleep. Tearing in margin of right foot, with tension. Paralysis of the feet; weakness and trembling; worse mornings in bed, better from rising and walking. Ulcerative, boring pains in heels (*Puls.*); worse when walking than when sitting. Painful chilblains on the feet (Agar., Nitr. ac., Puls.). Profuse sweat on the feet (*Nitr. ac.*, Sep., *Sil., Sulph.*). Stitches in toe-joints. Sprained pain in bends of toe-joints.

Generalities.—*Twitching and jerking in various muscles* (*Agar., Cic.*). Pain seems to be between the skin and the flesh. Great heaviness, weakness and lassitude; mornings in bed. *Jerking through the whole body during sleep at night.* Violent throbbing through the whole body (*Glon., Puls.*). Formication on the skin.

Sleep.—Unrefreshing sleep; disturbed by frightful dreams; with *screaming* and startings; *limbs and body jerk.*

Fever.—Febrile shivering down the back. Shaking chill in the evening. Heat all night, with sweat. Night sweats.

Aggravation.—*Most symptoms appear after dinner and towards evening. From wine* (Nux vom.); during rest; while sitting; in open air.

Amelioration.—*From camphor;* on walking; while eating; from sweat.

Compare.—Arg., Bell., Carb. v., *Cupr.*, Ign., Nux v., *Plumb.*, Puls., Stram. Zinc. is followed well by Ign., but not by Nux v., which disagrees.

Antidotes.—*Camph.*, Hep. s., Ign.

Zinc Antidotes.—Baryt. c., Cham., Nux v.

THERAPEUTICS.

Zinc is a valuable remedy in the neuroses, and for various diseased states, resulting from profound disturbance of the nerve-centers of the brain and spinal cord, especially exhaustion. A valuable remedy in chronic headaches and hemicrania, with symptoms above mentioned. Neuralgic headache from brain-fag, with blurred vision; school children who have been over-taxed, threatening meningitis. Hydrocephalus. Hydrocephaloid, following cholera infantum. Meningitis, from suppressed exanthemata, or during teething. Cerebral exhaustion. Softening of the brain; paralysis; chorea, caused by fright or suppressed eruptions, great depression of spirits and irritability. Beginning of locomotor ataxia, when lightning-like pains are marked and intense. Epilepsy, especially in young children. Convulsions from suppressed eruptions, suppressed menses or from fright. General paralysis. Neuralgia. Spinal irritation. Spine sensitive to touch; especially in lower dorsal region. Neuralgia after zoster, better from pressure. Zinc is often useful in melancholia, and other forms of insanity, resulting from softening of the brain or other cerebral disease. The patient is usually lethargic, stupid, paralytic feelings in the limbs, sometimes convulsions. Sometimes there is a suicidal tendency, and great apprehension and fear, especially of being arrested for crime. Anæmia of teething children, with hydrocephaloid symptoms. Brain exhaustion, and nerve weakness so that in children they are not able to develop exanthemata. It is therefore indicated in exanthematous diseases, especially scarlet fever, when the eruption develops slowly and imperfectly, and cerebral symptoms are manifest, or profound exhaustion, with rapid, almost imperceptible pulse. In all such cases the patient at once improves if the eruption appears. It is characteristic of Zinc that relief comes from the appearance of discharges or eruptions. The patient always suffers less during menstruation, the chest symptoms are relieved by expectoration, the abdominal and head symptoms by diarrhœa, all symptoms, but more especially head symptoms, by the appearance of eruptions. Zinc is a valuable remedy for varicose veins. On this point Allen says (*op. cit., p. 1152*) the remedy is "extremely valuable, especially in the sub-acute or chronic condition which underlies and determines the development of the disease. It works well when associated with Puls.; the two drugs should never be given together, but consecutively; Zinc follows Puls., acting better after Puls. has relieved some of the acute symptoms; neither of these drugs, however, is often indicated in acute phlebetis."

Eczema, Erysipelas, especially of the head and face, with brain symptoms. Catarrhal conjunctivitis, worse at inner canthus (outer canthus, Graph.) Granular lids after ophthalmia neonatorum. Corneal opacities. Pterygium. Blurred vision with cerebral exhaustion, especially brain-fag. Earache, chronic especially in children (Puls.). Gastric derangement from drinking wine or from eating too many sweets. Atonic dyspepsia, with flatulence and "gone" feeling in stomach before noon (Sulph.). Lead colic. Enteralgia. Flatulent colic, especially evenings. Liver enlarged and sore. Enlarged spleen. Cholera infantum with hydrocephaloid. Chronic dysentery. Vermicular affections. Reflex symptoms from floating kidney. Paralysis of the bladder. Occasionally useful in Bright's disease. Sexual weakness, with erethism; seminal emissions; hypochondriasis. Spermatorrhœa; emissions without dreams, face pale, sunken, blue rings around the eyes. Orchitis, from a bruise. Neuralgia of the testicles, worse when walking. Useful in various disorders of menstruation; menorrhagia, amenorrhea, dysmenorrhea. Vicarious menstruation. Leucorrhea. Pruritus vulvæ, causing onanism. Unnatural sexual excitement. Ovarian neuralgia, left side, boring pains, better from pressure, but only entirely relieved during the menstrual flow. Chronic metritis, better during menses. In all uterine and ovarian disorders demanding Zinc we usually find the peculiar mental depression and nervous restlessness of the drug, especially a continual nervous, fidgety moving of the feet. This also is one indication of the drug in hysteria, where we also get the globus hystericus, rising from the pit of the stomach, often retention of urine, and other Zinc symptoms. Useful in spasmodic coughs, when it seems as if the cough would draw the chest in pieces; aggravated by eating sweets; every time the child coughs it puts its hands on the genitals. Bronchitis. Asthma. Bronchitis with asthmatic symptoms, and constriction of the chest. Intercostal neuralgia. Sometimes useful in rheumatism, especially affecting the lumbar region, hips and thighs. Sciatica, with nervous restlessness of the feet. Has proved curative in somnambulism, with general Zinc symptoms.

ZINGIBER.

Synonyms.—Zingiber Officinalis. Amomum Zingiber. *Natural order.*—Zingiberaceæ. *Common name.*—Ginger. *Habitat.*—Native of Asia, but cultivated in the tropical regions of South America, Western Africa, Australia and the West Indies. *Preparation.*—Tincture from the dried root.

GENERAL ANALYSIS.

Through the cerebro-spinal system Zingiber exerts its chief action upon mucous membranes, especially of the digestive and respiratory systems, giving rise to irritation and catarrhal inflammation, causing in the one instance symptoms of disturbed digestion, and in the other laryngeal irritation, hoarseness, and cough.

CHARACTERISTIC SYMPTOMS.

Head.—Head feels too large (Arg. nit., Cimic., Glon.). Frontal headache over eyes and at root of nose (Hydras., Kali bi.); also when he exerts himself. Headache worse over left eye; aching over eyebrows, followed by nausea; later over right eye and pressing in left occiput; worse in warm room, but continued in cold, damp air, in motion or sitting. Heavy pressure in head, from without inward, when walking in cold, damp air.

Eyes.—Smarting and burning in eyes; sensitive to light; feeling as of sand in eyes (*Ars., Caust., Sulph.*).

Nose.—Coryza, watery, sneezing, more in open air. Dryness and obstruction in posterior nares, with discharge of thick mucus.

Face.—Drawing pain in left lower jaw and teeth. Exhausted look, blue under eyes, before menses.

Mouth.—Slimy, bad taste in mouth in morning. Mouth smells foul to herself, as from disordered stomach.

Throat.—Increased mucous secretion; no fever.

Stomach.—Much thirst; mouth dry. °Headache and pressure

ZINGIBER.

in stomach after eating bread. °Complaints from eating melons. Belching and diarrhœa. Nausea. Vomiting of slime; in old drunkards. Weak digestion, stomach heavy like a stone.

Abdomen.—Contracting colic passes through abdomen while standing; soon after desire for stool. Great flatulency; constipation. Sharp pain in left iliac region.

Stool.—°Diarrhœa from impure water; of brown mucus; worse mornings; worse from deranged stomach; °from damp, cold weather. Burning, redness, itching at anus and higher up the back.

Urinary Organs.—Urine thick, turbid; dark-brown, of strong smell. While urinating pain in orifice of urethra.

Male Organs.—Increased sexual desire; nightly emissions.

Female Organs.—Menses too early and too profuse; dark, clotted, irritable.

Respiratory Organs.—Hoarseness. Smarting sensation below larynx, followed by cough, with mucous expectoration. Painful respiration; worse at night, must sit up in bed; worse two or three hours every morning; °asthma. Dry, hacking cough, from tickling in larynx on left side of throat; from smarting or scratching; with pain in lungs; difficult breathing; morning sputum which is copious. Stitches in chest; pleuritic pains (Bry., Kali c., Squil.).

Heart.—Stinging, pressing pain in region of heart.

Back.—Backache, as from weakness; worse sitting and leaning against something; lower part of back lame, as if beaten, or from walking or standing; feels stiff.

Limbs.—Dull, heavy, lame feeling; numbness. Rheumatic, drawing pains. Joints feel weak, stiff, lame. Painful swelling of feet.

Generalities.—°Foaming at mouth; free urination; spasms. Faint, weak, wants to lie down. Nervous, fidgety feeling at night.

Sleep.—Sleepy and exhausted. Sleepless, wakes at 8 A.M.; falls asleep again late in morning (*Nux v.*).

Fever.—Chilly in evening; in open air. Hot and chilly at same time.

Antidote.—Nux v.

ZINGIBER.

THERAPEUTICS.

Zingiber has been found useful in colds in the head; coryza; conjunctivitis; ozœna; asthma; dyspepsia; vomiting of drunkards; diarrhœa; chronic intestinal catarrh, etc., the symptoms agreeing.

CLINICAL INDEX.

Abortion.—Aletris, Bell., *Caul.*, Caust., *Cim.*, Erig., Gels., Helon., Kali c., Op., Plumb., Rhus tox., *Sab.*, *Secale*, *Sepia*, Ustil., Vib. op.
Abscess (*Acute*).—Acon., *Apis*, *Ars.*, Bell., Bry., Calc. c., Colch., Crotal., Eucal., Hep s., Iod., Kali brom., Lach., Lyc., *Merc.*, Phos., Sil., Stram., Sulph. (*Chronic*).—Ars., Calc., Cinch., Hep s., Iod., Lach., *Merc.*, Phos., Rhus tox., *Sil.*, *Sulph.*
Acne.—*Ant. crud.*, Ant. tart., *Carb. an.*, Gnaph., *Hep s.*, Hydrocot., *Kali brom.*, Kali iod., *Merc.*, Natr. mur., Nux v., Phos. ac., Rhus tox., Sep., Sil., *Sulph.*
Adenitis.—(See Glands, Inflammation.)
Addison's Disease.—*Ars.*, Calc., Caust., Ferr. iod., Kali c., Kali iod., Nitr. ac., Phos., Sec., Sil., Spig., Sulph.
Adiposis.—(See Obesity.)
After-pains.—Acon., Bell., Caul., Cham., Cim., *Gels.*, Secale cor., Vib. op., Xanth.
Agalactea.—Acon., Agnus, Asaf., Bell., Bry., Calc., Caust., Cham., Phyt., *Puls.*, Rhus tox., Urt.
Ague.—(See Fever, Intermittent.)
Albuminuria.—(See Bright's Disease.)
Alcoholism.—Anac., *Kali brom.*, Led., Lob., *Nux v.*, Zinc.
Alopecia.—Ambr., Ars., *Bar. c.*, *Calc. c.*, Carban, Carb. veg., Caust., Coni., Ferr., *Fluor. ac.*, Graph., *Hep.*, Ign., Kali., Lyc., *Merc.*, *Nitr. ac.*, Petrol., *Phos.*, Sep., Sil., Staph., *Sulph.*, Sulph. ac., Thuja, Zinc.
Amaurosis.—Aur., *Bell.*, Calc., Caust., Chin. con., Chin. sulph., Cic., Euphras., Gels., Meny., *Merc.*, Natr. mur., Nux v., Phos., Plumb., Puls., Sep., Sil., Sulph.
Amenorrhœa.—(See Menstruation, Suppressed.)
Anæmia.—*Acet. ac.*, Aletris (in chlorosis), Arn., *Ars.*, Arum., Baryt. c., *Calc. c.*, *Calc. phos.*, Carb. v., Cedron, *Chin. s.*, *Cinch.*, Cocc. c., Cyc., Digit., *Ferr.*, Hell., *Helon.*, *Hydras.*,

(805)

Kali brom., Kali iod., Lyc., Mang., Merc., Natr. mur., Nit
ac., Nux m., *Phos.*, Plumb., Puls., Secale cor., Sep., Spong
Stan., Sulph., Verat. alb., *Zinc.*

Anæsthesia.—Acon., Can. ind., *Kali brom.*

Anæsthetic Vapors, *Bad effects of.*—Acet. ac.

Angina Pectoris.—*Acon.*, Am. c., *Amyl. nit.*, Arg. nit., Ar
Ars., Aur., Cact., Cim., Glon., Hep. s., Kalmia, Lack
Lact. v., Lob., Lyc., Naja, Nux v., Ox. ac., Spig., Spong
Tab.

Anthrax.—Apis, *Ars.*, Bell., Canth., Crotal., *Kreos.*, Lack
Lyc., Merc., Mur. ac., Nitr. ac., Phytol., Rhus tox., Seca
cor., Sil., Sulph.

Anus, *Fissure of.*—Hydras., Ign., *Graph.*, *Nitr. ac.*, Merc.

Anus, *Itching of.*—*Ars.*, Carb. ac., Ign., Nitr. ac., Mur. a
Petrol., *Sulph.*

Anus, *Prolapsus of.*—Aloes, Æscul., Ign., Merc., Nux v., Pod
Sulph.

Aphonia.—Acon., Am. c., *Carb. v.*, *Caust.*, *Hep. s.*, Gels., K
bi., Nux m., Op., *Phos.*, Spongia.

Aphthæ.—Arg., Arg. nit., Bapt., *Borax*, Canth., Carb. a
Hep. s., Hydras., Eup. perf., Kali bi., *Kali chlo.*, Mag.
Merc., Merc. cor., Mur. ac., Natr. mur., Nitr. ac., Nux
Phytol., Staph., Sulph. ac., Thuja.

Apoplexia.—*Acon.*, Agar., Arn., Baryt. c., *Bell.*, Chin. sulp
Glon., Hyos., Lach., Lauro., *Nux v.*, Op., Phos., Plum
Stram. *Ver. vir.*

Arsenic, *Vapors of, Ailments from.*—Kali bi.

Arthralgia.—(See Gout.)

Arthritis.—(See Gout.)

Ascarides.—(See Worms.)

Ascites.—Acet. ac., Acon., *Apis*, *Apoc. c.*, *Ars.*, Dig., Fer
Fluor. ac., Jabor., Phos., Sen. (See also Dropsy.)

Asphyxia, neonatorum.—*Ant. tart.*, Tab.

Asthenopia.—Agar., Alum., Am. c., Apis, Calc. c., Cina, Cro
Gels., Jab., Kali carb., Kalmia, Led., Lil. tig., Lith., Ly
Natr. mur., Phos., Rhod., Ruta, Senega, Sep., Spi
Sulph.

Astigmatism.—Physos.

Asthma.—Ailanth., Ambra, Am. c., Amyl. nit., *Ant. ta
Aral.*, Arg. nit., *Ars.*, Arum., Ars. iod., Asaf., Bad., Bar

CLINICAL INDEX. 807

c., Benz. ac., Bell., Cact., Calad., Camph., Can. sat., Carb. v., Card. m., Cinch., Cistus, Colch., Con., Cor. rub., Cupr., Dulc., Eucalp., Ferr., *Ipec.*, Hepar., Kali bi., Kali c., Kali iod., *Kali nit.*, Lach., Lil., *Lob.*, Merc., Mosch., Naja, Natr. mur., Natr. sulph., Nux v., Phos., Puls., Ranunc., Sabad., Samb., Sang., Sticta, Stram., Sulph., *Tab.*, Thuja, Verb., Zinc.

Ataxia, *Progressive locomotor.*—*Alum.*, *Arg. nit.*, Calc. c., Cim., Gels., Kali brom., Lach., Nux v., *Phos.*, Physos., *Plumb.*, Rhus tox., Stram., *Zinc.*

Atrophy.—Ars., Baryt. c., Calc. c., Cinch., *Iod.*, Phos., Physos., Plumb., Sulph.

Balanitis—Can. sat., Canth., Cor. rub., *Merc.*, *Puls.*, Sulph., Thuja.

Belladonna, *Abuse of.*—Hyos., Op.

Bed-sores.—Arn., Carb. ac., Fluor. ac., Hydras., Merc., Sil., Sulph., ac., Tereb.

Bilious Disorders.—Æsc. hip., Æthusa, Aloes, Asar., Berb., Bry., Caul., *Chel.*, *Cinch.*, Cocc., Dig., Dios., Eup. perf., Gels., *Iris*, *Lept.*, *Merc.*, Myrica, *Nux v.*, *Podo.*, Ptelea, Puls., Sep., Sulph., Tarax.

Bladder, *Catarrh or inflammation of.*—(See Cystitis.)

Bladder, *Paralysis of.*—Bell., Canth., *Caust.*, *Con. mac.*, *Gels.*, *Hyos.*, Nux v., Secale, Uran. nit., Zinc.

Bladder, *Spasms of.*—*Bell.*, Canth., Con. mac., Gels., *Hyos.*, Nux v., Sulph.

Blepharitis.—Alum., Ant. c., *Arg. nit.*, Clem., *Graph.*, *Hep. s.*, Kreos., Magn. c., *Merc.*, *Merc. cor.*, Merc. iod., Natr. mur., Petrol., Phytol., *Puls.*, Sang., Sep., Sil., Staph., *Sulph.*

Blepharoplegia.—(See Ptosis.)

Blepharospasmus.—Agar., *Bell.*, Gels., *Hyos.*, *Nux v.*, Ign., Physos., Puls.

Blood, *Complaints from loss of.*—Chin. sulph., *Cinch.*

Boils.—Arn., Ars., *Bell.*, Crotal., *Hep. s.*, Kali iod., Led., Lyc., *Merc.*, Mur. ac., Phos. ac., Phytol., Pic. ac., Rhus tox., *Sil.*, *Sulph.*

Bones, *Affections of.*—*Asaf.*, *Aur.*, *Calc. c.*, *Calc. phos.*, *Fluor., ac.*, Hep. s., *Kali iod.*, *Merc.*, Mez., *Nitr. ac.*, Phos. ac., *Phos.*, Phytol., Ruta, Sil., Staph., Stillin., Sulph., Thuja.

Brain, *Anæmia of.*—Zinc.
Brain, *Atrophy of.*—Plumb., Zinc.
Brain, *Concussion and compression of.*—Acon., *Arn.*, Bell., Bry., Cic., Ham., Hell., *Hyper.*, Op.
Brain, *Congestion of.*—Absinth., *Acon.*, Ascl. cor., Aster., Bell., Bry., *Chin. sulph.*, Cupr., Ferr., Gels., Glon., Hyos., Nux v., *Op.*, Rhus tox., Sulph., Ver. vir.
Brain, *Paralysis of.*—Zinc.
Brain, *Softening of.*—Am. c., Ars., Cinch., Ferr., Kali brom., Nux v., *Phos.*, Plumb., Zinc.
Brain, *Sclerosis of.*—*Plumb.*, Zinc.
Brain Fag.—(See Neurasthenia.)
Bright's Disease.—Acon., Amyl. nit., *Apis,* Apoc., Arg. nit., *Ars.*, Aspar., Berb., Can. ind., Can. sat., *Canth.*, Carb. ac., Digit., Dulc., Eup. perf., Ferr., *Hell.*, Helon., Jab., Kali iod., Kali nit., Kalmia, Lith., *Lyc.*, Merc., *Merc. cor.*, Nux v., Osm., Petrol., Phos., Phytol., Plumb., *Tereb.*, Sulph., Uran., Zinc.
Bronchitis (*Acute*).—*Acon.*, Alum., Am. c., *Ant. tart.* (*capillary*), Ascl. cor., Bell., *Bry.*, Cact., Canth., Chel., Cina (*capillary*), Cinch., Con., Dros., Eucalyp., Ferr. phos., *Hep. s.*, Ipec., *Kali bi.*, Kali c., Lact. v., Led., Lob., Lyc., Merc., *Merc. cor.*, Nat. sulph., Nux v., Osm., Phos. ac., *Phos.*, Puls., Rhus tox., *Rumex*, *Sang.*, Senega, Sep., Squilla, Spong., Stan., Sticta, Tereb., Ver. alb., Ver. vir., Zinc.
Bronchocele.—(See Goitre.)
Bubo.—(See Syphilis.)
Bunion.—Agar., Am., Benz. ac., Carb. ac., Iod., Sil.
Burns and Scalds.—Acet. ac., Acon., *Canth.*, Euphorb., Stram., Urtica.

Cæcum, *Inflammation of.*—(See Typhlitis.)
Calculi, *Biliary.*—(See Gall-stones.)
Calculi, *Renal.*—Bell., *Berb.*, Benz. ac., Canth., Calc. c., Cocc. cac., Coloc., Con., Dios., Eup. perf., Hydras., Lyc., Nux v., Pareira, Sars., Sep., Tab., Uran. nit.
Cancer.—*Ars.*, Carb. an., *Con.*, Eucalypt., Euphorb., *Hydras.*, Iod., *Kreos.*, Lach., Lyc., Mag. m., Merc., Nitr. ac., Phos., Plat., Phyt., Sil.
Cancrum Oris.—*Ars.*, *Bapt.*, Bell., *Kali chlo.*, Merc.

CLINICAL INDEX.

Cankers of the Mouth.—(See Aphthæ.)
Carbuncle.—(See Anthrax.)
Carcinoma.—(See Cancer.)
Cardialgia.—(See Gastralgia.)
Cardiac Diseases.—(See Heart.)
Caries.—Arg nit., *Asaf.*, Am., Calc. c., Calc. phos., Caps., Fluor. ac., Hep. s., Kali iod., Lyc., *Merc.*, Mez., Nitr. ac., Phos. ac., Phos., Sep., Sil., Ther.
Catalepsy.—*Can. ind.*, Gels., Ign., *Nux m.*, Stram.
Cataract.—Baryt. c., *Calc. c.*, Caust., *Con.*, Lyc., Magn. c., *Phos.*, Physos., Sep., *Sil.*, Sulph.
Catarrh of Upper Air Passages.—Absinth., *Acon.*, Æsc., Allium. cepa, Alum., Am. c., Am. m., Ant. c., Ant. tart., Aral., Arg. nit., Ars., Ars. iod., Ascl. cor., Ascl. t., Aur., Baryt. c., *Bell.*, Brom., Calad., Colc., Camph. (*incipient*), Caps., Carb. ac., Carb. v., Caust., Cham., Chel., Chin. ars., Cinch., Cocc. c., Cor. rub., Dios., *Dulc.*, Eryng., Eucalyp., Euphorb., Eup. perf., Euphras., Ferr. phos., Fluor. ac., Gels., Graph., Hep. s., *Hydras.*, Iod., Ipec., *Kali bi.*, Kali carb., Kali iod., Kreos., Lach., Lyc., Mag. m., Mang., Meny., *Merc., Merc. bin.*, *Merc. cor.*, Merc. iod. fla., Merc. iod. rub., Mez., Milef., Myrica, Natr. ars., Natr. carb., Natr. mur., Natr. sulph., Nitr. ac., *Nux v.*, Op., Paris, Petrol., Phos., Phytol., *Puls.*, Rhus tox., Rumex, Sab., Samb., *Sang.*, Senega, Sep., Sil., Spig., Spong., Squilla, Sticta, Sulph., Ther., Thuja, Verb., Zinc.
Chancre (*Chancroid*).—Ars., Carb. ac., Caust., Cor. rub., Iod., *Merc.*, Merc. cor., Merc. iod. fla., Mur. ac., *Nitr. ac.*, Phos. ac., Phytol., Thuja.
Change of Life.—(See Menstruation.)
Chapped Hands and Lips.—Ars., Calc. c., Caust., Graph., Hep. s., Merc., Natr. carb., Rhus tox., Sil., Sulph.
Charcoal Vapors, *Effects of.*—Bor., Op.
Chilblains.—Acon., *Agar.*, Arn., Ars., Bad., Canth., Carb. ac., Crotal., *Merc.*, *Petrol.*, Zinc.
Chicken-pox.—(See Varicella.)
Chlorosis.—Abrot., Absinth., *Aletris*, Alum., Arg. nit., Ars., Calc. c., Calc. phos., Carb. v., *Chin. sulph.*, *Cinch.*, Cupr., Ferr., Ferr. iod., Graph., *Helon.*, Lob., Lyc., Iod., Natr. mur., Phos., Plumb., *Puls.*, Sep., Sil., Sulph., *Zinc*.

Cholera (*Asiatica*).—Acon., *Ars.*, *Camph.*, *Cupr.*, Eupho cor., Euphorb., Ipec., Lauro., Phos., *Secale*, Tabac., *Ve alb.*

Cholera Infantum.—Acon., *Ars.*, Ars. iod., Æth., Bell., Bi Bry., Calc. c., *Camph.*, *Cham.*, Cinch., Coloc., Crot. tig Cupr., Elat., Euphor. cor., Ferr. phos., Hell., Ipec., Ka brom., Kreos., Lauro., Œnoth., Plumb., *Podo.*, Op., Robin Secale, Stram., Tab., *Ver. alb.*, Zinc.

Cholera Morbus.—*Ars.*, *Camph.*, Elat., Euphor. cor., Ipec Phos., *Ver. alb.*

Chorea.—*Agar.*, *Ars.*, Arg. nit., Asaf., Aster., Bell., Calc. c Caul., Caust., Cedron, Cic., *Cim.*, Cina, Coccul., Cup Croc., *Gels.*, Hyos., *Ign.*, Kali nit., Lach., Lauro., Merc *Mygale*, Puls., Sil., Sulph., *Tarant.*, Ver. alb., Ver. vir., Zin

Choroiditis.—Agar., Croc., Gels., Kali iod., Merc., Merc. co Phytol., Sil.

Climacteric.—(See Menstruation.)

Coffee, *Ill effects of.*—*Bell.*, Cham., *Ign.*, *Nux v.*

Colic.—Acon., Absinth., Ars., *Bell.*, Calc. c., Calc. phos., *Cham* Cinch., Coccul., *Coloc.*, Cupr., *Dios.*, Dulc., Iris, Lyc., Mag c., Merc., Nux v., Op., Plat., Plumb., Podo., Puls., Spig Sulph., *Ver. alb.*, Zinc.

Colic, *From lead.*—*Alum.*, Natr. sulph., Nux v., *Op.*, *Pla* Sulph., Ver. alb., Zinc.

Concussion.—(See Brain.)

Condylomata.—Ant. c., Kali iod., Merc. iod., *Nitr. ac.*, Pho ac., Phyt., *Staph.*, Sulph., *Thuja*.

Conjunctivitis.—(See Ophthalmia.)

Constipation.—*Æscul.*, *Alum.*, Aloes, Ambr., Am. m., Ant. c Ars., *Bry.*, Calc. c., Carb. v., Carls., Caust., Collin., Dolic Graph., Hydras., Ign., Iod., Iris, Kali carb., Lept., Ly Magn. c., Mez., Nat. c., *Nat. mur.*, Nat. sulph., Nitr. a *Nux v.*, Op., *Phos.*, Phytol., *Plat.*, Plumb., Podo., Ptele Puls., Selen., Sep., Sil., *Sulph.*, *Ver. alb.*, Zinc.

Consumption.—(See Phthisis.)

Contusions.—Acon., *Arn.*, Calend., *Con.*, Ham., *Hyper.*, Rut

Convulsions (*Infantile*).—Absinth., Æthusa, Ant. tart., *Bel* Calc. c., Camph., *Cham.*, Cina, *Cupr.*, *Gels.*, Glon., He Hyos., *Ign.*, Kali brom., Merc., Millef., Nux m., Œnan., O Plumb., Stram., Ver. alb., Ver. vir., Zinc.

c., Carls., Chel., Cinch., Coccul., Digit., Eup. perf., Euphorb., Hep. s., *Ipec.*, Iris, Kali bi., Kali carb., Lyc., Magn. m., *Merc.*, Mez., Natr. ars., *Nux v.*, Petrol., Phos., Ptelea, *Puls.*, Robin., Rumex, Sep., Sulph., Tarax.

Gastritis.—*Acon.*, Ant. c., Ant., t., *Ars.*, *Bell.*, *Bis.*, *Bry.*, Canth., Cham., Cinch., Cupr., Euphorb., Graph., Ipec., Iris, Kali chlor., Lyc., Merc., Natr. mur., *Nux v.*, Ox. ac., Phos., Podo., Puls., Sab., Sang., Sulph., Ver. alb., Ver. vir., Zinc., Zing.

Glands, *Inflammation, swelling and induration of.*—Ars. iod., Baryt. c., Bell., Brom., Bufo, *Calc. c.*, Calc. phos., *Carb. an.*, *Carb. v.*, Cistus, Cham., Con., Graph., Hep. s., *Iod.*, *Kali iod.*, Lyc., *Merc.*, Merc. cor., *Merc. iod. rub.*, Natr. carb., Natr. mur., Nitr. ac., Phos., Phos. ac., Phytol., Rhus tox., Secale, Sil., Staph., *Sulph.*

Glaucoma.—Acon., *Ars.*, Aur., *Bell.*, Bry., Cedron, Colch., Coloc., Kali iod., Merc., Osmium, *Phos.*, Physos., Rhod., Spig., Sulph.

Gleet.—Agnus, Arg. nit., Ascl. cor., Benz. ac., Canth., Chin., Elat., Equiset., Hydras., Kali iod., *Merc.*, Mez., Natr. mur., Pareira, Petrose., Stil., *Sulph.*, Thuja.

Glossitis.—Acon., Apis, Ars., *Bell.*, Canth., Kali chlor., Kali iod., Lach., *Merc.*, Merc. cor., Nitr. ac., Sulph.

Goitre.—Badiaga, Brom., Calc. c., Calc. iod., Ferr., Fluor. ac., *Iod.*, Kali iod., Lyc., *Merc.*, *Merc. iod.*, *Spong.*, Sulph.

Gonorrhœa.—Acon., Agnus, Alum., Arg. met., Arg. nit., Ascl. cor., Benz. ac., Camph., Can. ind., *Can. sat.*, *Canth.*, Caps., Clem., Crotal., Digit., Elat., Equiset., Ferr., Gels., Graph., *Hydras.*, Kali bi., *Merc.*, *Merc. cor.*, Merc. iod. rub., Mez., Natr. mur., Natr. sulph., Nitr. ac., Pareira, Petros., Phytol., *Puls.*, Sep., Spong., Stilling., *Sulph.*, Tereb., Thuja.

Gout.—Abrot., Ant. c., Arg. met., Arn., Ars., Benz. ac., Berb., Bry., Calc. c., Caust., Cinch., Coccul., Colch., Coloc., Gnaph., Guai., Kali iod., Led., Lith., Lyc., Mang., Merc., Nux v., Ox. ac., Phytol., Plumb., Puls., Ranunc., Rhod., Rhus tox., Sab., Sars., Staph., Sep., Sulph.

Gravel.—(See Calculi, Renal.)

Grippe.—(See Influenza.)

Hæmatemesis.—Acet. ac., Acon., Arn., Ars., Cinch., Crotal.,

Camph., *Canth., Chim.,* Coc. cact., Caps., Clem., Digit., Dulc
Equiset., Eryng., Eucal., Eup. purf., Ferr., Ferr. phos
Kali iod., Lach., Lyc., Merc., *Merc. cor.,* Nitr. ac., Nux v
Pareira, Petrol., Phos., Puls., Rhod., Rhus tox., Sars
Senec., Senega, Sep., Squilla, Sulph., Tereb.

Dandruff.—Ars., Badiaga, Calc. c., *Canth.,* Fluor. ac., Graph
Hep. s., Kali m., Kali s., Lyc., Merc., Natr. m., Sil., *Sulp.*
Deafness, *Acute.*—Acon., Bell., *Canth.,* Gels., Iod., *Merc*
Phos., Puls.
Deafness, *Chronic.*—Ars., Calc. c., Calc. phos., Graph., Iod
Merc., Pic. ac., Puls., Sil., Sulph., Tellur., Verb.
Debility.—Anac., *Ars.,* Calc. phos., Carb. v., *Chin. sulph*
Cinch., Colch., Coccul., *Ferr.,* Helon., *Iod., Phos., Phos. ac*
Selen., *Sulph.,* Sulph. ac., Uran.
Delirium Tremens.—Absinth., Agar., Ant. tart., Arn., *Bel*
Calc. c., Can. ind., Cim., Crotal., *Hyos., Kali brom.,* Lach
Nux v., *Op.,* Ranunc., *Stram.,* Zinc., Zing.
Dentition, *Disorders of.*—*Acon.,* Æthus., Apis, Ars., *Bel*
Borax, Bry., *Calc. c., Calc. phos., Cham.,* Cinn, Cupr
Dolich., Gels., Graph., Hell., Ipec., Kreos., Magn. c., Mag
m., *Merc.,* Phos., Phytol., *Podo.,* Rheum, Sil., Sulph.
Diabetes.—Arg. met., *Arg. nit., Apis,* Ars., Carb. ac., Cor
Eup. purp., Fluor. ac., Helon., Iod., Jab., *Kali brom.,* K
nit., Kreos., Lac. ac., Lycopus, Lyc., Merc., Natr. mur
Nat. sulph., Nitr. ac., Nux v., *Phos. ac.,* Plumb., Si
Squilla, *Uran. nit.*
Diaphragmitis.—Acon., Bry., Cact., Colch., Hep. s., Stram
Sulph., Uran.
Diarrhœa.—Acet. ac., Acon., Æthus., Agar., *Aloe,* Am. n
Ant. c., Apis, Apoc., Arg. nit., Arn., *Ars.,* Asaf., Ascel. co
Ascl. tub., *Bapt.,* Bell., Benz. ac., Berb., Bism., Bora
Bry., *Calc. c., Camph.,* Canth., Caps., Carb. ac., Carb.
Cham., Chel., Cina, *Cinch.,* Cistus, Colch., Collin., Colo
Crotal., Crot. tig., Cupr., Dios., Dulc., Elat., Eucal., F
phorb., Ferr., Ferr. phos., Gamb., Gels., Graph., Gra
Hell., Hep. s., Hydras., Hyos., Ign., Iod., *Ipec.,* Iris, K
c., Kali nit., Kreos., Lach., Lauro., *Lept.,* Lyc., Lycop.
Magn. c., *Merc.,* Mez., Mur. ac., Natr. ars., Natr. car
Natr. mur., Natr. sulph., Nitr. ac., Nuph., Nux m., *Nux*

CLINICAL INDEX. 813

Œnoth., Oleander, Op., Ox. ac., Petrol., Phos., Phos. ac., Phytol., Plumb., *Podo.,* Ptelea, Puls., *Rheum,* Rhod., Rhus tox., Rumex, Sab., Sang., Secale, Sep., Sil., Staph., *Sulph.,* Sulph. ac., Tabac., Tereb., Thuja, *Ver. alb.,* Zinc.

Diphtheria.—*Ailanth.,* Ant. c., *Apis, Ars.,* Ars. iod., Arum., Bapt., Bell., Brom., Canth., Caps., Carb. ac., *Chin. ars.,* Crotal., Hydras., Hepar. s., Ign., *Kali bi., Kali chlor.,* Kali iod., *Lach.,* Lachnan., Lac. ac., Lyc., Merc., Merc. cor., Merc. iod. fla., *Merc. iod. rub.,* Mur. ac., Naja, Natr. ars., Nitr. ac., Op., Phytol., Rhus tox., Sang., Sep., Sulph., Sulph. ac.

Dropsy.—*Acet. ac.,* Acon., *Apis, Apoc., Ars.,* Ascl. cor., Aspar., Bry., Cact., Calad., Cedron, *Cinch., Colch.,* Collin., *Dig.,* Dulc., Elat., Ferr., *Hell.,* Helon., Jabor., Kali c., Kali nit., Lach., Led., Lept., Lyc., Mag. m., Merc., *Merc. cor.,* Natr. ars., Natr. mur., Phos., Rhus tox., Samb., Sil., Squilla, Stram., Sulph., Tereb., Uran., Zinc.

Dysentery.—*Acon.,* Agar., *Aloes,* Arg. nit., Arn., Ars., *Bell., Bapt.,* Bry., Canth., Caps., Carb. ac., Colch., *Coloc.,* Crotal., Eucalyp., Ferr. phos., Gambo, Hep. s., Ipec., Kali bi., Kali chlor., Lept., Lycop. v., *Merc., Merc. cor.,* Mur. ac., Nitr. ac., Nux v., Ox. ac., Podo., Puls., Rhus tox., Sang., Secale, Sulph., Tereb., Zinc.

Dysmenorrhœa.—(See Menstruation, Painful.)

Dyspepsia.—Abies c., Abies n., Absinth., Acet. ac., Æsc., Æthusa, Agar., Alet., Alum., Ant. c., Arg. nit., Arn., Ars., Asar., Asaf., Ascl. tub., Bapt., *Bism.,* Bry., Calc. c., Calc. phos., Carb. ac., Caps., Carb. an., *Carb. v.,* Carls., Caust., Cham., *Chel.,* Chin. sulph., *Cinch.,* Coccul., Colch., Collin., Con., Crotal., Cycl., Dios., *Ferr.,* Ferr. phos., Fluor. ac., Gamb., Graph., Hep. s., Hydras., *Ign.,* Iod., Ipec., Kali bi., Kali brom., Kali carb., Kali nit., Kreos., Lach., Lac. ac., Lith., Lob., Lyc., Magn. c., Merc., Natr. ars., Natr. carb., Natr. sulph., Nitr. ac., Nux m., *Nux v.,* Petrol., Phos., Phos. ac., Podo., Ptelea, *Puls., Robin.,* Rumex, Ruta, Sang., Sep., Sulph., Sulph. ac., Ver. alb., Zinc.

Dysuria.—*Acon., Apis,* Arg. nit., Benz. ac., *Can. sat.,* Camph., Canth., *Chim.,* Equiset., Erig., Eup. purp., Gels., Kali nit., Lith., Mez., Puls., Sars., Senega, Tereb., Vib. op.

Earache.—*Acon.*, Ars. iod., Baryt. c., *Bell., Cham.,* Dulc., Led., Mang., *Merc.,* Nat. sulph., Nux v., Plat., *Puls.,* Rhod., Rhus tox., Ver. vir., Zinc.

Eczema.—Anac., Ant. c., Bov., Calc. c., Canth., Carb. ac., Carb. v., Cistus, *Clem., Crot. tig.,* Dulc., Eucal., Euphorb., *Graph., Hep. s.,* Hydras., Hydrocot., Iris, Kali chlor., Led., Lyc., *Merc.,* Mez., Natr. mur., Natr. sulph., Nitr. ac., Olean., Petrol., Phytol., Phos., *Rhus tox.,* Sep., Sil., Staph., *Sulph.,* Telluer., Thuja, *Viola,* Zinc.

Elephantiasis.—*Ars.,* Ant. c., *Hydrocot.,* Lyc., Merc., Nit. ac., Sil.

Emissions, *Seminal.* (See Spermatorrhœa.)

Emotions, *Bad effects of.*—Acon., Cham., Croc., Hyos., *Ign., Gels.,* Nux v., Op., Plat.

Emphysema.—Am. c., *Ars.,* Bell., Brom., Camph., Chin. ars., Carb. v., Dig., Lach., Lob., Natr. mur., Nit. ac., Sulph.

Encephalitis.—(See Meningitis.)

Endocarditis.—(See Heart.)

Enteralgia.—(See Colic.)

Enteritis.—*Acon.,* Aloes, *Ars., Bell., Canth.,* Coloc., Cupr., Euphorb., Ipec., Lyc., *Merc.,* Merc. cor., Nitr. ac., Nuph., Nux v., Ox. ac., Phos., Podo., Rhus tox., Sulph., Ver. vir.

Enuresis.—Angust. v., Bell., Benz. ac., Calc. c., Canth., *Caust., Cina,* Cupr., Dig., Equiset., Elat., Eup. perf., Ferr., Gels., Graph., Hep. s., Kali nit., Kreos., Merc., Nux v., Podo., *Puls.,* Sep., Sil., Sulph., Verb., Viola.

Epididymitis.—Clem., Merc., Puls., Rhod., Spong.

Epilepsy.—Absinth., *Agar.,* Amyl. nit., Arg. nit., Asaf., Artem., Aster., *Bell.,* Bufo, Calc. c., Camph., Caul., Caust., Chin. ars., Cic., Cim., Cina, Coccul., Crotal., *Cupr.,* Gels., Glon., Hell., Hyos., *Ign., Kali brom.,* Lach., Lauro., Magn. c., Nux m., *Nux v.,* Op., Œnanth., Plat., Plumb., Secale, Sil., Stan., Stram., Sulph., Taran., Ver. vir., Zinc.

Epithelioma.—*Ars.,* Carb. ac., Con., Kreos., Merc. ac., Phos., Sil., Thuja.

Epistaxis.—Acet. ac., Acon., Art., *Bell.,* Bor., Calc. c., Carb. v., Cinch., Cinam., *Croc.,* Crotal., Erig., Ferr., Ferr. phos., *Ham.,* Hydras., Ipec., Kali chlor., Kali iod., Lach., Lac. ac., Millef., Nux v., Phos., Rhus tox., Sulph., Zinc.

Erysipelas.—Am., Am. c., *Apis, Ars.,* Arn., *Bell.,* Borax, Bry.,

Canth., Carb. an., Euphorb., Graph., Hep. s., Kali c., Lach., Merc., Mez., *Rhus tox.*, Sil., Stram. Sulph., Zinc.

Erythema.—*Acon.*, Apis, Arn., Ars., Bell., Bry., Crot. tig., Gnap., Graph., Hydras., Merc., *Rhus tox.*, Sulph.

Excoriations.—Graph., Hep. s., *Hydras.*, *Lyc.*, Merc., Rhus tox., Sulph.

Exophthalmus.—(See Goitre.)

Exhaustion.—(See Neurasthenia.)

Exostosis.—Ars., *Dulc.*, Hep. s., Iod., *Kali iod.*, *Merc.*, Merc. iod., Mez., *Phos.*, Sil., Zinc.

Fatty Degeneration.—Aur., *Phos.*

Fever, *Bilious.*—Aloe, Bry., Cham., Chel., *Cinch.*, Crotal., Eup. perf., *Gels.*, Hydras., Ign., Ipec., Iris, Lach., Lept., *Merc.*, *Nux v.*, Phos., *Podo.*, Rhus tox., Sang., Sulph., Ver. vir.

Fever, *Catarrhal.*—*Acon.*, *Ars.*, Ascl. tub., Bell., Bry., Eucal., Eup. perf., *Gels.*, Hep. s., *Merc.*, *Puls.*, Rhus tox., *Sang.*

Fever, *Gastric.*—Acon., *Ars.*, Bell., Bry., Caps., *Cinch.*, Gels., Hydras., Ign., *Ipec.*, Lach., Merc., Nux v., *Puls.*, Sang., Sulph., Ver. vir.

Fever, *Hectic.*—Acet. ac., *Acon.*, Arg. nit., *Ars.*, Ars. iod., Calc. c., Carb. v., Cham., *Cinch.*, Gels., Hep. s., Iod., Lach., Lyc., Merc., Mur. ac., Natr. ars., Nit. ac., Phos., Rhus tox., Sang., Sil., Stan., Stram., Sulph., Sulph. ac., Ver. vir.

Fever, *Inflammatory or asthenic.*—*Acon.*, *Bell.*, Bry., Mur. ac., *Ver. vir.*

Fever, *Asthenic.*—(See Typhoid.)

Fever, *Intermittent.*—Am. m., Angust. v., Apis, Aran., *Ars.*, Bry., Cact., Caps., Carb. m., Carb. v., *Cedron*, *Chin. ars.*, *Chin. sulph.*, Cina, *Cinch.*, Coccul., Crotal., Cupr., Elat., Eucal., Eup. perf., *Ferr.*, *Gels.*, Hell., Hydras., Ign., *Ipec.*, Kreos., Lach., Lob., Lyc., Meny., Merc., Mur. ac., Natr. ars., *Natr mur.*, Nitr. ac., Nux v., Op., Petrol., Phos. ac., Podo., Puls., Rhus tox., Sab., Sang., Sep., Stram., Sulph., Taran., Ver. vir.

Fever, *Miliary.*—*Acon.*, *Puls.*, Sulph.

Fever, *Puerperal.*—*Acon.*, Ars., Bapt., *Bell.*, Cim., Cinch., Crotal., *Gels.*, Hyos., Lach., Merc., Mur. ac., Op., Phos., Rhus tox., Secale, Sil., Sulph., *Ver. vir.*

Fever, *Typhoid.*—Acet. ac., Æthu., Agar., Ailanth., *Apis,* **Arn.**

c., Carls., Chel., Cinch., Coccul., Digit., Eup. perf., Euphorb., Hep. s., *Ipec.*, Iris, Kali bi., Kali carb., Lyc., Magn. m., *Merc.*, Mez., Natr. ars., *Nux v.*, Petrol., Phos., Ptelea, *Puls.*, Robin., Rumex, Sep., Sulph., Tarax.

Gastritis.—*Acon.*, Ant. c., Ant., t., *Ars.*, *Bell.*, *Bis.*, *Bry.*, Canth., Cham., Cinch., Cupr., Euphorb., Graph., Ipec., Iris, Kali chlor., Lyc., Merc., Natr. mur., *Nux v.*, Ox. ac., Phos., Podo., Puls., Sab., Sang., Sulph., Ver. alb., Ver. vir., Zinc., Zing.

Glands, *Inflammation, swelling and induration of.*—Ars. iod., Baryt. c., Bell., Brom., Bufo, *Calc. c.*, Calc. phos., *Carb. an.*, *Carb. v.*, Cistus, Cham., *Con.*, Graph., Hep. s., *Iod.*, *Kali iod.*, Lyc., *Merc.*, Merc. cor., *Merc. iod. rub.*, Natr. carb., Natr. mur., Nitr. ac., Phos., Phos. ac., Phytol., Rhus tox., Secale, Sil., Staph., *Sulph.*

Glaucoma.—Acon., *Ars.*, Aur., *Bell.*, Bry., Cedron, Colch., Coloc., Kali iod., Merc., Osmium, *Phos.*, Physos., Rhod., Spig., Sulph.

Gleet.—Agnus, Arg. nit., Ascl. cor., Benz. ac., Canth., Chin., Elat., Equiset., Hydras., Kali iod., *Merc.*, Mez., Natr. mur., Pareira, Petrose., Stil., *Sulph.*, Thuja.

Glossitis.—Acon., Apis, Ars., *Bell.*, Canth., Kali chlor., Kali iod., Lach., *Merc.*, Merc. cor., Nitr. ac., Sulph.

Goitre.—Badiaga, Brom., Calc. c., Calc. iod., Ferr., Fluor. ac., *Iod.*, Kali iod., Lyc., *Merc.*, *Merc. iod.*, *Spong.*, Sulph.

Gonorrhœa.—Acon., Agnus, Alum., Arg. met., Arg. nit., Ascl. cor., Benz. ac., Camph., Can. ind., *Can. sat.*, *Canth.*, Caps., Clem., Crotal., Digit., Elat., Equiset., Ferr., Gels., Graph., *Hydras.*, Kali bi., *Merc.*, *Merc. cor.*, Merc. iod. rub., Mez., Natr. mur., Natr. sulph., Nitr. ac., Pareira, Petros., Phytol., *Puls.*, Sep., Spong., Stilling., *Sulph.*, Tereb., Thuja.

Gout.—Abrot., Ant. c., Arg. met., Arn., Ars., Benz. ac., Berb., Bry., Calc. c., Caust., Cinch., Coccul., Colch., Coloc., Gnaph., Guai., Kali iod., Led., Lith., Lyc., Mang., Merc., Nux v., Ox. ac., Phytol., Plumb., Puls., Ranunc., Rhod., Rhus tox., Sab., Sars., Staph., Sep., Sulph.

Gravel.—(See Calculi, Renal.)

Grippe.—(See Influenza.)

Hæmatemesis.—Acet. ac., Acon., Arn., Ars., Cinch., Crotal.,

Erig., Ferr., *Ham., Ipec.*, Kreos., Lach., *Millef.*, Nux v., Phos., Sulph. ac., Tereb., Trill.

Hæmatocele, *Pelvic.*—Arn., Croc., Ferr., Ipec., Sab., Sec., Thlaspi.

Hæmoptysis.—*Acalpha ind.*, Acet. ac., *Acon.*, Arn., Ars., Ars. iod., Bell., Cact., Carb. v., *Cinch.*, Crotal., Dig., *Erig., Ferr., Ham., Ipec.*, Lach., Led., Lycop. v., *Millef.*, Nitr. ac., Op., Phos., Plumb., Puls., Sang., Stan., Sulph., Sulph. ac., Tereb., Trill.

Hæmaturia.—Bell., Cact., *Canth.*, Cocc. c., Elat., Equiset., Erig., Ferr., Ham., Ipec., Lyc., Nitr. ac., Nux v., Petrol., Phos., Plumb., Sulph., *Tereb.*

Hæmorrhage, *From the intestines.*—Acet. ac., Arn., Cact., Bell., Cinch., *Erig.*, Ferr., Ham., Ipec., Millef., Sulph. ac., *Tereb.*

Hæmorrhage, *From the uterus.*—Bell., Caul., Cinch., Cin., *Erig.*, Ferr., *Ipec.*, Puls., Sab., *Sec., Trill., Ustil.*

Hæmorrhoids.—*Æscul., Aloes*, Apoc., Bad., Brom., Caps., Carb. v., Caust., *Collin.*, Dios., Erig., Ferr., Ferr. phos., Ham., Hydras., Ign., Kali c., Lach., Magn. m., Merc., Millef., Mur. ac., Natr. mur., Nitr. ac., *Nux v.*, Petrol., Phos., Phytol., Podo., Puls., Rhus tox., Sil., *Sulph.*, Thuja.

Hair, *Falling off.*—Ars., Calc. c., Ferr., Fluor. ac., Graph., Hep. s., Kali c., Kali iod., Merc., Natr. mur., Natr. sulph., Phos., Sep., Sil., Sulph. (See Alopecia.)

Hay-fever.—(See Asthma.)

Headache, *Neuralgic.*—Amyl. nit., Ars., Bis., Cact., Epiph., *Gels.*, Iris, Lach., Melilo., Meny., Natr. mur., Paris, Ver. alb., Zinc.

Headache, *Rheumatic.*—Acon., *Bry.*, Cic., Colch., *Gels.*, Kali iod., Merc., Puls., *Rhus tox., Spig.*, Staph., Sulph., Ver. vir.

Headache, *Menstrual.*—Bell., *Cim.*, Coccul., Ferr., *Gels.*, Ign., Natr. mur., Nux m., *Puls.*, Sep., Ustil.

Headache, *Catarrhal.*—Acon., Ars., *Bell.*, Bry., Camph., Dulc., Eup. perf., *Gels.*, Hep. s., Kali bi., Merc., Natr. mur., Nux v.

Headache, *Gastric or bilious.*—Ars., Bell., *Bry.*, Carb. ac., Chel., Cinch., Cupr., Eup. perf., *Gels.*, Ipec., *Iris*, Lept., Melilo., Merc., Natr. mur., Nux m., *Nux v.*, Podo., *Puls.*, Robin., *Sang.*, Sep., Tarax., Ther., Ver. vir.

CLINICAL INDEX. 819

Headache, *Nervous.*—Ars., Asclep., Bell., Bry., Can. ind., Cim., Cinch., Coca, Coccul., *Coff.*, Cupr., Epiph., *Gels.*, Glon., *Ign.*, Iris, *Kali brom.*, *Melilo.*, Merc., Natr. carb., Natr. mur., Nux m., Nux v., Pic. ac., Puls., Robin., Sang., Selen., Sep., Sil., Stan., Sulph., Therid., Val., Ver. vir., Zinc.

Heart, *Inflammation of.*—*Acon.*, Apis, Ars., Ascl. t., Bell., Bry., *Cact.*, Can. sat., Collin., Colch., *Digit.*, *Gels.*, Kali c., Kali nit., Kalmia, Lith., Lyc., Lycop. v., Naja, *Spig.*, Spong., Ver. vir.

Heart, *Debility of.*—Amyl. nit., Angust. v., Arg. met., Ars., Collin., *Dig.*, Kali nit., *Kalmia*, Lach., Lil. tig., *Lycop. v.*, Phos. ac., Tabac., Verat. alb., Ver. vir.

Heart, *Hypertrophy of.*—Acon., Amyl. nit., Angust. v., Arn., Ars., Aur., Brom., Cact., Collin., Dig., Ferr., Kalmia, Lach., Lycop. v., Naja, Natr. mur., Phos., Rhus tox., Spig., Spong., Ver. vir.

Heart, *Valvular disease of.*—*Cact.*, Collin., Corral., Caps., Dig., Iod., *Kalmia*, Lach., Lycop. v., Naja, Natr. mur., Rhus tox., *Spig.*, Spong., Ver. vir.

Heartburn.—(See Dyspepsia.)

Helminthia.—(See Worms.)

Hemicrania.—(See Headache, Nervous.)

Hemiopia.—Aur. (*horizontal*), Lith., Lyc. (*lateral*).

Hemiplegia.—(See Paralysis.)

Hepatitis.—Acon., Æsc., Ars., *Bell.*, Bry., Cact., Chel., Cinch., Hep. s., Kali carb., Lach., Lyc., Merc. cor., Natr. sulph., Nux v., *Phos.*, Plumb., Podo., Ptelea, Puls., Sulph.

Hernia.—Bell., Coccul., Dig. (*incarcerated*), Lob., Lyc., Mur. ac., *Nux v.*, *Op.*, Plumb., Sulph. ac., *Tabac.*, Ver. vir.

Herpes.—Ars., Bad., Bor., Calc. c., Canth., Cistus, Clem., Dolich., Dulc., Graph., Hep. s., Iris, Kalmia, Led., Lyc., Merc., Mez., Natr. carb., Nat. mur., Nitr. ac., Olean., Petrol., Phos. ac., Phytol., Ranunc., Rhus tox., Sars., Sep., Sil., Staph., Sulph., Tellur., Thuja.

Hiccough.—Agar., Am. c., Amyl. n., Cistus, Cocc., *Cupr.*, Gels., Hyos., Ign., *Kali brom.*, Lauro., *Mosch.*, *Nux. v.*, Stram., Sulph. ac., Ver. vir.

Hip Joint Disease.—Ars., *Coloc.*, Calc. c., *Calc. phos.*, Hep. s., Kali c., Kali iod., Lyc., Merc., Natr. sulph., Phos. ac., Sil., Stram., Sulph.

CLINICAL INDEX.

Hoarseness.—(See Aphonia.)
Hordeolum.—(See Stye.)
House Maid's Knee.—(See Synovitis.)
Hour Glass Contractions.—*Bell.*, Secale.
Hydrocele.—Abrot. (*of children*), *Aur.*, *Apis,* Calc. c., Dig Graph., *Iod.*, Kali iod., Merc. iod. rub., Natr., mur., Puls Rhod., Sil., Sulph.
Hydrophobia.—*Bell.*, *Hyos.*, Lach., Naja, Nux v., Stram.
Hydrocephalus.—Acon., *Apis, Apoc.*, Ant. tart., Ars., *Bell.* Calc. c., Calc. phos., *Glon.*, *Hell.*, *Hyos.*, Hep. s., Lyc. Si Stram., Sulph., Zinc.
Hydrocephaloid.—*Cinch.*, Hell., *Podo.*, Zinc. (Also see H drocephalus.)
Hydrothorax.—Am. c., *Apis,* Apoc., *Ars.*, *Colch.*, Coral. rul *Dig.*, Dulc., Fluor. ac., Ham., Hell., Jab., Kali c., Kali iod Lach., Lact. v., Lyc., Ranunc., Sang., Senega, Star Sulph.
Hypochondriasis.—Anac., Arg. nit., Asaf., *Aur.*, Arg. nit Ars., Calc. c., Cic., Cim., Coccul., Con., Hell., Helon., Hyos *Ign.*, Kali brom., Lach., Lil. tig., Lyc., Melilo., Natr. carb Natr. mur., *Nux v.*, *Plat.*, Phos. ac., Puls., Sab., Selen Sep., Staph., Sulph., Taran., Ver. alb., Zinc.
Hysteria.—*Ambra,* Am. c., *Asaf.*, Aur., Baryt. c., Cau Cedron, Cham., Cic., *Cim.*, *Coccul.*, Coff., Con., Cor. rul Croc., Cypr., Gels., Hyos., *Ign.*, Lach., Lil. tig., Lot Magn. m., Natr. carb., Nux m., Phos. ac., Pic. ac., Pla Plumb., Puls., Sat., Selen., Sep., Stan., Staph., Stict Stram., Sulph., Taran., Ther., Val., Ver. vir., Vib. op Xanth.

Icterus.—(See Jaundice.)
Ileus.—Acon., *Bell.*, *Nux v.*, Opi., Plumb., Thuja, Ver. vir.
Impetigo.—Ant. tart., Ars., Calc. c., Clem., Dulc., Graph., He s., Iris, Kali bi., Lyc., Merc., Mez., Rhus tox., Sulph., Viol
Impotence.—Arg. nit., Aur., Baryt. c., Bufo, Calad., Co Calc. c., Cinch., Eup. purf., Eryng., Graph., Kali. brom Kali iod., Lyc., Merc., Natr. carb., Natr. mur., Nuph., N v., *Phos.*, Phos. ac., Salph., Selen., Sep., Zinc.
Incontinence of Urine.—(See Enuresis.)
Indigestion.—(See Dyspepsia.)

CLINICAL INDEX. 821

Influenza (Grippe).—Acon., Ant. tart., Ascl. cor., *Ars.,* *Camph., Cepa,* Dulc., Eup. perf., Euphor., Gels., Ipec., Iris, Kali bi., Merc., Merc. cor., Merc. iod., Nux v., Sang., Squilla, Sulph., Stict.

Infra Mammary Pain.—(See Pleurodynia.)

Intermittent Fever.—(See Fever, Intermittent.)

Intertrigo.—Caul., *Hydras., Lyc.,* Petrol., Sulph.

Insomnia.—Ambra, Bell., Calc. c., Cim., Coca, Coccul., *Coff.,* Gels., Hyos., Iod., *Kali brom.,* Sen.

Injuries, *Bad Effects from.*—*Bruises and Contusions:* *Arn.,* Bad., Hyper., Ruta. *Spinal:* Hyper. *Sprains: Rhus tox.* *Lacerated wounds:* Hyper., *Calend. Punctured wounds:* Hyper, Led. *Incised wounds:* Staph. *Chafing,* etc.: Hyper., *Lyc.,* Merc., Natr. mur., Ruta, Sulph. ac.

Insanity.—(See Mania.)

Iritis.—Asaf., Aur., *Bell.,* Clem., Colch., Gels., Hep. s., Iod., Kali bi., Kali chlor., Merc., Merc. cor., Merc. iod. fla., Natr. mur., Nit. ac., Physos., Puls., Terebin., Thuja.

Iron, *Bad Effects of.*—Bell., Cinch., Hep. s., Ipec., Merc., Puls.

Itch.—Apis, Ars., Hep. s., Led., Lyc., Merc., Natr. mur., Rhus tox., Rumex, Senega, Sep., Sil., Spig., Staph., *Sulph.*

Jaundice.—Aloes, Am., Berb., Bry., Card. m., *Chel., Chin. sulph.,* Cinch., Crotal., *Dig.*, Dolich., Elat., Gels., Hydras., Iod., Lach., Lept., Lyc., Magn. m., *Merc.,* Myrica, Naja, Natr. sulph., Nit. ac., Nux v., Phos., Plumb., Podo., Sang., Sep., Sulph., Tarax.

Keratitis.—Acon., Arg. nit., Apis, Ars., Bell., Calc. c., *Chin. ars.,* Euphras., Hep. s., Kreos., Lach., Merc., Merc. cor., Natr. mur., Nux v., Physos., Rhus tox., Sep., Sil., Sulph., Thuja.

Labor, *Abnormal.*—Bell., *Caul.,* Cim., Gels., Ign., Nux v., Puls., *Secale,* Ustil., Ver. vir.

Laryngismus Stridulus.—*Acon.,* Bell., Brom., Cor. rub., Chlorine, Cupr., Lach., Op., Samb., Spong.

Laryngitis.—*Acon.,* Ant. tart., Apis, Arg. met., Arg. nit., Arum., Bell., Brom., Bry., Carb. v., Carb. ac., *Caust.,* Cocc. c., Dios., Eup. perf., Ferr. phos., Hep. s., Ipec., Kali bi., Kali c., Lact., Lact. v., Mang., Merc. iod. rub., Paris, Phos.

ac., *Phos.*, Puls., Rhus tox., Rumex, Samb., Sang., Selen. *Spong.*, Stan., Stillin., Sulph.
Lead, *Ailments from.*—*Alum, Op.*, Petrol.
Leprosy.—(See Elephantiasis.)
Leucocythemia.—(See Anæmia.)
Leucorrhœa.—Æscul., Agn., Alet., Aloe, Alum, Am. c., Am. m., Ant. c., Aral., Arg. nit., Ars., Ars. iod., *Borax,* Bov., *Calc. c.,* Calc. p., Carb. an., Carb. v., Carb. ac., Cham., Cim., Cinch., Clem., Coccul., Con., Eucal., Ferr., Ferr. iod., Graph., Helon., *Hydras.*, Ign., Kali bi., Kreos., Lil. tig., Lyc., Magn. m., Merc., Merc. iod. fla., Merc. iod. rub., Mez., Natr. carb., Natr. mur., Nitr. ac., Nux m., Orig., Pareira, Phos., Phos. ac., Pic. ac., Podo., *Puls.,* Sab., Sang., Senecio, *Sep.,* Sil., Stan., Stillin., Sulph., Thuja., Trill., Ustil., Vib. op., Zinc.
Lithiasis.—*Con.,* Elat., Eup. perf., *Lyc.,* Natr. sulph., *Sars.,* Sep., Uva ursi.
Liver, *Congestion of.*—Am. m., Agar., Aloes, Ars., Bell., Berb., Bry., Card. m., Chel., Cinch., Gels., Hep. s., Iod., Iris, Lact. v., Lauro., Lept., Lyc., Magn. m., Merc., Nux v., Phos., Podo., Sen., Sil., Sulph., Ther., Zinc.
Liver, *Enlarged.*—Absinth., Æsc., Ars., Calc. c., Cedron, Chin. sulph., Cinch., Digit., Fluor. ac., Iod., Lauro., Lyc., Kali brom., Kali c., Kali iod., Magn. m., *Merc.*, Merc. iod., Natr. mur., Nux m., *Nux v.*, Phos., *Podo.*, Selen., *Sulph.*, Tarax.
Liver, *Acute yellow atrophy of.*—Merc., Podo., Phos.
Lochia, *Suppression of.*—*Acon.,* Aral., *Bell.*, Bry., Caul., Cham., Cim., Dulc., Gels., *Puls.*, Rhus tox., Secale, Trill.
Locomotor Ataxia.—(See Ataxia.)
Lumbago.—*Acon.,* Æscul., Ant. tart., Ascl. tub., Bell., Bry., Cim., Ferr., Kali c., Kali iod., Lyc., Merc., Nux v., Puls., *Rhus tox.*
Lupus.—*Ars.,* Hydras., Hydrocot., Iod., Kali bi., Kali iod. Kreos., Lyc., Merc., Phytol., Phos., *Thuja,* Sulph., Uran.

Mania.—*Anac.,* Am., Aur., *Bell.*, Canth., Camph., Can. ind. Cic., Cim. Euphorb., Gels., Glon., *Hyos.*, Kali brom., Lach. Lil. tig., Plat., *Stram.*, *Ver. alb.*, Ver. vir., Zinc.
Marasmus.—Abrot., Ars., Calc. c., Calc. phos., Hep. s., *Iod.* Mur. ac., Natr. mur., Nux m., Phos., Sars., Sil., *Sulph.*

Mastitis.—Arn., Ars. iod., *Bell., Bry.*, Cham., Graph., Hep. s., Lach., Merc., Phos., Phytol., Puls., Sil., Sulph.

Mastodynia.—Acon., Bell., Calad., Cim., Con., Crot. tig., Gels., Phytol., Ver. vir.

Measles.—*Acon., Allium cepa,* Anac., Ant. tart., Apis, Ars., Bell., *Bry.*, Crotal. (*hæmorrhagic*), Dios., Euphras., Ferr. phos., *Gels.*, Ham., Hep. s., Kali bi., Merc., *Puls.*, Rhus tox., Sab., Squilla, Sticta, Stram., Ver. vir.

Melancholia.—(See Hypochondriasis.)

Meningitis.—*Acon.*, Ailanth., Am. c., *Apis, Bell.*, Bapt., Bry., Carb. ac., Cic., *Cim.*, Cinch., Crotal., Cupr., Dig., *Gels.*, Glon., Hyos., Hep. s., Kali brom., Lact., Lachnan., Plumb., Stram., Sulph., *Ver vir.*, Zinc.

Menopause.—(See Menstruation, Cessation of.)

Menorrhagia.—(See Menstruation, Profuse.)

Menstruation, *Painful.*—Acon., Æscul., Agar., Alet., Am. c., Am. m., Aral., *Bell.*, Berb., Borax (*membranous*), Brom. (*membranous*), Cact., Calc. phos., Caul., Cham., *Cim.*, Coccul., Collin., Coloc., Crotal., Cyc., Dios., Ferr. phos., Gels., Gnap., Graph., Guai., Ham., Ign., Kali carb., Kreos., Lach., Lauro., Magn. c., Merc., Natr. mur., Nux v., Phos. ac., Plat., Plumb., *Puls.*, Rhus tox., Sab., Senecio, Sep., Sil., Sulph., Ustil., Ver. alb., *Vib. op.*, Xanth., Zinc.

Menstruation, *Delayed, Irregular, Scanty, or Suppressed.*—*Acon.*, Agnus, Ant. c., Bell., Bry., Cact., Calc. c., Caul., *Cim.*, Coccul., Coloc., Cyc., Digit., Ferr., Ferr. iod., Gnap., Guai., *Graph.*, Helon., Ign., Kali c., Lach., Mag. c., Natr. mur., Nux m., Op., Ox. ac., Phos., *Puls.*, Secale, Senecio, Sep., Sil., Staph., Sulph., Ustil., Ver. alb., Vib. op., Xanth., Zinc.

Menstruation, *Profuse.*—Acet. ac., Agnus, Alet., Aloe, Am. c., Amyl. nit., Apoc., *Bell.*, Borax, Bovis, Bry., Cact., *Calc. c.*, Calc. phos., Carb. an., Carb. v., Caul., Cham., *Cinch., Cinam.*, Coccul., Croc., Erig., Ferr., Ham., *Helon.*, Hyos., Ign., *Ipec.*, Kali c., Kreos., Lach., Lyc., Magn. m., Mang., Merc., Millef., Nitr. ac., Nux m., Nux v., Phos. ac., Phos., Phytol., Plat., Sab., Sang., Secale, Sen., Sep., Sil., Sulph., Tril., Ustil., Xanth., Zinc.

Menstruation, *Cessation of.*—Cinch., Coccul., Cyc., Gels., Graph., Lach., *Lyc.*, Puls., Sab., Sang., Ustil., Zinc.

Menstruation, *Vicarious.*—Bry., Calc. c., Ferr., *Ham.,* Puls
Phos., Sen., Sep., Sulph., Tril., Zinc.

Mercurial Affections.—*Asaf.,* Aur., Carb. v., Clem., Dulc
Fluor. ac., Guai., *Hep. s., Iod.,* Kali bi., Kali chlor., *Kal*
iod., Lach., Lyc., Merc. iod. rub., Mez., *Nitr. ac.,* Podo
Sars., Staph., Stil., Stram., Sulph.

Metritis.—*Acon., Bell.,* Bry., Caul., Cinch., Gels., Ham., Ka
carb., Lach., Lil. tig., Lyc., Merc., Merc. iod. rub., Nux v
Puls., Phos. ac., Rhus tox., Sab., Sep., Secale, Tereb
Ver. alb., Zinc.

Metrorrhagia.—(See Menstruation, Profuse.)

Migraine.—(See Headache, Nervous.)

Milk Crust.—(See Crusta Lactea.)

Morning Sickness.—(See Pregnancy, Vomiting of.)

Mortification.—(See Gangrene.)

Mouth, *Inflammation of.* (See Stomatitis.)

Mumps.—(See Parotitis.)

Myalgia.—Acon., *Arn.,* Bry., *Cim.,* Gels., Rhus tox., *Rut*
Ver. vir.

Myelitis.—Acon., Arn., Ars., *Bell.,* Con., Dulc., Gels., Hyper
Lach., Ox. ac., Nux v., Phos., Physos., Rhub., Rhus tox
Ruta, Secale, Sulph., Taran., Ver. vir.

Myopia.—Agar., Calc. c., Jab., Phos., Physos.

Muscæ Volitante.—*Agar.,* Arn., Bell., Calc. c., Ferr., Hyos
Kali iod., *Merc., Phos.,* Sulph., Sil.

Nævus.—Acet. ac., Fluor. ac., Lyc., Thuja.

Nasal Catarrh.—(See Catarrh of Upper Air Passages.)

Nephritis.—*Acon.,* Apis, Apoc., Ars., Bell., Benz. ac., *Berb*
Can. sat., Canth., Chim., Cocc. c., Colch., Dig., Dios., Dulc
Ferr., Hell., Helon., Iod., Kali bi., Kali carb., Kali iod
Kali nit., Lact., Lith., Lyc., Merc., Merc. cor., Nux v
Phytol., Pic. ac., Plumb., Samb., Sen., Squilla, Sulph
Tereb., Uran.

Nettle Rash.—(See Urticaria.)

Neuralgia.—Acon., Agar., Allium cepa, Amyl. nit., Ars
Aster., Bell., Can. ind., Caust., Cedron, Cham., Chel., *Chi*
sulph., Chin. ars., Cic., Cim., *Cinch., Coff., Coloc.,* Cro
(ciliary), Crot. tig., Cupr., Dulc., Dolich., Eucal., Ferr
Gels., Glon., Gnaph., Graph., Guai., Ham., Hell., Hyper

CLINICAL INDEX. 825

Ign., Ipec., Iris, Kali bi., Kali brom., Kalmia, Lach., Lil. tig., Lycop. v., Magn. m., *Merc.,* Merc. cor., Mez., Naja, Natr. ars., Natr. mur., Natr. sulph., Nux m., Nux v., Osmium, Ox. ac., Paris, *Phos.,* Phytol., Plat., Plumb., Puls., Ranunc., Rhod., Spig., Stan., Staph., Sulph., Tarax., Ther., Thuja, Ver. alb., Vib. op., Xanth., Zinc.

Neurasthenia.—Anac., Arg. nit., Calc. c., *Cinch.,* Coca, Coccul., *Gels.,* Hyper., *Kali brom.,* Phos. ac., *Phos., Pic. ac.,* Sil., Stan., Sulph., *Zinc.*

Nodes.—Gnaph., *Fluor. ac., Iod., Kali iod., Merc., Merc. iod.,* Mez., Nit. ac., Sil., Stillin.

Nymphomania.—Ambr., *Canth.,* Cinch., *Hyos.,* Kali brom., Orig., Phos., *Plat.,* Sab., Stan., Taran., *Ver. alb.,* Zinc.

Obesity.—Agar., Amm., Ant. c., Ars., Baryt. c., *Calc. c.,* Graph., Lyc., Merc., Sulph.

Odontalgia.—(See Toothache.)

Œsophagismus.—Asaf., Bell., Cupr., Lact., Merc. cor., Naja.

Œsophagitis.—Acon., *Bell., Merc.,* Phos., Sab., Ver. vir.

Onanism, *Bad effects of.*—Agnus, Arg. met., *Cinch.,* Coca, Con., Eryng., *Phos., Phos. ac.,* Selen., *Staph.,* Sulph., Zinc.

Onychia.—Arn., Calc. c., *Fluor. ac.,* Graph., Hep. s., Kali iod., Merc. iod., Natr. sulph., Phos.

Ophthalmia.—Absinth., *Acon.,* Alum., Ant. c., Apis, *Arg. nit.,* Ars., Ars. iod., Aur., Bad., *Bell.,* Calc. c., Chin. ars , Cistus. Clem., Coloc., Con., Euph., Gnaph., Graph., *Hep. s.,* Hydras., Ipec., Kali bi., Kali chlor., Led., Lith., Lyc., *Merc., Merc. cor.,* Merc. iod. fla., Merc. iod. rub., Natr. ars., Natr. carb., Natr. m., Natr. sulph., Nitr. ac., Nux v., Phos., Phytol., Pic. ac., *Puls.,* Rhus tox., Sang., Senega, Sep., Sil., Spig., Staph., Sticta, *Sulph.,* Sulph ac., Thuja, Viola, Zinc., Zing.

Opacity of Cornea.—Calc. c., Colch., Euphras., Phos., Physos., *Sil.,* Sulph., Thuja, Zinc.

Orchitis.—Acon., Arg. met., Aur., *Bell.,* Cham., *Clem.,* Con., Gels., *Ham.,* Kali iod., Merc., *Puls.. Rhod.,* Spong., Staph., Sulph., Zinc.

Otalgia.—(See Earache.)

Otorrhœa.—*Aur., Calc. c.,* Caust., Crotal., Fluor. ac., *Hep. s.,* Hydras., Iod., Kali bi., Kali carb., Lyc., *Merc.,* Mez., Natr.

carb., Natr. sulph., Nitr. ac., Petrol., *Puls.*, Sil., Sulph., Tellur., Thuja.

Ovaries, *Dropsy of.*—*Apis,* Ars., Jab., Iod., Kali brom., Sulph.

Ovaritis.—Ambra, *Apis, Bell.*, Brom., Bry., Canth., *Cim.*, Cinch., Coloc., Ferr. phos., Gels., Guai., Ham., Lach., Lil. tig., Lyc., Merc., Phos. ac., *Plat.*, Podo., Puls., Sab., Sep., Sulph., Thuja, Ustil., Zinc.

Ovaralgia,—*Bell.*, Chin. sulph., *Cim., Coloc.*, Ferr. phos., Gels., Ign., Kali brom., Lach., Lil. tig., Merc., Puls., Sep., Ustil., Ver. vir., Xanth., inc.

Ozœna.—Arg. nit., *Aur.*, Calc. c., Crotal., Eucal., Fluor. ac., Hep. s., *Hydras.*, Iod., *Kali iod.*, Kreos., Mag. m., Merc., Merc. iod., Mez., Natr. carb., *Nitr. ac.*, Petrol., Phos., Puls., Sang., Sep., Sil., Sulph., Thuja, Zinc.

Panaritium.—(See Whitlow.)

Pancreas, *Disease of.*—Ars., *Iod., Iris,* Merc., Phos.

Paralysis.—Acon., *Arg. nit.,* Arn., Ars., Baryt. c., *Bell.*, Caust., Coccul., Colch., *Con.*, Crotal., *Cupr.*, Dulc., Ferr., Gels., Hyos., Ign., Kali brom., Kali carb., Kali nit., Lach., Laur., *Merc.*, Natr. mur., Nux m., *Nux v.*, Oleander, Op., Ox. ac., *Phos.*, Physos., Plat., *Plumb.*, Rhus tox., Secale, Stan., Sep., Sil., Staph., Stram., Sulph., Tarent., Ver. alb., Ver. vir., Xanth., Zinc.

Paralysis, *Agitans.*—Gels., Hyos., Merc., Phos., Physos., Plumb., Tarent., Zinc.

Parotitis.—*Acon.*, Am. c., *Bell.*, Hep. s., Jab., *Merc.*, Merc. cor., *Puls.*, Rhus tox.

Pemphigus.—Apis, Ars., Canth., Dulc., Kali iod., Lach., Merc., Ranunc., Rhus tox., Sulph., Thuja.

Pericarditis.—*Acon.*, Am. c., Ars., Ascl. tub., Bell., Bry., *Cact.*, Canth., *Colch.*, Dig., Iod., *Kalmia*, Lach., Naja, Spig., Spong., Ver. vir.

Periostitis.—Aran., Asaf., Aur., Bell., Calc., *Kali bi., Kali iod.*, Mang., *Merc.*, Mer. cor., Mez., *Nit. ac.*, Phos. ac., Phytol., Ruta, Sil., Staph., Stillin.

Peritonitis.—*Acon.*, Apis, Arn., Ars., *Bell.*, Bry., Canth., Coloc., Hyos., Kali nit., Lath., Mang., Merc., *Merc. cor.*, Ranunc., Rhus tox., Sulph., Tereb., Ver. alb., *Ver. vir.*

Pertussis.—Ambra, Ant. c., *Ant. t.,* Arn., Asaf., Bad., *Bell.,* Carb. ac., Chel., Cina, Cocc., Con., *Cor. rub.,* Crotal., Cupr., *Dros.,* Dulc., Eucal., Iod., *Ipec.,* Kali brom., Kali c., Kreos., Lach., Lact. v., Lauro., Led., Lob., Naph., Merc., *Mosch.,* Nux v., Osm., Phos., Puls., Samb., Sang., Senega, Sep., Spong., Squilla, Sticta, Stram., Sulph., Ver. alb.

Pharyngitis,—Æscul, Alum., Arg. met., Arg. nit., Bell., Canth., Caps., Cocc. c., Ferr. phos., Iod., Hep. s., Kali bi., Kali carb., Kali chlor., Merc., *Merc. iod.,* Merc. cor., Natr. sulph., Nitr. ac., Petrol., *Phytol.,* Sang., Senega, Stan., Sulph.

Phlebitis.—Acon., Apis, Arn., Bapt., Bell., Ham., *Lach.,* Merc., *Puls.*

Phlegmasia.—(See Phlebitis.)

Photophobia.—*Acon.,* Ars., Aur., *Bell.,* Clem., Con., Euph., Graph., Gels., Hyos., *Merc.,* Natr. carb., Natr. mur., Natr. sulph., Nux v., *Puls.,* Rhus tox., *Sulph.*

Phthisis, *Pulmonalis.*—Acon., Am. c., Am. mur., Ars. iod., Bapt., Bell., Bry., *Calc. c.,* Calc. phos., Carb. v., Carb. ac., Caust., Chin. ars., Cinch., Dios., *Ferr., Ferr. iod.,* Guai., Hep. s., Hydras., Iod., *Ipec.,* Jab., Kali c., Kali iod., Kali nit., Kreos., Lauro., Lob., Lyc., Lycop. v., Mang., Merc., Merc. iod. rub., Millef., Natr. ars., Natr. sulph., Nitr. ac., Phos. ac., *Phos.,* Plumb., Puls., Rumex, *Sang.,* Selen., Sep., Sil., Spong., *Stan.,* Sticta, Sulph., Sulph. ac., Ther.

Pityriasis.—Ars., Kali iod., Fluor. ac., Merc., Merc. iod., Nitr. ac., Sil., Sulph.

Placenta, *Retained.*—Ars., Bapt., Caul., Cinch., Cim., Kreos., Lach., Merc., *Sab.,* Secale, Ustil.

Pleurisy.—*Acon.,* Ant. t., Arn., Ascl. t., Bad., Bell., Borax, *Bry.,* Cact., Canth., Colch., Dig., Ferr. phos., Ham., Hep. s., Kali c., Natr. mur., Phos., *Ranunc.,* Squilla, Stan., Sulph., Ver. vir.

Pleurodynia.—Acon., Arn., Ascl. t., Borax, Bry., *Cim.,* Lycop. v., Nux v., Puls., *Ranunc.,* Ruta, Rhod.

Plica Polonica.—Arg. m., Borax, Graph., Lyc., Natr. mur., Sulph., Viola.

Pneumonia.—*Acon.,* Am. c., *Ant. tart.,* Arn., Ars. iod., Ascl. t., Bell., Brom., Bry., Cact., Can. sat., Carb. an., Carb. v., *Chel., Cinch.,* Dig., Ferr. phos., Hep. s., Iod., *Ipec.,* Kali c., Kali iod., Kali nit., Kreos., Lach., Lachnan., Led., Lyc.,

Melilo., Merc., Natr. mur., Osm., Phos., Rhus tox., Sang., Senega, Sil., Spong., *Squilla*, Stan., *Sulph.*, Ver. vir.

Polypi.—*Calc. c.*, Con., Iod. (*uterine*), Kali nit., Lyc., Merc., *Mar. v.*, Merc., Merc. iod. rub., *Nitr. ac., Phos.*, Sang., Sep., Sil., Staph., Sulph., *Thuja*.

Pregnancy, *Vomiting of.*—Aletris, Anac., Ant. c., Apomorph., Asar., Carb. ac., Cim., Coccul., Dig., Ferr. phos., Graph., Ign., Ipec., Iris, Kreos., Lact. ac., Lob., Magn. c., Merc., Nux. m., Nux v., Petrol., Phos., Puls., Sang., Sep., Sulph. ac., Tab.

Proctitis.—Acon., Aloes, *Bell.*, Colch., Collin., Merc., *Merc. cor.*, Nux v., Phos., Podo., Sulph., Tereb.

Prolapsus Ani.—(See Anus.)

Prosopalgia.—Acon., Amyl. nit., Angust. v., Arg. nit., *Ars., Bell.*, Chin. ars., *Chin. s., Cinch., Coloc.*, Ign., Ipec., Iris, Kalmia, Lach., Magn. c., Meph., *Merc.*, Merc. cor., Mez., Nux v., Phos., Plat., Rhod., Rhus tox., Sab., Sang., Sep., *Spig.*, Stan., Stram., Sulph., Thuja, Ver. alb., Verat. vir., Xanth.

Prostatitis.—Acon., Æsc. hip., Dig., Hep. s., Iod., Kali iod., Lith., Lyc., Merc., Natr. sulph., Nitr. ac., Puls., Sil., Sulph., Thuja, Uva ursi.

Prurigo.—Ars., Carb. ac., Sab., Kali bi., Kali brom., Kreos., Lil. tig., Merc., Mez., Natr. mur., Rhus tox., Rumex, *Sulph.*

Pruritus Ani.—(See Anus, Itching of.)

Pruritus Vulva.—Ambr., *Calad.*, Calc. c., Collins., Helon., Hydras., Merc., *Plat.*, Sulph.

Psoriasis.—*Ars.*, Ars. iod., Bor., Carb. ac., Graph., Hep., s., Hydroc., Kali iod., Lyc., Mang., Merc., Mez., Natr. mur., Nitr. ac., Petrol., Phos., Sep., *Sulph.*

Pterygium.—Arg. nit., Ars., Calc. c., Sulph., Zinc.

Ptyalism.—Cinch., Dulc., Hep. s., Iod., Iris, Jab., Kali iod., *Merc., Merc. cor., Nitr. ac.*, Podo., Sulph.

Puerperal Convulsions.—(See Convulsions, Puerperal.)

Puerperal Fever.—(See Fever, Puerperal.)

Puerperal Mania.—(See Mania.)

Ptosis.—Caust., Con., Gels., Natr. ars., Nat. carb., Naja, Nux m., Rhus tox., Sep., Spig., Zinc.

Purpura.—Ars., Carb. veg., Crotal., Ham., Kali iod., Lach., Naja, Natr. ars., *Phos.*, Rhus tox., Secale, Sulph. ac., Tereb.

CLINICAL INDEX.

Pyæmia.—Arn., *Ars.*, Bapt., Carb. ac., Carb. v., Chin. sulph., Crotal., Eucal., Hep. s., *Lach.*, Merc., Mur. ac., Phos.
Pyrosis.—Bis., Calc. c., Caps., Cinch., Hep. s., Iris, Lyc., Merc., Nux v., Puls., Rob., Sulph.

Quinine Cachexia.—Eucal., *Ferr.*, Natr. m., Ver. alb.
Quinsy.—(See Tonsilitis.)

Rachitis.—Asaf., *Calc. c., Calc. phos.*, Fluor. ac., Hep. s., Iod., Kali iod., Lyc., Merc., Phos., *Sil.*, Sulph., Therid.
Ranula.—*Ambra*, Calc. c., Fluor. ac., Merc., *Nitr. ac., Thuja.*
Remittent Fever.—(See Fever, Intermittent.)
Red Gum.—*Acon.*, Bry., Calc., Cham., Merc., Rhus tox.
Retinitis.—*Bell.*, Crotal., Dig., Gels., Glon., *Lach.*, Lyc., Merc., Merc. cor., Nux v., Phos., Physos., Puls., Sulph.
Rhagades.—Calc. c., Fluor. ac., *Graph.*, Hep. s., Merc., Nitr. ac., Petrol., Sars., Sil., Sulph.
Rheumatism.—Abrot., *Acon.*, Agar., Arg. nit., Ars., Ascl. cor., Ascl. t., Aspar., Bell., Benz. ac., Berb., *Bry.*, Cact., Calad., Calc. c., Calc. phos., Carls., Caul., Caust., Cham., Chin. sulph., Chel., Cinch., *Cim., Colch.*, Coloc., Crotal., Dulc., Elat., Eucal., Eup. perf., Ferr., Ferr. phos., Gels., Gnaph., Hyper., Iod., Kali bi., Kali c., Kali iod., Kali nit., *Kalmia, Lact. ac., Led., Lith.*, Lyc., Lycop. v., Mang., Teuc. m. v., Merc., Mez., Natr. ars., Natr mur., Natr. sulph., Nitr. ac., Nux. v., Ox. ac., Petrol., Phos., *Phytol., Puls., Ranunc., Rhod., Rhus tox., Ruta*, Sang., Sars., Sill. Spig., Spong., Stil., Sulph., Tarax., Thuja, Ver. alb., Ver. vir., Zinc.
Rheumatism of Small Joints.—*Actea sp., Caul., Colch.*, Led., Kali bi., Lact. ac., Led., Lith., Rhod., Sticta.
Ringworms.—(See Herpes.)
Rupia.—Ars., Clem., Nitr. ac., Kali iod., Phytol., Sulph., Thuja.

Salivation.—(See Ptyalism.)
Scabies.—(See Itch.)
Scald Head.—(See Crusta Lactea.)
Scarlet Fever.—Acon., Alianth., *Am. c., Apis*, Arg. nit., Ars., Arum., Bapt., *Bell.*, Bry., Caps., Carb. ac., Chin. ars., Crotal., Gels., Hell., Hyos., Lach., Lachnan., Merc., Merc.

CLINICAL INDEX.

iod. rub., Mur. ac., Natr. mur., Nitr. ac., Paris, Phytol., *Rhus tox.*, Stram., Sulph., Tereb., Ver. vir., Zinc.

Sciatica.—Absinth., Acon., Am. m., Ant. t., Ars., *Bell., Bry., Cim., Coloc.*, Dios., Elat., Eup. perf., Gels., Gnaph., Ign., Iris, Kali bi., Kali c., Kali iod., Lach., Led., Mang., Merc., Natr. ars., Nux. v., Phos., Phytol., *Plumb.*, Rhus tox., Stil., Sulph., Tellur., Thuja, Val., *Xanth.*, Zinc.

Scirrhus.—(See Cancer.)

Sclerosis.—(See Myelites.)

Scorbutis.—Am. c., Ars., Ber., Carb. v., Ferr., Kreos., *Merc., Mur. ac., Natr. mur.*, Phos., Staph., Sulph.

Scrofula.—Asaf., Aur., *Bad.*, Baryt. c., Bor., *Calc. c., Calc. phos.*, Camph., Chin. ars., *Cistus, Clem.*, Con., Dulc., Ferr., Graph., Hep. s., Iod., Kali bi., Kali iod., Kreos., Lyc., Merc., Merc. cor., Merc. iod. rub., Mez., Nux v., Phos., Sep., *Sil.*, Staph., *Sulph.*, Stilling., Tellur., Ther., Viola.

Scurvy.—(See Scorbutis.)

Sea Sickness.—Apomorph., *Coccul.*, Glon., Kali brom., Kreos., *Nux m., Nux v., Petrol., Tab.*, Ther.

Seminal Emissions.—Agnus, Arg. nit., Arum., *Cinch.*, Con., Dig., Eryn., Gels., Phos., *Phos. ac.*, Sulph., Staph.

Septicæmia.—(See Pyæmia.)

Shingles.—(See Zona.)

Sick Headache.—(See Headache, Nervous.)

Singultus.—(See Hiccough.)

Small-Pox.—Acon., Am. c., Am. m., *Ant. t.*, Apis, Bapt., Bell., Carb. ac., Crotal., Ham., Hep. s., Hydras., Lach., *Merc.*, Mur. ac., Phos., Rhus tox., Sulph., Thuja, Ver. vir.

Somnambulism.—Cis., Kali brom., Nux v., Puls., Sulph., Zinc.

Spasms.—(See Convulsions.)

Spermatorrhœa.—Acet. ac., Agnus, Ars., Canth., Cinch., Eryng., *Kali brom.*, Meph., Merc., Natr. mur., Nuph., Nux v., *Phos. ac.*, Phos., Staph., Sulph., Zinc.

Spina Bifida.—Calc. phos., Iod.

Spinal Irritation.—Acon., *Agar.*, Arg. nit., Arn., Caul., Chin. sulph., Can., Coccul., Cupr., Gels., *Hyper.*, Ign., Kali c., Natr. mur., Naja, Nux v., Ox. ac., Phos., Physos., Puls., Secale, Sil., Sulph., Taran., Tellur., Ther., Zinc.

Spine, *Concussion of.*—Acon., *Arn.*, Con., *Hyper.*, Nux v., Physos., Ver. vir.

CLINICAL INDEX.

Spine, *Curvature of.*—Calc. c., *Calc. phos.*, Phos., *Sil.*, Sulph.
Spine, *Congestion of.*—Absinth., Acon., *Agar.*, Arn., *Gels.*, Hyper., Nux v., Phos., Sil., Sulph.
Spine, *Softening of.*—*Agar.*, Coccul., Crotal., *Ox. ac.*, Phos.
Spine, *Sclerosis of.*—Alum., Arg. nit., Coccul., Nux v., Plumb.
Spleen, *Enlargement of.*—Absinth., Agar., Aral., *Ars.*, Ars. iod., Calc. c., Cedron, Chin. ars., *Chin. sulph.*, *Cinch.*, Ferr., Iod., Kali iod., *Merc.*, Natr. mur., Natr. sulph., Phos., Sulph. ac., Sulph., Zinc.
Spleen, *Inflammation of.*—Acon., *Ars.*, *Cinch.*, *Chin. ars.*, *Chin. sulph.*, Iod., Kali iod., Merc., Natr. mur., Nat. sulph., Nux v., Sulph.
Sprains.—Acon., Am. c., Am. mur., Arn., *Led.*, Phytol., *Ruta*, Rhus tox.
Staphyloma.—Apis, Physos.
Stammering.—Bell., Hyos., *Stram.*
Sterility.—Agnus, Aletris, Aur., Borax, Canth., Con., Iod., Kreos., Natr. mur., Nux m., Phos., Plat.
Stings and Bites of Insects.—Acet. ac., Am. c., Ant. c., Apis, Carb. ac., Camph., Crotal., Lach., Led.
Stomatitis.—*Ars.*, Arg. nit., *Bapt.*, Bell., Benz. ac., Borax, Caps., Hyd., *Kali chlor.*, *Merc.*, *Merc. cor.*, Mur. ac., Nitr. ac., Nux v., *Sulph.*
Strabismus.—*Bell.*, Cic., Cina, *Cyc.*, Hyos., Jab., Lach., Merc., *Stram.*
Strain.—(See Sprain.)
Strangury.—*Acon.*, *Apis*, Bell., Camph., *Can. sat.*, *Canth.*, Caps., Chin., Dig., Gels., Nux v.
Styes.—*Apis*, Bell., Graph., Ham., Hep. s., Merc., Natr. mur., *Puls.*, Staph., Sulph., Thuja.
Sun Stroke.—Acon., *Amyl. nit.*, *Bell.*, Gels., *Glon.*, Tab., Ther., Ver. vir., Zinc.
Suppuration.—(See Abscess.)
Syncope.—Amyl. nit., Dig.
Sycosis.—Ars., Merc., *Natr. sulph.*, *Nitr. ac.*, Phos. ac., Plat., Staph., Thuja.
Synovitis.—Acon., Apis, Bry., Calc. c., Cinch., Fluor. ac., Hep. s., Iod., Kali iod., Led., Merc., Puls. Rhus tox., Ruta, Sulph.
Syphilis.—Arg. nit., Asaf., Aur., Bad., Benz. ac., Carb. ac., Cor-

rub., Crotal., Fluor. ac., Guai., Hep. s., Iod., Kali bi., *Kali iod.*, Lach., Merc., *Merc. cor., Merc. iod. fla., Merc. iod. rub.*, Mez., *Nitr. ac.*, Petrol., Phytol., Plat., Sars., Staph., Stil., Sulph., Thuja.

Tabes Dorsalis.—(See Ataxia.)
Tabes Mesenterica.—Arg. nit., Ars. iod., Baryt. c., *Calc. c., Calc. phos.*, Cinch., Iod., *Hep. s.*, Kreos., *Merc.*, Natr. sulph., Nitr. ac., Phos., Sil., Sulph., Zinc.
Testicles, *Hypertrophy of.*—Agnus, Aur., Clem., *Con., Iod.*, Lach., *Merc., Mer. iod.*, Puls., Sulph.
Tetanus.—Amyl. nit., August. v., Ars., Bell., Crotal., Gels., Hydroc. ac., *Hyos.*, Hyper., *Kali brom.*, Lach., Lauro., Nux v., Op. Physos., Plumb., Stram., Val., Ver. alb.
Tic Douleurex.—(See Prosopalgia.)
Tinea Capitis.—(See Crusta Lactea.)
Tinnitus Aurium.—Acon., *Bell.*, Calc., Calc. phos., *Chin. sulph.*, Cinch., Graph., Kali iod., Merc., Puls., Sil.
Tonsilitis.—Baryt. c., *Bell.*, Benz. ac., Berb., Canth., Caps., Cistus, Ferr. phos., Guai., Hep. s., Hydras., Ign., Kali bi., *Lach.*, Lyc., *Merc.*, Merc. iod. rub., Merc. iod. fla., Natr. sulph., Nitr. ac., Phytol., Rhus tox., Sab., Sil., Sulph., Sulph. ac.
Tonsils, *Enlarged.*—Baryt. c., Calc. c., *Colch.*, Iod., Merc. iod., Sil., Sulph.
Toothache, *From Cold.*—Acon., *Bell.*, Cham., Coff., Kali carb., Merc., Nux m., Puls., Rhod. *From Indigestion.*—Ant. c., Bry., Euphorb., Kreos., Merc., Nux m., Puls. *Nervous.*—Ars., Bell., Cham., Cinch., Coff., Guai., Hyos., Ign., Merc. c., Nux v., Plat., Spig., Verat. alb., Zinc. *In Pregnancy.*—Magn. c., Nux m., Puls., Sep., Staph. *From Decay.*—Carb. ac., Hep. s., *Kreos., Merc.*, Mez., Sil., Staph., Thuja.
Tympanitis.—Ars., Asaf., Carb. v., Cinch., Coccul., Colch., Coloc., Ferr., Lyc., Nux v., Phos., Phos. ac., Plumb., Secale, Taran., Tereb., Val.
Typhoid Conditions.—(See Fever, Typhoid.)
Typhlitis.—*Acon.*, Ars., *Bell.*, *Bry.*, Colch., *Hep. s.*, Kali iod., Lyc., *Merc.*, Merc. cor., Natr. sulph., *Natr. sulph.*, Op., Rhus tox., Sulph.

Ulcers.—Ars., Asaf., Aster., Bufo (*malignant*), Canth., Carb. v., Carb. ac., Cistus, Clem., Eucal., Fluor. ac., Graph., Hep. s., Hydras., Iod., Kali bi., Kali brom., Kali iod., Kreos., Lach., Lyc., Merc., Merc. cor., Merc. iod. rub., Mez., Mur. ac., Naja, Natr. c., Natr. mur., Natr. sulph., Nitr. ac., Phos., Phos. ac., Phytol., Ranunc., Sang., Sars., Sec., Sep., Sil., Staph., Stil., Sulph., Thuja.

Uræmia.—Am. c., Apis, Apoc., Ars., Ascl. c., Benz. ac., Can. ind., Cupr., Kali iod., Kali nit., Lith., Op., Phos., Phytol., Plumb. Stram., Uran., Ver. alb.

Urethritis.—(See Gonorrhœa.)

Urinary, *Calculi.*—(See Calculi, Renal.).

Urticaria.—*Apis*, Ars., Bor., Carls., Dulc., Graph., Hep. s., Kreos., Led., Lyc., Natr. mur., Nitr. ac., Nux v., Puls., Ranunc., Rhus tox., Sulph., Tereb., *Urtic. ur.*

Uterus, *Atony of*—Aletris, Aloes, Alum., Bell., *Caul.*, Ferr. iod., *Helon.*, Lil. tig., Millef., Puls., Sec., Sep., Tril., Ustil.

Uterus, *Displacements of.*—Absinth., Aletris. Alum., Am. m., Apomorph., Arg. met., Aur., Bell.. Calc. phos., Cim., Collin., Ferr., Graph., Helon., Iod., Lach.. *Lil. tig.*, Natr. mur., Nux m., Nux v., Plat., Podo., Puls., Rhus tox., *Sep.*, Stan., Staph., Sulph., Thuja, Tril.

Uterus, *Ulceration, etc., of.*—Arg. nit., Ars.. Bapt., Carb. ac., Hep. s., *Hydras.*, *Kreos.*, Merc. iod. rub., Mez., Mur. ac., Natr. carb., Nitr. ac.. Phos., Phytol., Sang., *Sep.*, Sulph., Thuja, Zinc.

Uterus, *Subinvolution of.*—Calc. c., Calc. phos., Ferr. iod., Hydras., Iod., Kali brom., Kali iod., Kreos., *Lil. tig.*, Merc. iod., Natr. mur., Phos., Plat., Podo., Sab., *Sep.*, Sec., Ustil., Vib. op.

Vaccination, *Bad effects of.*—Apis, Ars.. Crotal., *Sil.*, Thuja.
Vaginitis.—Acon., Ars.. Berb., Calad., Canth., Can. sat., Ham., Hydras., Kreos., Merc., Natr. mur., Nitr. ac., Sep., Sulph.
Vaginismus.—Ars., Aur.. Bell., Berb.. Calad., *Ham.*, Kali brom., Kreos., Merc., Plat., *Plumb.*, Sulph. Teuc. m. v.
Varicella.—*Acon.*, Ant. t., Apis, Ars.. Bry., Ipec., Merc., *Puls.*, Rhus tox.. Sulph.
Varices.—Arn., Calc., Carb. v., Caust., Collin., Ferr., Fluor.

ac., *Ham.*, Hydras., Hep. s., Lyc., Merc., Mellif., Natr. mur., *Puls.*, Sulph., Thuja, *Zinc.*

Variola.—(See Small-Pox.)

Varicocele.—(See Varices.)

Vertigo.—Ambra, Ant. t., Arg. nit., Ars., Bry., *Bell., Calc. c,* Calc. phos., Chel., Chin., Cinch., Coccul., Coff., *Con.*, Lyc., Dig., Gels., Ferr., *Glon.*, Iod., Ipec., Kali c., Merc., Natr. carb., Nux v., Oleander., Petrol., Phos., Phos. ac., Puls., Sulph., Tab., Zinc.

Vermicular Affections.—(See Worms.)

Vulvitis.—Acon., Apis, Ars., Bell., Canth., Crot. tig., Lach., Merc., Rhus tox., Sab., Sep., Sulph., Urtica, Zinc.

Warts.—Acet. ac., Ant. c., Calc. c., Caust., Dulc., Kali iod., Merc., *Nitr. ac.*, Phos. ac., *Staph.*, Sulph., *Thuja.*

Whitlow.—Am. c., Apis, Ars., Crotal., *Fluor. ac., Hep. s., Merc.*, Merc. iod., rub., Natr. sulph., *Sil.*, Stram., Sulph.

Whooping Cough.—(See Pertussis.)

Worms.—Acon., Calc. c., Cham., *Cina*, Dolich., Ferr., Ign. (*convulsions*), Mang., Merc., Natr. m., Nux m., Sab., Spig., Stan., Sulph., Tereb., Teuc. m. v., Zinc.

Wounds.—(See Injuries.)

Wry Neck.—*Lachnan.*, Lyc., Nux v.

Yellow Fever.—(See Fever, Yellow.)

Zona.—Ars., Crot. tig., Dolich., Graph., Merc., Mez., Puls., Ranunc., Rhus tox., Sulph.

Printed in the United States
87959LV00003BB/28/A